GEORGIA JOURNEYS

Georgia Journeys

Being an Account of the Lives of Georgia's
Original Settlers and Many Other Early
Settlers from the Founding of the Colony
in 1732 until the Institution of
Royal Government in 1754

By
SARAH B. GOBER TEMPLE
and
KENNETH COLEMAN

Published in Athens, Georgia, by
THE UNIVERSITY OF GEORGIA PRESS
MCMLXI

MRS. MARK TEMPLE, nee SARAH BLACKWELL GOBER

Cobb County pioneers were trail breakers imbued with love of the land, and they early developed characteristics of leadership and ideals on which later generations have built. Mrs. Temple shared this fine inheritance. A special legacy from her talented father was her zeal for learning and for accurate research. Through the pages of this work shines her love of Georgia, and on every page is evidence of her monumental research. Her pen was stilled before the manuscript took final form. As a long-time personal friend of Mrs. Temple, I feel that this publication serves as an appropriate and useful memorial.

B. C. YATES

Kennesaw Mountain Battlefield Park
Marietta, Georgia

Paperback edition, 2010
© 1961 by the University of Georgia Press
Athens, Georgia 30602
www.ugapress.org
Printed digitally in the United States of America

The Library of Congress has cataloged the hardcover edition
of this book as follows:
Library of Congress Cataloging-in-Publication Data
LCCN Permalink: http://lccn.loc.gov/61018514

Temple, Sarah Blackwell Gober.
    Georgia journeys, being an account of the lives of Georgia's original settlers
    and many other early settlers
    348 p. illus. 25 cm.
    1. Frontier and pioneer life—Georgia. [from old catalog] 2. Georgia—History—
Colonial period, ca. 1600–1775. I. Coleman, Kenneth, [from old catalog] joint
author.
F289 .T4
61–18514

Paperback ISBN-13: 978-0-8203-3529-2
ISBN-10: 0-8203-3529-0

Contents

Preface

No MAN is the hero of this book; instead its heroes are the men, women, and children whose hard work, heartaches, failures, and successes in Georgia's first two decades began the colony. Historians have written little about the obscure, ordinary men and women whose lives are not spectacular but whose work is so essential to any area. Certainly the first colonists, who came to Georgia on the *Ann* in 1732, were such people. It is hard to find out about such people; they left few records. Usually they were too busy living and making a living, especially in a new area like Georgia, to record their doings and thoughts. They wrote few letters and almost no diaries. Most of them got into the records seldom unless they caused trouble. Yet from the records of the Trustees the outlines of the lives of many of these colonists can be made out. The story is incomplete, yet it tells enough of the doings of "the poor" in early Georgia to make the retelling worthwhile.*

Usually co-authors work together; however, at times they must work at a distance with little personal knowledge of each other. For them never to meet is more unusual. I know my co-author only through a little that other people have told me of her and through the work which she did on this book.

I first heard of Mrs. Temple when I was asked to finish the study of Georgia's earliest settlers, which her death had not allowed her to complete. The manuscript impressed me with the

---

*This paragraph is the sense of "Notes for Preface" found among the manuscripts of Mrs. Temple.

thoroughness of the research and the many interesting facts she had discovered about Georgia's little known original settlers. Most of the story had been written, but the manuscript was in an unfinished condition. Following Mrs. Temple's tracks through the sources soon convinced me even more that she had been a careful researcher who knew well how to extract the value from the documents. The story here offered is essentially Mrs. Temple's story told in her own way. Yet I have made numerous changes. Parts have been changed slightly, others rewritten, and some written for the first time.

In quoted matter original spelling is adhered to throughout this study. Only when the word seems not clear is its modern English equivalent given in brackets. Spelling was not nearly so standardized in the eighteenth century as it is in the twentieth. Even educated people showed great variance in their spelling; the uneducated who are often quoted in this study would be expected to show more variation and individuality. The original spelling has been retained in the belief that it gives more of the individuality of the writer and the atmosphere of the period than modernized spelling would. Spelling of proper names also varied greatly in the eighteenth century, and no single correct spelling could always be arrived at. The most common spelling of names was adopted unless no such could be determined, in which case an arbitrary decision was made.

When Georgia was settled the English world still used the Julian calendar, though most of Western Europe was using the Gregorian calendar (the one now used in most of the world) at that time. Under the Julian calendar the new year began on March 25, instead of January 1, and the Julian calendar was eleven days behind the Gregorian in actual dating of days in the eighteenth century. The colonists arrived at Yamacraw Bluff on February 1, 1732, so far as they were concerned. Yet when the English-speaking world adopted the Gregorian calendar in 1752, this date became February 12, 1733. In this study dates between January 1 and March 24 have been cited as to year by the Gregorian calendar but the day of the month has not been changed. Thus a date given in a source as February 15, 1734, would be cited as February 15, 1735. Dates between March 25 and December 31 have not been altered at all. Dates given in footnotes are exactly as stated in the documents but all between January 1 and

March 24 are clearly indicated Old Style [O.S.] unless written, as they often were, with both years, thus, 1732/3.

Mrs. Temple and I owe a debt of gratitude first to the Georgia settlers whose lives we recount, for what they did and for the record they originated, to the British Public Record Office, the Earl of Egmont, and others who preserved these records through the years. We have received much willing and encouraging assistance from Mr. W. W. DeRenne, Mr. John Bonner, Mrs. Susan B. Tate, and others at the University of Georgia Library; from Mrs. Lilla M. Hawes of the Georgia Historical Society; the staff of the Manuscripts Division of the Library of Congress; the staff of the Georgia Department of Archives and History; Miss Florence Weldon Sibley, Clarke Library, Marietta, Georgia; Mr. B. C. Yates, Kennesaw Mountain Battlefield Park, Marietta, Georgia; and other keepers of records and interested people. Miss Martha Gramling deserves thanks for the jacket drawing of early Savannah, and Mrs. Susan B. Tate for the tedious but necessary job of proof reading. We owe the staff of the University of Georgia Press thanks for help in the editing and publication of the book. Perhaps our greatest debt is to Mrs. Temple's sister, Miss Eilleen Gober, who watched this study with interest from its inception and without whose interest it would probably never have been published.

KENNETH COLEMAN

University of Georgia
Athens, Georgia

Introduction

GEORGIA was founded with three main aims in view: to aid the unfortunate, to advance mercantilism for Britain, and to strengthen imperial defense by securing control of the debatable land between South Carolina and St. Augustine which Spain also claimed. Though concern for debtors had much to do with the origin of the idea for a new colony, by the time the charter was issued the designation "debtors" began to be expanded to include any unfortunate Englishmen or non-English protestants. Few, if any, debtors came to Georgia, but certainly many "unfortunates" did come at the expense of the Trustees, the charity colonists of the early years. Mercantilism, the prevailing eighteenth-century economic system, demanded that European countries have colonies to produce items not produced easily at home. Britain was especially anxious to secure silk, wine, and various tropical and semi-tropical products from her American colonies. These had been tried rather unsuccessfully in Virginia and the Carolinas; and there were great hopes that they could be produced successfully in Georgia. Spain had first laid claim to the Georgia area with the founding of St. Augustine in 1565 and had maintained her claim throughout the seventeenth century with missions and presidios along the Georgia coast and up the Chattahoochee River. By the time of the founding of Georgia there were no Spanish north of the St. Marys River, though Spain still claimed the Georgia territory. Hence there was constant fear that the Spanish would invade Georgia and try to drive out the colonists. The problem of the Spanish in Florida was not to be solved until 1763, a date beyond the limits of this study.

Georgia was founded and was to be controlled for twenty-one years by a board of twenty-one Trustees who could neither occupy any office nor own any land in the colony. The Trustees could be recompensed for their efforts and money spent on Georgia only by the satisfaction of having been a help to the unfortunate or to the empire. The three-fold purpose in the colony's founding made for regulations in the colony that sometimes seemed in conflict. Philanthropy and mercantilism were paramount in the thinking of the Trustees, and they concerned themselves mainly with regulations concerning these two aims, leaving imperial defense to the British government. Social and economic experiments must be controlled if they are to accomplish their purposes. Controls were easier to specify with the controlling body a considerable distance from the area and people to be controlled. The Trustees remained in England, except for Oglethorpe, the only one who ever came to Georgia.

The Trustees were so concerned with their social and economic ideas that they almost forgot that government is necessary when men live together. Hence they never developed a full-fledged government for Georgia. At the founding of the colony they did provide for a town court of Savannah, which was clearly municipal in character and not suited to govern an entire colony. During his first year in Georgia, Oglethorpe was in essence the government though he bore no title and was given little specific power. After this year he turned more and more to defense, and the civil government had to be carried on by the officials appointed by the Trustees. Since these originally were from among the charity colonists, they often were not very outstanding administrators or political leaders. Besides, the Trustees gave the officials in Georgia only limited powers, keeping all real authority in their own hands in England.

The Trustees always demanded more information than they received about what was happening in Georgia until William Stephens arrived as their secretary in the colony in 1737 and began to send them in regular installments his detailed journal. Acknowledgment that there might be insufficient government in Georgia was made by the Trustees in 1741 when they proposed the two-county (Savannah and Frederica) system and put the Savannah County government into operation. William Stephens became president with a Board of Assistants. When Oglethorpe left Georgia in 1743 Frederica County was abolished—its government had never been created—and the government in Savannah was extended to include the entire colony. But the president and the assistants never had power comparable to that of a governor and his council in a royal colony. They were merely agents of the Trustees, who kept all real power in their hands.

In 1751, just before they gave up their power to the King, the Trustees called an elected assembly in Georgia which was intended to advise but not to legislate. This is as close as Georgians came to having any self-government during the period of this study. Evidently the Trustees thought that all power of decision should reside in them in England, and that none should be given to the colonists in Georgia. The representations and objections which the "malcontents" sent from Georgia to England might well have been prevented had there been any machinery through which Georgians could express themselves and have a share in their own government. The Trustees seemed incapable of realizing that Englishmen were used to participating in their government and that one way for the Georgia settlers to progress was to be given some authority and responsibility in controlling their own affairs.

To prevent a recurrence of the misfortunes which had made the charity colonists poor and unfortunate, the Trustees adopted numerous regulations. One of the first and most emphasized was the prohibition of the sale or consumption of rum in the colony. Oglethorpe attributed the deaths during the first summer to the drinking of rum, and the Trustees forthwith insisted that rum be prohibited. However, this regulation was never really enforced. Rum was sold and consumed in Georgia despite all the regulations that the Trustees might enact in London and their insistence that these regulations be enforced in Georgia.

Regulations to which the colonists objected much more strenuously were the land regulations, which the Trustees were in a much better position to enforce than the prohibition against rum. Land was not granted in fee simple but through tail male, a system held over from feudal times. The Trustees felt that many of the unfortunate might lose their land should it be granted in fee simple, and so they made provision for land to be granted through tail male, a feudal and military tenure forbidding women to inherit. According to the Trustees' plan, fifty acres of land was assigned to every adult male, who was to be available to fight in case of Spanish or Indian attack. These provisions may have kept some colonists from coming to Georgia, but in practice the tail male provisions were not always enforced and the Trustees almost always allowed women to inherit land when there was no male heir. However, special application was necessary in every case. Land could not be sold or exchanged without the Trustees' permission, and though permission was usually given upon application, the requirement was a limitation upon ownership that made land harder to dispose of in Georgia than in other colonies. The absence of fee simple land titles made the mortgaging of land difficult. Charity colonists were given fifty acres of land, and people who had paid their own passage over could receive up to 500 acres. These limitations were contrary to the general land ownership pattern in the southern colonies and limited the economic activity of many. Peasant proprietorships where every man could live under his own vine and fig tree (or mulberry tree in Georgia) were envisioned by the Trustees. They never seemed to realize that conditions in a new country might not fit this idea and that much of the land granted could not be used effectively this way. Some land was swampy, some was sandy, and much was inferior. Often more money could be made from timber cutting and cattle raising than from farming. The forty-five-acre farm lots which charity colonists received were insufficient to make a living on. The Trustees seemed to think that all land was capable of being used in the same way and that a colonist who did not diligently cultivate his lot was not deserving of additional land or further consideration.

The only regulation about mercantilism which applied to all the colonists was the requirement that each should plant one hundred white mulberry trees upon his forty-five-acre farm lot. The leaves of these trees were to be used to feed the silkworms which it was hoped would loom large in Georgia's economic life. The young mulberry trees were to be furnished from the Trustees' Garden in Savannah. The making of wine and other items which the Trustees hoped would be produced in Georgia was not to be forced upon all colonists as was silk production.

Defense was the reason for the original idea of settlement in compact towns or villages rather than on isolated farms or plantations. The initial plan was carried out at Savannah and its outlying villages. Compactness would certainly make for easier defense, for better social life, and for efficiency in enforcing the controls which the Trustees prescribed. The original idea worked with some success only in Savannah and not perfectly there. For a new colony this was perhaps a good idea, but it necessitated settlers' taking land which was assigned to them instead of picking their own land as frontiersmen generally did.

In the prohibition against slavery can be seen a combination of the three reasons for Georgia's founding. Poor people would not be able to purchase slaves. The Trustees insisted that the charity colonists work diligently, and the presence of slaves in the colony might discourage hard work. Silk and wine production were not thought to require hard labor; so the labor of slaves would not be as necessary as in the plantation colonies. Slaves could not be used as soldiers in time of need, and their presence in the colony could only weaken it from a military standpoint. But the Trustees omitted several points from their calculations. The temperature in Georgia was much hotter than in England, and it was generally thought that whites could not labor in the summer sun. Negro slaves were in use in South Carolina, and Georgians knew about them and the work that they could do.

One point which seems to have been entirely ignored by the Trustees is that almost none of the original settlers were farmers who knew how farming was done in England, let alone in Georgia. Being tradesmen of various sorts, the colonists were not used to the hard physical labor connected with clearing land and cultivating it. Apparently a new chance in Georgia was supposed to inspire the colonists immediately to hard physical labor that few of them had been accustomed to.

The fact that farming was not very easy in Georgia was made clear by Hector de Beaufain of Purrysburg, South Carolina, just across the river from Georgia, to the Earl of Egmont while Beaufain was in London in 1741. He pointed out the great labor necessary in clearing land before cultivation was possible, in fencing to keep out wild animals, in building barns, and in cultivating and harvesting the crops. Great damage was done by crows, turkeys, squirrels, and other small animals, which must be guarded against even at night. Mulberry trees needed to be fenced and otherwise cared for if they were to do their best. Besides, land wore out soon so that the clearing of new ground was a continual process. Beaufain summed it all up by saying, "what I intend by this tedious narrative was to shew that these things [silk and provisions] cannot be raised without Labour, nor will make a return till after some years, I might have taken notice, that let a man be ever so industrious, a bad Season or accidents may disappoint him of his crop, and that till he is Season'd to the Climate; he may probably lay out more with the Doctor, than he can get by his work, but I believe I have said enough to convince you of the difficulty of the undertaking, and that further helps and encouragement are necessary—"[1] The letters and lives of many of Georgia's early settlers bear out the truth of Beaufain's statements. Certainly the colonists continually asked for "further helps and encouragements." One wonders what difference it might have made had the Trustees been given such information before the settlement of Georgia.

Beaufain points out something seldom mentioned by the early settlers or by the Trustees—"that till he [the colonist] is Season'd to the Climate; he may probably lay out more with the Doctor, than he can get by his work." This adjustment to the difference in climate between Georgia and England, Salzburg, Scotland, or wherever the settlers came from was a matter of major importance. More of the deaths in the first year can probably be blamed on the climate difference than on rum, drinking river water, or the other reasons given in Georgia and England. The fact that climate is almost never mentioned leads one to think that Georgians themselves probably did not realize what a great, and often fatal, problem it was.

A brief chronological outline of happenings in Georgia's first twenty years will assist readers to put events mentioned throughout this study in their correct chronological setting.

When the 112 original charity settlers arrived on the *Ann* at the site of Savannah on February 12, 1733, they found nothing but a pine-covered bluff above the Savannah River with the small tribe of Yamacraw Indians living there under their old chieftain Tomochichi. Oglethorpe and Colonel William Bull of South Carolina laid out the town, and the colonists set to work felling trees and building their houses. Oglethorpe remained in Georgia until May, 1734, directing the colonists in most of their endeavors. Through the intermediary Mary Musgrove, the half-breed wife of an Indian trader, Oglethorpe made an agreement with Tomochichi that the colonists might settle at Savannah. Later he se-

---

1. Egmont Papers, Phillipps Collection (University of Georgia), Vol. 14212, pp. 105-13, reprinted in Kenneth Coleman, "Agricultural Practices in Georgia's First Decade," *Agricultural History*, XXXIII, 4 (1959), pp. 196-99.

cured the agreement of the Creek Indians, who controlled the
area of southern Georgia, that the land between the Savannah
and Altamaha rivers as far up as the tide ebbed and flowed
might be used by the whites, except for a tract near Savannah
and the islands of Ossabaw, Sapelo, and St. Catherine. Regulations for Indian trade were also agreed to. Oglethorpe immediately established himself as a successful Indian diplomat, something of great value to Georgia. The fast friendship of Tomochichi for Oglethorpe, which lasted until the Indian died in 1739,
helped Oglethorpe's success; but his own abilities should not be
overlooked.

Besides establishing good relations with the Indians, Oglethorpe in his first year surveyed the colony with an eye to its
defense. The first outpost to be established was Fort Argyle at
the point on the Ogeechee River where the Indian trading path
crossed that river. Here a fort was built and ten families settled.
Oglethorpe surveyed the coast, picking out places for future
fortifications and towns. He also selected the sites and began the
settlements of outposts around Savannah which were intended
for its defense.

Having settled the colonists, begun the town government at
Savannah, surveyed the defenses of the colony, sketched plans for
further execution, and settled the Salzburgers outside the immediate area of Savannah, Oglethorpe embarked for England in
May, 1734. Tomochichi, his wife and nephew, and several other
Indians went with Oglethorpe, to be impressed with England and
to impress England with Georgia. Oglethorpe succeeded in securing a Parliamentary appropriation and additional settlers, and
generally in impressing Georgia upon the English world of the
day. In early 1736 he returned to Georgia with "the great embarkation," two vessels loaded with Georgia settlers under convoy
of a man-of-war. John and Charles Wesley and a group of Moravians came with Oglethorpe, as well as additional Salzburgers
and colonists from England.

A group of Scotch Highlanders who had preceded Oglethorpe
to Georgia were settled at Darien at the mouth of the Altamaha
River, as far south as Georgia extended according to its charter.
Frederica was laid out on St. Simons Island, Oglethorpe being
oblivious to the fact that it was south of the Altamaha River and
therefore not in Georgia. Frederica was on the inland passage and
conceived of by Oglethorpe as the chief defense of the colony

against any possible Spanish attack from St. Augustine. Other
fortifications south of Frederica were built and manned with a
few defenders. Not content with fortifying the coastal frontier of
Georgia, Oglethorpe also had laid out and built the fort and town
of Augusta some one hundred and fifty miles up the Savannah
River from Savannah at an important point for Indian trade and
diplomacy. Truly Oglethorpe's main interest in Georgia had
changed from philanthropy to imperial defense. Henceforth he
was so much taken up with military matters that he had little
time for the civilian affairs of the colony, though he did not
stop giving directions to the civil officers, none of whom dared
openly to oppose him.

    In January, 1737, Oglethorpe again returned to England to
secure additional funds, especially for Georgia's defense. It was
on this trip that he was made commander-in-chief of the military
forces in South Carolina and Georgia and colonel of a regiment
which he raised before returning to Georgia in October, 1738.
This regiment was stationed at Frederica, and here Oglethorpe
spent most of his time, being seen less and less in Savannah.

    War between England and Spain (the War of Jenkins' Ear, to
be merged with the War of the Austrian Succession or King
George's War, as it was called in America) began in 1739 and
took up all Oglethorpe's time as well as creating much excitement
and concern in Georgia. In the late spring of 1740 Oglethorpe
began his first invasion of Florida. After a siege of over a month
at St. Augustine, he was forced to abandon operations in late
July and retire to St. Simons Island. In the summer of 1742, the
Spanish invasion of Georgia created such fear throughout the
colony that many people refugeed to South Carolina or elsewhere. The military activity on St. Simons Island culminated with
the Battle of Bloody Marsh and the withdrawal of the Spanish.
Oglethorpe made another unsuccessful attempt to capture St.
Augustine in March of 1743 before he returned to England permanently in the summer. The war was actually over in Georgia,
but there were alarms and fear of further Spanish invasions for
the next several years. With the signing of a general peace in
1748, the danger was ended for the time being.

    With the exit of Oglethorpe, the most outstanding and dominat-
ing personality that Georgia had seen to date, there was no one
left to dominate or to give central control to the actions in the
colony. President William Stephens and his two successors could

not fill Oglethorpe's place. In reality Oglethorpe himself had ceased to dominate except in military matters. Georgia was no longer a one-man operation by 1743.

The ending of the fear of invasion led some people who had fled the colony to return, and the population increased. By now the Trustees' original restrictions were weakened or gone. No attempt was made to restrict or prevent the consumption of rum. Land policy was much more liberal so far as actual grants were concerned, and ownership in fee simple was possible by 1750. The prohibition of slavery was the last restriction to go, but it was weakening in 1750 and was dead by the time the Trustees gave up control of Georgia. Now Georgia could follow in what might be called her natural direction, copying to a considerable degree the economy of South Carolina, planting rice on the coast and European small grains in the upcountry. Lumber and cattle continued important.

By the late 1740's the Trustees were having a harder and harder time securing sufficient funds to finance their operations in Georgia. Most of their funds had from the start come from Parliamentary grants, but in 1751 both Parliament and the King refused to give any further financial help to the Trustees, whose charter had only about one year yet to run. Since the Trustees could not continue to operate without funds, they gave up their control to the King on June 23, 1752. With this action the period set for this study ends.

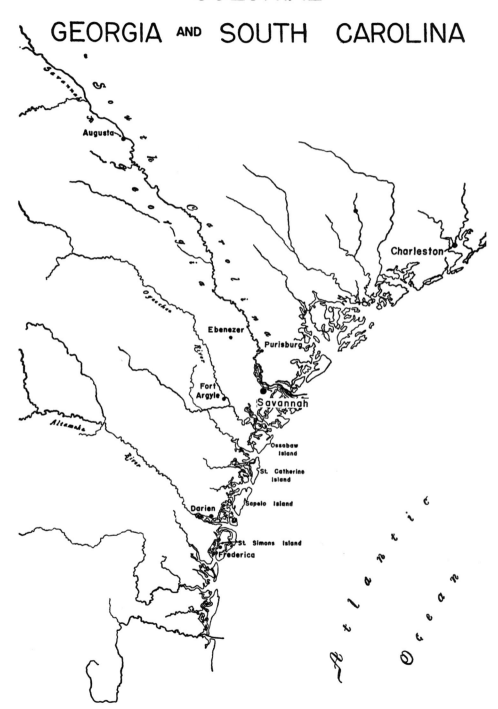

COLONIAL
GEORGIA AND SOUTH CAROLINA

Savannah River

South

Carolina

Georgia

Augusta

Ogeechee

River

Charleston

Ebenezer

Purisburg

Altamaha

Fort
Argyle

Savannah

River

Ossabaw
Island

St. Catherine
Island

Sapelo Island

Darien

Atlantic

St. Simons Island

Frederica

Ocean

SAVANNAH AND VICINITY
EARLY SETTLEMENTS

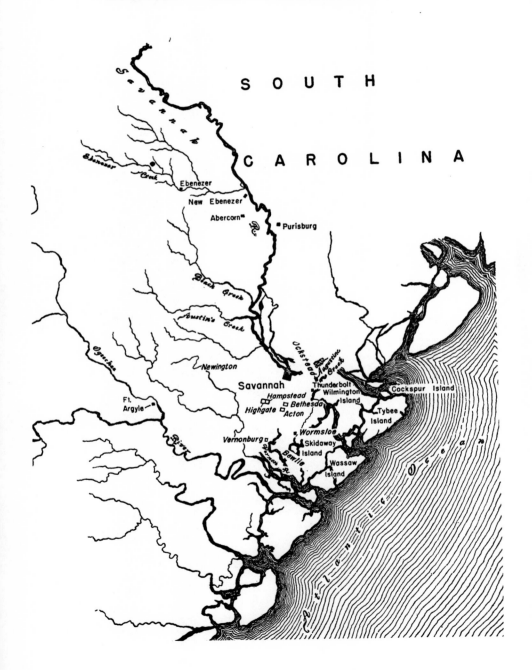

CHAPTER ONE

Atlantic Crossing

THE SETTLERS for the new colony of Georgia in America sailed from England in November of 1732, a year afterwards memorable to them—memorable with bitterness or with gratitude depending upon the personality of the individual or his future success. These passengers and others who followed them left home with mixed emotions and varying attitudes toward this great philanthropic experiment. Some had only their memories to increase their sadness in quitting England. Others had great hopes for a new life in a new world where many of the failures of the old might be recouped. To some a new land and new opportunities could mean little. Their lives had been so shaped by past misfortunes that they could not share the hope of the young in spirit. Others, whatever their misfortunes in the past, rebounded and entered into a new life with zest.

On October 23, 1732, the group met in London in the office of the Trustees for Establishing the Colony of Georgia in America. They and many others had been interviewed during the preceding weeks. So many had wanted to go that the Trustees had advertised, "Great Number of Unfortunate People having attended . . . in order to be sent to GEORGIA, this is to acquaint all Persons in like Circumstances (to prevent their losing their time in Attendance) that there is no Possibility of admitting any more at present, since out of several Hundreds whose Names are already enter'd, the Trustees can send Seventy Persons this Season, their Cash not as yet enabling them to provide comfortably for more."[1]

This meeting was a solemn occasion for the settlers and the

Trustees who now saw as a group the frail human instruments chosen to carry out their plans across the ocean. The future colonists were given a final review of the terms they must accept. Four immediately decided not to go. The objections of four others to the system of land tenure in tail male were smothered over with some concessions, but were to cause trouble later. Another soon decided not to go, since "his Friends had proved kinder to him, and offer'd to provide for him." Replacements were soon secured, one because he insisted so loudly upon being taken. All signed a statement pledging themselves to submit to the Trustees' laws and the form of government in the colony, to stay at least three years, and to assist each other in clearing land and building their houses the first year.[2]

The people at the meeting were perhaps unaware of the plans which led up to their assembly, nor would they have been greatly concerned had they known. They were occupied with the momentous step they were about to take, with their own troubles and plans, and not with those of philanthropically inclined gentlemen who had envisaged this new settlement in America. To begin with, these gentlemen saw the settlement as a colony for debtors; by the time this narrative opens the plan was enlarged and it was for "such as were in decayed Circumstances, and thereby disabled from following any Business in England; and who, if in Debt, had Leave from their Creditors to go, and such as were recommended by the Minister, Church-Wardens, and Overseers of their respective Parishes."[3]

When the people came out of the meeting that afternoon, they knew that their time in England was now short. Much had to be done, including taking leave of friends and relatives, many of whom they might never see again. Theirs were grave decisions, for no man lightly quits forever the land of his birth. Life in a new colony would be different, but could not, they thought, be harder than theirs had been already. Some were well aware of the opportunity before them in a new land.

"The *Ann* Galley, of above 200 Tons," an announcement the following Monday read, "is on the point of sailing from Deptford, for the new colony of *Georgia*, with 35 Families, consisting of Carpenters, Bricklayers, Farmers, &c. who take all proper Instruments. The men were learning Military Discipline of the Guards, as must all that go thither, and to carry Musquets, Bayonets, and

Swords, to defend the Colony in case of an attack from the Indians." A possibility of more cheerful life was the statement, "She [the *Ann*] has on Board 10 Ton of Alderman Parsons' best Beer, and will take in at the *Maderas* 5 Tun of Wine, for the Service of the Colony."[4]

The people embarked at Gravesend on November 6, their goods in a chest, or if they had enough, in two chests, their places on the *Ann* chosen by lot. The following day it was announced that James Oglethorpe, member of Parliament for Haslemere in Surrey and one of the Trustees, "will go on Board a Ship in the River Thames, in order to proceed to Georgia in America, to give the finishing Instructions for the happy Settlement of a new Colony there: He will be accompanied by near a Hundred Persons. And we hear a Hundred more will soon follow him."[5]

On the last Sunday in England "a Sermon [was] preach'd at Gravesend, by the Rev. Mr. Herbert, to the several Passengers on board the *Ann* Galley, Captain Thomas, Commander, bound for the new Settlement in Georgia; they came all ashore in three Gravesend Boats, and after Divine Service and the Sermon was ended, return'd again on board in the same manner. The said Mr. Herbert goes over at his own Expences, in order to officiate as Minister of the Colony to be establish'd in the said Country." Henry Herbert, son of the late Lord Herbert of Cherbury, volunteered to serve as minister until the Trustees could afford to pay the salary of a clergyman.[6]

Finally, on Thursday, November 16, seven Trustees went to Gravesend where Oglethorpe presided at the meeting on board the *Ann*, at which were "Settled sevll. things in relation to the Colony." Accommodations on the *Ann* were inspected. The ship was described as "being Tight & Strong & well Manned, Tackled and Provided fitt for Merchant Service." The latest benefactions to the colony were noted, the Trustees thanked by the passengers, and the roll of the passengers was called.[7] This roll is contained in the Appendix to this study. On his list Captain Thomas marked down a total of 114 passengers, or 91 heads.[8] After the roll was called, the Trustees "left the People very well satisfied." The troubles of the voyage began that night, when "The Pilot being in Liquor was set ashoar & another Ordered in his Room."[9]

Little remained to be done. Aid, if needed, was already requested from the governors of colonies in America and from the

ships at sea.[10] Viscount Percival noted several days before that
"as for provision, medicines, tents, arms, etc., nothing is wanting."
He termed those about to sail "able, sensible men," and went on
to write, "Thus, I hope that with the blessing of God, this noble,
charitable, disinterested and profitable design to the nation will
take root and flourish, having taken all the care possible for its
success."[11] Did Lord Percival think then of a recent conversation
in which he joined at Court? The talk then was of "curbing
the New England people," and one opinion expressed about the
colonies was that " 'tis to be feared they will one day withdraw
their allegiance, growing too headstrong."[12]

So the day came when the settlers left England, sailing from
Gravesend on Friday, November 17, 1732, about nine o'clock in
the morning, falling down the Thames with the tide. Friday
night the *Ann* anchored "between the Nore and the Downs, the
Pilot not chusing to venture over the Flats in the night time."
On Saturday morning the anchor was weighed early. The wind
blew fresh and strong and the *Ann* sailed down the coast of Kent
to Deal, where, about eleven o'clock, it stopped briefly to take on
board some fresh provisions and send away letters. Several passengers took advantage of the last chance to buy brandy offered for
sale on the *Ann* by local dealers. "Yesterday came down and sailed
through, . . . the *Ann*, Thomas, for———," was the newspaper statement from Deal on November 19. Two days later
the *Ann* anchored briefly at Dover, and the next day, November
21, was opposite the Isle of Wight. Landmarks soon faded from
sight as the *Ann* sailed through the Channel and out into the
Atlantic.[13]

Soon many of the passengers were seasick, and this continued
throughout the voyage with bad weather. The sick were given
water gruel with sugar and white wine in it, sage tea, and chicken
broth. The ship was ordered sprinkled once a week with vinegar.[14] The colonists had need of patience for theirs was a journey
stripped to stark essentials. The Trustees had little money for
the expenses of the new colony, and such refinements as gifts for
women and children and candles for the passage came only from
kind-hearted well-wishers.[15]

By the terms of the charter party, £4 sterling was paid by the
Trustees for each passage on the *Ann*. Each passenger over 12
years of age was a whole passage, children between seven and
twelve were counted half a head, those between two and seven

were counted three for one, and children under two received a free ride.[16]

The passengers slept in wooden cradles with boarded bottoms. On later passages mention is sometimes made of flock mattresses having been supplied, but there is no record of mattresses having been used on the *Ann*. These cradles, the charter party specified, were five feet eight inches in the clear inside and were hung be-,tween decks. A canvas curtain was hung four feet below the beam from the bulkhead of the lazaretto to the bulkhead of the gun room on both sides.[17] The passengers must have been crowded as they slept, the youngest placed alongside their mothers in any cracks available, so that dawn of each winter's day was welcomed by both young and old alike. Perhaps, though, the quarters were no more meager than what some of them al-ready were inured to; certainly they had the advantage of being temporary.

If the *Ann's* youngest passengers slept in cracks, they must also have been fed on crumbs. Before the *Ann* left the Thames her part owner, Samuel Wragg, and Captain Thomas contracted to put on board "a Convenient & Sufficient Quantity of Provisions Vizt. Eighty four Butts of Water eight Tons of Beer forty Hundred Weight of Beef nineteen hundred Weight of Pork Sixty hundred Weight of bread with a Sufficient Quantity of Fish Flower Pease Butter Suett & plumbs. . . ." Food was rationed on the basis of a six weeks' passage; the ten days' delay in the Thames, from November 6, doubtless accounted for the purchase of provisions costing £52.13.10 when the *Ann* paused at Deal.[18]

The passengers ate beef four days a week, pork two days, and fish one day. The daily allowance for each mess of five was, on beef days, four pounds of beef, two and a half pounds of flour, and half a pound of suet or of plums. On pork days, five pounds of pork and two and a half pints of peas were issued; on fish days, two and a half pounds of fish and half a pound of butter was the ration. In addition each head received seven pounds of bread a week, bread being weighed at fourteen ounces to the pound, though all other provisions were sixteen ounces to the pound. Each head received two quarts of beer a day. Water ration for drinking and bathing was not specified, though both water and beer rations were reduced toward the end of the voyage, pre-sumably because supplies were running short. To supplement the standard diet, carrots and potatoes were sometimes issued

and onions were ordered once a week. Vinegar, wine, and
molasses were at times given out. Celebrations brought extra
allowances of food and drink.[19]

The *Ann* ploughed across the Atlantic, small, lonely, and remote. She sailed to the southward, thus lengthening her passage
but avoiding, for part of the journey at least, the fury of the
winter winds. The voyage must have been tedious on the
crowded vessel. However, several days of celebration stood out.
On November 23 the Trustees' bounty provided three quarts of
flip per mess and a handsome supper to celebrate the christening
of Georgius Marinus Warren, to whom Oglethorpe stood god-
father. To celebrate Oglethorpe's birthday on December 21 there
was a pint of punch to each head as well as mutton and broth, and
cudgel was played for a pair of shoes. On Christmas there were
prayers and a sermon before the dinner of mutton, beef broth,
and pudding, with a pint of flip per head. The weather was
noted as being "exceedingly hot" or the hottest that passengers
had ever known. Toward the end of the voyage the men were exercised with guns and bayonets. When several people fell out with
each other, Oglethorpe ordered a pint of rum punch for each
head and told the people to drink and be friends again.[20]

Except for seasickness, the passage was accounted a healthy
one. People fell and bruised themselves, Joseph Hughes had
several fits on December 17, and Peter Gordon was reported
desperately ill of the colic. James Cannon and James Clark, two
infants, died in passage. The two little boys "were very weakly
when I came on Board and had indeed been half starved thro'
want before they left London as many others were who are recovered with Food and Care but these were so far gone that all
our Efforts to Save them were in vain . . . ," Oglethorpe wrote.
Their deaths were duly noted in London, yet it was a matter
of congratulation that only these two had died. Oglethorpe and
Dr. Cox saw to the needs of everyone. Whatever Dr. Cox thought
the sick needed was ordered out of Oglethorpe's private stores
if the ship did not afford it otherwise. Once when Oglethorpe
caught a dolphin, he "being Aprised of some Big-Bellyd. Women
in the Ship Longing, gave it all amongst them withot. tasting any
himself."[21]

The *Ann's* passengers were in good health when they neared
their journey's end, except Francis Scott, bruised by a fall when
the last storm struck the *Ann*. But storms at sea would soon be

but a memory. Before eight o'clock on the morning of Saturday, January 13, 1733, the passengers on the *Ann* saw land, the coast of South Carolina in the vicinity of Charles Town. They knew that the sea part of their journey was nearly done. Governor Robert Johnson of South Carolina had warned that the people should not come ashore at Charles Town. A hundred inconveniences would ensue, he observed diplomatically, and with this the Trustees agreed.[22] It was the first of those reiterated cries when colonists were sent: Do not let them see Charles Town, else they will be charmed and never go to Georgia.

The *Ann's* passengers waited on board, searching with intent gaze the line of shore, while their leader James Oglethorpe went ashore. Governor Johnson met Oglethorpe when he landed, for the two had much business to discuss after Oglethorpe presented a copy of Georgia's charter and the King's instructions to help the new colonists. Details concerning the practical help which South Carolina's General Assembly would give the new colony were arranged.[23] Oglethorpe's reception was cordial, as well it might be, for the men and women on the *Ann* would in some degree relieve South Carolina of her role of border colony and take from her the partial brunt of enmities and incursions from Spaniards in Florida and Indians to the south and west.

With Mr. Middleton, the King's pilot, on board to show Captain Thomas his route through unfamiliar waters, the *Ann* sailed on January 14 towards Port Royal Island, South Carolina. Here the passengers landed on January 20. Oglethorpe had preceded the *Ann* and, together with Lieutenant James Watts of the Independent Company, was fitting out the new barracks at Beaufort as the temporary home of the colonists.[24] Watts that day met his future wife from off the *Ann*, though she then was married to another man. Now began the business of disembarking the passengers and the stores.

"We were just a week in our Passage from Charles Town to Port Royal where we Landed and were Lodged at some new Barracks that are there intended for a new Fortification about 3 miles from Beaufort Town. At our Landing Mr. Oglethorpe ordered me to take all the Stores into my Care and to keep an Account of them. And in that office I shall continue which takes up my whole time," Thomas Causton wrote to his wife. His time was so occupied that he "could not so much as go to See the Town or Stir half a mile from the Place. But the Accot. I have from other People is enough for me to believe that the Houses there are all of Timber and very few have Glass Windows or Brick Chimneys. But notwithstanding that the People are very Gallant and generous and seem to live in a plentifull manner. Some of our Company who went to the Town were entertained in a very elegant manner and every one found some body to entertain them in some Shape or other." Causton added, "We have five or six familys amongst us that are deserving a Gentleman's conversation."[25]

Some of the people of Beaufort and its vicinity paid visits to the colonists, showing them various kindnesses, while Oglethorpe made a quick trip to the Savannah River where he selected the site for the settlement, conforming to the Trustees' stipulation that it be as near as possible to the Savannah River. This made it as far as possible from the Spaniards at St. Augustine, and as close as could be to Carolina, so that the colonists could both assist and be assisted by that province.[26] Near the site he chose, Oglethorpe found a small Indian tribe, the Yamacraw, whose chief, Tomochichi, gave Georgia an allegiance from which he never wavered. Such allegiance was important in itself and for its influence on other Indians in the protection of the colonists' lives; it also caused Tomochichi to step upon a larger stage and eventually to occupy an honored place in Georgia's history.

The South Carolina General Assembly generously resolved to give the settlers of Georgia 100 head of breeding cattle, five bulls, twenty breeding sows, four boars, and twenty barrels of rice. Protection by scout boats and rangers, transportation by boat, and the assistance of Colonel William Bull, delegated by the governor and council to accompany the colonists to Georgia, were additional signs of South Carolina's friendship.[27]

Oglethorpe returned to Beaufort on January 24. On Sunday, January 28, a celebration of thanksgiving was held, attended not only by the *Ann's* passengers but by a number of people from Beaufort. The colonists gave thanks for their safe arrival, for protection from the perils of deep waters, and for their present blessings, which included a favorable site for their settlement and friendly Indian neighbors. They heard a sermon by the Reverend Mr. Jones of Beaufort, for their own minister, Henry Herbert, preached by invitation that day in Beaufort. They had a bountiful meal from four fat hogs, eight turkeys, fowls, English beef and other items, a hogshead of punch, a hogshead of beer,

and a large quantity of wine, "and all was disposed in so regular a Manner that no Person was Drunk nor any Disorder happen'd."[28]

On January 30 the colonists embarked in a seventy-ton sloop
and five small boats, with the scout boat and Captain MacPherson
and fifteen of his rangers for their protection. They camped the
first night, somewhat hurriedly because of a storm, at a place
called the Look-out, and the second night on Johns Island, where
they ate a supper of venison and slept in huts prepared for
them. The next afternoon they disembarked at the foot of a
bluff on the Savannah River and stepped for the first time upon
Georgia's soil. Up went four large tents, and in went the bedding;
when darkness fell on Thursday, February 1 (February 12, new
style), and tired people lay down to rest, English men and
women had taken possession and the colony of Georgia was
begun.[29] The prelude to the Georgia journey of 112 people was
ended.

CHAPTER TWO

Birth Pains of a Colony

EARLY the next morning the settlers had a long look at the place which was to be their home. "It is impossible to give a true Description of the Place because we are in a Wood," Thomas Causton wrote, "but I can't forbear Saying that it is a very pleasant one." Oglethorpe too thought the place was pleasant but he dwelt particularly on the healthfulness of the site, on high ground with springs of water nearby; "it is sheltered from the Western and Southern Winds (the worst in this Country) by vast Woods of Pine-trees, many of which are an Hundred, and few under Seventy Feet high." There was, however, "no Morse [moss] on the Trees," he said, such as he had seen in Carolina. This must have been written after a cursory view, for around the site of Savannah moss was later described as growing in quantities and hanging three or four yards from the boughs; "it gives a noble, ancient and hoary Look to the Woods. . . ."[1] Another description said, "The River washes the Foot of the Hill, which stretches along the Side of it about a Mile, and forms a Terrass 40 Feet perpendicular above High Water.

"From the Key, looking Eastward, you may discover the River as far as the Islands in the Sea; and Westward, one may see it wind thro' the Woods above 6 miles.

"The River is 1000 Feet wide; the Water Fresh, and deep enough for Sloops of Seventy Tons to come up close to the Side of the Key."[2]

In the center of Yamacraw Bluff, a mile-long plain of dry and sandy soil was to be the town of Savannah. Opposite was an island, Hutchinson's Island, where rich growth promised pasturage for cattle. About fifteen miles downstream the river ran into the sea at Tybee Island. About half a mile away from the town site was the village of the friendly Yamacraw Indians with the trading house of John and Mary Musgrove. The Indians and the Musgroves were the only inhabitants.[3] To the south stretched unexplored woods. "The Landskip is very agreeable," Oglethorpe observed; but it was a landscape requiring much hard work to make it habitable. The Trustees had said that they had sent none but people inured to labor, who were prepared to undergo hardships cheerfully.[4]

From the tents early in the mornings the men and boys emerged to work. No one could be idle. Their needs defined their tasks: unload boats, bring up stores, cut down trees, clear land, sow seed, build houses. In and around the tents the children played. They were not allowed to stray; for no one knew what dangers might lie within those woods.

All hands worked the first week on a crane intended to expedite the transfer of goods from the river up the bluff. But much of the goods had to be tugged up by humans; by the end of the week work on the crane was stopped as consuming labor sorely needed elsewhere. Oglethorpe divided the people into three groups: some to clear land for planting, some to begin the fort and palisade, the remainder to fell trees where the town would be.[5]

As in all new colonies, labor was of paramount importance. The tall pines were not easily sent crashing to the ground. Before the *Ann* sailed, the Trustees had asked Governor Johnson of South Carolina to hire twenty Negro laborers and four pairs of sawyers to assist in clearing the ground.[6] Determined as the Trustees were never to allow slaves in the colony, the need for additional labor was compelling.

On February 7 trees began to be cut on the town site, and on February 9 Savannah was laid out; Oglethorpe and Colonel William Bull marked out one square, several streets, and 40 house lots. Only half of the site was cleared of trees immediately. The town plan, Thomas Causton wrote back to England with pride, was drawn by Oglethorpe's direction.[7] Years later some of the bitterest critics the colony ever had, said "The Plan of the Town was beautifully laid out in Wards, Tythings, and publick Squares left at proper Distances for Markets and publick Buildings, the whole making an agreeable Uniformity."[8]

The people had been divided into tythings on board the *Ann,* and each of the four large tents into which they moved on the day they landed represented one tything. The town was to consist of tythings of ten houses each, and of wards of four tythings each. In each tything, ideally, were eleven men able to bear arms—a tything man with his ten men—who took their turns in keeping watch. Before more colonists arrived, each tything must keep guard every fourth night. Each ward was overseen by a constable to whom the four tything men reported. One of the four constables was responsible each twenty-four hours for keeping peace and order, reporting on these matters to the chief, or first, constable.[9]

On the day when Savannah was laid out, the first house was begun. Now began a busy time for the men expert in building: Thomas Milledge, whom Oglethorpe spoke of as the best carpenter, James Goddard, and Noble Jones. They worked closely with Colonel William Bull and several other gentlemen from South Carolina, Bull "Himself measuring the Scantlings and setting out work for the Sawyers, and giving the Proportion of the Houses." Colonel Bull "also gave the work of his Four Servants for the said month."[10] "We have very great Assistance from the Gentlemen of Charles Town," Thomas Causton wrote in March, [we] "have always some of them with us who bring us Workmen to help forward with our Works; they have assisted Mr. Oglethorpe in laying out most of the lands already." Causton thought there would be a fine prospect when the woods were clear. The houses were to be a short distance from the bluff above the river, 60 yards being reserved there.[11]

By the middle of March most of the town site was cleared of trees, two clapboard houses were built and three sawed houses framed. The crane, the battery of cannon, and the magazine were finished. This was all they had been able to do, Oglethorpe wrote, because of the smallness of their numbers, sickness, and people unused to labor. Now, he thanked God they were then pretty well and not one soul had died since their arrival.[12]

A Charles Town merchant, Samuel Eveleigh, during a March visit to Savannah was impressed by Oglethorpe's abilities and the regard in which the settlers held him. "He is extremely well beloved by all his People; the general Title they give him is Father." He comforted the sick and settled arguments. He "keeps a strict Discipline; I never saw one of his People drunk, or heard one swear, all the Time I was there: He does not allow them Rum, but in lieu gives them English Beer. It is surprising to see how chearfully the Men go to work, considering they have not been bred to it: There are no Idlers there; even the Boys and Girls do their Parts . . . he hopes, when he has more Sawyers . . . to finish two Houses a Week . . . . He was palisading the Town round, including some Part of the Common, which I do suppose may be finished in a Fortnight's Time. In short, he has done a vast deal of Work for the Time, and I think his Name justly deserves to be immortalised."[13]

The progress of the building was delayed by the difficulty of hiring slave sawyers. At least three escaped before they reached Georgia. However, twenty pairs of sawyers were hired that spring, and building proceeded more rapidly.[14] The place must have been heaven for boys big and little: trees crashing, logs being sawed, chips flying, shavings curling, houses growing before their fascinated eyes, and the good clean smell of cut pine.

By the latter part of May, clearing had progressed until the trees were cut for a distance of 100 yards around Savannah. Four ground saw pits were in operation. Now, not quite four months after the arrival in Georgia, two clapboard houses and nine framed houses were finished. Thomas Causton described them as "of one Floor, only a Cock Loft over it Sufficient to hold two Beds, the lower part will make one large Room and two smaller ones and stands in a piece of Ground which with the intended Gardens is 20 Yards broad in front and 30 Yards long in depth." The houses (twenty-four feet long, sixteen feet wide, and eight feet high exclusive of the garret) were built of feather-edged boards and roofed with tarred shingles. The floors were made of one-and-a-half-inch planks and stood on log foundations two and a half feet above ground.[15] A newcomer, later describing the house Oglethorpe occupied in Savannah when he finally moved from his tent, remarked that it was "the same as the common Freeholders Houses are, a Frame of sawed Timber, 24 by 16 Foot, floored with rough Deals, the Sides with feather-edged Boards unplaned, and the Roof shingled."[16]

By the latter part of May, there were also finished a guard-house thirty-six feet long and twenty-four feet wide, the sides covered with thick slabs and the top with bark; and two block-houses, proofed against musket shot, with four portholes for cannon and one piece of cannon ready to be put into each. Further

defence was afforded by a battery of six cannon on the riverside
and on the eastern side of Savannah a palisade then 140 feet
long and seventeen feet high.[17]

The town had then, by Oglethorpe's estimate, a population of
160 head, of which seventy were able to bear arms. Many of
the arms brought from England on the *Ann* were burned in a
fire earlier in the spring which also destroyed a quantity of tools
sorely needed. Additional arms and tools were purchased in
Charles Town. Each man had to take his regular turns in standing guard. Most of the *Ann's* passengers were inexperienced in
the use of arms. To increase their skill, Oglethorpe made a com-
petitive sport of target practice, putting up a turkey or other
game as both target and prize.[18] If the bird was not too mutilated,
it proved a welcome addition to the winner's larder. Certainly
the practice with arms must, in the midst of their hard work, have
formed a grateful interlude, with many resulting pleasantries.

From the time of the original landing, some of the settlers
had been set to clearing land for raising food. By the middle of
March about ten acres of land had been sowed. Later in the
month, in the opinion of Charlestonian Samuel Eveleigh, one
piece of land which had been planted in wheat gave promise of
a good crop. Also several gardens were sowed "with divers
Sorts of Seeds . . . Thyme, with other sorts of Pot-herbs,
Sage, Leeks, Skellions, Celeri, Liquorice &c. and several sorts of
Fruit-trees." The town site itself was barren land but a mile
back was very rich ground, Eveleigh said, "and on both Sides,
within a Quarter of a Mile of the Town is choice good Planting-
land. Colonel Bull told me, That he had been Seven Miles back,
and found it extraordinary good." But, said Eveleigh, people
could not live without corn and it would be difficult for white
people to tend corn in the summer-time when the heat was as
great as ever he had felt it in Jamaica in the summer. He thought
the Trustees made a mistake in barring Negro slaves who could
advance the crops as well as clear more land.[19]

Eveleigh thought the fare enjoyed by Oglethorpe and the
colonists "is but indifferent, having little else at present but
salt Provisions . . . ." Yet in those first months the colonists
felt no pinch of hunger. "We are plentifully provided with
Victuals," Causton wrote, "and the Men have a Pint of Strong
Beer every night after work besides other frequent Refreshments, as Mr. Oglethorpe sees Occasion." The Indians "have al-

ways Parties out hunting and they bring us Venison, for which
Mr. Oglethorpe pays at a very moderate rate." In fact, Causton
continued, "Our Situation is indeed very pleasant, and tho' we
want for nothing we have some Grumbletonians here also."
Fish and game were certainly plentiful. Eveleigh "saw Six or
Seven large Sturgeon leap, with which Fish the River abounds,
as also with Trout, Perch, Cat and Rock Fish, &c. and in the
Winter Season there is Variety of Wild Fowl, especially Turkeys,
some of them weighing Thirty Pounds, and abundance of
Deer."[20]

Much of the food consumed by the colonists came from South
Carolina. The Assembly there gave some rice to help the new
settlement. Oglethorpe soon began to supplement the colony's
stores with food purchased in Charles Town or from ships which
offered at Savannah. For payment he drew on the Trustees in
London, a practice to which they were soon to raise objections.[21]

The people's basic diet of meat and flour was supplied by the
Trustees for those sent at their expense. In the spring and later,
the Trustees asked Oglethorpe to estimate the expense of subsistence for a family yearly; but his reply, that he was unable
to determine the exact amount as some needed or deserved more
than others, was of little help to men in London endeavoring
to plan for the future of the colony.[22]

The original plan of the Trustees to subsist the colonists for
one year only, or until the first crops were in, was soon seen to
be impractical. The next year those who could not maintain
themselves were to have subsistence continued if approved by a
committee composed of Thomas Causton, the storekeeper,
Thomas Christie, and John Vanderplank. Subsistence then would
not exceed fifteen bushels of Indian corn and a barrel of beef
a year to such persons as that allowance should be necessary.
In addition, sixty-four quarts of molasses, twelve quarts of
lamp oil, and one pound of spun cotton—all items in the original
year's allowance—were to be continued, but "if any Person shall
drink Rum, notwithstanding such Allowance of Molasses to
prevent him, his Allowance of Molasses must immediately be
stopped."[23]

During the first year little was written from the colony about
food crops. Much was written from London about exotic plants
which were to be tried out in the Trustees' Garden. The *Ann's*
passenger list gives only three colonists who were experienced

in growing food. John Gready was entered as "understanding farming," John Penrose as a husbandman, and Joseph Fitzwalter as a gardener. However little the settlers knew about farming, much was expected of them. By the spring of 1734 when the admiration of some of the Trustees for Oglethorpe was perceptibly waning and the strain of meeting his bills drawn for the colony was becoming great, some of them thought "that by the ill management in settling the English now there, the expense has greatly exceeded what we imagined, and we know not how much it may cost more, especially since they have not cultivated their lands as was expected, so that they will be another year charged upon us to maintain them, which was not in our scheme, for after the first year they were to maintain themselves out of the produce of their lands, but that cannot be since they have spent their time in building houses, and not in reducing the land."[24]

The colonists certainly had not spent all of their time in building houses, but neither had they produced adequate food for the next year.

Spring brought other problems which had not been apparent when the *Ann* sailed on a cold November day. Many of the colonists did not have suitable clothing. "I shall want Thread or Cotton Stockings," Thomas Causton wrote back to England, "Some good Checqued Linnen of a dark blew and Strong Linnen for Waistcoats and Trowsers. . . . We have very heavy Rains sometimes but tho' it rains a whole Day and Night it makes no Dirt. We are much pestered with a little Fly they call a Sand Fly. I have seen it in England about the Horse Dung. But every Insect here is stronger than in England. The Ants are half an inch long and they say will bite desperately. As for Alligators I have seen several but they are by the Sides of Rivers. Our Town is too high Ground for them to Clamber up, we have killed one. I find the Camphire very good against the Stings of the Flies. I now begin to be something hardened against them."[25]

Any progress and hope of further progress in Georgia rested largely upon the assumption of Indian amity. The Trustees' policy towards the Indians was from the first based on the assumption that the settlers would need the Indians more than the Indians would need them, and that disaffected Indians would greatly harass the English and discourage settlers from coming to Georgia. Before the *Ann* sailed the Trustees asked

Governor Robert Johnson of South Carolina to inform the Indians adjacent to the site of the intended settlement of the colonists' arrival and dispose them to friendship.[26]

One of Oglethorpe's first acts after the *Ann* reached South Carolina was to visit the Yamacraws, the only Indians within fifty miles of Savannah, and engage their friendship before the settlers arrived. Besides friendly acceptance of the new settlers by the Yamacraws, it was desirable that in ranging through those great wooded tracts surrounding this pinpoint of English settlement, they discover hostile persons or spies. No one knew when the Spaniards and their Indian allies might creep up to have a look. In fact two supposed spies were taken, on their way from Georgia to St. Augustine, within two months after the colonists arrived. A little later the Yamacraws stopped two more suspicious persons, to whom Oglethorpe showed the battery of cannon on the riverside, the block-houses, and the colonists under arms; he bade the two tell the governor of St. Augustine what they had seen. The spies were not supposed to know that the ranks of colonists were considerably augmented by men from South Carolina, come to help in building and planting.[27]

When the Yamacraws, a refugee or outlaw band from the Lower Creeks, settled in 1730 on the bluff later named for them, they numbered only about seventeen or eighteen families, or about forty men, under the leadership of Tomochichi. The Trustees' Indian policy, suitably re-inforced with the necessary presents, was initiated with the Yamacraws. "Mr. Oglethorpe has behaved towards them with so much good Conduct and prudent Generosity," Thomas Causton wrote, "that tho' Some amongst them were ready to Grumble at our Coming yet he has both gained their Love & encreased their fearful Apprehensions of us." Causton thought then the Yamacraws totaled about 100. "They seem to be sober judicious men, Straight and Strong almost naked; But the King and the Chiefs wear Cloaks and Drawers and a piece of cloth tied about their Legs like Boots. The Queen and her Daughters wear common printed Calicoe Jacket and Petticoat without any Head Cloaths. They maintain very little Distinction . . . ."[28]

The *Ann's* passengers could scarcely have imagined anything more strange than when the Yamacraws "came to bid us welcome and before them came a Man dancing in Antick Postures with

a spread Fan of white Feathers in each hand as a Token of
friendship, wch. were fix'd to small Rods about four foot long,
Set from Top to Bottom with small Bells like Morrice Dancers
which made a jingling whilst the King and others followed making a very uncouth Hollowing. When they came near, Mr.
Oglethorpe walked about ten Steps from his Tent to meet them;
then the man with his feathers came forward dancing and talking,
which I am informed was repeating a Speech, the Acts of their
Chief Warriours, and at times came close and waved his Fans
over him & Strok'd him on every Side with them; this continued
more than a Quarter of an Hour. Then the King & all the men
came in a regular manner & Shook him by the hand; after that
the Queen came and all the Women did the like. Then Mr.
Oglethorpe conducted them to his Tent and made them Sit down;
the next day he made them some Presents to make them Cloathing."[29]

If Oglethorpe could give gifts, so also could Tomochichi. Here
is a little present, he said to Oglethorpe in his first speech,
proffering a buffalo skin, on the inside of which was painted the
head of an eagle. Tomochichi continued through his interpreter:
Accept this, because the English are as swift as the bird and as
strong as the beast since like the first they fly from the utter-
most parts of the earth over vast seas and like the second nothing
can withstand them. The feathers of the eagle are soft and
signify love; the buffalo's skin is warm and signifies protection;
we ask you to love and protect our little families.[30]

The news went back to London that the Yamacraws were
most surprisingly inclined to friendship; in fact they desired to
be subjects of His Majesty King George and to have their children taught in Christian schools. They ceded the site of Savannah and adjacent acres, and Oglethorpe marked off the land
which they reserved for themselves. He cemented the friendship
further by organizing two companies to Tomochichi's men as
Indian allies and at their request commissioned Tuscaney, or
Tuskenca, as captain of the first company, and Skee as captain
of the second company. These two companies consisted of forty
men whose pay was one bushel of corn a month for each man
while Oglethorpe employed them in war or hunting, one blanket
a year, and a gun at the enlistment of each man.[31]

The real test of the colony's Indian relations would come when the Lower Creeks arrived to make their treaty. They must approve Tomochichi's cession and make others of their own if the colony was to have needed land and a measurable degree of security; the Creeks, Upper and Lower, could be the colony's most dangerous enemies. However close were Tomochichi's ties of friendship with the Lower Creeks, all would not be well until this treaty was signed.

Oglethorpe wrote to the Trustees on May 14 that all was at peace with the Indians. He was then in Charles Town, where he had taken Tomochichi and his nephew and adopted son, Toonahowi. The *South-Carolina Gazette* diplomatically complimented Toonahowi on being a sprightly youth "of a very apt Genius," who had progressed in his English education to the point of being able to read his letters and figures.[32] Nothing could have pleased Tomochichi more.

Oglethorpe returned from Charles Town on May 18 to find fifty-four Creeks waiting for him in Savannah. The Indian Traders John Musgrove and Thomas Wiggan interpreted, while the visiting Creeks, as well as Tomochichi and his men, conferred with Oglethorpe in one of the new houses. Long speeches were made; one of the head warriors thanked Oglethorpe for his attentions to Tomochichi; Tomochichi in his turn praised the English. Oglethorpe gave the visitors presents, graded according to rank: laced hats, laced shirts, duffel and other material for clothing, guns, bullets, and cutlasses with gilt handles. For all of them there were a cask of tobacco, provisions for their homeward journey, and eight kegs of rum.

The visitors ceded the needed land; the treaty of alliance, friendship, and commerce, to last as long as the sun shines or the waters run in the rivers, was signed on Monday, May 21. Oglethorpe at the end of the year could say: "The Creeks adhere firmly to us." In the autumn of 1733 the Trustees ratified the articles of friendship and commerce and Lord Percival observed with some pride when he saw the treaty, "Our part is finely wrote upon vellum and ornamented with festoons, birds, etc., in water colors to take the eye."[33]

Oglethorpe returned to Charles Town on business the same day the treaty was signed in Savannah, leaving the colony in the care of Francis Scott and James St. Julien, the latter one of the Carolina friends of the colony who helped to forward planting and building.[34] The Indians left; excitement died down; normal work routines were again observed; and the settlers faced the summer.

Saturday, July 7, was the high spot of the first year in Georgia, the anniversary of which was to be celebrated in years to come. At first light of that summer's day the settlers met together on the strand and there near the river heard prayers of praise and thanksgiving read. They then went to Johnson Square where the ceremony of naming the streets, wards, and tythings of Savannah was held and each freeholder was put in possession of his lot. Whatever the Trustees' limitations on ownership, on this day each Georgian had tangible evidence of a new strength and status, his own land.

In Derby Ward only twenty-one houses were built by that day in July. Thomas Milledge and James Goddard, the two chief carpenters, offered in the name of themselves and seventeen of their helpers, to take the nineteen vacant lots and to give the built-upon lots to others not so able to help themselves. "But alas!" Oglethorpe wrote, "five of them dyed within one week."[35] Milledge and Goddard could not fulfill their offer.

The day was marked by a hearty dinner. In the afternoon the Trustees' grant for establishing a court of record for trying both civil and criminal cases was read, the court was opened, a jury impanelled, and a case tried. Appointments to be officers of the civil government were read and oaths of allegiance, supremacy, and abjuration administered by Oglethorpe. Peter Gordon, William Waterland, and Thomas Causton were made bailiffs, or magistrates; Thomas Christie, recorder of the court; Joseph Fitzwalter and Samuel Parker, constables; John West and John Penrose, tythingmen. Conservators of the peace were Peter Gordon, William Waterland, Thomas Causton, Thomas Christie, George Symes, Richard Hodges, Francis Scott, and Noble Jones. Afterwards the Trustees said of their appointment of bailiffs that they "chose for Magistrates such as appear to them the most prudent and discreet; but amongst a Number of People, who were all upon a Level at their first setting out, it was impossible to make any Choice or Distinction, which would not create some future Uneasiness among them."[36]

In case of the death of an officer or failure to perform his duty, substitute appointments were signed by the Trustees. Peter Gordon would be replaced by George Symes; William Waterland by Richard Hodges; Thomas Causton by Francis Scott; Thomas

Christie by Noble Jones; Joseph Fitzwalter by Richard Cannon;
Samuel Parker by Joseph Coles; John West by Francis Mugridge;
and John Penrose by Thomas Young. Thus was established the
government by bailiffs, constables, and tythingmen. The laws
of England were to be in force in the colony.[37]

A second court was held on July 28 at which William Waterland and Thomas Causton presided. Joseph Fitzwalter, constable for Derby Ward, humbly prayed the direction of the court
in the affairs of Joshua Overend, who had died on June 28.

Overend was found to be legally entitled to one built dwelling
house with garden in Derby Ward, one five-acre lot and one of
forty-five acres not yet cleared or cultivated. As he had no
children, his wife, Mary, in England, was entitled to the house
lot and one-half of the fifty acres for her life time, the other
half to descend immediately to Overend's next male heir. His
cow, calf, and steer were directed to be sold to pay his debts
of £1. 1. 17, and his personal possessions to be sent to his wife
in England.

Overend's personal possessions, which he would have brought
with him on the *Ann*, were found to be a scarlet great
coat, a white cloth coat, a black coat, a red rug coat, a sailor's
jacket, seven stocks, one linen handkerchief and a woman's
handkerchief, a pair of black stockings, a pair of grey stockings,
a worsted damask nightgown, black waistcoat and breeches,
a pair of woolen breeches, five ruffled shirts, an old speckled
shirt, one black velvet cap, one linen and one woolen cap, one
light tie wig and one bob wig, a pair of old slippers, and some
old gloves. He had also a razor, wash ball, one and a half dozen
brass buttons, a clothes brush, a pair of scissors, a small red pocket
book, two linen bags, a pillow without pillowcase, a pair of ordinary sheets of different sorts, one old speckled sheet, and two pairs
of silver buckles put up in a leather bag. These, with his Bible,
a Book of Common Prayer, a copy of *The Whole Duty of Man*,
three account books, a printed interest book, a day book, and a
clasp knife, completed his possessions.[38]

Overend's occupation was not given on the *Ann's* passenger
list but Thomas Causton spoke of him as having lived in
Aldersgate Street in London, "and did live in Cox's Court,
he is a married man, has lived well in the Mercery [mercer's]
way, and has left his wife in England."[39]

Before Overend died, two others of the first colonists were

gone. Dr. William Cox was the first to die, on April 6, leaving his wife, Frances, and two children, Eunice and William. Mrs. Cox was pregnant during that long hot summer. The new baby, Mary, was born in October but lived only ten days. In June, 1734, Mrs. Cox married Lt. James Watts of the Independent Company but he died the same month. Later in the year Mrs. Watts returned to England with the two Cox children.[40]

Dr. Henry Herbert, the minister, was ill in the early spring, probably at the time when ten colonists were ill with bloody flux, thought at the time to be caused by cold and living in tents. Dr. Herbert wrote back to England about this time that he must go to Charles Town about his health. He embarked in Charles Town for England early in May on the *Baltic Merchant* but died at sea on June 15 "of a fever and bloody flux."[41]

Before these colonists were gone, the first English child was born in Georgia on March 17, 1733, the daughter of Henry and Hannah Close. They named her Georgia. James Hume, of South Carolina, had promised a silver boat and spoon to the first child born in the colony, which Georgia Close now received. Conceived in England and born in Georgia, the baby survived various hardships before she opened her eyes in a tent on the banks of the Savannah River. She came early enough to receive the ministrations of Dr. Cox and Dr. Herbert and undoubtedly also of Mrs. Joseph Stanley, a midwife. Georgia Close must have been an important little person, with her own silver and bearing the same name as the colony, the object of interest and concern on the part of the first colonists during her short life.[42]

The summer of 1733 became for most Georgians a time of tragedy as death and disease struck with increasing swiftness and severity in July, August, and September. The colonists were literally weighted down with grief and concern for their loved ones.

Husbands lost wives; wives lost husbands; sometimes both died and some of the children. The *Ann's* passenger list quickly diminished. James Goddard died early in July, probably shortly after the first court day on the seventh. Mrs. Goddard died on July 28, leaving Elizabeth and John, aged about five and nine years. John was apprenticed to Joseph Fitzwalter, the gardener; Elizabeth was placed in the care of James Carwell and his wife to whom Oglethorpe planned to allow £3 a year for her care, while the Trustees allowed subsistence to Carwell and £5 after subsistence was discontinued. This arrangement did not last for Mrs. Carwell herself died early in September.[43]

William Littel, or Little, and his five-year-old daughter, Mary, both died on July 12. Littel's widow, Elizabeth, left with a two-year-old son, William, married John West on August 28. West's wife and child had died in July. But this second marriage brought West little happiness, because Elizabeth Littel West died on September 26.[44]

Samuel Parker, Richard Hodges, Thomas Milledge, Robert Johnson, and John Mackey died in July. John Sammes and John Warren died in August. Mrs. Warren lost three members of her family that summer: her son John, aged two, in June; her husband John, in August; her son William, aged six, in September. After she left the colony in the winter of 1733-1734 her house was used as an infirmary for the many sick people.[45] On September 7, both Mrs. James Carwell and her daughter Margaret, born in June, died. Daniel Thibaut died in October and Timothy Bowling in November. On December 14, Henry Close died, to be followed two weeks later by little Georgia.[46] Short was her fame, and only in Georgia.

Others of the *Ann's* passengers died as well as settlers who arrived on later vessels. Probably between thirty and forty Georgians died that first summer. The illness brought great physical and mental anguish to many who survived and caused real concern for the welfare of the weak colony which could so ill afford to lose any workers. Many must have found themselves in the condition of one man who, ill with fever the following year, ruefully declared that it "left me reduced to a Skelet."[47]

Not only illness troubled the colony that summer. A new spirit was manifest, different from that which the people had shown when they sailed on the *Ann*. Some of it may have merited the term insubordination, which was freely used to characterize it as time went on. Some of it undoubtedly was the result of growing pains. Neither the Trustees in London nor Oglethorpe in Georgia seem to have made any allowance for the growth of individuals, loosening of old bonds, forming of new ties, stirring of ambition in the colonists for themselves and for Georgia, or for the response to the stimulus and challenge of a new and unspoiled environment. This change was in reality the first evidence of a spirit of independence, even if shown on so small a scale as wanting provisions issued by a different system. Philanthropists are often unable to accept evidences of this spirit, so disconcerting when shown by "the poor," as the *Ann's* passengers were labelled. Oglethorpe termed the spirit "This Petulancy."

He wrote confidently in the spring that he had brought all the people to desire the prohibition of Negroes and rum.[48] Upon his return from Charles Town on June 18, he was greeted with demonstrations of joy, yet as *The South-Carolina Gazette* remarked, "During his Absence there have been some small Divisions and Differences . . . . " Oglethorpe himself was amazed at the change: "Some of the People began to be intemperate and then Disobedient so that at my Return I hardly knew them." He was even more emphatic: "the People were grown very mutinous and impatient of Labour and Discipline."[49]

A reason must be found for these untoward happenings. Why should they be petulant in spirit, these people whom the Trustees had described as sober, moral, and industrious men? Why, for that matter, should they be sick, on this site that he had selected and praised for its healthfulness? After all, despite his and the other Trustees' plans, this colony could fall apart by mounting deaths and petulancy. What tales there would be then in England, what questions asked in Parliament!

But he had an answer: the cause of the petulancy and of the illness was rum punch. Within its potent depths, he discerned the source of disease, death, and all troubles. Rum punch must have been a truly powerful drink to produce so horrifying a list of ills, both of body and spirit. "This Petulancy was owing chiefly to several of them having got into drinking of Rum," Oglethorpe wrote. Rum even explained the business about the provisions: "Some of the more artfull . . . stirred them up . . . the Silly People desired their Provisions that they might be able to gratify their Palates by Selling a large Quantity of wholesome Food for a little Rum Punch."[50]

The Trustees' plan of joint labor was also beginning to die. Oglethorpe had to acknowledge this to the extent of paying the men to work on the storehouse and other public buildings if the work got done.[51]

A visitor from South Carolina, Jean Pierre Purry, told Lord Percival in London that the causes of what he termed the uneasiness of the people at Savannah were the system of land tenure, by which wives and daughters did not inherit; the prohibition of slaves; and there being many lazy fellows and some unable to work. Those who worked stoutly thought it unreasonable that the fruits of their labors should be enjoyed by others who, when the land was cleared, would have an equal chance when lots were cast for determining each person's holdings.[52] It was ever thus in planned utopias!

"By Degrees I brought the People to Discipline," Oglethorpe wrote, "but could not revive the Spirit of Labour; Idleness and Drunkeness was Succeeded by Sickness." He sent away the Negro sawyers, thinking they might encourage idleness; he allowed a moderate amount of wine to alleviate thirst and staved all the rum he could find in town. John and Mary Musgrove, at their trading house less than a mile from town, sold rum in spite of Oglethorpe's prohibition. He had no wish to anger them, especially as they were his only Indian interpreters. "However at present I must either Suppress them or our People must be destroyed, we having lost twenty People within a month since the drinking of Rum was come into fashion; whereas we lost but one Person in five months whilst I was here and kept the People from excessive Drinking."[53] A dispatch from Savannah in *The South-Carolina Gazette* was doubtless inspired by Oglethorpe: "Some of the People having privately drank too freely of *Rum* are dead; and that Liquor which has always been discountenanced here, is now absolutely prohibited."[54]

At the new settlement of Purrysburgh, not far from Savannah but in South Carolina, it was conceded that some deaths there were attributable to rum but some also were due to "exposing themselves to the air during the great heats."[55] In Savannah Oglethorpe saw only one cause. Poor Overend, he remarked, was dead with rum, and most of the others owed their deaths to the same cause. "Milledge our best Carpenter is dead of a burning Feaver which on his Deathbed he confessed he contracted at the Indian Trading House; he drank there Rum Punch on the Wednesday, on Thursday was taken ill of a burning Feaver and on the seventh day, the Crisis of that Distemper, dyed."[56] Whether extorted or voluntary, this death-bed confession by a patient, with the degree of fever implied, seems to lack validity.

If Oglethorpe's explanation for these deaths of men, women, and children is accepted, the idea of children toddling in and out of the trading house continually and blissfully sipping rum

punch seems overdrawn. But Oglethorpe could explain all.
"But the Illness being once frequent became contagious. It appeared chiefly in burning Feavers or else bloody Fluxes attended
by Convulsions and other terrible Symptoms." There was no
doctor. Noble Jones helped to look after the sick until he was
himself taken ill. Women who had some experience in nursing
gave willing service until they became ill and some of them
died. Indian roots, rhubarb, diascordium, and laudanum were
administered to small effect. In the middle of July more than
sixty people were so ill that it was thought most of them could
not recover.[57]

But God, so the people must have thought, took heed of their
needs. On July 11, an unexpected ship arrived among
whose passengers of the Jewish faith was Dr. Samuel Nunis. The
ship had not been sent by the Trustees, and its passengers were
not acceptable to the Trustees. Yet Dr. Nunis went immediately
to work, refusing pay for his services. "He proceeded by cold
Baths, cooling Drinks and other cooling Applications. Since which
the Sick have wonderfully recovered," Oglethorpe wrote, "and
we have not lost one who would follow his Prescriptions." However, with the evidence of the doctor's skill and the effectiveness
of his treatment before him, Oglethorpe added, "Next to the
Blessing of God and the new Regimen I believe one of the greatest
Occasions of the people's Recovery has been, That by my constant
watching of them I have restrained the Drinking of Rum."
Several months later he said again, "Their excessive Drinking
was followed with Sickness which raged for some time most
terribly amongst us. . . . " Ten years later he was still at-
tributing all illness to rum and kindred spirits. "The mortality
in America is chiefly owing to distilled liquors. . . ."[58]

Oglethorpe gave no hint that the people may not have agreed
with him; some people thought the climate was to blame, he
said. Mrs. John Warren probably spoke for more of the colonists
than herself when she told Lord Percival in London that they
attributed their illness and death to drinking the river water,
which gave them the flux. Peter Gordon, back in England for
a time, supposed the illness to have been caused by drinking the
river water and remarked on the improved health of the people
since a well was dug in the middle of town and a pump placed
in it. This was the well which Oglethorpe described as being
20 feet deep, built with bricks sent by the Trustees, and afford-

ing excellent water. But he did not dwell upon it as a health asset.[59]

This well may have shared the fate of those mentioned by that group known as "the Scotch" who wrote a vigorous indictment of Oglethorpe for the lack of a proper water supply. Wells were immediately choked up, they said, the want of properly dug ones forcing the inhabitants to drink the river water "which all the Summer over is polluted with putrid Marshes, and the numberless Insects that deposite their *Ova* there, together with the putrified Carcases of Animals and corrupted Vegetables; and this no doubt occasioned much of the Sickness that Swept off many."[60]

The spirit of petulancy which so amazed Oglethorpe in that summer of 1733 was harmonized to a certain extent, for early in 1734 a report went back to London that the first people were working quietly and with courage.[61] In the year or more since their arrival some of them had left the colony, more had died, and the lives of most were changed by the new environment and associations.

CHAPTER THREE

Other Worthy Poor

SHORTLY after the *Ann* sailed from England, the Trustees sent four more colonists and more stores to Georgia on the *Volant*, Captain Edmund Smyter. The ship must have sailed about the middle of December, 1732, for the Georgia passengers were already on board at Gravesend on December 14. The *Volant* reached Charles Town the latter part of February and arrived in Georgia in early March, having been eleven weeks in her passage. Captain Smyter unloaded his stores and returned to Charles Town. He had cleared this port by April 7 and was back in London by June 26.[1]

The new colonists were John Vanderplank and Samuel Grey, the latter with two apprentices, Cornelius Jones and Chetwyn Furzer. Vanderplank, then forty-eight years of age, had been at sea for a number of years, and proved to be a dependable man in the colony where he held several offices.[2] Samuel Grey, sent by the Trustees as a silk throwster, was thirty years of age, while his apprentices were fifteen and sixteen years old respectively. Oglethorpe evidently was not impressed by Grey, who he remarked "pretended" to understand the silk business. In any event, Grey's stay in the colony was short. Oglethorpe, returning from Charles Town in June and disconcerted by the dissatisfaction which he found, decided that Grey had been an instigator of mutiny. Francis Scott, one of the justices of the peace, had ordered him set in the stocks while Oglethorpe was away, the first record of this punishment being used in Georgia. Grey proposed to Oglethorpe that he would leave the colony unless certain conditions were met; Oglethorpe ordered him to be gone in twelve hours and he accordingly left for Carolina, the first of many to change to that colony.[3]

The Trustees had planned to reinforce the first colonists with larger groups than were sent on the *Volant*. In London the Trustees continued to receive benefactions from charitably disposed persons and to interview people who might wish to go to Georgia. One thing was certain, the number of the first colonists must be augmented. The Trustees were convinced of this even before they heard of the depletion by death in the summer of 1733. The security of the remaining colonists depended in large measure upon the sending of other colonists.

Some of the captains of ships that brought colonists that year— Captain Yoakley, Captain William Thomson, Captain Henry Daubuz—made repeated trips to Georgia and became one of the chief sources of information about conditions in the colony. They were shrewd people whose first-hand observations are still valuable despite the fact that they sometimes glossed over events in the colony, not wishing to give reports too discouraging or to disagree too openly with those who questioned them.[4]

Captain Yoakley's ship, the *James*, the next one to sail after the *Volant*, was even smaller than the *Ann*, one hundred ten tons and six guns. Her passengers on the charity list, eleven persons or ten heads for whom the Trustees paid passage of £4 a head, were mustered aboard off Rotherhith on January 28, 1733. Six of these men were sawyers; the seventh was a blacksmith. Lord Percival had but a small opinion of the sawyers, "miserable objects," he said, for "one of them had for sickness been forced to sell his bed, another must sell his tools to pay his debts." Several other passengers paid their own way. One of these was Botham Squire who had been master of a ship. Squire was to be given provisions for the first year or until he could make a crop. Long range plans were not necessary for Squire; he left the colony only three months after his arrival.[5]

The *James* arrived at Savannah on May 14, having touched first at Port Royal. Between the two points the foremast men mutinied and threatened to run away with the ship. Lieutenant James Watts of the Independent Company at Port Royal came out in the garrison boat and put "the Ringleader of them, who had formerly been a Pirate, and had taken the Benefit of the Act of Grace, into Irons. . . ." After this excitement, Captain

Yoakley brought the *James* to Savannah and unloaded his passengers, stores, and ammunition. Oglethorpe awarded him the
prize offered by the Trustees for being the first vessel to unload
at Savannah.[6] Captain Yoakley's accomplishment was not one
to be repeated often; few kind words were said of the channel
of the Savannah River for many years.

Two of the *James's* passengers died within two days of each
other in July during the great illness. One of these, Peter Tondee, paid the expenses of passage for himself and his two sons,
Charles and Peter. After the father's death, the boys were
added to the growing list of orphans in the colony. In later
years the name became well-known, for Tondee's Tavern was
famous in the town and countryside, but the boys' start in
their new life was an unhappy one.[7]

The Trustees were gratified that some people were willing to
pay their own way and risk at least some of their own money
by settling in the new colony. A part of one such group
arrived in July, 1733—Philip Bishop and Joseph Hetherington
of London with their wives and indentured servants and possibly also Theophilus Hetherington. The member of the group
who opened negotiations with the Trustees, Roger Lacy, and the
steadiest one of the lot as time was to prove, did not arrive until
the following February with his wife Mary and his brother James,
their mother having preceded them a few weeks earlier. On the
basis of their taking four servants each, they were granted
500 acres of land each. Special consideration, supposed to enable
them to obtain servants more easily, was the agreement that
when the indentures expired the servants would be granted
twenty-five acres of land each instead of the customary twenty
acres. The Trustees promised to supply these colonists with
arms not exceeding thirty firelocks, and ammunition as it should
be required for their defense; also to supply provisions for
thirty people for a year from the date of their arrival in Georgia at the rate of five pounds of flour and of meat for every
person weekly. Concessions in land tenure were that their land
would descend to their wives in tail male if they died without
male issue. Roger Lacy got further special consideration about
inheritance.[8]

However, no relaxation of the usual terms of grants was
made in their favor. They would pay an annual quit rent at the
rate of ten shillings for every hundred acres, payment to be-

gin at the end of ten years; if they did not clear and cultivate
100 acres of each 500 acres in ten years and within twenty
years did not clear 300 other acres of each grant, the land would
revert to the Trustees. The grants contained other detailed
provisos, even one relating to their morals, all with the threat
that if they were not complied with, the grantees would
lose their land. Particularly must they, in common with all other
colonists, plant 1000 white mulberry trees upon each 100 acres
as soon as it was cleared, "to breed Silk Worms in Order to
Produce Silk . . . for and in consideration of the great Advantage that May Accrue to the Kingdom of Great Britain by
producing so valuable a Commodity in one of the Colonies
thereto belonging . . . ."[9]

These were the customary terms for grants. The unusual favors
extended by the Trustees regarding tenure of land were perhaps
due in some measure to a plan which they thrust upon the new
colonists. Roger Lacy seems to have planned to make potash
besides engaging in farming. But suddenly the meager records
begin to mention these men's entering into the production of
raw silk, and thereafter the emphasis is on that. Which people,
if any, in this group knew anything about silk is never revealed.
But the pressure on them must have been considerable, and any
efforts in this direction would redound to the Trustees' credit.
They proposed to "make silk Yarn," Lord Percival remarked,
"wherein if they succeed we shall have done a notable service
in this kingdom." The Trustees even decided that Roger Lacy
should take over to Georgia as apprentices in the silk business
twenty charity children, indentured to him until they were
twenty-four years of age; but the scheme did not materialize.[10]

Bishop and one or more of the Hetheringtons with wives and
servants sailed on the *Pearl,* Captain William Thomson, on April
20, 1733, and arrived at Charles Town June 12, after a nine
weeks' passage. The *Pearl* sailed to Jamaica, while the approximately thirty passengers for Georgia arrived in Savannah on July
7. This was the time of illness, and Mrs. Joseph Hetherington
died on July 27. Oglethorpe settled this group at Thunderbolt
where they soon set to work to build the fort needed at that point
and there they were joined by the Lacys the following February.[11]

On July 21 the passengers on the *Peter and James,* Captain
Cornish, arrived. Among the seventeen passengers, or fourteen
and a half heads, sent by the Trustees were Samuel Quincy,

the new minister, and his servant James Middleton, who died in October. Less than a week after the *Ann* sailed in November 1732 with Dr. Henry Herbert as the temporary minister, the Trustees asked the Society for the Propagation of the Gospel in Foreign Parts to supply Georgia with a missionary, with the usual salary, books, and furniture given to their missionaries in the colonies. The Trustees had already allotted the glebe and planned to build a church. Samuel Quincy, whom the Trustees thought a young man of modest appearance with excellent references, applied for the place of missionary. Quincy had been educated in New England and in England and had served for several years as an Independent preacher and as a Presbyterian minister before he took orders in the Church of England. He had a wife and one child but did not propose to bring them to Georgia with him.[12]

It was decided that Quincy should go on the *Peter and James* on April 4 with the other passengers. Because of his ministerial status he was given passage in the great cabin and was allowed £5 by the Trustees for refreshments during the voyage. Oglethorpe wrote later that Quincy, Hetherington, Bishop, Fletcher, and Pennefeather had arrived and that he was forced to lend them provisions out of the Trustees' store to prevent their suffering.[13]

Captain John Pennefeather, gentleman, of Dublin, had a grant of 300 acres of land from the Trustees, but soon crossed the river to settle in Purrysburgh, South Carolina. In London, Captain Pennefeather's "abandoning the colony" was used by Trustee James Vernon to emphasize the need for changing the system of land tenure so that daughters or collateral branches might inherit land in Georgia. No change was made at the time, though Vernon thought that people were discouraged from going to Georgia because inheritance by women was not allowed.[14]

Two men named Fletcher came on the *Peter and James*. Thomas Fletcher, his family, and servant came at his own expense but because of illness soon removed to Charles Town. The other Fletcher was Henry, a dry salter from Leeds, to whom the Trustees made a grant of 200 acres of land on provision that he was to take over one man-servant and plant mulberry trees as his land was cleared. His servant would have a grant of twenty acres of land upon the expiration of his indenture.

The Trustees paid the passage of Fletcher, his wife, son, and two daughters and were to pay the passage for two servants but he brought three. Probably this was allowed because of the £20 which was paid in to the Trustees for his benefit by a friend or relative.

Fletcher originally had small good and much worry from his servants. While the passengers on the *Peter and James* were in the barracks on Port Royal Island waiting for transportation to Georgia, James Hewitt and Thomas Holemark, two of the servants, escaped in a canoe, probably the first instance of indentured servants escaping from Georgia colonists. Hewitt, or Hewet, about thirty-five years old, was "a thin Man about 5 Feet 4 Inches high, and was formerly a Schoolmaster in *New England,* and understands something of Sea Affairs, and had on when he went away a handsome chocolate colour'd Coat and pair of Breeches, a black Wastecoat, and is supposed to be in those Cloaths, or a Sailor's Habit. . . . " Holemark was about twenty-five years old, five feet eight inches tall, and very much marked by smallpox. He was by trade a clog-maker but had been employed in felling and sawing timber, which experience would have made him especially valuable to Fletcher. His clothing, when he left in the canoe, was "a light colour'd Drab Coat, with flat metal Buttons, and a blue pair of Breeches, and is supposed to have on those Cloaths or a Sailor's Habit." A reward of £50 South Carolina currency for both or £30 for either one was offered if they were delivered to Oglethorpe or to the provost marshal in Charles Town. Their arrival is duly listed with the other passengers on July 21; evidently they enjoyed but brief freedom.[15]

Six non-British passengers on the *Peter and James* were Nicholas Amatis, brother of Paul Amatis who had come on the *Ann,* and the Camuse family, numbering five. Jacques Camuse came as a servant to assist Nicholas Amatis, an Italian who was to engage in the silk business.[16] The relationship of master and servant did not last long. There was never anyone in the colony like Mrs. Camuse. In times serene or troubled she swims vigorously to the surface of affairs—a most redoubtable woman.

In late August, 1733, there arrived in Georgia the largest embarkation yet sent since the *Ann,* on board the *Georgia.* The Trustees determined in May to send fifty able men with all possible speed. For some weeks afterward they interviewed

prospective colonists and had those they accepted sign the
articles. Passengers were mustered on board the *Georgia* on
June 15, eighty-four persons or seventy-two and one-half heads
at that count. The *Daily Advertiser* in London gave the number
as ninety when the ship sailed, and that number may
be correct.[17]

The *Georgia*, owned by the English firm of Peter and John
Symonds, was a pink, one of those small ships characterized
by a narrow stern. Captain Henry Daubuz brought her to the
colony on a number of trips. The Trustees might speak of her
formally as the *Georgia*, but soon she was called the *Georgia
Pink*, and by this charming name she continued to be known.
In the opinion of the Trustees she was large and airy; she drew
but ten and one-half feet of water and they planned to have
Captain Daubuz sail her, if possible, up the Savannah River
and land the passengers at the town.[18]

She was only 138 tons and was a stuffed little ship on her
first voyage to Georgia. Besides her passengers she carried cannon, muskets, powder and ball, swords, vinegar, beer, water,
oatmeal, bedding, tarpaulin for tents, drugs, nails, "engines for
pulling up roots of trees when felled," knives, hatchets, lucerne
seed, and £20 worth of Indian presents, described by the Trustees
as trinkets. Among the drugs on board for the use of colonists
in Georgia was a box of tellicherry bark, an infusion of which in
white wine was recommended to the Trustees as the best remedy,
in the East Indies at any rate, for the flux.[19] The mixture would
have had to be potent indeed to counteract the effects of animal
life imbibed in the Savannah River water.

Scarcely a ship came to Georgia without religious and instruc-
tional books donated by well-wishers in England for the poor
people in the new colony. The *Georgia Pink* had a number of
copies of *The Great Importance of a Religious Life Considered*,
The Duty of Man, Bibles, and prayer books. An anonymous
benefactor contributed in May several hundred devotional
books, horn books, primers, and catechisms. Perhaps from this lot
the *Georgia Pink* carried some of the two hundred copies of
Friendly Admonitions to the Drinkers of Brandy.[20] Presumably
these admonitions applied also to rum.

Four men were appointed to act as constables on board but
only three of them sailed—Henry Parker, James Turner, and
John Barnes. These three and William Brownjohn were appointed

additional constables for Savannah and its precincts. Brownjohn was to act as steward on the ship and several days before sailing he was instructed to have sage and mint on board for the embarkation.[21]

The *Georgia Pink* sailed out of the Thames on June 15. Three days later, Brownjohn and Thomas Gapen wrote from the Downs that all were in good health. The women, having been served with sage and sugar, were somewhat recovered from their seasickness. Robert Hainks was seized with a violent fit of apoplexy in which he fell down a ladder, but Samuel Pensyre bled Hainks who thereupon recovered. That day they washed the ship, read prayers, and then broached a barrel of strong beer, every mess being served. They drank the healths of the King and Queen, the Prince of Wales and all the Royal Family, the Trustees, Oglethorpe, and all benefactors and well-wishers of their undertaking. By that time they were enormously pleased with themselves and all about them, with Captain Daubuz who was very careful and tender of them, and with their provisions. "Our utmost endeavors," they assured the Trustees, "shall be to obey your Honors' directions."[22] And so they set forward on their Georgia journey.

At Deal unfavorable winds delayed sailing for several days. On Saturday, June 23, the *Georgia Pink* sailed. Two lives were lost in the passage, Robert and Anne Hainks's son Robert died, and Daniel Preston was washed overboard in a storm.[23]

Captain Daubuz brought the *Georgia Pink* directly from England to Savannah, where he arrived August 29. For this direct voyage he received a prize from Oglethorpe for the Trustees. The men in the embarkation had varied skills. Five of them were carpenters. We hear of one of these, James Papot, from time to time. Stephens reported that he went to Carolina but returned to Georgia, where he was always seeking to improve his wages. They evidently did not improve enough in Georgia, for he was reported dead with his grown sons in Charles Town during an epidemic in September, 1739. Another, John Desborough, is mentioned a few times before he and his family "quitted to Carolina" in 1739 where Desborough died in September and his wife in 1740.[24]

Four farmers were among the passengers. John Graham, both a tanner and a farmer, earned the designation of a riotous fellow. In September, 1734, he kept his hat on in court, for which offense he was fined. Both Graham's sons died within three months after landing and the family moved to Carolina a few years afterward.[25]

William Brownjohn, one of this group, was a very good gardener. He must have had some qualities to impress the Trustees because he was appointed a constable before he sailed. His younger brother Benjamin and an apprentice, Leonard Whiting, joined him in 1736. Brownjohn was so good a farmer that he was irked by the inferior quality of the land granted to him and at one time prospected in South Carolina for better soil and was consequently called a malcontent by Stephens. However, he remained in Georgia, improved his land, and experimented to determine which crops were best suited to the soil and climate. His farming activity so favorably impressed Stephens that he interceded with Thomas Causton, the storekeeper, to pay the passage of a servant of Brownjohn's which the latter could not pay. In 1738 Brownjohn's wheat, barley, oats, and fruit trees were so flourishing that he was accounted one of the most valuable freeholders in Savannah and his advice was sought by others on planting. When he died on August 13, 1738, after a lingering illness, William Stephens said of him: "he was a Man generally well spoken of, and one whom I knew to be a Pains-taking Man, never idle, but addicted to improve his Land; which he did in so exemplary a Manner, that though he did not boast of so many Acres cleared as some, yet in Spite of the Poverty of the Land where his Lot was fallen, few could show such a Product." This was high praise; indeed, none higher could be given of a colonist and it was particularly pleasing to the Trustees to learn that a man could take poor land and make so much of it.[26]

The *Georgia Pink* brought upholsterers, tailors, peruke makers, shoemakers, a sawmill wright, an alehouse keeper, and shopkeepers. Two passengers knew something of the care of grapevines, Peter Baillou, who was also a hatter, and Jeremy Papot. These would help in the hoped-for production of wine, but Jeremy Papot did not have a chance to prove his skill, for he died in less than two months after his arrival.[27]

Among the passengers were Robert Moore and John Davant, who were cabinet makers and might have been expected to make some needed furniture in intervals when not farming their land. However Davant built no furniture in Georgia. He died almost as soon as he arrived. William Parker, a silversmith, the brother of Henry, and Lewis Bowen, a bookseller, also came on the *Georgia Pink*.[28] Neither of these could hope to engage in their trades in the infant colony. A colonist's first business was to be industrious, and by that the Trustees meant that he should clear and plant his land. Every man was expected to feed his family from his land. The emphasis on this idea was to be greater as the Trustees saw that some colonists continued to need food from the public store after their first year.

Bowen apparently planned some kind of shop, for in 1734 he had "raised his Frame" and having given security for his return was given permission to go to Charles Town to buy goods. Death in Charles Town in August or September, 1734, prevented his return to Georgia.[29]

One of the *Georgia Pink's* passengers was a surgeon, Samuel Pensyre, who had a son, Tiberius, born not long after landing, who lived less than a month.[30] Members of some of the other *Georgia Pink's* families lived only a few weeks after landing; others died in the autumn.

The next group of colonists, six at the Trustees' expense, came on the *Susannah,* Captain Bailey or Baillie. The *Susannah* sailed from London in May, 1733, but did not leave England until late June or July. Her arrival was not registered at Savannah until September 23. She brought with her a silver chalice and paten to be used in the church not yet built in Savannah. These were gifts of an anonymous donor through the Reverend Mr. Samuel Wesley, who had himself procured and sent out earlier a pewter chalice and paten.[31]

Three wives came to join husbands who had come on the *Ann*: Mrs. Mary Overend, to find her husband Joshua three months dead; Mrs. Elizabeth Bowling and her daughter Mary, aged eleven years, to join Timothy Bowling, who would die early in November; and Mrs. Martha Causton, with her young son Thomas Mancer Causton, and her niece, Sophia Christiana Hopkey. Thomas Causton had written earlier to his wife, "You must needs think I long to hear how Affairs stand and how You do in Health, and how my little Boy does, whether he grows and how he reads; and think likewise, That as my Heart is immovably fixed on the well doing of Miss Sophia and my Dear Jacky I long to hear from them and till then am betwixt Hope and Despair.''[32] Miss Sophia's charms were to precipitate something of a crisis in the colony later.

Edward Jenkins, a hosier from Shepton Mallet, Somerset, paid the passage of his family on the *Susannah* and of his two servants, Frank Duren and James White, who had already come on the *Georgia Pink*. He had a grant of 100 acres. Of his family of six, a son died in January and a daughter in February.[33]

The *Susannah's* passengers came without mishap.[34] After them no more groups came for several months, though a few colonists came in singly or by twos and threes.

In the spring of 1733 when the Trustees presented their petition to Parliament for funds for the colony they encountered some opposition to sending more settlers. Several members thought the Trustees, though disinterested and well meaning, did not know the scarcity of inhabitants in the country. Instead of sending Englishmen over to America, it would be far better to make some good laws to regulate the poor and keep them useful in England where their labor was needed and where they could not repeat the impertinences of the New England colonies, which one member wished sunk beneath the seas.

Sir Joseph Jekyl spoke generously of Georgia. How commendable it was, he said, to transplant indigent persons to where they could strengthen England's power in the West Indies and prove useful to their mother country by producing materials like silk, wine, and potash that did not interfere with manufacture in England. It seemed a particular design of Providence to erect at this time a colony which would become also a haven for persecuted Protestants from Salzburg. Sir John Barnard hoped that Parliament would give even more funds to take off the numbers of poor, especially children, that pestered the streets of London. Horace Walpole thought that great advantage might arise to England from the plantation of Georgia, especially since the Trustees were gentlemen who could have no private gain from it. Lord Percival said that there was no danger of the Trustees' depriving England of useful hands, "for those we have sent and shall send, are a sort of middle poor, . . . decayed tradesmen, or supernumerary workmen in towns and cities, who cannot put their hands to country affairs or are too proud to do it, and being ruined or eating one another up by

the multiplicity of workmen of the same trade . . . if they
remain, fall a charge with their families on their parishes."[35]

Sir Robert Walpole tepidly relayed the King's lack of objection to whatever Parliament should give the colony, and the
Trustees received their grant of £10,000 for sending over foreign and other Protestants. In the hope of it, they proceeded
with their plans to send over new colonists before Oglethorpe
returned to England. They wrote to Oglethorpe that Savannah,
so pleasantly and conveniently situated, must be enlarged and
made the metropolis of the country. As many people should be
settled in Savannah as were needed to complete it. Then a new
village to be a part of the precincts of Savannah should be
begun on a stream where sawmills could be tried. Preferably a
high and healthy place should be selected for the village.[36]

Plans began to mature for bringing over Salzburgers, persecuted Protestants from the Archbishopric of Salzburg in the Holy
Roman Empire. Other people applied during the summer.
Among those accepted were some who were rejected at the last
minute because their creditors appealed to the Trustees. To
William Wise, described as an unfortunate gentleman recommended by several bishops, Lord Percival said that unless he had
money to pay his passage and subsist servants to cultivate land,
he must perforce go on the charity list, which, said the viscount
frankly, "was the meanest foot that could be"; but Wise was
undeterred: better do anything than starve, he said.[37]

The report in London was that the Trustees would send about
300 families. Sermons were preached exhorting parishioners to
contribute towards the colony. It was spoken of as "that Religious Purpose" and one church announced that "As the Persons
chose by the Trustees for this Settlement are such as come well
recommended, it is hop'd will prevail with all good Christians to
assist in so good and laudable a Design, in providing for so
many honest poor Families." In another church a little later the
colony of Georgia was zealously recommended by the rector and
the lecturer in their sermons. "The Gentlemen were so fully
convinc'd of the Charity and Excellence of this Undertaking,
that they resolv'd, with great Unanimity, to collect from House
to House for the Promotion of it."[38]

The Trustees used no solicitations to induce people to go to
Georgia,[39] nor did they need to. The next embarkation proved

so popular that all the passengers and stores could not be accommodated on the *Savannah*, Captain Lionel Wood. On September 11, 1733, on this little ship 128 passengers were mustered; 103 were British and twenty-five were foreigners; there were thirty-seven men, thirty women, thirty-four boys, and twenty-seven girls, totalling ninety-four and one-half heads sent by the Trustees. Captain John Thomas, who had been captain of the *Ann,* was captain of the *London Merchant* for his second trip to Georgia. He carried five passengers and stores for the colony when it left Gravesend on September 21. The *James,* Captain Yoakley, also making his second trip to Georgia, mustered on board on September 28 thirty-one British and seventeen foreign passengers: twenty-one men, nine women, eight boys, and twelve girls, or forty and one-third heads. The original total of fifty was lessened by two passengers who left the ship just before it sailed.[40]

Captain Wood on the *Savannah* was wind bound in the Downs for a day. Captain Thomas was delayed a week by contrary winds at Deal, and it was October 4 before he sailed. Captain Yoakley was more fortunate; he brought the *James* down to Deal and passed without stopping in the early morning of October 6. The *Savannah* arrived at Savannah on December 15, Captain Wood being complimented on the conduct of his ship and the health of his passengers of whom only two children died on the trip. Early in January a visitor to Savannah saw the ship riding at anchor before the town and wrote to her owner, the Symonds firm in London, to compliment it on her brave appearance.[41]

The passengers from the *London Merchant* were registered in at Savannah on January 12 and those from the *James* on January 14, 1734. From all three ships they were a varied lot—some would cause trouble, some would die within a short time after arriving, some would live on for a few years, others for a normal lifetime making little stir but putting down the roots by which men, and therefore a colony, make foundation in a new land.

CHAPTER FOUR

Impregnable Bastion and Rock of Help

BEFORE the *Savannah*, the *James*, and the *London Merchant* arrived with their passengers, Oglethorpe did not have enough people to carry out his plan of settlement. The plan was conceived before he received the Trustees' directions to make a new village, part of the precincts of Savannah. Oglethorpe's idea was to make a series of small settlements with Savannah as the hub. Each new settlement was to consist of ten families with a small fort or guardhouse. This would push the frontiers of the colony out from Savannah and provide other areas for settlement and cultivation. Defense would be improved by intelligence being sent from these settlements to Savannah at the approach of danger. Whatever happened to the out-settlements, Savannah must be saved at all costs. Here the Trustees' effort centered; the village was already known by name in England from propaganda about Georgia to get more public subscriptions for the Trustees.

The original plan seems to have been for Savannah to serve as a refuge for inhabitants of the out-settlements in case of attack, with each group of four villages forming a ward related to a ward in town. In case of danger, the people from an out-settlement would move to its related ward in Savannah and use its square as a camping place and refuge. This was largely a theoretical use of Savannah's squares, of which little further mention was made in this connection. Other people must have agreed with Samuel Eveleigh who remarked in the autumn of 1734 that the out-settlements would securely defend Savannah from any surprise.[1]

41

Before the passengers from these three ships arrived, a beginning was made towards the new settlements. In mid-June, 1733, before the illness of that summer became so great that his presence was required in Savannah, Oglethorpe began some exploration of the adjacent country. Taking with him Captain James MacPherson and a detachment of his rangers, in the pay of South Carolina and detailed for the protection of Georgia, Oglethorpe went about forty miles west of Savannah. Here "he chose a Post which Commands the Passages, by which the *Indians* used to invade *Carolina,* in the late Wars." The situation was "a very happy one, being an Eminence which commands all the Country round, with a great and deep River at the Foot of it." This was the stream which Joseph Avery, the surveyor, later termed "that Excellent River Ogeche. . . ."[2]

Oglethorpe engaged Captain MacPherson to build a fort here and by the middle of August, 1733, Fort Argyle, the first fort to be built outside of Savannah, was well under way. It was supplied from Savannah with cannon, ammunition, and provisions. In a southerly direction from Fort Argyle a fort on Thunderbolt Creek was to be started on August 11.[3] When once these out-settlements were started they had to be continued; one was of little use and indeed would be too dangerous, for its inhabitants who would have to be protected from Savannah rather than protect it. Even before Fort Argyle was finished, it was used as a jail, there being none in Savannah. A man who had stolen a horse in Virginia was tried in Savannah, sentenced to three years hard labor at Fort Argyle, and sent there immediately.[4]

This fort, which came to be called First Fort, was about half finished when work on it was stopped, because the Ogeechee River below the fort became choked with trees carried down by the water. This rendered impossible passage by boat up the river. The labor involved in clearing the mass of timber and brush from the river was too great, in Oglethorpe's opinion; to build another fort he thought more feasible. He ordered another Fort Argyle begun ten miles lower down the river; and by the middle of September it was finished, the guns mounted, the houses built, and six families and the garrison settled there. Boats of fifteen tons burden had by then successfully negotiated the river.[5] Visitors to the fort in February, 1734, considered it very defensible and complimented Captain MacPherson on his diligence. The fort was considered well flanked and was fortified with four cannon. It had palisades six inches thick and eight feet above ground, and a breastwork of earth gave additional protection. Within the fortified area were a stable for thirty horses and twelve houses. John Wesley later described the fort as "a Small Square wooden Building, Musket proof with Four little Cannon."[6]

First Fort on the Ogeechee was abandoned with its unused building material. Although it does not seem to have been a place of settlement, it was one of the points from which the rangers patrolled. MacPherson's mounted rangers were divided into three groups of ten each. MacPherson in 1734 commanded ten rangers at Fort Argyle; Lieutenant William Elbert, another ten at First Fort; the other ten men were stationed on the Carolina side of the Savannah River at Palachocolas. Patrols were maintained between these points. The scout boat sometimes patrolled up the Ogeechee. The Carolina garrison was Fort Prince George, but this name was seldom used in Georgia; it was usually referred to as the Palachocolas garrison. In 1734 it was commanded by Lieutenant, later Captain, Aeneas Mackintosh and, after his return to Scotland, by his brother.[7] Three men and one wife, possibly more, from Captain Lionel Wood's ship, the *Savannah*, were sent to settle at Fort Argyle. It was evidently too much for the wife; she returned to England a year later.[8]

In 1734 another settlement was made up the Ogeechee River. Oglethorpe directed that the group thereafter known usually as "the Scotch" should settle there. His decision was unfortunate for these men and for the colony because of the animosities engendered on both sides which continued for years. Among these men were William and Hugh Stirling, Andrew Grant, and John Baillie, who came at their own expense, the Stirlings bringing ten servants each and receiving 500 acres each, while Grant and Baillie had 400 acres each. Dr. Patrick Tailfer, a member of this group, had his 500 acres laid out nearer Savannah.[9] The Stirlings and their associates and servants were a considerable addition to the settlement and man-power of the Ogeechee region and long after adversity had forced them to leave, their place was still known as Stirling's Bluff.

Fort Argyle was about twenty miles back of Savannah. A route about forty miles long was marked out to facilitate the

rangers' patrol and to open land communication from Fort
Argyle to the Palachocolas garrison. In the course of clearing the
trail for the rangers' horses, a site was discovered which lent
itself well to a new settlement. It was named Abercorn and ten
families were settled there. At least six of these men were passengers who came on the *Savannah*. This ship also furnished
settlers for another point called Highgate and two families coming on the *James* settled there. One of the latter earned the
ultimate in praise: James Landry, a gardener, was spoken of as
being remarkably industrious. Near Highgate another ten families were settled and the place called Hampstead. Highgate and
Hampstead were about five miles south of Savannah,[10] and the
way to them had to be hacked out of trees and undergrowth,
across swamps and streams to dry land.

At each of these three settlements were ten huts and a guardhouse; Abercorn's guardhouse boasted two pieces of cannon.[11]
Oglethorpe described these settlements as villages, but they were
scarcely that. The people originally lived in huts. Several years
later an attempt was made to differentiate the types of housing in
Savannah. The standard house, which most of them were, was
twenty-four feet long and sixteen feet wide. A small tenement
was a frame building smaller than the standard size; a large
house was one exceeding the standard dimensions. A hut was
usually built without framework, of round poles and split
boards, and was smaller than a house.[12] The huts at these new
out-settlements must have been similar to those in or near
Savannah.

These settlements were on the land side of Savannah. On the
water side, three were soon established. The first was that
made by the Lacy-Hetherington-Bishop families, whose grants
Oglethorpe fixed at Thunderbolt, five to seven miles southeast
of Savannah on Augustine Creek. Oglethorpe considered Thunderbolt a strategic point and here the colonists began in August,
1733, a hexagonal fort with earthen breastworks and a battery
of four cannon. In the vicinity six houses were built.[13] This fort
and settlement was one of three guarding the water passage
by which the Spaniards at St. Augustine could come to Savannah. Settlements on Skidaway and Tybee Islands guarded these
approaches also.

Thunderbolt was apparently the first settlement made outside of Savannah, Fort Argyle the second, and Tybee Island the

third. "Tyby is a very pleasant Island," remarked one visitor who did not have to live there, "and has a beautiful Creek to the Westward of it, so that a Ship of any Burthen may lye safe at Anchor. . . ." In September, 1733, Oglethorpe ordered ten families settled on Tybee, and a communal house was built in which they lived until they could build their own huts or houses.[14] Location on Tybee brought expressions of anguish from those assigned to farm its sands. Land was land to the Trustees, who thought that settlers should cultivate it, whatever its nature. After discouragement had left a deep imprint on many colonists and others had left Georgia the Trustees became more realistic about the nature of lands granted. In the early years whenever Oglethorpe was in the colony, by the Trustees' direction he selected the sites for individuals. Defense was his chief consideration in the selection of early outsettlements. The Trustees' rule was to subsist none who did not intend to cultivate lands for their own subsistence.[15]

At least nine of the families settled on Tybee were from Captain Daubuz's passengers on the *Georgia Pink,* arriving the last of August, 1733. One of the men deserted and for this offence was committed to Fort Argyle. John Davant died in September and his wife a few months later. Four men and two wives died in 1734, two more in 1735. Oglethorpe might write back to London with justifiable pride of the new settlements but putting ten families at each did not mean that ten families remained. They died, not killed by marauding Indians or Spaniards, but by illness. Six years later William Stephens wrote of a man who was, he thought, trying to slip out of the colony in mysterious circumstances but who insisted that by the advice of his physician he was merely going to Tybee for a change of air, "which we thought was not probable, Tybee being a Place so exceedingly pestered with Musketoes, by Reason of the adjacent Marshes, that no Person would ever be fond of taking his Abode there. . . ."[16]

Among the settlers on Tybee was Samuel Pensyre, surgeon. He went back to Savannah, for "as to my Lott at Tybee I Can no way improve it by Reason that I have Nothing but a Salt Marsh that is overflowd at every spring tide. . . ." He had been allowed two shillings a day at Tybee for taking care of the sick people, but Thomas Causton refused to continue this allowance after Pensyre returned to Savannah because Causton

had no orders to pay Pensyre except at Tybee. Isaac King
Clark, an apothecary who was one of Captain Wood's passengers on the *Savannah,* was evidently supposed to care for the
sick at Savannah. "Mr. King Clark he has been unCapable of
Doing any thing, by Reason of his been ill Most part of ye time
that he has been in Georgia but never the Least he has the profit,
and I have the Labour for my paine . . . ," Pensyre wrote. Besides that, he had to buy his medicines at a dear rate.

All of this was unfortunate, but in his letter to Oglethorpe,
then in England, Pensyre showed himself really saddened because of a message Oglethorpe sent by another colonist which
"Tells me that yr Honor is very Angry with me to which I
should be very Sorrow to inCur yr Honors Displeasure, upon
any acCount be whatever, Sir in a few Lines I will acquaint
you of ye whole truth of it, for why I did do, what I have done,
having been Maried to that woman about ten years, and Lived
very happy for about Seven years, Butt she got acquainted with
Some people; that was Debauchd in ye way of drinking that
Cursed Liquor Called Geneva, and when She once got in, in that
way of Drinking She Could not Leave it off, and Generally Got
Drunk almost every Days, and all that I Could do to hinder her,
of that abominable way of Drunkness still was in vaine . . . at
Last my life began to be very Troublesome to me, and I was
ashamed of her, both for her Drinking and Curssing and Swearing that I Could not bare it any Longer that I was, in a manner
forced to go away from her, on purpose to find peace and Rest
in my mind, after a while meeting with this woman Now at
present in Georgia with me, Seeing her of Good Beheaviour, and
Sober woman, apperceiving no ill Course in her, and by that
mean wee Concluded both to go to Georgia, where Sir I Can
assure yr Honor, that She has Caried her Self as Sober and
Cheast as any woman in Georgia ever did, or ever will do. . . ."
Still, if Oglethorpe would insist on sending his lawful wife to
him in Georgia, he wrote resignedly, "I Shall Receive her, I Cannot say willingly receive her, by Reason I Know very well
that She will never Keep her Selfe from Drinking, and when Shes
Drunk She is also Mad, But in Case that She Come I will send this
present woman away . . . then I am Sensible that I Shall not
be Capable of doing what I have been oblige to do, that is to
take Care of ye Sick people in Savannah as I have done either
to. . . ."

His character was never stained in anything before this, he said; people spoke well of him in Georgia for his diligence and good behavior; he liked the colony, it was improving, and "I thought I Should been happy in it and live a sober life but my mind is very Much Disturb. . . ." He remarked gently but pertinently to Oglethorpe, "yr Honor is very sensible that no Body would Leave his native Country if they had not som Crosses or Misfortune to venter their lives in Crossing ye ocean. . . ."

He said parenthetically but proudly of the woman introduced as Mrs. Pensyre, "She has two fine Boys. . . ."[17] Tiberius Pensyre had lived less than a month in 1733; eleven months later Francis Joseph Pensyre was born; and there was another boy. Samuel Pensyre was anxious lest they send his wife from England and he have to enter again that old and tragic life occasioned by her affliction. To this would be added the sorrow of breaking up his present happy family. He need not have worried. Death solved it all for him in June, 1735.[18]

Oglethorpe planned a fort for Tybee in the summer of 1733, and remarked that when the island was fortified, it with Argyle and Thunderbolt would make Savannah "pretty safe."[19] Tybee was also to have a beacon, or lighthouse to aid shipping, erected on the southeast of the island fronting on the inlet where a creek divided Skidaway and Tybee islands.[20] The beacon, under construction in Savannah in the autumn of 1733, was examined with admiration by visitors. One of them observed that a fine lighthouse was making by Oglethorpe's order; another described it as "a Tower of Wood of prodigious Height, that the Ships that are bound to Georgia may know the Bar. . ."; while another observed that it would be of great service to shipping bound for either Georgia or Carolina "for the Land of all the Coast, for some hundred Miles, is so alike, being all low and woody, that a distinguishing Mark is of great Consequence."

The beacon was an octagonal wooden structure ninety feet high, twenty-five feet wide at the bottom, twelve and one-half feet wide at the top. The foundations were secured with cedar piles, and the tower was weatherboarded to a height of twenty-six feet, the rest being open. Oglethorpe described it as being made of the best light wood, later identified as white pine. In November completion was anticipated by the following March, but this was not to be.[21] Elisha Dobree remarked to the Trustees early in 1735, "I am Sorry that I have to inform your Honble Board that the Workmen at Tybee are almost Continually Drunk & that the Light House is not like to be Quickly built: of Course it must go on Slow Eno; & no Ways Answer the Cost of that Dear Peice of Building."[22] The lighthouse became, in some men's minds, a still dearer piece of building. Fifteen hundred pounds sterling spent on it, they said later in 1735, and not up yet.[23]

William Blitheman, a carpenter who was one of the original group of Tybee settlers from the *Georgia Pink,* was in charge of the work. Since the first Tybee settlers were nearly all dead, men had to be brought down from Savannah to work on the lighthouse at mounting costs. In an effort to cut down expenses and to increase the settlers at Tybee, Thomas Causton by the summer of 1735 discharged the workmen from Savannah and had the work proceed with men who were willing to settle on Tybee.[24]

Oglethorpe, planning to leave England in the early winter of 1735 for Georgia, knew that the beacon was not yet up. When he arrived in February, 1736, the report went back to London that he was mightily incensed at the workmen who had not completed it. He "imprison'd the chief Man and threatened to hang him, But Suppose at his Instigation Mr. Vanderplank and Other's interceded for him, and became Body for Body that he Should finish it in five Week's Time, upon wch He Strenuously apply'd himself to the Work, and in Sixteen day's has done more than what He did in Sixteen Months before. He has finished the Foundation and raised the four Corner Post's so farr as to be A Very good Signal at Sea for Vessel's bound in, it is to be hoped he'el finish the Same by a Limitted Time." The lighthouse was finished that spring of 1736.[25] But this did not end lighthouse troubles in Georgia, for the structure always seemed to be falling down, in need of repairs, or just repaired. By August, 1741, Stephens said of it "the Old one (weak as it is) yet holds up its head. . . ." Others said that the beacon had fallen, and the *South-Carolina Gazette* remarked that "this fine piece of Workmanship, so beneficial to all those who fell in with the Coast of *South-Carolina* and *Georgia,*" had fallen to the ground for want of £100 worth of weatherboarding to protect a £1500 structure from the elements. Already a new lighthouse at Tybee was being built which Stephens thought would be better and last longer than the old one.[26]

In spite of Oglethorpe's plans for the settlement of Tybee, the island did not prosper. John Wesley observed gloomily in 1737 that after most of the inhabitants had drunk themselves to death the others went away. The island, he summed up, "is now as before a Settlement of Opossums, Racoons and the like Inhabitants."[27]

Oglethorpe's plan of protecting the approaches to Savannah included settling families on Skidaway Island and building a guardhouse there. In the summer of 1733 he contracted with Captain Ferguson, of the Carolina scout boat, to build a guardhouse;[28] but it was not until after Captain Yoakley's ship, the *James*, arrived in January, 1734, that he could make the settlement. He assigned to the Skidaway settlement six single men and five with families from the *James*. Two of these died almost immediately. By trade these men were perukemakers, clogmakers, ropemakers, weavers, dyers, victuallers, and bookbinders. One was an erstwhile soldier, William Johnson Dalmas, whose passage and part of his maintenance were paid by the Duke of Kent. The guardhouse on the northern end of Skidaway provided housing for the people until they could build their own houses. Here two pieces of cannon were placed and a boat with sails and oars stationed. At the southern end of the island a fort was begun in 1734, to be built by Captain Ferguson and his scout boat crew who patrolled these waters and up the Ogeechee to Fort Argyle.[29]

Skidaway was the only one of the out-settlements to have any especial alarm that year. Some of the Indians in the vicinity of Savannah, when hunting on St. Simons Island, met a party of Spaniards and Indians who declared they were deputed to search for settlements. A false report reached Savannah that Spaniards and Yamassees were landed on Skidaway. Freeholders from Savannah went to the aid of Dalmas, the tythingman on Skidaway; Thomas Causton sent the scout boat down toward the Altamaha River to search for enemies; Savannah men patrolled to the south in the Skidaway boat but they never caught sight of the intruders.[30] Dalmas was sufficiently impressed by the report to increase Skidaway's meager fortifications by adding a square redoubt on the northern point, with an intrenchment inside; one carriage gun and four swivel guns commanded the river and approaches to the huts. Dalmas was pleased with the increased protection but not with the spirit of the people, only six of whom would help with the work unless they were paid.[31]

Stout hearts were needed to struggle with Skidaway. They were possessed by the largest family coming over on the *James* who settled on the island, Thomas Mouse, a clogmaker, his wife Lucy, and five daughters. The only clue to the ages of the young Mouses—Anne, Catherine, Elizabeth, Mary, and Lucy—is that Mary Mouse was seven years old and Lucy was six in March, 1740, when they were taken to Bethesda Orphanage. Lucy may have been the baby born after they arrived in Georgia, or she may have been a very young colonist still in her mother's arms. Only two or three other children were among the first Skidaway settlers, though a new baby was born in April, 1734, to Thomas and Frances Smith. They named her Anne Skidaway Smith and years afterward she prided herself on being the eldest female born in the colony.[32]

Some of the settlers on Skidaway complained, as did those on Tybee, of the quality of their land and wished to have other grants more susceptible of cultivation, but the Trustees decided that the Skidaway people must remain where they were posted by Oglethorpe. The decision was to have cruel results. The Trustees did relent later in 1734 to the extent that they ordered the people on Skidaway, as well as those on Tybee, trying to farm the salt marshes to have provisions given them for another year; and, as a further encouragement, the Trustees sent them shoes and clothing.[33]

In spite of discouragement the Skidaway people made some progress. Captain George Dunbar, whose ship, the *Prince of Wales*, brought new colonists on December 27, 1734, went southward at the request of the Trustees to make a reconnaissance with eleven white men and four Indians. Some time before, a group of Spanish Indians had come up from the south and killed nine Euchee beyond the Ogeechee River. Captain Dunbar went to determine whether trouble was brewing along the coast south of Savannah and whether on the islands below those settled by Georgia colonists the Spaniards and their Indian allies were poised for mischief. Captain Dunbar's trip revealed nothing threatening. On Skidaway, January 9, 1735, he discovered that the people had made much greater progress in their houses and lands than he had expected. They were so regular in their watch that by night or day no boat could pass undetected, and their battery of three carriage guns and four swivels was in good order.[34]

In the same month Thomas Mouse, who had been in the colony a year, wrote his only known letter to Oglethorpe in England. "You being well acquainted with our Settlement at Skidaway, I have made bold to Informe your Honour of the Improvement belonging to my own Lott, which I call ye House Lott, it is pailed in, and I have two large hutts built thereon one is Twenty four by Sixteen and is sett all around with large upright Loggs, the other is Twenty one by fourteen with Clapboards only, which I propose as a Store House with a Yard and Conveniencys for Breed, where I keep my Fowls, of which I have about thirty, besides what I have Sold which came Chiefly from the Fowls which your Honour was pleased to give me, but I have not had altogether such good luck with my Sow, she has had two litters of Piggs, the first Died being nine, and the last Litter five, only two Living, which are large thriving Piggs, The Cows & Calves which we had are all run into the woods, and cannot bring them up, having so few hands that pretend they cannot Spare time to Hunt for them & theirs.

"I am now to informe your Honour that the Ground brings forth plenty of Callavances, Potatoes & Indian Corn, and will I dont doubt produce many other things which I intend to Try. I hope your Honour will not forget to send over some more Settlers for our Island, It being very hard for a Man (who has a large Family) to watch continually every third or fourth Night, and for refusing one Night, I have been tied Neck & Heels by Mr. Delmas our Tything Man. . . . I am informed that It is in his power to Tye me Neck and heels when he pleases, wch I submit to If deserved, but If a Man is to be Governed by an Officer, who will Reign Arbitrary, it is very hard to Submitt to, and if it is to be so," Thomas said stoutly, "I most Humbly beg your Honr please to permit me and my Family to proceed for England, altho' I like Skidoway better than any place I have seen in the Collony, I really declare that I think it very hard to be used as a common Soldier as I like my Place of Settlement so well, and to leave the Same after I have taken so much pains for my Family's sake is still more hard to me.

"I take the freedom to acquaint Your Honour," Thomas continued with modest pride, "that I do not mention out of Vanity, but I do Assure you I have made ye most Improvement on my Lott of any one, in ye Settlement," and remarked that "our Land which is belonging to us is lately rund out ye 17th December." Mr. Causton had informed him that the Trustees would allow the Skidaway people another year's provisions, "for which Great favour, your Honours have mine and my Familyes Humble Thanks."

Not until the last paragraph does he mention his wife Lucy Mouse. "My Spouse is in Dayly Expectation of being brought to Bed, and is now in Savanna where she Intends to Lye in—She and my Family Joins me in Humble thanks to your Honr and the Rest of the Honble Trustees."[35]

This forthright and informative letter is the expression of a self-respecting Englishman who had regard for his dignity, whose family's welfare was a present concern, and who was an industrious workman. His wife Lucy surely must have worked as hard as her industrious Thomas, during a pregnancy which covered the major portion of her first year in the colony. Mouse was hopeful and trying his best to succeed. Thomas Causton, who went a little later to look at Skidaway, was not pleased with what he saw. The people he reported were generally idle, and Captain Ferguson thought some might try to desert. Orders were given to seize any who should attempt this. Causton reversed his opinion the following year when he reported that three of the original settlers—Thomas Mouse, Samuel Ward, and John Stonehewer—had improved some of their land. Ward and Stonehewer both returned to England a few years later, Stonehewer with the help of friends.[36]

Several people spoke of the healthfulness of Skidaway Island, and some thought it more healthful than Savannah. However, this prospect enticed no settlers from Savannah to Skidaway. William Johnson Dalmas, the tythingman, said in early 1735, "I am Situated upon one of ye Pleasantess Islands in America (as indeed all ye Country is beautiful) and will with ye Smallest Industry answer all the ends proposed. . . ."[37] By mid-March Dalmas was dead. His death probably had little to do with Skidaway's healthfulness but resulted from an illness of which he had complained since his arrival in Georgia. A visitor to the island early in 1736, after inspecting the village, guardhouse, and battery of cannon at the northern point of Skidaway, spoke cheerfully of the settlers' prospects and the richness of the land; however, he had not tried to cultivate it.[38]

Some settlers died, a few new ones came, more went, but the Thomas Mouses persevered on Skidaway. At one time they kept a public house on a very small scale to eke out their scanty living. A Yamacraw Indian woman complained to Thomas Causton in 1737 that, when she was on Skidaway, one of Mrs. Mouse's daughters had beaten her. The Mouses had from time to time bartered with the Indians and in this instance the latter received what was described as strong liquors, with which they were drunk. Lucy Mouse was severely reprimanded for dealing with the Indians and giving them liquor and was told by Thomas Causton that if this occurred again she and Thomas would not only lose their license but be prosecuted. "The Indians seemed very well satisfied," Causton observed, "and Mrs. Mouse promis'd to take care for ye. future."[39]

John Wesley, who with his brother Charles had partaken of Mouse hospitality on Skidaway, described the island as computed to be of 6000 acres with a village at the east point with a fort, one house, four huts, and twenty acres of oak-land cleared. A mile westward were two families, a small fort, a hut, and ten acres of cleared oak-land. Nine of the ten families originally settled in the village were dead or gone, the forts and huts hastening into ruin.[40]

The tenth family remaining was the Mouses. Thomas's life had been such as to win the highest praise the Trustees could accord him; he was a very industrious man. In 1739 Oglethorpe decided to give Mouse one of the German indentured servants brought over by Captain William Thomson as an encouragement to the out-planters.[41] But it was too late for Thomas Mouse, much too late. The years from 1734 to 1740 on Skidaway took too great a toll. Thomas and Lucy Mouse had seen most of their plans and hopes dissolve and their neighbors leave the island.

One young man, William Ewen, worked his land on Skidaway with high hopes from 1736 through 1739. His first year on Skidaway he planted about sixteen acres of land cleared by others who had gone. While clearing his own land he employed four German servants whose sole work was on the land. But since he could not maintain them by produce from his land he returned them to the Trustees' store in Savannah, and so was left singlehanded. In 1739 he had a very bad crop: nine bushels of corn, one-half bushel of peas, but no rice or potatoes; in 1740 he "raised 90 bushels of corn; but had no pease, nor pottatoes."

"It was now very low with me," he wrote. He had bad luck with his cattle, his calves died, many of his hogs ran away, "which kept me poore; for I could gett none to Sell; and many times none for my own use." He sold the boards and shingles which he had planned to use for his own house; "this money furnished me with Shoes to my feet; and Other things which I much wanted. . . ." All of the inhabitants were gone except Thomas Mouse and Ewen, and Mouse "was reduced so low, that he had Scarce cloathes to cover him, he haveing a large family. . . ."

William Ewen made a telling point in this letter. The Trustees emphasized raising mulberry trees, olives, grape vines, and various exotic plants which they hoped the colony could produce. "I need not amuse your Honrs. with the many Curiossities; that may be raised here (with care, and pains) as well as in Europe, but those are things that will not Satisfye a man when he is hungry; nor cloathe him; when he is Naked; for many times: I have had: no other provisions to eat but Homony and Salt; tho I have used my utmost endeavours."

Ewen continued: "I had now: almost broak my Constitution; with hard working; and hard Liveing and could not see any prospect; of any return of my Labour; now I am Obliged to leave my Settlement (tho, much against my Inclination) and Skidaway; without Inhabitants." His stay on Skidaway he summarized by the statement that he must now go back to Savannah, "after that I had spent, all my time; all that I was worth; and had brought my self in Debt. . . ."[42] Thomas Mouse could have told almost the same story.

By now even the Mouses had experienced all they could on Skidaway and went with Ewen to Savannah to find work. The two men wrote an account of the island's settlers, what they had done, and what became of them. They were now all gone. The cleared land was grown up in weeds and small trees and had now become a strange place to all the inhabitants. The guardhouse was in ruins, the guns taken away.[43] Seven years were sufficient to convince the settlers, even the persistent Mouses, of the futility of struggling against an unfavorable environment. Thomas Mouse, had the turns of fate been a little different, might have been successful. There was good land in the colony, and there was poor. Whatever grant a man was given, he was expected to produce on it. Land suitable for farming was not at first designated as such. A man could break his heart as well as his health on poor land. The breaks could never be mended, the time never retrieved. This the Trustees in England never seemed to realize.

In Savannah Lucy Mouse, always one to turn her hand to whatever had to be done, found work as a midwife. She also took in sewing. Thomas was employed at George Whitefield's new orphanage. This may have been the reason why two of the Mouse children were admitted to the orphanage, for Mary and Lucy, aged seven and six years respectively, were admitted in March, 1740.[44] The measure of Thomas and Lucy Mouse's struggle to maintain themselves is shown by this step; they must have been unable to provide for themselves and the children. Two of the girls married. Anne married Francis Brooks and presented Thomas and Lucy Mouse with twin grandchildren who were baptized on October 29, 1738. Elizabeth Mouse married Isaac Young, Jr., whose father, a miller and maltster from Gloucestershire, had a grant of 100 acres and brought his family at his own expense to the colony in 1736.[45]

In the summer of 1742 "a Malignant Feaver of the worst sort, and near Epidemical" raged in Savannah and carried off Thomas Mouse on August 17. On Friday, October 29, Elizabeth Mouse Young died.[46] Lucy Mouse might well say, as indeed she did, that she had suffered many misfortunes and bred up a large family with great difficulty. She had in 1747 two daughters dependent upon her still, one of them a widow, for Francis Brooks was killed by a Spaniard in February, 1740. Her house on Skidaway was destroyed, the boards of the house stolen, the frame burned by the Indians. She must make her living in Savannah "where She has not an House but that of her Son in Law." Lucy Mouse was too independent for this to suit her; she wanted a lot of her own. "She has no House any Where, and must follow her business in Savannah. . . ." She also wanted to be paid for her share of the cattle on Skidaway, which the settlers had agreed to sell.[47] Eventually she received £8.10.0 from the sale of the cattle but the lot she had set her heart upon could not be granted to her as there were heirs to that property. She continued as a midwife in Savannah and finally on November

10, 1752, she was granted a lot. The time and the place of her death are not known, though it evidently occurred in Savannah, where in court records of 1768 she is referred to as Lucy Mouse "deceased."[48]

The most permanent of the early settlements made outside of Savannah was that of the Salzburgers. Georgia was intended as a refuge for the King of England's poor subjects and for foreigners who were willing to become his subjects. All were guaranteed liberty of conscience, and all Protestants free exercise of religion. The Prince-Archbishop of Salzburg had recently expelled his Protestant subjects, and their welfare was of concern to many in Protestant England. The Trustees were interested in these unfortunate Lutherans and had considered sending some of them to Georgia before the Society for the Propagation of Christian Knowledge asked in October, 1732, if Salzburgers might find asylum in Georgia. The Trustees were willing for them to go where "they shall be so mingled with English men as in time to become one people with us."[49]

The Trustees also listened with interest to the plans of Jean Pierre Purry for settling a colony of Swiss on the Carolina side of the Savannah River, not far from what would be the village of Savannah; they subscribed individually to aid his colonists, and heard later with satisfaction that Purry arrived safely with his people in Charles Town in December, 1732.[50]

By the latter part of December, 1732, the Trustees had agreed to send fifty families of Salzburgers to Georgia and empowered the Reverend Samuel Urlsperger at Augsburg to collect the families. The Trustees agreed to defray the costs of passage and provisions for 300 heads, furnish them tools, seed to plant, and food until they made a harvest. Each man was to be entitled to three lots, one each for his house, garden, and farm. Freedom of religion was promised and the full enjoyment of the civil and religious rights of the free subjects of Great Britain. The Salzburgers would be expected to obey such orders and regulations as were necessary for maintaining peace, property, and good government; and, when they arrived, to engage in joint labor in clearing land and building houses. A minister and a catechist, who would officiate in the German language, were to be supported by the S.P.C.K. This Society would pay the expenses of the Salzburgers from Germany to Rotterdam.[51]

Early in November the Trustees sent one of the Symonds

ships, the *Purisburgh,* to Rotterdam to meet those who wished to go to Georgia. The ship returned to Dover about December 12 where the Salzburgers occasioned considerable interest. "The Contentment and Resignation of these Saltzburghers under their Sufferings," remarked a man who was at Dover at the time, "the chearful Gratitude they express'd for what they had, was so visible in their Countenances, that every Body in our Company seem'd touch'd with Tenderness towards them, and not a little pleas'd that they are now in a way to be happy."

Some one, thought to be one of the Trustees, gave a plentiful dinner of roast beef and plum pudding for the Salzburgers, to which they marched from the ship with their leader, Baron Von Reck, at the head. The ministers, John Martin Bolzius and Israel Gronau, closed the procession, which sang German hymns along the way. "I own to you," the writer observed, "it seems a Glory peculiar to Protestant Countries, and particularly to Great Britain, that her Dominions are a refuge to such People. . . ." Others were impressed by the piety and order of the Salzburgers and made them gifts with many good wishes for their journey.[52]

The *Purisburgh,* Captain Fry, sailed from Dover with a fair wind on Tuesday morning, January 8, 1734. Besides the Salzburgers, other colonists on board made a total of seventy-three persons, or fifty-nine and one-sixth heads—twenty British and fifty-three foreign passengers for whom the Trustees paid. Not all of the latter were Salzburgers. In November the Trustees thought that only thirty-six Salzburgers would go, but more must have been added, for when the ship arrived in America, she was reported to have forty-seven Salzburgers, still considerably less than the fifty families the Trustees had agreed to send initially.

Captain Fry came to anchor off Charles Town on Thursday, March 7, 1734. Von Reck, Bolzius, and Gronau went into the city and met Oglethorpe, who showed Von Reck a map of Georgia from which he might choose the place of settlement for the Salzburgers. He chose a site about twenty-one miles above Savannah, "where there are Rivers, little Hills, clear Brooks, cool springs, a fertile Soil, and plenty of Grass."[53]

The *Purisburgh* sailed from Charles Town on the morning of March 9. The following day Von Reck wrote: "God blessed us this Day with the Sight of our Country, our wish'd-for Georgia,

which we saw at ten in the Morning; and Brought us into the
Savannah River, and caused us to remember the Vows we made
unto him, if He did through his infinite Goodness bring us
hither." The river, he thought, was wider than the Rhine and
from sixteen to twenty-five feet deep, abounding with oysters,
sturgeon, and other fish. "Its banks were cloathed with fresh
Grass; and a little beyond were seen Woods, old as the Creation;
resounding with the Musick of Birds, who sung the Praise of
their Creator." Bolzius, the minister, whom Oglethorpe called a
very wise man and who was destined to grow in the esteem of
the colonists and the Trustees as the years went by, wrote that
day, "And lying in fine and calm Weather, upon the Shore of
our beloved Georgia, where we heard the Birds sing melodiously,
every Body in the Ship was joyful."[54]

The *Purisburgh* came up the river on the morning of March
12 to Savannah. Captain Fry saluted with five guns; Savannah
responded with three. Everybody rushed out to look; in fact,
"all the Magistrates, the citizens, and the Indians, were come to
the River side." From the land came loud huzzahs; from the
English and the sailors on the *Purisburgh* came loud huzzahs.[55]
In the incomparable beauty of a spring day on the Georgia coast,
the sun shone and the birds sang; the Salzburgers had arrived
and everybody was proud and happy. They had come a long
way, to settle among people whose language they did not speak,
whose customs they did not know, but where they would have
religious freedom and economic opportunity.

They were received, Von Reck said, with all possible demonstrations of joy, friendship, and civility. The Indians reached
out their hands to touch him, as a testimony of their joy at the
people's arrival. A dinner and "very good and wholesome
English strong beer" was given them. The Salzburgers were lodged
temporarily in a tent pitched in Johnson Square. Von Reck,
Bolzius, Gronau, and Dr. Zwefler lodged with Samuel Quincy, the
minister. Von Reck was eager to look at the rising town of
Savannah and found it "regularly laid out, divided into four
Wards, in each of which is a spacious Square, for holding of
Markets and other public Uses. The Streets are straight, and
the Houses are all of the same Model and Dimensions, and well
contrived for Conveniency; For the time it has been built, it is
very populous, and its Inhabitants are all White People. And
indeed, the Blessing of God seems to have gone along with this

Undertaking; for here we see Industry honoured, and Justice strictly executed, and Luxury and Idleness banished from this happy Place, where Plenty and Brotherly Love seem to make their Abode, and where the good Order of a Nightly Watch, restrains the Disorderly, and makes the Inhabitants sleep secure in the midst of a Wilderness." Of the regulations governing the colony, Von Reck thought that one of the best was that prohibiting rum, "that flattering and deceitful Liquor which has been found equally pernicious to the Natives and new Comers which seldom fails, by Sickness, or Death, to draw after it its own Punishment."[56]

The Salzburgers were admonished to abstain from drinking this deadly beverage and told that it had occasioned the deaths of many people. They learned from the English to brew "a sort of Beer of Molasses, with Sassafras, and the Tops of Firr-Trees, instead of Hops, which they boil in a Kettle, with Water; some add Indian Corn; The Inhabitants here reckon this Liquor to be wholesome, and the drinking of Water unwholesome; but we prefer Water to this Mixture, and find our selves well after it; sometimes we mix it with a little Wine."

Bolzius, thinking of his people's future, was concerned with the productivity of the land. "All that is sowed," he remarked, "grows in a short Time." In the Savannah gardens he saw fruit trees and herbs but noted the lack of greens. All the houses and gardens were laid out in a mathematical equality, which he thought would make a fine show when they came to perfection. The people had horses, cows, and fowls. Yet he found milk, eggs, and other victuals, except pork, much dearer than in Germany; for the people did not kill the cattle, rob the calves of milk, or take the eggs from nests, being anxious to increase the stock. From the nearby woods, where the cows were turned out, he could hear the tinkle of cowbells.[57]

Oglethorpe returned from Charles Town to Savannah on March 14 and took Von Reck with him up the country to find the place of settlement, tentatively chosen in Charles Town from a map. Accompanied by the Indian captain, Tuscaney, they made an arduous journey, part of it by boat up the Savannah River, part of it on horseback, camping at night. Trees had been blazed to show the route of future roads and to mark the parts of the river already found passable. On March 17 they arrived at the site which the Salzburgers were to settle and call Ebenezer, rock of help. Von Reck was enthusiastic about it. Here were fine meadows on which hay could be made; here were woods of cedar and walnut, pine, cypress, oak, and myrtle trees, the berries of which, he was told, were used to make a green wax for candles. The earth seemed to him very fertile and "very fit for Vines," fertile enough to bring forth anything planted in it. The earth was "of several sorts, some sandy, some black, fat and heavy, and some of a claiey nature. The first is good for Potatoes and Pease; the second for all sorts of Corn; and the third to make Bricks, Earthern Ware, & etc." He noted many kinds of game: eagles, turkeys, deer, wild goats, hares, partridges, and buffaloes.[58]

By degrees the Salzburgers moved up to their future home. An advance party went first to build houses for the women and children, two bark tents forty feet long. The rest of the settlers went to Abercorn to stay in two tents until a road was built to Ebenezer and it would be possible to move their baggage there. Until this was done some had to carry provisions the twelve miles from Abercorn to Ebenezer on their backs.

Martin Lackner was the first Salzburger to die in Georgia. He died at Abercorn on Good Friday, April 12, "of a Ptisick [tuberculosis] and a wasting Fever: He died in the Lord whom he loved with his whole Heart, in Health and Sickness." People would have made a coffin for him, but the Salzburgers thought it unnecessary, "being accoustomed to bury no Body in a Coffin, but Women that die in Child-Bed: So they dressed the Corps, after it was washed, in his own Cloathes, laid him upon a Board, and after he was brought to his Grave, in an orderly Procession, they wrap'd him in a Cloth, and let him down into the Ground." Lachner's money was put into a box for relief of the poor and of Indian children. Before the Salzburgers left Savannah, their first child born in Georgia, James Frederick Rothe, had been added to their number.[59]

By April 19, the road between Abercorn and Ebenezer was finished, ten days after it was begun. The English were surprised that a twelve-mile road with seven bridges could be built through the forest in so short a time.

In the meantime sawyers arrived from South Carolina at the Trustees' order to saw boards for the first houses at Ebenezer. Governor Johnson also sent four horses, and the Lord provided a young strong horse with no master that came out of the woods at Ebenezer. These could pull the sledges the people had made to carry their baggage to Ebenezer. By May 1, lots were drawn for. A dozen cows and calves plus seed soon arrived, and the cleared land was under cultivation. Indians sometimes brought deer for the settlers. By May 12 a chapel of boards was finished for worship, and on the 13th a day of Thanksgiving was held before Von Reck left to return to Germany.[60]

Like the earlier settlers, the Salzburgers were soon troubled with sickness in their new home. Bolzius noted in May that "The People in *Abercorn* as well as in *Ebenezer* are troubled with Loosnesses. It is thought that drinking too much in hot Weather, is the Reason of it. They are too bashful to tell it in the Beginning when the Evil might have been prevented. Some have had great Benefit by our Physick." He thought that river water would not agree with the Salzburgers, being too full of trees and leaves. They intended to dig a well, and Bolzius was sure that Providence led them to the discovery of a brook whose good and wholesome water saved them this labor.[61]

Ebenezer was described in February, 1736, as containing four good framed timber houses built at the expense of the Trustees for the two ministers and the schoolmaster, and for a public store. A chapel and guardhouse as well as a great number of split board houses had been built by the people. The settlers were well supplied with cattle and poultry. Some crops had been successful, but the corn had failed because of improper cultivation. Despite all this apparent good luck the Salzburgers were dissatisfied because of the inaccessibility of the place and the marshy ground. Von Reck returned to Georgia with Oglethorpe in February, 1736, and with the Ebenezer ministers immediately brought to Oglethorpe a petition of the people to move to a better location. Oglethorpe went to Ebenezer and tried to dissuade the Salzburgers from moving. When he saw that they were determined, he allowed them to move a few miles to the junction of Ebenezer Creek with the Savannah River, a much more accessible location; and soon Old Ebenezer was but a memory as its former inhabitants set to work to build a new and more permanent town.[62]

Commissary Von Reck remained only a short time on his second stay, his enthusiasm for Georgia greatly lessened because of the hardships of his co-religionists.[63] Yet Salzburgers continued to come to Georgia, and Ebenezer under the leadership of Pastor Bolzius became truly a "rock of help," whose inhabitants worshipped God in their own way, educated their children, and proved that the Trustees' dream of self-sufficient white farmers could be achieved in Georgia.

CHAPTER FIVE

The "Unfortunate Poor" as Rulers

T HE PEOPLE who came on the *Ann*—the First Forty, as they were sometimes called—found their members augmented and a plan of settlement under way. People in the little settlements might die, but others arrived to take their places. New settlers replaced those dead in Savannah, who soon were only a fading memory. The plan of settlement was carried out because Oglethorpe could not leave the colony at the time that he had originally planned. He thought in June, 1733, that he would return to England by early July, as soon as he had put the people in possession of their lots and held the first court.[1] When he announced his intentions in a speech to the South Carolina Assembly in June, Governor Johnson thought Oglethorpe's absence would discourage and disquiet the Georgia people. Johnson, fearful that Georgians would grow disorderly with Oglethorpe gone and would desert to South Carolina, promised to do all possible to prevent trouble.[2]

When illness grew so great in the summer of 1733, Oglethorpe saw that he could not go. With so many people ill he thought that if he abandoned them they would be thrown into despair and the distemper might become fatal. He stayed, "lest it might seem that I left them in distress and for fear of Sharing the Sickness. . . ."[3] By November he thought everything was so well settled that he could go immediately. About a month later he planned to leave within a week after returning from a trip to the Altamaha River. He had prolonged his stay awaiting the Salzburgers but he said that if they had not arrived when he returned to Savannah he must leave for England anyway.[4]

He was in Charles Town on the point of embarking for England when the Salzburgers arrived there on March 7, 1734. He returned to Georgia and attended to settling them. Then he sailed from Charles Town on a man-of-war, the *Aldborough,* on Tuesday, May 7, 1734, and arrived in London on June 20. On this trip Oglethorpe was accompanied by Tomochichi, the latter's wife, Senauki, his nephew Toonahowi, other Indians, and an interpreter.[5]

Oglethorpe came on his second visit with the largest of the embarkations to Georgia, arriving at Tybee on February 5, 1736, and reaching Savannah the following day. Much of his second stay in Georgia was spent, not in Savannah, but south of it at the new town of Frederica. On November 23, 1736, Oglethorpe again sailed from Savannah on the brigantine the *Two Brothers,* Captain William Thomson, for England.[6] He returned to the colony in 1738, on the *Blandford,* Captain Burridge, in company with five transports bearing his regiment which he had enlisted in England. On September 13, the *Blandford* was nearing Frederica on St. Simons Island, where the regiment was to be stationed. The date of this arrival was variously reported as September 15, 18, and 19.[7] He remained in Georgia until 1743 but was so engaged with military affairs in the southern part of the colony that he could give little time to civil affairs in the northern part, and Savannah saw him only briefly. He left Georgia for the last time on July 22, 1743, on the guard-ship commanded by Captain William Thomson. The *South-Carolina Gazette* reported that he put in at Virginia and there embarked on a forty-gun ship for England.[8]

These relatively long absences from the colony and his concern with military affairs show that much of the early life of Georgians was not determined by Oglethorpe. In fact he never assumed general oversight in the colony after his first return to England in 1734. The fact that Oglethorpe was the only Trustee in the colony and that his was a forceful personality did in practice give him enhanced power, but this was not through any formal action of the Trustees. Oglethorpe was never governor in Georgia; as a Trustee he could hold no civil office in the colony. He acted as an agent of the Trustees with limited stipulated powers. To a man who ascribed authority to Oglethorpe superior to that of the magistrates, the Trustees said forcefully that "no single Trustee has any Power at all as a Trustee, and no Person Whatsoever can have any Power in the Civil Government of the Province, except what is devolv'd by the Collective Body of the Trust, nor any Authority but what is derived from them. . . ."⁹ The Trustees, "who are the governors" as they said in 1734, alone could give directions in the colony. Their instructions must be obeyed, and they will support those who obey them.¹⁰ The Trustees never appointed a governor or developed a full colonial government in Georgia. They kept most political power in their hands regardless of the inconveniences that delays in communication entailed. "As the Trustees cannot desire Genl. Oglethorpe's interposing in their Civil Concerns while he is imployed in his Military Ones which are distinct Services," they wrote in 1740, "they expect their Orders to be pursued by those to whom they are given Without their giving the General the trouble of being consulted or waiting for his Directions therein whc. the Trustees themselves do not expect from him, nor reasonably can."¹¹

After Oglethorpe returned to Georgia in 1738 with his regiment the war against the Spanish in Florida became more and more important to him and civil affairs of the colony receded. His military appointment was from the King and not the Trustees. The Trustees realized that some form of government was necessary and that Oglethorpe could be depended upon less and less to carry out their desires. They tried to solve in two ways the problems arising from the absence of a central administrative officer. They asked Oglethorpe to suggest someone in the colony to superintend it in his absence. They sent over a man of unquestioned loyalty to them who would influence the trend of events in their favor and report in detail on people and affairs in Georgia. With his reports the Trustees could then reprove, admonish, deflate, or advance the people they thought deserved such treatment. This new Trustees' agent was William Stephens, sent to Georgia with the title of Secretary for the Affairs of the Trust in 1737.

"He was in Queen Anne's reign a member of Parliament," Egmont observed, "but fallen to decay." The journal which Stephens had kept on a trip to South Carolina impressed Egmont; it was "extremely well wrote, and it were to be wished it could be brought about to make him Governor of Georgia."¹² The Trustees had no idea of making him governor of Georgia; they wanted some one who would tell them in detail everything that went on in the colony, since they could not wring the desired information out of Oglethorpe. Indeed, they reached depths of pessimism in which they thought they could not carry on the colony, and so told Oglethorpe. Stephens received his appointment as Secretary to the Trustees in Georgia on April 18, 1737, and was given a grant of 500 acres of land and instructions regarding his duties of gathering and transmitting information about the colony to the Trustees. Egmont remarked with satisfaction that "we shall have from him by every ship an account of the state and transactions of the Colony."[13]

Stephens sailed on the *Mary Ann,* Captain Thomas Shubrick, in August, 1737, arriving at Charles Town on October 20 and Savannah on November 1. Stephens's third son, Thomas, came on a later ship, the *Minerva,* Captain Nicholson, to Charles Town and reached Savannah on December 21. Thomas Stephens remained in the colony until August 3, 1739, and returned later; William Stephens remained in Georgia until his death in 1753 at the age of eighty-three.[14] He wrote a journal and letters to the Trustees, which gave them great satisfaction because of the details of life in the colony which both journal and letters contained.

When Oglethorpe was planning to return to England in 1733, long before he finally sailed, the Trustees inquired "in whom you judge proper to lodge the Power of Superintending the People when you come away." Learning from Oglethorpe of the "petulancy" he thought was so manifest, they were "therefore more sollicitous to have some Man of Abilities, of Spirit and Temper as Super Intendent over them." By the time this letter arrived on the *Georgia Pink* on August 29, Oglethorpe had decided to nominate for this thankless and onerous job Thomas Causton.[15]

Thomas Causton is noted in the List as "Age 40; calico printer"; he had come over with the original embarkation on the *Ann.* His wife, Martha, an infant son Thomas, and his wife's niece Sophia Hopkey, did not arrive in Georgia until September 23, 1733, at which time the family was reunited. One of the most interesting and informative letters about Georgia's beginning was written by Causton to his wife; it shows a man of some education and ability who evidently loved his wife and son.[16]

Causton's first official position in Georgia was his appointment as third bailiff (or magistrate) on November 8, 1732, before the

Ann sailed.[17] On January 19, 1733, the day before the *Ann* arrived at Port Royal Island, South Carolina, Oglethorpe ordered him "to take all the Stores into my Care and to keep an account of them. And in that Office I shall continue which takes up my whole time," Causton wrote. On the arrival of the colonists at Savannah, Oglethorpe continued him in office to deliver out, as the occasion demanded, all of the Trustees' stores; they needed "a pretty Deal of Care," Causton remarked. In September, 1733, Joseph Hughes died and Causton, already doing much of Hughes's work, was appointed public storekeeper in his place.[18] In this position, he was responsible for giving out the allowances of food, tools, and other items to the people. The Trustees fed the people until they could make a crop, or longer as it often turned out. Many tools and other necessities for life in a new area also came from the stores through Causton.

In March, 1734, before leaving for England, Oglethorpe, according to Causton, authorized him to do whatever was necessary in Oglethorpe's absence to support the settlement under any difficulties which might arise and to preserve peace, safety, and lawful properties.[19] These were evidently verbal instructions, and the Trustees must have been informed of them when Oglethorpe reached England. Acceptance of this delegation of authority to Causton seems evident from the Trustees' letters to him; for they heaped more responsibility upon him, and it was to him that their orders for the colony were sent. As Causton began to feel the weight of the responsibility in his various offices he became uneasy. This uneasiness was aggravated by the lack of adequate help in the store, where every mistake was blamed on him. He said later that he ought to have been more particularly instructed and his real authority made public to the colonists.[20]

When Oglethorpe returned to the colony in February, 1736, he expressed his approval of Causton's actions in his absence, Causton said later. Causton now asked to be relieved of his duties. By then there had been many complaints of the people about the store, and Causton knew that in many respects his position was untenable, but Oglethorpe refused to allow him to resign.[21] Causton saw difficulties ahead in the development of some of Oglethorpe's plans. Because of his intimate relationship with the people and their daily lives, by 1736 Causton's knowledge of their abilities and desires far surpassed Oglethorpe's. But he could not resign without permission, and that permission was refused. Indeed instead of relieving him of any of his duties, the Trustees gave him additional ones.

William Waterland, the second magistrate, after presiding with Causton at one or possibly both courts in July, 1733, was turned out of his office for misbehavior on August 2, 1733. He was "Brother to Dr. Waterland the Kings chaplain, who for his drunkenness would take no notice of him—" a hint as to the possible cause of his removal. Waterland left for South Carolina in February, 1734. He must have taught school in Savannah, for in 1735 the Trustees were reminded that there had been no instructor of youth in Savannah since Waterland left. In Carolina he pursued the same vocation, advertising that he taught writing and arithmetic in all its most useful parts and the rudiments of grammar, "but more particularly English, of which great care is taken, and by such methods as few Masters care to take the trouble of, being taught grammatically."[22]

The career in Georgia of the first bailiff, Peter Gordon, was one from which neither he nor the Trustees derived satisfaction. He was not present at the court in July, 1735,[23] and left the colony in November to return to England. Upon his arrival there on February 25, 1734, he gave as his reason for coming that he must be operated on for a fistula. The Trustees questioned anyone coming from the colony who could give them information; Gordon's report was optimistic. He praised Oglethorpe for his indefatigable zeal and reported that forty houses were built in Savannah. He described the battery of twelve guns on the Savannah River, the two blockhouses, each in an angle of the town, with four guns each, and the town house in which Samuel Quincy preached. He had great hopes for the production of silk and wine. The Trustees were greatly pleased with Gordon's sketch of Savannah as it was when he left in November, 1733, which they bought from him for sixteen guineas and ordered engraved. Gordon also reported that not as much land was cleared as expected because of the time spent in building houses, and he predicted that the Trustees would have to support the colonists again the next year.[24]

Gordon, his wife, and two servants returned to Georgia on the *Prince of Wales*, Captain George Dunbar, their expenses paid by the Trustees. Another embarkation of Salzburgers conducted by John Vat came by this ship, as did a number of other colonists, and Tomochichi and his party after having been to London to see the King and Queen. Gordon was in charge of the passengers, who arrived on Saturday, December 28, 1734.[25]

Gordon must have had the details of his ensuing procedure clear in his mind when he returned; perhaps the interest with which the Trustees listened to him in London led him to think that he could influence them further in his own behalf. Soon after his arrival he began to gather complaints about the colony, particularly about Causton, to take back to England. He had been in the colony about two months, when he left for Charles Town, reportedly to sell some goods brought with him from England. From that port he sailed for England with ten or twelve complaining letters from colonists.[26]

Others besides Causton must have been relieved when Gordon left. He had stirred up considerable trouble. "As I am now informed Mr. Gordon is Sailed for England," Causton wrote the Trustees, ". . . I beg leave to say, That when he arrived, I rece'd him, as one I wisht for, I mean a person capable of assisting me, with hopes that he would Save me the Trouble of Acting (on every Occasion) in the office of Magistrate; and I communicated to him, Such parts of Your Honour's Orders to me as concerned the publick Administration.

"I expected, he would have enforct the former Orders, which till then, had been peacable Submitted to; But to my great Surprize, encouraged Complaints and Raised Discord, As if he came with some great Commission, And there is not one Materiall thing done, but he has endeavoured to Expose it. . . .

"But thus it is, He has made a Voyage to Georgia, Staid here about a Month, Encouraged Complaints against the Administrations of Justice, helped Villifye, Ridicule, and Oppose all former Management, hearing One Side without the other, and then left us; Without letting us know his Sentiments, (or Staying) whereby to prevent those things which he pretended to Complain off.

"I hope Your Honours will not be Offended, if (with great Submission) I say, That this Treatment by Mr Gordon, has given me so great Uneasiness that I had Rather Choose, the most ordinary Servitude Than Execute a Publick Office on Such Terms."[27]

Before Gordon reached England, Oglethorpe told the Trustees that reports from the colony told of "a great deal of murmuring and uneasiness" from the time Gordon arrived in December, 1734; Oglethorpe thought this proceeded from Gordon, who was suspected of being a papist, which the Trustees planned to inquire into, "as a matter of very great consequence." The Trustees did not feel kindly towards Gordon since he had come over without leave; they ordered him to appear before them, which he did on May 10, delivering the complaining letters he brought over.[28] In his own written statement he began: "Finding upon my Arrivall at Savannah the Affairs of the Colony in Such A Situation, as required an emediate representation to this Honble Board, by which means alone they can be redress'd, and the evile consequences, which at present threatens the Colony prevented. I thought I could not better express my duty to Yr Honours nor my affection and hearty good Wishes for the Success and prosperity of the Colony, thane by returneing to England and laying them before You, that thereby the ill consequences that might attend the delayes and uncertainties of letters coming Safe to yr hands may be prevented."

Gordon brought several specific complaints. Noble Jones, the surveyor, was slow in running out people's land, with consequences that people must live in town and pay high prices for food. The cause of these high prices was the feastings and clubs encouraged by the magistrates, at several of which fifteen or sixteen pounds sterling had been expended. He himself had paid five or six pence a pound for fresh meat, ten pence for butter, the same for candles, and two or three pence a pound for bread. People were reduced to great want, selling clothes and other necessities in order to eat.

Courts were held too frequently, thereby taking too much of the people's time and losing one-third of the labor of the colony. Ten tythingmen under arms were obliged to attend each court; besides these were the jury, witnesses, "and many idle Spectators who are drawn there out of curiosity and whose labour is likewise lost. . . ." Gordon criticised Causton's conduct of the court and his personal conduct as most arbitrary. He presented complaints from three people whose licensed public houses were frustrated by a Mrs. Penrose, who with no license boldly kept a public house where rum and punch were sold in quantities despite several fines in court. Causton took strangers there when they must be regaled, and public feasts were held there, to the envy and detriment of two of the first forty, Mrs. Hodges and James Muir, who had licenses. Thomas Christie, the recorder, sold rum. Causton sold rum in the store; he was blamed for selling rum to workers, because drinking caused them to do little work. The lighthouse at Tybee was greatly neglected. Gordon thought that unless one of the Trustees came over and put affairs to rights, there was danger that people would leave the colony. If they did so and reported the usage they had from Causton, others would not go to settle in Georgia, however great misfortunes they had labored under before.

The Trustees considered that Gordon had behaved ill in leaving Georgia without permission and in countenancing complaints against the other magistrates. They took no action about Gordon's criticism, delaying until Oglethorpe returned to Georgia and investigated the charges.[29] However little they may have thought of Peter Gordon's complaints, the Trustees, as was their custom when criticisms were made of the colony, wrote immediately to state the complaints and demand an answer. To Causton they wrote, "The Trustees are very sensible of the great fatigue you have had in the administration of Justice; & they hoped by Mr. Gordon's return to Georgia it would have eased you in some degree of the burthen; but in that have found themselves disappointed by his not having assisted you in enforcing the Trustees' Orders & quitting their Service without Licence." They directed that, as originally ordered, court for hearing civil cases should be held every six weeks and not oftener.[30]

The magistracy of the colony underwent other changes. In case of necessity the Trustees had originally provided by dormant commissions that George Symes was to replace Gordon, Richard Hodges was to replace Waterland, and Francis Scott was to replace Causton.[31] Whether Symes ever served as a magistrate is not known, nor is the date of his death known. Symes, an apothecary, at fifty-five was the oldest man to come on the *Ann*. His wife died in the summer of 1733, and he married in 1735 Elizabeth Gray (Grey), a woman who came from Scotland as an indentured servant. She died two years later of "a violent Flux, wch. she had laboured under about a month." His daughter Amy married Robert Johnson, who came on the *Ann* indented to Thomas Christie; Johnson died in July, 1734; his widow married in 1735 Morgan Davis, an indented servant to Roger Lacy and died herself about 1738 or 1739.[32] Little is known of Symes except what he said in two letters written to Oglethorpe in 1735: "I Disser a Small faver from your honor if you please to Send Me one Man Servant or a boyer it will be of greate youce to Me in My

Agge. . . ." He was having financial troubles; people would not
pay him for treating them, hence he could not pay for his house.
He was thankful for all the favors he had received and was himself in good health, "ixceapte my Rupter that will be on me
whill in this world."[33] After that he vanishes from the records,
probably through death.

Richard Hodges, who was to replace Waterland, died in July,
1733, and Francis Scott, who was to replace Causton as third
Bailiff, died on January 2, 1734. The Trustees elevated Causton
to be second bailiff in October, 1734, and made Henry Parker
third bailiff at the same time. On the removal of Gordon as first
magistrate because of his unseemly conduct, Causton was promoted to the first magistracy on September 24, 1734, Henry
Parker to the second, and John Dearne was appointed third
magistrate.[34]

Causton, who had been the senior magistrate present in Georgia
for most of its life, remained in the colony during his entire term
as first bailiff and worked hard at this job and that of storekeeper.
In fact, outside of Oglethorpe and William Stephens after his
arrival in 1737, Causton was the most important official in Georgia
until late in .1738. As first magistrate and storekeeper Causton
was concerned with most happenings in the colony. He was the
main channel of communication between the Trustees and Georgia, except for those things which Oglethorpe handled personally,
and was given many important jobs by the Trustees.[35] However,
he was in no sense a chief executive or governor, but rather the
servant of the Trustees.

There were numerous complaints that Causton was partial at
the store, that he did not give everybody equal treatment, that
he was domineering, and that he was generally hard to get along
with. The Trustees sent over the complaints which they received
to be answered after their usual custom, but there is no indication
that they or Oglethorpe were dissatisfied with Causton's actions.[36]
Because he came into contact with most of the people as storekeeper, Causton was in a vulnerable position to be complained
about. He seemed able to take responsibility and to get things
done, abilities not uniformly displayed among Georgia's early
colonists. He undoubtedly had a hot temper and probably favored
some colonists over others. That he had ability seems obvious
from what both his enemies and his friends said about him.
After the arrival of William Stephens in the colony as secretary,

he and Causton had much business and some social contact. Stephens, who said what he thought of most Georgians, apparently got along well with Causton. Just how close their personal relationship was is not obvious, but that one existed is clear. Perhaps John West summed up Causton best when he told the Trustees that Causton was "a passionate man, but resolution was necessary to keep up the authority of the Trustees and to repress the insolency of many of our people."[37]

Causton developed his plantation at Ockstead (Oxted) into one of the best in Georgia in the first decade. He kept several servants at work there, developed a fine herd of cattle, planted corn and other crops, grew mulberry trees, and generally pursued the kind of farming operations that the Trustees desired but in which so few Georgians succeeded.[38]

Another of the *Ann's* passengers held the office of magistrate. John West held it reluctantly and longed to be rid of it after his appointment in October, 1733. "He was a broken blacksmith by trade," Lord Percival wrote of him, "and relieved out of jail by the Debtors' Act, swearing himself not worth 10 1. We found him an honest, sensible man, and sending him over with the first embarkation with Mr. Oglethorpe made him one of the bailiffs or chief magistrates of Savannah town."[39] West was one of the colonists upon whom trouble bore heavily in the sickness of 1733. His wife and little son died in July. He married Elizabeth Little in August, but she died in September. He married Elizabeth Hughes, the widow of Joseph Hughes and an *Ann* passenger, in April, 1734, and wrote proudly in December that "my wife is brought to bead with a Sone on ye 28 of this Enstont. . . ."[40]

Two months before, he wrote a cheerful letter to Oglethorpe: "I have mad bould to trobell your Honour with thes leattor to a quaint you that wee are All in a good State of Health wee have not bureyed three of our pepell for thes Seaverell months past . . . the most of our pepell are Vearey indosttros & goos on Vearey well with thayer belding & Colteyvating thayor Lands & as to my own part I have my health heare beattor than Ever I had in England & Soo Sayes a maney more I know nott hoow too Express my Self with gratitude a nofe to your Honour & the reast of ye Honnorobell & worthy gentlemen the trostees for the grate faver Doon me to Send me heare wheare I ingoys both pease & Plentey. . . ." He asked leave to come to England the following spring on some business, after which he would return.[41]

In the same month that West wrote this letter, the Trustees, being informed of his desire to retire from the magistracy, permitted him to 'do so and appointed Henry Parker to that office as a reward for being "very diligent in cultivating his Lands, and Active in maintaining the public Peace. . . ."[42] West had behaved very well in the magistracy, the Trustees thought; hence they gave him leave to return temporarily to England. West and his wife sailed on July 8, 1735, with the usual bundle of mail to the Trustees, friends, and relatives in England.[43] The Trustees were delighted with West; here was an example of what an industrious man could accomplish in their colony. Only a few years before he had been in debtors prison and not worth £10, while in Georgia he was reported to have made £10 a week as a blacksmith. They were ready to accede to his request to sell his own house and lot and give him a gentleman's grant of 500 acres. His report on the colony was good except on the religious disposition of the people; he reported that some Sundays not ten people were at church. As for Causton, the first magistrate, West said that he was "a passionate man, but resolution was necessary to keep up the authority of the Trustees and repress the insolvency of many of our people."[44]

With a grant of 500 acres of land and £60 borrowed from the Trustees, West and his wife returned to Georgia, arriving February 2, 1736. He was in financial difficulties occasioned partly by his trip to England and partly by the loss of business while away.[45] Misfortunes accumulated. His three-year-old son Joseph was drowned on June 10, 1737. He could not pay his promissory note for £10 given to the Trustees while in England. Causton answered the Trustees' demand for payment by saying that it was with great difficulty that he could keep West from being torn to pieces by his creditors. West said in the summer of 1738 that he had spent two years and considerable money constructing the first brickworks in the colony and was now capable of producing 120,000 bricks a year if needed. He had neglected everything else to bring the brickworks to perfection and hoped the Trustees would give him time to repay his loan.[46]

William Stephens reported that West was going to give up work as a smith, finding he made no profit in it. This lack of profit, Stephens said, was due to West's own neglect.[47] John West was a sick man; time was running out for him. He told the Trustees he had been very ill since returning to Georgia. If only he could

return to England! His return might be the means of his recovery. His letter showed how homesick he was. If the Trustees
would permit, he would sell his lot and all his improvements upon
which he had laid out so much money—his farmhouse, kiln,
outhouses—all of it. He would deliver up his 500-acre grant; "itt
can be of noo youse to me now. . . ." But above all he pleaded
for quick permission to return to England.[48] The Trustees gave
the desired permission on June 6, 1739, but news of it arrived
too late. He died on Friday afternoon, July 27, "of a Consumption,
wherewith he had been wasting for near a Year past. . . ." He
died insolvent with his great hopes for himself and the colony
unfulfilled.[49]

Mrs. West, who had been Elizabeth Hughes when she came
with her husband Joseph on the *Ann,* died the following year.
Some people said that she married Will Kellaway after West
died; others said no, she merely lived with him. Perhaps if Kellaway had been in Savannah when she died he might at the last
have helped her reputation a little. He could have let people
know whether they actually had been married up at Purrysburg.
But Kellaway, who spoke Spanish, was down in the south with
Oglethorpe as an interpreter. In any event, Elizabeth, dying on
the morning of June 5, 1740, was buried that evening, the time
when most funerals took place. George Whitefield returned from
a trip that day, and after some hesitation finally consented to
officiate at the funeral. Whitefield gave a discourse over Elizabeth's grave on the evil effects of "a loose and debauched Life
and Conversation; not sparing the Deceased, as one who had
given publick Scandal to good People by her Deportment for
some Time past. . . ."[50]

CHAPTER SIX

Scandals, Savages, and Tangled Clerical Love Affairs

SEVERAL upheavals shook the colony in its early years, in each of which some of the *Ann's* passengers were concerned mildly or disastrously. Most of the original settlers still living in Georgia felt the effects in some way. Two of these events, occurring in 1734 and 1735, concerned a group of people who were trouble makers in the colony.

The first event was the arrival of Irish transports (convicts to be sold as indentured servants) late in December, 1733, or early in 1734. The master of the vessel was refused permission to land at Jamaica, and probably elsewhere, because the authorities feared trouble from these convicts. When the sloop was forced into Savannah through stress of weather and lack of food, with only forty of the original lot surviving and they about to perish, Oglethorpe saw a chance to obtain needed labor and said he thought it an act of charity to buy the servants from the master. He drew a bill on the Trustees for £200 sterling to pay for the convicts' indentures at £5 per head. He gave one servant to each of the women widowed the previous summer, to help in cultivating food. Each magistrate might have one servant at cost to compensate for the loss of time devoted to public service.[1]

Oglethorpe said several months later, when explaining the large bills he had drawn upon the Trustees, that the Irish transports had grown very useful. This was far from being the opinion of that shrewd observer, Samuel Eveleigh, when he went to Savannah in the autumn of 1734. Causton had a great deal of business, Eveleigh said, so much, in fact, that he was fatigued from morning to night. The Irish transports, being constantly in trouble and requiring punishment, gave him much disturbance. It was the general opinion, Eveleigh told Oglethorpe, that "buying those convicts was the worst action you did whilst here, though people said it was with a good design."[2]

One trouble caused by an Irish transport concerned William Wise. Wise, though in 1733 reduced to dire straits, was descended from the ancient family of Sir Edward Wise of Sydenham and "besides my serving a Clarkship to ye Law, & always delighting in Learning, was brought up in Farming, dressing & planting of Land, & feeding Cattle, wch had been my chief business."[3] The "unfortunate gentleman," as Percival described Wise, had brought letters from bishops to recommend him as a Georgia colonist. Because of his poverty, Wise said he would go as a charity colonist, which he said was considerably better than starvation.[4]

Wise embarked on the *Savannah*, Captain Lionel Wood, in September, 1733. Scarcely had the voyage begun when a scandal broke; the Trustees found that Wise had taken on board a female described as a woman of the town, passing her off as his daughter. He was reported to have occasioned great disturbances on the ship—just how is not clear—sufficient for the Trustees to send orders to ports where the *Savannah* might touch to have him set on shore. These orders did not catch up with the *Savannah*, but at the ports where she put in, stories came back to London of distractions among the passengers, which the Trustees blamed on Wise. The Trustees were fearful that he might cause distractions in Georgia and ordered that he should be sent back to England at their expense.[5] What happened to the woman Wise is reported to have taken on the ship in England is not revealed. In fact, she is mentioned only once, with no indication if she remained on the ship and had anything to do with the disturbances during the voyage which were attributed to Wise. It seems doubtful that she came to Georgia and even more doubtful that she remained if she did. She certainly was not punished like a woman of similar reputation, Elizabeth Malpas, who came on the *James*. Within ten days after arrival, she was given sixty lashes at the cart's tail and carried through Bull Street and back again. The man, William Bully, who brought her over as his wife was ordered to give security for his good behavior while in the colony.[6]

Despite specific orders to do so from the Trustees, Oglethorpe did not send Wise back to England. Instead he was allowed to remain in Georgia, and no further mention of any misbehavior on his part has been found. Having arrived on December 16, 1733, Wise settled on Hutchinson's Island, which lay directly in front of Savannah and was described by Oglethorpe as one of the most delightful spots he ever saw. Most of it was a natural meadow, which he planned to use for cattle; the remainder was covered with trees, many of which were bays more than eighty feet tall. In 1733 Oglethorpe ordered that a walk, the breadth of the town of Savannah, be cut through the woods on the island. Later a similar clearing, known as the vista, was ordered at Savannah. Joseph Fitzwalter remarked, "The Vistoe from the Town to the other Side of the Island is Cutt Through and Lookds Extream Pleasant." By the end of 1733 Oglethorpe had an overseer and four servants on the island to work there and to guard against enemies and thieves passing on the Savannah River.[7]

Wise could perhaps have had a contented life on Hutchinson's Island. Here were cattle to be tended, land to be dressed, and the love of learning to be indulged in his spare time. Perhaps he thought that his new life now might be better than his previous years of misfortune. Two of the Irish transport servants on the island, Richard White and Alice Ryley or Riley, gave Wise some personal care after he became incapacitated soon after his arrival. From his bed he would call in the morning for water in which to bathe as best he could; White would come in at the call and later would help Wise in combing his hair. Wise wore his own hair, in which he took considerable pride because of its length. He would lean over the side of the bed so that it might be combed more easily. On the morning of March 1, Alice Riley brought the bucket of water. White came in also and under pretense of assisting Wise, now leaning over the side of the bed preparatory to the combing, gave a quick twist to Wise's neckerchief to strangle him. Alice Riley seized his head, plunged it into the water "& he being very weak it Soon Dispatched him. . . ."[8]

Alice Riley was sentenced to death on May 11, 1734.[9] However, because she was pregnant her hanging was delayed until the birth of her child. A son, James, was born on December 21 and died in February. The birth of the child determined the date of the hanging. Alice Riley, the first woman to be hanged in Georgia, died on the gallows on January 19, 1735, denying to the last that she had murdered Wise.

At an undetermined date White broke out of jail. The knowledge that a murderer, who was reported to have defied ten men to take him, was loose created uneasiness among the people of Savannah and its vicinity. But he was taken with no real difficulty. Edward Jenkins described the capture in somewhat breathless fashion: "Mr Henery Parker and his Brother william was at woork at my Lot to pay me for what woork I had doon for him, as we was woorking one of my men sd yonder Goes a man very fast, I looked & saw ye man & said I believe its White that Brook out of Prison If it is Let us Go & take him, the two Parkers agreed not knowing where it was he or no Left ye men at woork All the weapons we had was two hooks & an ax we was at woork with, I desired one of them to be about 10 yards at my right hand & the other at my Left keeping the distance without speaking a word—And as Soon as Came to him I woud Cease him & if he offered to reble they shoud kill him immediatly—So we persued him tell we came into about twenty yards of him, At first sight of us was much Surprised, I told him your Name is White its in vain to Attempt & immediately I Ceased him, he fell on his nees & with many Blows on his Breast baged his Life, so I took him by one side of Coller & Mr. Henery Parker by ye other & William walked behind, we heald him very fast for we had often heard that the sarvant bid defiance two ten men to take him As we was Leding him to Town, we asked him where he had been & where he was Going He said he had been looking for some house out of Town to Get some Provitions. . . . As we was Leding him along he woud often beat his breast & bage his Life, we told him if we Let him Go he must perish In ye woods he said he would [be] Joyfull to perish in ye woods rather than dye on the Gallows[.]" Jenkins tried to elicit information concerning "any other vilony that ye Irish Sarvants . . . was inventing" but the most he could learn from White was that the Irish transports had a plan for breaking into the store. White was hanged on January 20 for, as Edward Jenkins continued, after they caught White they "Carryed him into Town he was had immediately to ye Gallows & Declared to ye last he was not Guilty of ye Murder. . . ." The unfortunate Wise was avenged, while Jenkins and the Parker brothers were rewarded with £50 by the Trustees for capturing White.[10]

Another troublesome affair in which the Irish transports played a part was one which gave the colony even more alarm than the death of Wise. This came to be known as the Red String Plot and occurred in 1735. Savannah and the near-by settlements were thrown into a state of intense excitement. In the succeeding charges and counter-charges, grudges, animosities, and gossip boiled up; and it was some time before some men's names were cleared.

On Sunday evening March 2, 1735, during church services John Vanderplank and some of the other constables and tything-men were hastily called out of church. Very soon afterward, the alarm bell rang. This was so unusual that men armed themselves and hastened to meet at the guardhouse. Thomas Christie, the recorder, was one of the first to reach the guardhouse and to him Vanderplank said that he had discovered a plot to surprise Savannah and kill its people and that John Musgrove and the Indians were concerned in it. However friendly Tomochichi and his Indians were, who really knew what they were thinking? As for Musgrove, was he not part Indian? One report was that fifty or sixty men in concert with Musgrove and the Indians would kill all the men and burn the town.

Christie, as one of the officers of the court, took charge. Joseph Fitzwalter, one of the constables, immediately started to Thunder-bolt to notify Thomas Causton, who had gone there that day; another was sent for Henry Parker, the other magistrate. In fifteen minutes after the alarm bell rang, nearly fifty armed men assembled at the guardhouse and were marshalled into formation by James Carwell. Vanderplank took a party to Musgrove's but found no one at home. By the time Vanderplank returned, suspicion was already directed elsewhere. Christie, by persistent questioning, had turned up another suspect, and, with the questioning of Elizabeth Gret, had heard the first mention of the red string, to be worn on the wrist to identify the plotters to each other.

Various unsavory pieces of scandal came out in the course of the examination. Christie sent men to round up anyone wearing the red string. As night came on, Causton returned, for Fitzwalter met him on his way back to Savannah, and together they hastened to town. Causton immediately gave orders for the defense of Savannah: two complete tythings of able men were to be on guard that night, three of the four cannon were charged and drawn out to flank the Strand on each side, and a guard was put about the magazine to protect the arms and ammunition stored there. The transport servants had already stolen several guns and some ammunition, found hidden in the woods; and it was determined that they should not gain access to more. Most of the men, Causton among them, joined the tythingmen to patrol the town that night. Search was made for indentured servants to determine whether they were at home and in bed, orders being given to send them to the guardhouse if found elsewhere, "especially the Irish Transports who if any Mischief had been on Foot we had no great Oppinion of . . . ," Causton remarked. Roger Lacy came through the dark woods from Thunderbolt in pursuit of two of his servants who ran away that evening. He brought news that a third, a maidservant, was about to leave when, being discovered with the red string on her wrist, she broke down and gave the plot away.

The night was quiet, Savannah was not burned, nor were its men killed. Monday morning, the magistrates began to try to unravel the plot and sift the charges and counter-charges. Tomochichi and his people convinced the magistrates that they had nothing to do with this affair; Musgrove gave assurance of his innocence and was believed. Both Christie and Causton were sure that if Vanderplank had not had the alarm bell rung so quickly, more of the plotters might have been discovered. For the future, it was decided no alarm was to be given in the day time without a warrant from the magistrates. Three men wearing red strings on their wrists were apprehended almost immediately, one or probably two of them Irish transport servants. The houses of Joseph Watson, Robert Parker, Jr., and several other men suspected by Causton were searched for evidence of plotting, but nothing of any moment was discovered.

On March 10, the grand jury indicted John Cos, Piercy Hill, and Edward Cruise, the latter Vanderplank's transport servant, for high misdemeanors and misprision of treason for their part in the Red String Plot. They were convicted and received sixty lashes each at the hands of the common hangman. A woman, Marg Hislop, received sixty lashes for her part in the plot. Robert Parker, Jr., was indicted by this grand jury because of publishing false stories concerning the colony.

Later, after the excitement died down, freeholders as well as Irish servants were thought to have been implicated in the plot, which in England was termed an insurrection. One of the first people, Francis Mugridge, was supposed to have been concerned in it. Some people said that no freeholders were involved; others averred that they were and that they planned, during the uproar if the plot succeeded, to desert the colony. The Red String Plot seems to have been two separate movements which fused. The Irish transports attempted to gain their liberty from indentured servitude and revenge themselves by murder and arson; some freeholders, if any were concerned, attempted to use the plot and its consequences as a means to desert the colony. This was due, they said, to their dissatisfaction with the land tenure. Causton said the plot resulted from freeholders too much in debt who while drunk swore to leave the colony upon pretense their titles were faulty. The plot was abortive and probably not so serious as it seemed to many in Georgia and England. The Irish transport servants were certainly not happy with their lot, and many settlers disliked intensely the land-tenure system. Both groups would seize anything that might offer relief from their objections. There is just a chance that the whole thing was the figment of the imagination of only a few people who craved excitement.[11]

The case of Joseph Watson was one of the greatest festering spots in the colony in the seventeen-thirties. A few men attached themselves to his cause from pity, others for selfish reasons, and a Watson party evolved. Watson was said to have lived at Grantham in Lincolnshire and to have been a sailor in his earlier years. Before he left Charles Town to come to Georgia, people said that his mistress's having jilted him had driven him mad.[12]

In February, 1734, Oglethorpe recommended Watson to the Trustees for a gentleman's grant of 500 acres. The request was unusual in that Oglethorpe specified that if Watson had no male heirs the land was to pass to his daughter Susannah, except that his widow was to be entitled to a life estate in the house and one-third of the land.[13] Watson seems never actually to have taken up the grant, but he settled on the land, located a few miles from Savannah and called Grantham. He went into partnership with John Musgrove in the Indian trade.

Watson evidently leashed his temper well enough until Oglethorpe left the colony in 1734. Not long after that Watson "gave himself to drinking, and was so seldom sober That it was hard to Guess if he was not Mad. He would be naked with the Indians, Drink with them lye down with them, and sometimes pretend to Baptise them." Watson became engaged in a long series of quarrels which frequently brought him into court. He quarrelled with

John Musgrove before Musgrove went to England as interpreter with Tomochichi and his party in 1734, and with Mary Musgrove while John was away. She haled him into court in August, 1734, for calling her a witch. Many men must have thought Mary Musgrove a witch though no other was fined six shillings eight pence for his opinion. Mary brought him into court again in August for trying to shoot her. This time the fine was £5 sterling and Watson was ordered to be bound for his good behavior. The following day he was tried and found guilty of beating an Indian, Esteechee, and defrauding him of his goods.[14] While this assault on Esteechee was no great matter in itself, anything that tended to cause Indian trouble was dangerous. Watson, by this time, had incurred Indian enmity through what they considered unfair dealing at Musgrove's trading house. Causton and Christie urged Watson to leave the colony and let his affairs at Musgrove's store be managed by others, but he refused.

Some Indians came one day to Musgrove's to have their skins weighed. Watson was locked in and refused to open the door to them. While they were trying to break in, Mary Musgrove persuaded Watson to leave for fear the Indians would kill him when they gained entrance. The Indians' anger was so aroused when they found that Watson had escaped that a little later Esteechee killed the Musgroves' Indian slave Justice.

Here was cause for alarm. To prevent Esteechee's relatives and friends from descending upon Savannah to aid him, Esteechee himself was taken to the town limits and urged not to return. Watson was asked again to leave the colony and remain away at least until the magistrates could have instructions from the Trustees as to their course. But Watson told around town that Causton was trying to steal his share of Musgrove's store, and that no one need be afraid of the Indians since hostages (Tomochichi and his party) could be held in England.

Samuel Eveleigh, an experienced merchant who did considerable business with Musgrove, came from Charles Town to Savannah to help in trying to straighten out the tangle which Watson had made of Musgrove's store before the business was ruined. Arbitrators were appointed to assess Watson's holdings in Musgrove's business, but Watson refused to accept their decision. Three uneasy months went by. The Indian Skee, whom Oglethorpe had made a captain of Indian militia, had become Watson's "chief companion" in his drinking bouts. Causton said that

Watson, seeming to apprehend some danger from Skee, made him a "particular friend" and drinking companion every day for a month. Skee was taken sick with flux, and Watson publicly boasted that "he had done Skee's business, and that he would dy." This was generally thought to be drunken talk, until Skee died.

Watson continued his boast after Skee's death. Causton warned him to stop such talk, as the Indians would believe it and might cause trouble. Watson's boast that he had killed Skee did reach Indian ears, and it was thought that Esteechee planned to murder Watson when he broke in Musgrove's store and killed the Indian slave. It was then that Causton "resolved either by fair or foul means to drive Watson off the Bluff; For it will be of ill and dangerous Consequence," Eveleigh remarked, if he should be killed by the Indians.[15] That had to be avoided! A white man killed by an Indian would bring trouble the end of which could not be seen. Watson's life would be safe from Indian methods of justice only if English law could prevail first.

The grand jury charged Watson with misdemeanors, and on November 21 he was tried and found guilty of publishing several unguarded expressions. But the court, "believing him to be Lunatick, recommended him to the mercy of the Trustees." Watson offered bail and Causton would have been glad to take it, "If the Security would have been bound, That he should not go out of Town." Where once Causton had urged him to go and he refused, he wanted now to go and Causton was no less anxious to be rid of him, but could not be since he had been tried. He was committed a close prisoner to lodgings of his own choice in Savannah until the Trustees' pleasure was known.[16]

Now began the espousal of his cause, which drew to it all the bad humors of the colony. Peter Gordon, returning to the colony from England the month after Watson was sentenced, found the case made to order as one of the complaints he would put before the Trustees. In general the behavior of the people had been very commendable, Causton wrote, "But when Mr Gordon unhappily, took part with Watson, and discovered to the People, that he had different Sentiments from me, They soon Concluded, That as he was First Bayliff, it was in his Power to Order everything, And every one, that had Beef, when they wanted Pork, was Countenanced by him with a great deal of Compassion and Complaisance." Gordon and others thought that a white man should not be imprisoned for the sake of an Indian.[17] The whole subject of Indian amity and its delicate balance was a closed book to them.

Watson said only that he believed Causton by his malice proposed to destroy him; his lodgings were searched in connection with the Red String Plot and "after serching they naild up my fore dore & Window and Keeps a Sentinell att my back dore with orders to Sufer noe person to come near nor speak to me att aney distance unless he hears our discourse or may i Evse pen inck or paper onley my Servt Maid is parmited to goe out & in, I have sent my Case to My Wife with orders to lay itt before ye Honr Trustees. . . . I realey epect Mr Causton will putt me out of this World by fowle practice . . . i must languish in this almost darck Jayl an perrish without reliefe or the World know aney part of my Storey i beg You as You tender the life of an inosent injured Man doe what on You lays to prevent my sufrings before Your return Ease some of my griefs and lett me have the Laws of my Nation to Condemn or aquitt Me I desier Noe ffafour but an Empartiall Treyall and Somebodey Skilld in ye Law to Plead my Cause That i May not be quibled out of my ffortune nor life. . . ."[18]

Other letters went to the Trustees concerning the case. Men hung their own failings, disillusionment, and dissatisfaction on the Watson case. When the flood of correspondence began to reach the Trustees, they first considered how far they could proceed against Watson by corporal punishment, fine, or forfeiture of his land.[19] The final decision was embodied in instructions to bailiffs and recorder, whose conduct the Trustees approved. They thought Causton acted very judiciously in regarding the general interest and safety by justly confining one man, rather than risking the safety of all Georgians. Watson's behavior appeared to the Trustees to be cruel and premeditated malice. His destroying Skee with rum and then boasting of it appeared to them murder aforethought with malicious design. The use of dangerous liquor made him just as guilty as if he had used a weapon.

"But as the Jury have brought him in Lunatick & therefore incapable of making his Defence The Trustees direct, that he should be confined as a Lunatick and proper Care taken for his Recovery; until he shall be in a Condition to take his Tryal. For which Tryal a special Commission will be sent over; And You at your Perils, must take Care that he shall be forth coming when such Commission shall arrive." No other proceeding must take place until the commission should arrive. The magistrates were wrong to have let Watson off with a slight fine when convicted of assault on Esteechee; it was too great a mildness and led to the death of Skee. "You see by this, a foolish Tenderness is the greatest of Crueltys, It has occasioned the death of two Men, and if that kind of Spirit should continue of not punishing the Guilty; You will destroy Yourselves. It is very surprising to the Trustees; That any Magistrate could think of Bailing a Murderer; for Murder is not bailable; And bailing of a Lunatick is an Act of Lunacy; for his Distemper makes his Confinement necessary for the benefit of Mankind.

"This new Started Opinion; That it is very cruel to Imprison on Account of an Indian, is Itself very cruel and pernicious. For if Injustice is done to an Indian, the Person who does it, should be more severely punished: for doing it to one who is helpless from his Ignorance of Our Language. And because it is a Breach of Treaty, and an Act of Ingratitude to the first Possessors of the Land, who have always been exceedingly friendly and kind to the Colony in its first Weakness and Necessitys.

"And as for the Opinion; That it is right to let a Guilty Man go out of the Province without Punishment. That is giving up at once those valuable Privileges of Trying all Facts committed in it; and declaring Your selves incapable of supporting a Civil Government. If a Man is guilty You should Punish him in the Province according to his Deserts; And if he is not Guilty, You should acquit him: But you have no such thing as a Power of banishing a Man from the Colony; nor ought You to let a Criminal Escape to another Colony in Safety."[20]

The Trustees ordered that Watson be kept in close confinement, that no person should converse with him lest his senses might be disturbed, and that he should so continue until the special commission or instructions for his trial should arrive.[21] There is no record to show that this commission was ever sent.

Many stories about the Watson case were told in Savannah. Causton received some bitter criticism for his actions as magistrate, though he was carrying out the Trustees' orders. Several years later one story still circulating said that the true reason for Watson's imprisonment was that upon arriving in the colony, Watson asked Oglethorpe what laws he intended to put into effect in Georgia. Oglethorpe's reputed reply was: Such laws as the Trustees thought proper; what business had poor people to do with law? Since Watson could testify that Oglethorpe had made this statement, people said, Oglethorpe had Watson imprisoned so that he might not open up Oglethorpe's arbitrary designs.[22]

The Watson case simmered down. Mary Musgrove was recompensed for the death of her Indian slave Justice by the gift of a Trustee servant, and presents were sent to the Indians to reconcile them. Though for some months angry letters continued to be sent to England excoriating Causton, they too finally diminished. Oglethorpe, while in the colony in 1736, conducted an examination of Watson and the Indians concerned[23] but this seems to have been of no great moment, unless to soothe the Indians by giving them a chance to talk. Certainly it seems not to have changed Watson's status.

Apparently Watson was forgotten by the Trustees until abruptly recalled to their attention in 1737. His wife, Sarah, in England appealed to members of Parliament for redress and petitioned the King against Causton, the Trustees, and Oglethorpe, citing her husband's unjust trial and his confinement as a lunatic.[24] Justification of the Trustees' procedure now became necessary. Legal talent was employed by the Trustees, and further investigations were made. Watson was released by order of the Trustees in November, 1737. William Stephens, talking to Watson shortly afterward, thought him "a little too much transported, and carried away with Flights sometimes in his Discourse, which had the Appearance of a distempered Head."[25]

After various troubles following his release, he returned to England and in 1743 petitioned the Trustees that he be again licensed for the Indian trade at Yamacraw for a period of three years and four months, the length of time he had been debarred from trading. The Trustees recommended to William Stephens, Commissioner for Indian trade, that such a license be given to Watson if there was no objection in Georgia. They also looked favorably on his request for a grant of 500 acres.[26] The Watson case had done the Trustees no good in England and probably they tried to make some amends.

Watson returned to Georgia the following year and President William Stephens and the Assistants began to inquire into his tangled affairs, according to the Trustees' instructions. Certainly his "extravagant way of talking which was generally esteemed the Effects of a disordered Brain" made their task a difficult one.

The Board did not wish to give Watson a license to trade with the Indians. Stephens, as commissioner for licensing the traders, had the power to withhold a license and looked still more adversely on Watson's efforts to obtain one after learning that he was already trading illegally, a procedure for which Watson was reproved by the Board and threatened with penalties.[27]

Watson was by now a pitiable figure but none the less troublesome, "whose dark manner of behaviour among us," Stephens said, "since his last arrival, gave me no small umbrage of some Mischief that he might be hatching." Others must have agreed with Stephens that Watson's behavior was a riddle, he "having no certain abode, but sometimes met walking the woods in an odd habit, with a sort of short Gown or Cassock made of the Coarsest black Cloth and gather'd at the Wrists, seeming to betoken some order; and the rather, because of his giving it out that he meant to convert the Indians. . . ."[28] Stephens thought, however, that Watson's purpose was much less to convert than to trade. Stephens and the Assistants were not anxious to refuse any request of the Trustees, but they postponed giving Watson a trader's license for a number of reasons, one of which was "That from the well known Disposition of Watson and his former Proceeding He is looked upon as One of the most improper Persons in the Colony to carry on a Trade with the Indians, his Life being in Danger to this Day for Disturbances which he has formerly made among them."[29] It is doubtful if even a suspended fine of £100 which he incurred for trading with the Indians without a license stopped him, however. Finally in March, 1745, the Trustees approved Stephens's refusal to give Watson a license.[30]

His land was the subject of prolonged inquiry. No proper records concerning it could be found in Georgia but it was conceded that he had occupied it, that no one else had been in possession, and that it was always spoken of as Watson's land. He sold this land to William Francis in 1755, one provision in the transaction being that the buyer was to have peaceable possession without hindrance from Watson's wife, Sarah.[31] When Watson died in 1758, his estate was appraised as: Cambridge Concordance of the Bible in folio, 10 s.; a small trunk, 2 s.; two old pictures, 10 s., 6d. Total £1: 2:6.[32]

The question of Watson's sanity remains unanswered. Certainly he was vain, boastful, malicious, mischievous, and unbalanced at times if not permanently. The reasons for and extent of his mental troubles are not clear. It was an unfortunate day for the colony when Oglethorpe asked for a grant for him.

The third upheaval in this series is the story of John Wesley's stay and troubles in Georgia. The Trustees had great difficulty in securing an adequate Anglican minister to officiate in Georgia. Dr. Henry Herbert, the first minister, soon left the colony because of ill health and died [...] back to England. The second, Samuel Quincy, arrived [...] 3, but soon proved unsatisfactory. The Trustee [...] ointment in October, 1735, before his letter as [...] urn to England could reach London.[33]

The Trustees appointed [...] ley minister in Quincy's place on October 1[...] ety for the Propagation of the Gospel in For[...] to continue to Wesley the £50 annual salary [...] d to Quincy.[34] With John Wesley there came [...] brother Charles, Benjamin Ingham, and Char[...] nn intended to become a missionary to the In[...] is brother-in-law, Westley Hall, decided not [...] at Savannah, Wesley was prevailed upon to [...] on temporarily until someone else could be found [...] harles was to be secretary to Oglethorpe, secretary of the Indian trade, and minister at Frederica. Ingham and Delamotte were to perform clerical and educational duties. When John Wesley first approached Ingham about going to Georgia, Ingham said, "I thought we had Heathen enough at home," and refused to go. Yet under Wesley's persuasion, he changed his mind and went.[36]

The Wesleys and their party came to Georgia on the *Symonds*, Captain Cornish, the ship upon which Oglethorpe returned with the great embarkation. The vessel anchored near Tybee Island on February 5, 1736, and landed its passengers the next day. A month later, March 7, John Wesley preached his first sermon in Savannah.[37] Neither Wesley nor Ingham ever preached to the Indians. Wesley said that whenever he mentioned going to the Indians Oglethorpe said, "You cannot leave Savannah without a minister." Wesley's objections that the appointment to Savannah was made without his solicitation or consent never got around Oglethorpe's view that Wesley had been appointed minister to Savannah and that this was his first duty.[38]

Upon arrival in Georgia, Wesley made a trip to Frederica with Charles and then began to consider in what manner he might be most useful to the little flock at Savannah. He advised the more serious among them "to form themselves into a sort of little society, and to meet once or twice a week, in order to reprove, instruct, and exhort one another. Then to select out of these a smaller number for more intimate union with each other, which might be forwarded, partly by our considering singly with each other, and partly by inviting them all together to our house; and this, accordingly, we determined to do every Sunday in the afternoon." Wesley held morning service at five o'clock, communion with sermon at eleven, and afternoon service at three. He began visitation at "the time when they [the parishioners] cannot work, because of the heat, viz. from twelve to three in the afternoon." As one of the parishioners said, Wesley went "from house to house exhorting the inhabitants to virtue and religion."[39]

Wesley preached several times in Frederica, where he expressed himself as fearful for the spiritual future of its people. William Horton, a leading citizen of Frederica, told him, "All your sermons are satires upon particular persons, therefore I will never hear you more; and all the people are of my mind, for we wont hear ourselves abused . . . as for you, they cannot tell what religion you are of. They never heard of such a religion before. They do not know what to make of it. And then your private behaviour—all the quarrels that have been here since you came, have been 'long of you. Indeed there is neither man nor woman in the town, who minds a word you say. And so you may preach long enough; but nobody will come to hear you." Inevitably Wesley likened himself to St. Paul and remarked, "If, therefore, striving to do good, you have done hurt, what then? . . . But shall you, therefore, strive no more? God forbid! Strive more humbly, more calmly, more cautiously."[40] The advice was good, but John Wesley did not take it. Neither did he remember later St. Paul's remark that "some things are lawful but are they expedient?"

Despite this opinion of the Frederica residents, Wesley returned there more frequently after his brother Charles left on July 26, 1736, to return to England. Once John's life was threatened in Frederica, and he left the place with "an utter despair of doing good there, which made me content with the thought of seeing it no more."[41] Benjamin Ingham followed Charles Wesley back to England in February, 1737, leaving only John Wesley and Charles Delamotte to labor in the Lord's vineyard in Georgia.[42]

Since John Wesley had come to Georgia he had had increasing contact with Sophia Hopkey, Mrs. Thomas Causton's niece, a girl of eighteen. She was certainly attractive to the thirty-three-year-old clergyman. Wesley liked "Miss Sophy's" company, and Sophy and the uncle and aunt were anxious for Sophy and Wesley to marry. It is not clear just what Wesley's state of mind was regarding Sophy. Perhaps he was not in love with her. Perhaps he was, but believed her statement that she never intended to marry. Perhaps he just never got around to such a secular consideration as deciding whether he was in love or not. Wesley's records of their relations, including a week-long boat trip from Frederica to Savannah, are mainly taken up with religious discussions and readings. When Wesley went so far as to tell Sophy that he would think himself most happy if he spent his life with her, Sophy told him to say no more of that, and his record seems to indicate that he took her at her word. The conversations at the breakfasts which Sophy took at Wesley's and Delamotte's lodgings in Savannah and during her French lessons from Wesley are not well recorded.[43] Regardless of Wesley's personal feelings about Sophy, he was most unpleasantly shocked when Mrs. Causton asked him to publish the banns for her niece's marriage to William Williamson. The aunt's request was Wesley's first knowledge of Sophy's interest in Williamson. The fact that this engagement might have been agreed to in order to force him into declaring his intentions about Sophy seems never to have entered Wesley's head.

Sophy was married to Williamson on March 12, in Purrysburg, South Carolina.[44] On April 5 Wesley went to Carolina with the intention of putting a stop to the proceedings of a clergyman in that colony who had married several of Wesley's parishioners without either banns or license. Whether this was the minister who married Sophia and Williamson is not known, but it seems highly probable that it was. Wesley was assured by the Reverend Alexander Garden, the Bishop of London's Commissary for South Carolina, and the other Anglican clergy of the colony that they would marry no Georgians without a request by letter from Wesley.[45]

For several weeks, whatever his emotional turmoil, Wesley

continued his daily routine much as usual. He had several routine conversations with Thomas Causton; he asked to have the glebe land laid out and fenced after it was surveyed; and he requested that a school room be built by his house. Causton arranged for John Desborough to undertake the job, and the £14 price agreed upon was to be deducted from his debt to the Trustees. In June Wesley told Causton that the latter was accused by some people of several acts of injustice, of taking revenge on some people in the colony, and of giving short measure at the store. These complaints were probably exaggerated by the colonists who made them to Wesley, but he took them seriously. Causton answered patiently and reminded Wesley that he had taken pains to uphold the minister's character to those who would lessen it. When Wesley complained to Causton of the presence of several deists in Savannah, Causton assured him that Wesley could set them right and could expect whatever help was necessary from the civil authorities.[46]

When Causton and the other magistrates asked Wesley to conduct the special service in commemoration of the first court day in Savannah, he also asked him the meaning of his letter of the previous day, which intimated that Causton might oppose Wesley in his duties as a minister. After a considerable pause Wesley said, "Suppose I should refuse to administer the Sacrament to some body in your family." Causton answered that if it was himself, his wife, or child he would expect to be acquainted with the reasons, and thought anyone in Savannah would have the same right under the canon law. Wesley replied that he hoped Causton should have no occasion to give himself any uneasiness about the matter.[47]

On July 3, after communion Wesley reproved Sophy for her behaviour, and Sophy turned away from him in anger. The next day Mrs. Causton tried to excuse Sophy's anger and asked Wesley to inform Sophy in writing what he disliked about her behaviour. He complied with this request at the same time he sent Causton the letter which puzzled him and the other magistrates. On August 3, Wesley brought the matter to a head when he "repelled" Sophy from Holy Communion.[48] Savannah was electrified at this open breach.

Constable Noble Jones served a warrant on Wesley on August 9 in which Williamson demanded £1000 damages for defaming Sophia by refusing to administer the Lord's Supper to her in public worship without cause. Wesley told magistrates Henry Parker and Thomas Christie that this was an ecclesiastical matter in which they had no right in interrogate him. Parker told Wesley that he must appear at the next court.[49]

Causton insisted that Wesley give his reasons for refusing to give the sacrament to Sophy. Hence Wesley wrote to Sophy that those who intended to take communion were required to notify the curate of this fact some days before. This she had not done. If any of those wishing to communicate had done wrong to his neighbor so that the congregation would thereby be offended, the curate would then notify him not to come to the Lord's table until he had openly declared himself to have repented. If Sophy offered herself at communion on Sunday, Wesley continued, he would advise wherein she had done wrong and when she had declared herself repentant, he would then administer the sacrament to her.[50] His only actual charge against her was that she had not notified him of her intention to partake of the communion.

Wesley told William Stephens that he had told Sophy not to offer herself at communion without conferring with him first. Stephens, who had lately come to the colony, said that he had found all Savannah divided into two parties on the matter and thought that the trouble first arose "upon young Williamson's marrying Mr. Causton's Niece, whom the Parson had a Liking to for himself." Before her marriage Sophy had received the sacrament which was administered weekly to some few who met privately with Wesley. However, since the marriage she had discontinued attendance at these small meetings at the insistence of her husband. When her attendance stopped, Wesley wrote her that she had lapsed from her duty.[51] Soon after this the incident of refusing the sacrament took place.

This affair became the greatest festering point yet evident in the colony. Wesley talked of it, hinted more, and allowed himself to become entangled with the disaffected of the colony. In London, letters, affidavits, and grand jury presentments on several points against Wesley poured in upon the Trustees. They found in the liturgy some justification for the clergyman's procedure. The accusations were sent to Wesley for his reply. The Earl of Egmont said, "It appears to me that he [Wesley] was in love with Mrs. Williamson before she married, and has acted indiscreetly with respect to her, and perhaps with respect to others, which is a great misfortune to us, for nothing is more difficult than to find a minister to go to Georgia who has any virtue and reputation."[52]

John Wesley never came to trial on the charge of defamation of character or the ten counts found against him by the grand jury. He asked trial at several courts, but it was always postponed, apparently at Causton's instigation. Wesley at length posted a notice in Johnson Square, as was the custom for those who wished to make public announcements, that he intended to return to England. Since his case was pending, public notice was given to the constables and tythingmen to apprehend him or any person assisting him, should he attempt to leave the colony.[53] He did leave on the night of December 2, 1737; in his own words, "Being now only a prisoner at large, in a place where I knew by experience every day would give fresh opportunity to procure evidence of words I never said, and actions I never did, I saw clearly the hour was come for me to fly for my life, leaving this place; and as soon as evening prayers were over, about eight o'clock, the tide then serving, I shook off the dust of my feet, and left Georgia, after having preached the gospel there with much weakness indeed and many infirmities, not as I ought, but as I was able, one year and nearly nine months. 'Oh that thou hadst known, at least in this thy day, the things which make for thy peace!' "[54]

After being lost in the woods while walking to Beaufort, Wesley arrived in Charles Town where he was asked to officiate in the church. He took ship for England on December 22, and must have thought over his Georgia experience on the homeward voyage. He "landed at Deal, it being *Wednesday,* FEBRUARY 1, the anniversary festival in Georgia for Mr. Oglethorpe's landing there." On that day he summarized his Georgia experience thus, "It is now two years and almost four months since I left my native country, in order to teach the Georgia Indians the nature of Christianity. But what have I learned myself in the meantime? Why, what I the least of all suspected, that I, who went to America to convert others, was never myself converted to God."[55] Though Wesley later expressed doubt about the accuracy of these sentiments,[56] he certainly must have been closer to his heart-warming experience in Aldersgate Street upon his return to England than when he left for Georgia.

CHAPTER SEVEN

Expenses, Extravagance, and Official Removals

THE FOURTH in this series of crucial events was the most serious, in that it effected a change which had far-reaching results for Georgia. The year in which the crisis took place, 1738, was a portentous one for the colony. Throughout most of the year events were shaping in England which came to a climax in Georgia in October.

The Trustees, always anxious for first-hand reports from the colony, plied John Wesley with questions when he returned to London in February, 1738. Wesley was a better educated man than the Trustees were accustomed to interrogate about conditions in Georgia. They had respect for his cloth, despite the recent turmoil in the colony. Troubles helped along by some of their policies in Georgia were now evident. One of these was a dispute with South Carolina concerning the Indian trade. Trustees' resignations showed a lessening interest in Georgia and caused Egmont to remark acidly that "When houses are falling the rats leave it. . . . In truth the bad account of Causton's behaviour brought over by Mr. Wesley, our minister at Savannah, is enough to make all of us quit; . . ."

For Wesley brought a very bad account of Causton. The Trustees judged Wesley guilty of indiscretion in Savannah but thought that Causton was much more to blame. Wesley charged Causton with gross mal-administration of his office as magistrate. This was opposite to the report brought over by Charles Wesley in 1736 when he told the Trustees that complaints submitted to Oglethorpe concerning Causton were "found to be absolutely frivolous."[1] However, Charles was in the colony only five months and had not become emotionally involved with a member of Causton's family.

Egmont himself had no great opinion of John Wesley and two months later the Trustees received his resignation "with great pleasure," Egmont remarked, "he appearing to us to be a very odd mixture of a man, an enthusiast and at the same time a hypocrite, wholly distasteful to the greater part of the inhabitants, and an incendiary of the people against the magistracy."[2] The Trustees particularly resented Wesley's interference with, or undue interest in, the conduct of the courts. When William Norris was to sail as the next minister in Georgia, Egmont noted the advice given to Norris by the Bishop of London, "not to split upon the rock his predecessor had done, meaning Mr. J. Wesley, and meaning his falling out with the magistrates and refusing the Communion to Mrs. Williamson."[3]

Some of the Trustees doubted the wisdom of the policy instituted by Oglethorpe at the beginning of the colony of certifying bills of exchange in Georgia to be paid by the Trustees in London. The Trustees begged Oglethorpe to notify them of the bills he had drawn, but he by no means always did so. Hence the Trustees were often confronted by bills for purchases of which they knew nothing and for which no provision for payment had been made. As early as February, 1734, they resolved that no bills drawn by any person should be accepted or paid without notification to them by the person who drew the bill.[4] Though this resolution was specifically aimed at Oglethorpe, it diplomatically left him unnamed. Oglethorpe's return to England that year allayed the Trustees' anxiety. Whatever verbal instructions Oglethorpe gave when he entrusted the general superintendency of the colony to Causton, who as the storekeeper was responsible for having on hand sufficient provisions to supply the colony, the Trustees themselves gave him explicit instructions concerning the bills which he must draw on them.[5]

A year later the Trustees thought they had arrived at a solution to their problem. They received permission from the Bank of England to issue to Oglethorpe sola bills, promises by the Trustees, that would pass as money in the colony and could be redeemed in England.[6] The advantage would be that once the Trustees had given Oglethorpe whatever number of bills they thought necessary, they would know exactly what he would spend, and the money could be set aside in London to redeem the bills.

It was a good enough plan but it did not work. Oglethorpe took with him £5000 in sola bills and money when he left for Georgia early in the winter of 1735. Yet he drew bills of exchange on the Trustees as formerly. Egmont said in June, 1736, "We were all extremely displeased that Mr. Oglethorpe having carried over that sum, should not employ it there, but drew upon us."[7]

Oglethorpe was making new settlements in the southern part of the colony, the expenses of which exceeded any estimate made in London. Even after Oglethorpe began the settlement of Frederica, the Trustees told him not to settle the new people on St. Simons Island, but nearer Savannah. Oglethorpe ignored these instructions, being intent on military defense. That year, 1736, Parliament appropriated £10,000 for Georgia though the Trustees asked for £20,000. The Trustees realized that the greatest frugality would be necessary. More than 590 people were still on the store in Savannah; 490 new colonists would reach Georgia in the great embarkation early in 1736, the great majority of whom would settle in the southern part of the colony and must have two years' subsistence until their lands could produce. Causton was instructed that no one should have continued maintenance from the Trustees' store in Savannah beyond the first year without the Trustees' order except in case of absolute necessity.[8]

Oglethorpe's bills of exchange caused considerable alarm in London as the amount grew—£2700 worth in payment for provisions by August. A bill for £210 for a cargo of provisions bought by Thomas Causton at Oglethorpe's order caused special concern, though the Trustees paid it.[9] They were displeased also that Causton wrote now concerning financial matters only, saying nothing of the general state of the colony. Some Trustees believed that Oglethorpe had given specific orders that no one but himself was to give general accounts to the Trustees while he was in Georgia. This lack of information was blamed for the decline of interest on the part of some Trustees. Causton's letters of this period show a change in tone and a brevity which might well have led the Trustees to think as they did. Another disquieting fact was observed, when a cargo list showed the Trustees "that luxury is already got into Savannah by the use of tea and coffee. . . ."[10]

The Trustees sent Oglethorpe more sola bills but ordered an advertisement in a London paper and in the *South Carolina Gazette* giving notice that as they had sola bills in Georgia to answer all expenses, they would not pay in London any bills drawn upon them. "Highly necessary," Egmont said, "for else we shall be drawn upon without end, neither Mr. Oglethorpe nor the magistrates of Georgia being able to know the state of our cash." The situation was summed up by Egmont as "The great difficulty we shall be under of answering Mr. Oglethorpe's bills if he continue to draw at this rate, and the dishonor if we do not, etc." The Trustees continued to beg that Oglethorpe would use their sola bills and not draw upon them. Resolved to put an end to the drawing of bills upon them, they finally told him that his presence in England was imperative to answer complaints about the colony, to give an account of its progress, and to justify the application of the sums already granted. They did not think they could carry on the settlement of Georgia or apply to Parliament for more money unless he returned to England to give this information.[11] Oglethorpe sailed for England in late November, 1736, soon after the receipt of this communication.

Oglethorpe was in England from January, 1737, until June, 1738. The Trustees paid the bills; Parliament made another grant and authorized a regiment for the defense of Georgia against the Spanish. Oglethorpe was the commanding officer of the regiment, and its expense would be borne by the English government, not the Trustees.

The Trustees had already learned that it was not an easy matter to run a colony. Affairs were growing increasingly complicated. Before Oglethorpe returned to the colony again, they made another effort to right their financial policies. On March 23, 1738, six members of the Common Council began meetings in London in which they went over Georgia matters rather thoroughly. "Thinking it high time to put the affairs of our Colony on a better foot than it has been of late, to remedy abuses, to prevent unnecessary and unknown expenses to us in Georgia," they resolved to cut expenses to the bone despite Oglethorpe's argument that this would hurt the colony and force people to leave. Because Parliament gave the money for settling, not defending, the colony, the Trustees would first strike off all expense of a military nature. A real attempt was made to make expenses fit the Parliamentary grant of £8000, by now the main source of the Trustees' income. Oglethorpe's presence had certainly helped to secure the Parliamentary grant yet his advice was to be largely ignored in spending it. Oglethorpe was busy with raising his regiment and drifted further from the Trustees' viewpoint.[12]

Throughout the past year Causton had been asking questions and giving information about Georgia that further aroused the Trustees. He had reported that many colonists refused to work their land and made pretense at store keeping or other types of work. This usually resulted in increased debts to the individual colonists, and Causton especially asked if he should stop the credit at the Trustees' store for these "idle." Causton was told to inform all people that those first entitled to the Trustees' favor were those who industriously cultivated their lands, which all were supposed to make their first concern. The Trustees said they knew the ill effect of too great credit in Georgia and would soon send over orders about regulating credit and suing for debt.[13]

Having answered this part of Causton's letters, the Trustees ignored his inquiries about punishment for crime; "Having found many Inhabitants of this place guilty of Offenses (which) rather than expose their Characters, I have (hitherto) in some Measure Overlookt I must Desire your Directions what will be a proper judgment to give in Petty Larceny Whoredom, Adultery, or any other Offenses which are generally punisht by the Laws of England with Whipping Imprisonment or fines, or Burning in the hand. And in regard to those judgments be pleased to give me leave to Observe That if, by fine, they may not be able to pay it, If by Imprisonment they are thereby rendered useless to the Colony and their familys may Starve, If by whipping or burning in the hand, those seem too Ignominious for a ffreeholder."[14]

The Spanish alarm, Egmont noted ruefully, was of great damage to the colony in retarding cultivation. People would thus be on the Trustees' store longer, an expense which the Trustees did not think they could support as such a contingency was not foreseen when the estimate of money needed was given in to Parliament.[15]

The Spanish threat also brought out evidence of independence in Savannah. The people started to build a fort for their protection. The first criticism from England was that the Savannah people, in their haste to erect a fort, had cut down the woods on the eastern side of town, woods which Egmont thought were an ornament and shelter to Savannah and the absence of which would render the town less healthy. Captain George Dunbar, of the *Prince of Wales,* reported that the people built the fort although Causton declared himself against it, fearing that the Trustees would not approve as they had not ordered it.[16] "I hope I have not erred in giving way to the Peoples Demands for building the Walls of a Fort," Causton wrote. "The Clamour on that Occasion was Inexpressable and having done what was absolutely necessary and answer'd their first demand, (vizt) a place of Retreat for the women and Children and Effects till Succours could come, I have possitively refused to do any thing more to it, till you shall give Orders, judging, that shod an Attack now happen It might be made Defenceable in a few hours, And if no Attack happen'd As your Honours would very probably think it necessary to build a New Magazine the old One being too Small and decrepid this might not be an unfit place as well for such an use, As also for a general Landing of Goods wch is now very expensive:".[17]

Whatever his misgivings concerning the Trustees' opinions of the fort, Causton had a certain pride in it. He sent Noble Jones's drawing of the fort, remarking that Colonel Bull approved it. Colonel Bull and Colonel Barnwell came from South Carolina and spent three days in the colony in March, 1737: "As the Continual Alarms, raised an Uneasiness in these (who Stile themselves Gentlemen) concerning a Proper Commander in Chief, I took this Opportunity to ask Colonel Bull (if Occasion sho'd happen to require) whether he remembered a former promise of his made to Mr. Oglethorp, to head the Militia of this Place: He told me he was allways ready to do what lay in his power to serve the Colony. And that he came on purpose to See how we did; He was extreamly well pleased with the preparacons we had made And the Account I had given him of the Peoples Vigilance particularly he says The Fort is the best of the Kind he ever saw of which I have enclosed Mr Jones Draught."[18]

The highly important question of a commander for a handful of militia inadequate to face an enemy invasion was thus nicely settled by Causton and by the man who had helped to lay out Savannah, Colonel William Bull. The command of the militia, by the terms of the charter vested in the Trustees in all ordinary cases, was in extraordinary cases when a commander might have to take the field, placed in the governor of South Carolina, "the Trustees not imagining that they should have People in Georgia capable of Commanding in Chief. . . ." If the Trustees could not approve the fort, they did propose one measure against the Spaniards, a fast day for a blessing on the people and for prayers to avert the danger of invasion.[19]

There was no lack of other exhortation as the need for economy grew increasingly evident. Have a care, the Trustees warned Causton, to exercise the greatest frugality but do not discourage the industrious nor be imposed upon by the idle who are drones eating upon the public and at the same time evil-mouthed of their benefactors. As for the great numbers of very honest and industrious people in the colony, show them the greatest countenance, do not stretch anything to make them uneasy, and interpret all orders in their favor as far as the words will bear it.[20] These exhortations to be frugal produced one result—the colony in 1737 did not have enough food. John Brownfield, factor in Savannah for the English firm of Pytt and Tuckwell and register for the colony, remarked in the spring: "I am sorry that the Colony in general seems so much dispirited: The want of Provisions has chilled Mens Endeavours extremely. . . ."[21]

Brownfield was concerned with an account in an English newspaper by which he said the colony was represented in a very unjust and too optimistic light. He thought the report was written by some person to insinuate himself into the Trustees' good opinion. "In my belief the Colony was never yet so low as at this time. The Necessitys of the People are so very open that every Stranger who comes hither must see them in the most plain undeniable manner." Public credit was at a standstill: Causton did not have enough cash to pay even the poor workmen engaged on the fort. The Trustees' store was out of provisions; he thought not a piece of meat was left. "The Peoples Wants are so great That if a Boat should come with Provisions hither I believe the whole Town could not purchase it And I wish that Hunger may not bring Distempers amongst us, more fatal than the Sword of an Enemy." Some of the best workmen were leaving to find employment in Carolina and to keep their families from starving. The fort was now left unfinished and "the Place which was intended for our Security against an Enemy may now be made use of by the Foe against us." Brownfield asked a pertinent question, "If such great Improvements have been made here and the Colony is so flourishing as our Publick Papers would persuade us; How comes this general Want?" Egmont, who read this letter in London with interest, remarked that he was told Oglethorpe had inserted the newspaper notice to which Brownfield referred.[22]

Early in 1738 the Common Council took action on certified bills sent by Causton for food supplies before he had any sola bills. The Trustees lacked funds to pay the bills and returned them to Causton with instructions to pay with sola bills which would soon arrive in Georgia. No more bills must be sent to England to be paid. Expenditures must be limited to the amount of sola bills available. Public notice would be given in Georgia that no money would be paid in England but only sola bills in Georgia. "You see the Confusion created by your making Expenses before You had Sola Bills to defray them," they scolded Causton.[23] A lack of proper calculation for the needs of the colony was evident. Supplies had to be in the Trustees' store if people were to be fed. There were few other sources in the colony.

It was about this time that Wesley had his first interview with the Trustees after his return. A little later, a Common Council Committee met to consider how to put affairs in Georgia on a better footing. The Committee agreed, but without as yet taking official action, that Causton should be dismissed as storekeeper. An inquiry into the conduct of Noble Jones, the surveyor, was ordered. Notices were ordered posted in Savannah and Frederica and published in London and South Carolina newspapers that all expenses of the colony should be met in Georgia by sola bills. No person would have authority to receive any provisions or stores or to contract any debts in the Trustees' name.[24]

"We could not but observe that Mr. Oglethorpe has been very careless of attending the Board of late," Egmont observed; "that is, since he knew the gentlemen were resolved to reduce the Colony's expenses, in which he told Mr. Verelst he desired to have no hand. He sees how cool many of the Trust are grown to the work, and that there is only one set who remain to carry it on, whom if he should disgust, the charter might fail for want of a sufficient number to support it, and therefore since he is not thoroughly pleased with our proceedings, he choses to be absent as often as he can with decency, without falling out with us."[25] If Oglethorpe was cool to the Trustees, they were no less so to him and showed it when only four of them accepted his invitation to watch the remaining part of his regiment march through London into Sussex on March 30. However, eleven of them dined with him on May 1, a farewell entertainment as he was to leave soon for Georgia.[26]

The Trustees now began to talk much of Causton's mismanagement, agreeing that he had used strangely the money entrusted to his care; the poor state of finances was laid to Causton. It was said that he had squandered money and bought ships' cargoes not from necessity but as a favor to the ships' owners, even with the suggestion that he might have been paid to do so. One dark thought brought on others darker still. Credit was given by Causton to several persons without orders from the Trustees. In the past year he had spent £11,000 for which he had not accounted, besides the certified accounts. The trouble was due to Causton's wasteful hand. He must be called to account. Yet the Trustees' committee thought he should be "further gratified for his past services."[27]

Thomas Jones, going over with Oglethorpe, was appointed storekeeper in place of Causton. "Mr. Oglethorpe proposes great advantage in having him as a companion," Egmont remarked, "for he looks upon him as a capable man to advise him, having as cool a head as the other's is warm." Egmont later characterized Jones, from accounts sent from Georgia, as "too hot and passionate."[28]

The Scots in Georgia had always disliked Causton and had never hesitated to say so. In the bitter and sometimes unsound denunciation of the colony which they published, they contrasted Causton and Jones: "And, as if the Inhabitants had not been sufficiently punished before by the *arbitrary* Government of *Causton*," they wrote, "The *Two* Offices of Store-keeper and Magistrate were again joined in *One* Person, which infallibly renders him, whoever he is, *absolute* in *Savannah*. And indeed if the Miseries and Hardships of the People could have received any Addition, they must have done so from the Person appointed to execute those Offices, namely, Mr. *Thomas Jones,* Third Bailiff . . . who surpassed Mr. *Causton* in every Thing that was *bad,* without having any of his *good* Qualifications. . . ."[29]

The Trustees did not yet display their full measure of resentment and distrust towards Causton. He was appointed one of the three men to fill up the sola bills by which all the colony's expenses were to be paid. Oglethorpe, in the civil affairs of the colony, could no longer make new expenses nor send certified accounts. All expenses were strictly itemized and must not exceed the estimate set by the Trustees. Any two of the three men, Causton and Henry Parker and William Stephens, were to fill up the

sola bills and sign the account of expenditures. Thus a move was
made toward a shared responsibility in the affairs of the colony.
All credit at the Trustees' store was to stop from the time Oglethorpe arrived in Georgia, only the Trustees' servants being
maintained henceforth by the Trust.[30]

Though Causton still had much authority, he was roundly
berated by the Trustees. His unsatisfactory conduct was said to
be the cause of their stopping credit. They accused him of
receiving every ship's cargo brought to Georgia whether the provisions were needed or not, with consequent enormous bills for
the Trustees to pay. These large quantities of provisions must
richly provide for all expenses of the colony for the time being
and provide also a surplus for the Trust's indentured servants.[31]

Bills certified by Causton continued to reach London after he
had received instructions to stop certifying. Most of these were
refused by the Trustees and ordered returned to Georgia for
payment. Egmont wrote gloomily, "This has an ill aspect for
Causton." However displeased the Trustees were with Causton,
they thought they saw a reason for his conduct, though they did
not excuse him. "It was the private sentiment of some of us that
Mr. Oglethorp had given him direction to act in this manner,"
Egmont observed, "for the sake of his regiment, that on their
arrival they might not want for provision, or the people there
encouragement; but in so doing (if that should prove the case)
he has acted very unadvisedly, and contrary to the Trustees' intentions, who when they sent orders to Causton not to draw any
more bills upon us, meant that their sola bills should alone answer
the expenses of the Colony, but this method of certifying accounts
is a manifest evasion of that order."[32]

Causton himself in November, 1738, only implied that Oglethorpe knew the reason for many of his expenditures. Later he
said that Oglethorpe sent him an open order by Lieutenant
Colonel James Cochran for assistance and accommodations of officers and men of the regiment which resulted in great expense.[33]
The Trustees' anger at Causton mounted as the bills increased.
Though their action was not known in the colony for some time,
at their meeting on June 7 they removed him as first magistrate,
appointing Henry Parker in his place. The removal order was
sent to Oglethorpe, who was told the removal was a suspension
until Causton's accounts were made up. The Trustees first directed that Causton be sent back to England with his books and

accounts to answer to them directly, but finding a legal complication here, they directed Oglethorpe to keep him in custody or on
sufficient surety in Georgia until they should give other directions.[34]

About four o'clock on the afternoon of Tuesday, October 10,
1738, Oglethorpe arrived in Savannah from Frederica, for the first
visit since his return from England two weeks previously. He
received a warm welcome from the Savannah people, after which
he immersed himself in business. Thomas Jones had preceded him
from Frederica and began after Oglethorpe's arrival to work on
the accounts of the Trustees' store, which was closed while
inventory was taken.[35] The closing of the store was inconvenient
and occasioned some distress. Tales flew about Savannah and
there was a general feeling that much more was about to happen.

On October 17 Oglethorpe called together the inhabitants of
Savannah and, by William Stephens's account, "made a pathetick
Speech to them, setting forth how deeply the Trust was become
indebted, by Mr. Causton's having run into so great Exceedings
beyond what they had ordered, which debts the Trust had nothing
left at present to discharge, besides what Goods and Effects they
had in the Store. . . ." Great mismanagement of the Trust
funds was apparent; the stock in the Trustees' store must largely
be applied to the debts; retrenchment was necessary. Oglethorpe's
words "had such an Effect, that many People appeared thunder-
struck, knowing not where it would end; neither could the most
knowing determine it."[36] Oglethorpe's speech marked a turning
point in the colony.

When news of the speech reached Egmont in England in a
round-about way before the Trustees were notified, he remarked,
"It gives me great satisfaction to find that Mr. Oglethorpe has
executed the Trustees' orders in this matter, which some of our
gentlemen feared he would not." His satisfaction was short-lived.
Ten days later the Trustees' solicitor told the Board of reading
a letter from New York describing the meeting at Savannah, at
which Oglethorpe told his audience "that it cut him to the heart
to be obliged to tell them, that he had the Trustees' order to
shut up the stores, and call on all who were indebted thereto to
give bond to the Trustees for repayment, after which they might
retire where they pleased, their subsistence being at an end. And
further, that he had orders to seize on Mr. Causton and send him
over prisoner to England to answer for his misapplication of the

stores, and disobeying their orders. But as it was necessary Mr. Causton should have time to make up his accounts, he would suspend sending him till that was done." "We could not but observe . . . that Mr. Oglethorp had not acted rightly in this affair," said the Earl, "for though our first direction was that he should send Causton over, we afterwards altered that purpose, and were more indulgent to him, which second resolution we imparted to Mr. Oglethorp before he left England, but by imparting the harshest of his orders and concealing the milder, he recommended himself to the people's good opinion at our expense."[37]

The people of Savannah were not in a cheerful mood, and neither was Oglethorpe. William Norris, the new minister, landing from the *Two Brothers,* Captain William Thomson, on Sunday evening, October 15, with "the Relish for land, which the sickly disagreeable State of a Sea-Life naturally gave me," met an inhospitable reception: "The unhappy Situation of ye Colony at this Time, & the Reception, so disagreeable to the Assurances of the Hon: Trustees, which his Excellcy. the Genl. gave me, seem'd both fataly instant to obviate the good Intents & Purposes of my coming & continuing here." Oglethorpe seemed to see him, Norris continued, "only as one who by the Supports &c I should necessarily require, if invited to stay here, would really contribute to, & must consequently bear a considerable Share in the present & growing Calamity of the People." Oglethorpe told Norris that unless he "could depend solely on him, who feeds the Ravens &c, he neither could or with Security might give me Credit here."[38]

The effect of gloom and calamity upon the newcomer to Georgia was still stronger upon those who lived in the colony. Blow followed blow. The day after the meeting, Oglethorpe sent formal notification to Causton of his dismissal, ordering him to turn over his books and accounts to Thomas Jones and to find security for his appearance to answer charges against him. The latter order, since it was difficult to find bondsmen in the colony, was tempered: Causton was allowed to make his own bond, assigning all of the improvements he had made at his plantation, Ockstead, or elsewhere.[39]

Oglethorpe fulfilled further Trustees' orders when he removed Causton as first magistrate, removed Noble Jones as surveyor, suspended Jones as first Constable, and dismissed Joseph Fitzwalter as gardener.[40] Speculations as to further changes were rife in Savannah. While some rejoiced at Causton's fall, others deplored it and the method used to effect it. The Trustees' action and Oglethorpe's speech shook the colony to its foundations. Frederica, newly settled, felt little of the effects of the removals except when it had to deal with Thomas Jones. In Savannah, the first people had come over with Causton and Noble Jones, and every one knew them. Their removal from offices, the heavy charges hanging over Causton, the closing of the store, and the swift and summary action were disquieting in the extreme. A cleavage became evident. The colony was never the same again.

Thomas Jones tried diligently to prove that Causton had been engaged in fraud to his personal advantage, but was never able to do so. He did insist that he thought the store accounts were so mixed purposely to prevent the true picture's being determined. Causton and Jones immediately began to hurl recriminations at each other and continued on the worst of terms for a long time. Both Oglethorpe and Stephens wrote the Trustees that they could find no personal fraud on the part of Causton, but thought he had allowed too much credit at the store and approved too much nonessential work for which colonists were paid out of the store.

Oglethorpe questioned him as to why he dared exceed the Trustees' orders and plunge the colony into its great difficulties. Causton replied that he had made no expenses except those necessary. He was forced by the people to build the fort for fear of the Spaniards; he had several times to provide for groups of new colonists whose expenses were not in the Trustees' estimate. Oglethorpe agreed with Causton that the prices of provisions were three times greater than those on which the Trustees' estimate was based, that the Spanish alarm obliged Causton to comply with the people's demands that food be laid in at high prices lest the time come when none could be procured. Causton insisted that he was not guilty of any fraud or of converting the Trustees' money to his own use.

Oglethorpe was very gloomy concerning the immediate future of Georgia. Industrious poor people who had saved something by their frugality and lodged it in the store, hoping to have provisions in their necessity, must perish if the store could not pay. The same misery must befall the Trustees' indentured servants, as well as those inhabitants who had been prevented by sickness or misfortune from making a crop that year. Oglethorpe reported that the remainder of the large stores laid in, which the Trustees

thought could be sold to support the colony, was small. Oglethorpe would not incur debts or draw bills; he could see nothing
but destruction to the colony unless some assistance was sent
immediately.[41]

Causton's own reply to the Trustees' charges shows a man beset
by difficulties in offices from which he had begged to be removed
when his common sense forced him to see his position as untenable because of often conflicting orders which could not be
successfully carried out. He never had enough help to make up
accounts which were behind. Frequent orders came to undertake
new ventures and supply new colonists for which sufficient funds
were not forthcoming.[42]

On October 24, Oglethorpe called together the civil officers at
his lodgings. Henry Parker was now first magistrate, Robert Gilbert was a new addition to the bench, John Fallowfield was first
constable, and Samuel Mercer was second constable. Oglethorpe
appointed new tythingmen, to bring the number up to eighteen.
He charged these officers, concerning their duties, particularly to
preserve the peace "at this Time, when ill disposed Persons,
taking Advantage of Peoples Uneasiness at those inevitable Pres-
sures they laboured under, and must necessarily for some Time,
might craftily incite them to an Insurrection. . . ."[43]

Oglethorpe returned to Frederica the following day, "leaving
a gloomy Prospect of what might ensue; and many sorrowful
Countenances were visible," William Stephens wrote, "under the
Apprehensions of future Want: Which deplorable State the
Colony was now fallen into, through such Means as few or none
had any Imagination of (my own entire Ignorance of it I truly
own) till the Trustees in their late Letters awakened us out of
our Dream; and the General, when he came, laid the Whole
open, and declared we were but little removed from a down-
right Bankruptcy."[44]

"This Day like many others," Stephens wrote on November 8,
"my Door was almost continually frequented by poor People of
divers Sorts, importuning me to intercede at the Stores for some
small Relief under their present Necessities; imagining, though
without Cause, that it lay in my Power to order it: And thereupon
the greatest Part of the Clamour fell to my share, which indeed
gave me great Disquiet."[45]

Stephens observed "a visible change in peoples looks & tempers;
and little Storeys continually flew about, to augment Fears and

Jealousys. . . ." Neither money nor credit was current at Savannah, he observed in December. Ships with cargoes no longer came to Savannah, in the changed state of affairs. Provisions being nearly exhausted by the middle of that month and "there being yet no Appearance how the Stores would be recruited, gave a melancholy Prospect of what might happen." Stephens might well speak, as he did, of the disorder of the civil economy and remark that it was a poor Christmas at Savannah in 1738, "kept as a Holiday (or rather as an idle Day) . . . a Festival without any Feasting."[46]

If the Trustees could explode a bomb among the people of Savannah, the people could explode one among the Trustees. Oglethorpe's speech produced a cleavage between the colony and the Trustees, who seem never to have thought beforehand of the effect the announcement of their action would have upon the people. Perhaps "the poor" were not expected to react to the decisions of their governors in England. Certainly some less severe and less shocking method could have been pursued. Causton's letter of May 26, 1738, begging the Trustees to fix an estimate of the expenses of the colony by which he might abide, to send him instructions for the regulation of credit, and acknowledging the receipt of their orders of January 11 and February 17 which ordered him not to certify any more accounts was received by the Trustees in July. They had evidence in June, before Oglethorpe left England, that Causton had refused to certify a bill in April. Yet no effort was made to change or modify the decision of April so that affairs might be kept on a more even keel in Georgia.[47]

When the colonists saw, at that meeting on October 17, two of the foremost men in Georgia, Thomas Causton and Noble Jones, ignominiously discharged from office, something must have stirred in many of them. Could this happen to any one of them? Each one, perhaps, had his own doubts and fears about himself and the colony. Objections to Trustees' policy and ideas about the future of Georgia which had been slowly forming in men's minds, now came to the fore and showed the amount of dissatisfaction in the colony.[48]

A representation to the Trustees, dated December 9, 1738, was drawn up. The document declared that most of its signers had settled in the colony because of descriptions circulated by the Trustees in England. They now found after several years' experience that the colony could never succeed if its present regulations were continued. None of those who planted their lands had raised sufficient produce to maintain their families, however great their industry. It was now obvious that people could not subsist themselves by their land. This was proved by trials and failures which could not be contradicted by any theoretical scheme of reasoning. Since the land could not subsist them, they must depend upon trade. The situation of Savannah was well adapted to it, they thought, yet they were debarred from trade by difficulties and restrictions. Timber was the only exportable item; they were obliged to fell it before planting their land. Yet it could not be made ready for export except at double the expense incurred by other colonies with slave labor. The cultivation of land in Georgia with white servants had proved too expensive; so would other endeavors. For the past two years not more than two or three persons had come into the colony to settle, other than those sent by the Trustees on charity or as servants. None, they were sure, would come until the colony was on a better basis. The signers wanted their lands in fee simple and the use of Negroes with proper limitations.[49]

The representation was signed by 121 men. Among them were twelve of the first arrivals and several other men married to women widowed after they arrived on the *Ann*. The signers, though a few were of no especial import to the colony, were a fair cross section of the inhabitants. Both the magistrates, Henry Parker and Robert Gilbert, signed, as did the recorder, Thomas Christie. The representation was the talk of the town both during the signing, at Robert Williams's house, and afterward. Stephens remarked on "the surprizing Concurrence it met with from almost every Body . . . it was left open at the House where it was wrote fair, viz. Mr. Williams's; all who came voluntarily might sign it, if they liked, or let it alone, if they pleased; so that it ran like Wild-fire, and seemed almost universal. . . . With such a Spirit was this Affair carried on, and such Confidence of Success, as perfectly amazed me: But the Consequences I feared."[50]

Previously reiterated grievances of certain men show in the wording of the representation, but the fact that future representations embodied the same main points shows that the opinions expressed at this time were not confined to the few to whom Oglethorpe, Stephens, and the Trustees attributed the paper. The

Scots and Robert Williams were active in the preparation of it. The Scots had grievances enough; and Robert Williams, a Bristol man with a grant in 1733 of 500 acres,[51] was a vigorous business man who was ahead of his time in the colony and found irksome the Trustees' restrictions on the trade which he hoped to develop. Williams and the Scots became the objects of Oglethorpe's, Stephens's, and the Trustees' ridicule and sarcasm and were never forgiven; rather, excoriation increased.

Stephens's views were mild enough at first. He remarked on "a general buzzing at the Corners of the Streets about what they had been doing; and forming such Events from it in their own Imaginations. as they conceived would follow." But when Oglethorpe expressed great resentment against the signers and displeasure with all of Savannah, Stephens's views began to change. By the first part of January, 1739, Stephens thought the scene in and around Savannah was one of confusion and disorder, following the events of October and the representation in December. The whole situation had, he said, a melancholy aspect, with little food at hand.[52]

Oglethorpe thought that if the representation was heeded, the colony was ruined; he insisted that if Negro slavery should be allowed or the land tenure changed he would have nothing further to do with Georgia. He blamed Robert Williams;[53] yet it was plain subsequently that Oglethorpe's and Stephens's later views over-emphasized the influence of Williams and the Scots, who were not sufficiently strong to have manipulated the opinions of all the men who signed this or later representations on the same subject. The Trustees themselves were not united on the question of land tenure. Egmont's diary shows their debates on the subject. The representation of 1738, coming at the end of that troubled year, was an evidence of independence on the part of more than a handful of men. It was the first real charge in a battle with the Trustees, which eventually gained for the colonists their two main points of holding their land in fee simple and using slave labor. It showed that Georgians were beginning to be adult enough to handle their own affairs and to chafe at the Trustees' leading strings.

"A very sawcy Memorial," Egmont said. The petitions in it were flatly refused by the Trustees, and the magistrates and officers in the colony were sharply reproved for signing or having any part in it. The representation was responsible for a change of officers in the colony, which in turn brought about a small storm.[54]

In the meantime the settlement of Causton's accounts proceeded slowly. Causton left Savannah for Ockstead and came to town on rare occasions. Thomas Jones "bespattered" Causton "daily with opprobious Stories" and continued to "almost" find evidence of fraud and to be sure that Causton was about to flee the colony, neither of which ever happened, to Jones's disgust. Savannah divided on the case. Some people thought Causton had been misjudged. Others, remembering old scores against him, were sure that he was guilty and should be punished. Reports were sent to the Trustees by both sides. Jones was never able to understand Causton's accounts and continued to lament their confused state.[55]

Lieutenant Colonel Cochran upon his arrival in England told the Trustees in May, 1739, "That Causton will not be found so very bad as we [the Trustees] think him, but he was partial and gave to those he favoured more than enough, which afterwards they sold for half value to drink out in rum and other liquors." Cochran did not think the great complaints from the colony would have arisen had not the Trustees' stores been closed. Yet others reported that most people were glad that Causton had been turned out of office.[56]

On April 2, 1739, the Trustees appointed William Stephens, Henry Parker, and Thomas Jones as commissioners to examine Causton's accounts and the debts owing by the Trustees in Georgia. The commission arrived in Savannah on June 23, but it was August 6 before the commissioners began their work. Small discrepancies were discovered, but no great sums and no fraud. Objections were made to Causton's mixing of public and private accounts. Some accounts approved by the commissioners were paid by the Trustees.[57]

Causton himself sent petitions and letters to the Trustees and went into more detail in his own defense than he had done originally. However, he presented few new facts or ideas, only a restatement of those already presented. In the summer of 1740 Stephens reported Causton "in a decaying State of Health; which (it is to be feared) a great Anxiety of Mind has contributed to; and now we heard . . . his Life was near an End." But he recovered in time for a new calamity in October when both his son and wife died within ten days of each other. Great personal sorrow was thus added to his existing troubles.[58]

In 1742 Causton's health improved, his grief lessened, and he became at times actually cheerful, something that Stephens often wondered about. Oglethorpe seemed friendly upon trips which Noble Jones and Causton, almost constant companions now, made to Frederica. Something which Stephens could not understand was when Noble Jones, Causton, and Thomas Jones began spending time together, perhaps on Causton's accounts. In December, 1742, Causton and Thomas Jones began to sound out Stephens, he thought, about certifying that nothing amiss was found in Causton's accounts. This was certainly a change in attitude for Thomas Jones, which neither Stephens nor the present writers can understand. In January, 1743, Causton insisted that the commissioners either point out some fraud on his part or certify his acquittal. Though the commissioners could determine nothing further from the accounts, Stephens in his usual cautious way refused to agree to an acquittal. Causton went to Frederica to see Oglethorpe and came back with an acquittal form which he and Noble Jones insisted had Oglethorpe's approval. Thomas Jones seemed ready to acquit Causton, but Stephens and Parker (probably at Stephens's insistence) refused. Instead they reported the proceedings to the Trustees for a final decision, which the Trustees had undoubtedly intended for the commissioners to make.[59]

Causton in disgust appealed to the Trustees for a final decision. The commissioners, he said, made all sorts of excuses for delay in a decision, and when pressed, "The answer of Collonel Stephens is, He dont understand accounts; Of Mr. Parker. That it seems a very tedious work; Of Mr. Jones, That he will take care to be in the way and their time should be his; When they were once all met about it at the Store Each person (as usual) declared that they knew not or beleiv'd that any Crime was or could be laid to my charge and after turning over a few leaves Mr. Parker moved for an Adjournment to the Ale house with a proposition to conclude thereon the manner and time of proceeding therein; But as Mr. Parker's proposal was not thought well of, the whole Debate dropt. . . . Thus by delay they pursue . . . a self Interested Scheme; . . . . But it is something more than probable that they cannot bear the thoughts of reporting what the truth is; That a large sum of money has been rais'd by my frugality for the necessary Support of the Colony, And that there was no just cause to publish me as a fugitive or to Imprison me." Causton, doubting that the commissioners would ever make a final report, urged the Trustees to accept his accounts, let him appear before them personally, or take some action to bring the matter to a decision.[60]

The Trustees ordered a new inquiry into Causton's accounts, apparently in reply to his letter of May 1; but Causton could not have known this when he sailed for England in November, 1743, to press his case in person. William Spencer, a new magistrate, was to make the major portion of this inquiry. Spencer began this investigation in January, 1744, but had given it up as an impossible task by the end of April.[61] On November 30, 1744, the Trustees considered Causton's petitions, reports from Georgia, and the whole case, with Causton present. It was decided that he should return to Georgia, at the Trustees' expense, and settle his accounts with the commissioners there. In May Causton, still in London, requested and the Trustees approved additional expense funds, the appointment of a special commission (James Habersham, Francis Harris, and William Spencer) for examining and stating his accounts, and instructions to the commissioners to prepare a full report thereon.[62]

In November, 1745, Causton embarked on the *Judith* for Georgia. In her eleven-week passage, there was an epidemic of spotted fever which killed the captain, one of the ship's company, and eleven passengers including Causton. The new commissioners decided after Causton's death not to pursue the matter of the accounts any further and so reported to the Trustees. Thus only by death and a watery grave in the Atlantic was Thomas Causton relieved of concern for his accounts after seven years. If St. Peter confronted him with the accounts in the next world, the records have not been discovered.[63]

CHAPTER EIGHT

Botanists, Trustees' Garden, and Gardeners

J OSEPH FITZWALTER was one of the three men of the *Ann's* passengers who lost their offices in the colony in October, 1738. In Georgia's history, Fitzwalter has been almost an unnoticed man. What record of him survives is because of the energy and enthusiasm in his few letters and occasional mention in the letters of others. He was thirty-one years of age when he sailed on the *Ann,* already appointed by the Trustees as gardener and one of the two constables. He undoubtedly enjoyed his work as gardener, despite various man-made vexations.

When the officers of the colony were sworn in on the first court day, July 7, 1733, Fitzwalter stoutly swore before Oglethorpe: "I Joseph Fitzwalter, Constable, of the town of Savannah & the Precincts thereof, Do swear That I will duely and faithfully execute the office of Constable to which I am nominated & appointed by the Common Council of the Trustees for Establishing the Colony of Georgia in America, and that I will in all things perform & Execute the same without fear, favour or affection. So help me God." The constable's duties were defined by the court: "all Juries Panells Inquisitions Attachments Precepts Mandates Warrants Judgements & Process whatsoever necessary to be had or done touching or Concerning the Pleas Suits & Actions aforesaid shall be summoned Done & Executed by the Constables. . . ." Fitzwalter pledged himself to obey the warrants, orders, and judgments of the bailiffs and recorder.[1]

The court had powers to try civil and criminal cases under the laws and customs of England. Property was as regularly recovered and criminals punished as in any court in Europe, Oglethorpe said with some pride at the end of 1733. Fitzwalter had to attend court held every six weeks or oftener for trying civil and criminal cases. Each panel of jurors was composed of twenty-four freeholders, of which each party in a trial might challenge six. In civil cases any of the magistrates upon complaint issued a summons, executed by one of the constables. The plaintiff and defendant appeared before the magistrates, where the matter might be settled by agreement or set for trial at the next court. If the defendant was a freeholder, he need give no security for his appearance; if he was a non-resident or non-freeholder, security was required. In criminal cases the magistrates could commit to bail, with the exception that in murder cases they must commit to prison, the tythingman on duty having charge of the prisoner.[2]

Fitzwalter would not have heard any lawyers in court; they were almost non-existent in the early days of the colony. Oglethorpe remarked in 1733 that each man was his own lawyer, and a newcomer to Georgia in 1736 commented admiringly that "there are no Lawyers allowed to plead for Hire, nor no Attornies to take Money but (as in the old times in *England*) every Man pleads his own Cause." A man would sometimes designate a friend to represent him in court. Samuel Eveleigh, after attending court in the autumn of 1734, observed that the grand jurymen came from all parts of the settlement "to Whom Mr. Caustin gave a very handsome Charge and then Proceeded to business," cases being tried very impartially "without the Jargon or the confused Quirks of the Lawyer's and without any Cost or Charges, and Yet (in my Opinion) consonant to reason and Equity, wch I take to be the foundation of all Laws."[3] Even after men with legal knowledge came into the colony they were often spoken of in derogatory terms. A part of the good opinion held of one man was that he was "very honest and sober, and is no attorney." It was no recommendation to William Stephens that William Aglionby was "bred a Smatterer in the law," for he was "looked upon as one of the greatest Mischiefmakers in the whole Town."[4]

Constables were fairly busy officials, even though there were four by the end of 1734. One constable mounted guard every day and was responsible for the peace for twenty-four hours. He must make returns of all boats that passed and all strangers arriving and where they stayed. Under the constable, a tythingman and his ten men went on guard every night. This guard posted sentinels, patroled Savannah, enforced the prompt closing of public houses at ten o'clock, and executed the police power necessary to deal with or prevent disorders. A tythingman did not always have his full complement of ten men, nor a constable four tythingmen.

A constable received from the tythingmen in his ward the names of the sick, which he reported to Thomas Causton. This procedure, probably instituted during the first summer when sickness was prevalent and death frequent, made the constables watch for the appearance of his people, especially those living alone. Causton had authority to hire a nurse to care for such sick people as had no relatives to care for them, and authority to rent a house for use as an infirmary.

By virtue of his office as constable, Fitzwalter was also an officer in the militia, which Oglethorpe estimated in late 1734 or early 1735 as consisting of about 400 men from Savannah and the out-settlements. The militia was exercised by constables and tythingmen, and arms were issued to each freeholder, who was required to keep them in good condition.[5]

Fitzwalter must soon have found out that as a constable he had ample opportunity to observe at first hand the seamiest side of life. The Mellichamp case, in 1735, was one which aroused excitement both in Georgia and Carolina. William Mellichamp, gentleman, arrived in the colony in March, 1734, bringing with him his wife, family, and two servants. One of Mellichamp's sons, Thomas, came with him; another, a minister, remained in England.[6]

In 1735 South Carolina officials informed Causton that some of the Carolina currency bills were being counterfeited. The counterfeiters were found by Carolina officers to be William Mellichamp and his son Lawrence at Winyah, in Carolina. The bills were found in Georgia, and Walter Augustine remarked ruefully that "we have had Sad doings here with Counterfeit money it being Suposed twas utered by Ould Malishamp I had no less than 33 £ and am ye Loser of 18 £ without Remedy. . . ."[7]

Causton was informed by Georgians that all counterfeiting was not ended when the elder Mellichamp returned to England. Thomas Mellichamp and Richard Turner were suspected, for Turner was known to have made a rolling press, which it was supposed they had used. Not enough evidence could be found at this time, and the two were admitted to bail. Since the case was one in which South Carolina was concerned, Causton requested the advice of that province's attorney general, James Abercromby, who came to Georgia in July to assist briefly with the trial. William Mellichamp and Richard Turner were indicted on three counts for counterfeiting and passing Carolina currency and making a rolling press and other instruments with which to counterfeit. William was gone; Turner stood trial on July 14, was convicted on the third count, was fined £200 sterling, and was jailed until payment was made. Turner now found himself suffering more than those who had employed him. He and his wife poured out the whole story, which resulted in another indictment of William and one of Thomas Mellichamp. Warrants were issued to seize the land and effects of the two in case they were found guilty, but confiscation was deferred until the Trustees' orders could be received.

Thomas Mellichamp did not intend to be tried. He fled. On Tuesday, August 19, a constable peered into the depths of a barn on Wadmellaw Island, South Carolina, where Thomas and a companion were busily at work. Thomas ran but was knocked down and taken in a nearby corn field. There in the barn were the press and the bills. Thomas and his companion were taken to jail in Charles Town to await trial. Thomas broke jail in less than a month and fled again.[8]

Thomas's father, William Mellichamp, in England, expressed himself strongly to the Trustees. The affair was an ill-natured aspersion thrown upon his family since he left America that should not prevent his return to make use of his salt pans there, to claim the land promised him, and maintain his poor distressed wife and children. The scandal, he said, might have hurt him temporarily in the Trustees' esteem but time would show that it was a plot to disparage him with the Trustees.[9]

Thomas Mellichamp was evidently caught and returned to jail, for in the summer of 1736 bail was arranged for him in Charles Town and he was set at liberty. The report was that he had returned to Georgia to marry Sophia Hopkey, Causton's niece, something he did not do. The news that he intended to come to Georgia caused an offer of £10 sterling to be made for his apprehension on the old forgery indictment.[10] Early in August he was arrested in Savannah, "together with a gang of Men of very vile characters, upon some of whom stolen Goods were taken; he is committed to Gaol for Forgery, the Grand Jury here having found a Bill of Indictment against him for that Crime, his Mother and Family, being concerned in the Proceedings of the Gang, and conveying away the Goods, are expelled from the Colony."[11]

Fitzwalter as a constable was not often involved in cases as important as the Mellichamp case. Still, there was William Watkins of Abercorn, a surgeon who arrived on Captain Lionel Wood's ship, the *Savannah*, in December, 1733. He married in April, 1735, a woman who came also on the *Savannah*, whose husband, James Willoughby, a peruke maker, died in October, 1734. Disconcerting news came that Watkins's first wife was alive and in blooming health in England. The Georgia marriage was secret so far, but Mrs. Willoughby was by now pregnant. Watkins in a quandary proposed to her "That as he had a Wife in England, he should be liable to be troubled, and therefore dared not own it; and as she was with Child, the world would soon discover it, and believe that she had played the Whore, Therefore, persuaded her to marry Richard Mellichamp." Mellichamp, discovering her condition after the ceremony, "and his own misfortunes in marrying her," solved the problem by offering her to the highest bidder at a convivial gathering at Richard Turner's. Five pounds she brought at the immediate auction and went away from the party with her purchaser. Despite this solution the grand jury indicted Mrs. Willoughby for bigamy and her purchaser and Watkins for misdemeanor. Mellichamp was acquitted as being a sufferer by the marriage. The purchaser was bound over for his future good behavior. Mrs. Willoughby was jailed, being with child and not punishable at the time, while Watkins "was whipt (unpittyed) on a Muster day at the Carts Tail around the Town, and remains in Gaol for want of Surety."[12]

Whipping, administered in the public view, was a common punishment of criminals in the colony. When it was discovered that a man and woman were not married as they claimed and the woman's conduct was sufficiently abandoned to cause conviction for leading a dissolute life, she was given sixty lashes at the cart's tail down Bull Street and back again. The man was ordered to give security and was bound over to his good behavior during residence in the colony.[13] Among the complaints which Robert Parker, Sr., sent the Trustees he spoke of punishments "wch in a New Colony in my Humble Opinion ought to be used very tenderly & as seldom as Possable, but at Savannah they are frequent & Shocking, even to Disgust the Neighboring Provinces. . . ."

This was a nicely calculated remark since the Trustees would not have had South Carolina criticize the administration of justice in Georgia. "I have seen a woman Sit in the Stocks for 3 Hours when it Rain'd hard, (& the only Dairy Wife we have to Supply the Colony with Butter) . . . she was taken out of the Stocks & Carried on Board a Sloop & Ducked, in Ducking Her they Bruis'd her so against the Vessel she was lame for 2 or 3 months. . . ."[14]

Other punishments besides whipping were administered at the whipping post. A woman who stole some chickens from Edward Jenkins was ordered to stand two hours at the whipping post with a paper pinned on her chest which told her misdeeds. She confessed, promised to mend her ways, and was forgiven. A fine of 10s. 6d. was paid to the mistress of a maid-servant by a man who got the maid with child. Too obvious revelry was punished by the revelers being set in the stocks. Warrants of hue and cry were issued upon the disappearance of indentured servants, run away in hopes of a freedom most of them never attained. Usually their taste of liberty was brief before being caught and returned to their masters.[15]

Fitzwalter was doubtless glad to share in the reward given by the Trustees in 1735 to the magistrates, recorder, constables, tythingmen, their families, and the widows and families of those who had held any of these offices. Each was allowed another year's provisions out of the Trustees' store because of the zeal of the magistrates in the public service "and out of regard to the various fatigues, which the Constables and Tything Men have gone thro' for the defending and preserving the Peace of the Colony. . . ."[16] The officers of the colony needed this help; the amount of time they spent on their public duties seriously hampered cultivation of their lands.

Though the Trustees' ideal of joint labor in the colony was not realized long, for some time the constables and tythingmen banded together to help each other in cultivating; they showed "an Unanimous disposition for Improving their Lands; they are entred into joint Labour, And constantly bestow two days in a week for clearing and fencing each others Lands, and each Member, has the benefit of their joint Labour in turn. This also excites other people to Industry of the same kind."[17] Fitzwalter must have found this agreeable, for however good a constable he was, he most enjoyed plants and planting. He was at heart a gardener.

The Trustees' garden, in which Fitzwalter was the first gardener, was a project on which great hopes were based. A report of the colony's first year defined the purposes of the garden: "Besides the several Works on which the People was employed at Savannah, as palisading the Town, clearing the place from Pine-trees, &c. and building of Houses, some other Works were carried on; viz. a publick Garden was laid out, which was designed as a Nursery, in order to supply the People for their several plantations with White Mulberry-trees, Vines, Oranges, Olives, and other necessary Plants; a Gardener was appointed for the Care of it, and to be paid by the Trustees."[18]

The Trustees' plan that Georgia should eventually supply England with many items then imported from Europe (among them silk, wine, potash, flax, hemp, cochineal, oranges, olives, and various drugs) strongly aided them in obtaining financial support from Parliament. If Georgia could produce these items for the mother country, particularly silk and wine, she would become a factor in making England more mercantilistic. No part of the colony but would produce these products, the Trustees decided on the basis of Oglethorpe's information to them. Two years after the colony was founded, they began to figure on produce worth eventually £500,000 a year. In the last of the thirteen colonies was to be tried again a scheme of planting similar to that tried earlier but unsuccessfully in Virginia and Carolina.[19]

The Trustees' garden was to be the starting point in this ambitious undertaking. Subscriptions to a special fund were begun by the Trustees in the summer of 1732 to defray the cost of encouraging and improving botany and agriculture in the colony. Even before the *Ann* sailed, the first botanist was engaged for three years at £200 a year. William Houstoun, doctor of physic of the University of St. Andrews, and late surgeon of the South Sea Company's ship *Don Carlos,* was instructed by the Trustees to proceed to Madeira, Jamaica, the Spanish settlements at Cartagena, Puerto Bello, Campeche, Vera Cruz, and Panama if possible, using his utmost diligence to procure seeds, roots, or cuttings of all useful plants wanting in the British colonies, among them "Ipecacuana, Jallap, Contrayvera, Sarsaparilla & Jesuits Bark; the Trees which yield the Peruvian, & Capivi Balsoms, the Gum Elemi &c. the Cochineal Plant with the Animals upon it; and all other things that you shall judge of use to the Colony of Georgia. . . ." Houstoun was instructed to study the process of wine-making in Madeira, the culture of grape vines, cinnamon trees, logwoods and barks for dying cloth, and the white mulberry tree which would provide food for silkworms. When Houstoun had made his collections, he would be expected to go to Georgia to take care of the cultivation of them.[20]

Houstoun made progress in his collecting but died in Jamaica on August 14, 1733, leaving a collection of plants, a few of which probably eventually reached the colony.[21] In February, 1734, the Trustees subscribed to the expenses of another botanist, Robert Millar (or Miller), recommended by Sir Hans Sloane, himself a contributor to the fund for improving botany and agriculture in Georgia and anxious for information about the plants and possibilities of this region. Millar, given similar instructions to those of Houstoun, was to spend two years collecting the desired plants. He was then to cultivate a farm in Georgia where he would experiment in growing plants best suited to the climate, from those which England was then purchasing from foreign countries.[22]

Returning to England in November, 1736, Millar was engaged by the Trustees for two more years. His travels took him over the route originally outlined for Houstoun, with some additions. His interesting letters give many details of his assiduity in collecting. The colony had little profit from his work, however. Some of his plants may have been among those sent later from England, but he did not bring them to Georgia nor have charge of an experiment farm as originally planned. He wished to stop traveling but was willing to bring his plants to Georgia before returning to England. The Trustees refused to accept his conditions, having become dissatisfied and thinking that Millar had provided fewer plants for them than for some of his other subscribers, among them the Apothecaries' garden at Chelsea.[23] Thus disappointment marked both botanists' work. The Trustees themselves sent over various seeds and plants to the colony from the first.

The Trustees' garden in Savannah had a parent garden in Charles Town where thousands of plants and seedlings were collected and grown to be transplanted to Georgia. Paul Amatis took a small house and a garden in Charles Town probably soon after his arrival with the first people on the *Ann,* for in the spring of 1733 he advertised in the name of the Trustees for silk balls to be brought to him in Broad Street, Charles Town. Amatis's garden was doing well by May when Samuel Eveleigh paid him a visit and found that he had sown tea seed, had nearly 3000 young white mulberry trees growing, and expected to obtain 3000 more mulberry cuttings from Eveleigh's brother's plantation. About 450 of the grapevines sent by the Trustees were flourishing, as were 500 orange trees, and a quantity of peach and other fruit trees. "Amythis" (as Eveleigh often spelled his name) was "now very Busie feeding his Worms some of which have worked themselves into Balls and he proposes a second Cropt. . . ."[24]

Oglethorpe acknowledged by the end of 1733 that the maintenance of the Charles Town garden as a nursery for mulberry and orange trees, grapevines, and so on was a large expense but justified on the basis that a sample of fine silk that had been made there showed what could be done in this region. "And we have gain'd one Year's Growth upon the Mulberry and Orange Trees which is inestimable in a new Settlement." Eveleigh found the garden in good order the next summer with the grapevines flourishing and Amatis expecting to have 100,000 mulberry trees from the seeds he had sown.[25] Amatis was to begin transplanting from the Charles Town garden in the autumn of 1734.

After the first week in February, 1733, when all hands at Savannah worked at unloading the boats and making the crane, the men were divided into three working groups, one of which cleared land for planting seed. Towards the end of March some vegetables, herbs, and fruit trees were planted in two or three gardens;[26] probably one of these was the Trustees' garden or its predecessor. By the latter part of the summer enough land was cleared so that some colonists began to plough. The tools brought on the *Ann* were so largely inferior that they proved useless and had to be replaced.[27] Whatever the tools, by the spring of 1734 the garden had taken shape. Von Reck, soon after he landed with the Salzburgers, went to visit it. "There is laid out, near the Town, by Order of the Trustees, a Garden for making Experiments, for the Improving Botany and Agriculture; it contains 10 acres, and lies upon the River; and it is cleared, and brought into such Order, that there is already a fine Nursery of Oranges, Olives, white Mulberries, Figs, Peaches, and many curious Herbs: besides which, there is Cabbages, Peas, and other *European* Pulse and Plants, which all thrive. Within the Garden there is an artificial Hill, said by the Indians, to be raised over the Body of one of their ancient Emperors."[28]

The tract of ten acres which comprised the garden was bounded on one side by the Savannah River and on another, by the unbroken forest. The garden lay partly on top of the bluff, where

the soil was sandy, and sloped down to a marsh on the east where
the soil was rich and moist and protected from the wind. Two cross
walks, thirty feet wide lined with orange trees, divided the garden
into four squares. In one of these squares the woods were left
as the colonists found them; in the other squares were planted
"Forreign Trees and plants in the Soils most adapted to them."
Among these were fifty olive trees, 2000 grapevines, and 40,000
mulberry trees, peach, pomegranate, fig, orange, and other trees.
Oglethorpe stated specifically in 1734 that the garden was the
nursery of the colony from which trees were given out to the
people as soon as their gardens were ready for them.[29]

By that time Fitzwalter had done much hard work. After the
Irish transports arrived, Oglethorpe assigned four of these servants
to the gardens.[30] Fitzwalter, early in 1735 after he had been in the
colony almost two years, wrote to Oglethorpe with gusto and appreciation about the state of affairs generally and the garden particularly. The Trustees should have valued his letter; not many of
its kind were written. "The Garden I have made great Improvements in—Most of the Trees Stumps I have Root upp planted the
front walk with Trees of Oranges Six foot Hight. which will bear
fruit some This Year; and all in Generall Thrive. . . .

"Some Orange Trees this last Season Shott in the Nussary four
Foot and the least Shott Two foot; I have a Thousand of them; of
Mulberry's plants I have Eight Thousand some of them this last
Season Shott fairly fifteen foot, and this Season will be capable of
feeding Abundance of the Worms—The Olive Trees like the Soile
and Situation for I have Some of them Shott Six foot this Season. . . ." It was agreeable certainly to report progress but he
could do better and describe every foot of growth. He must
often have called his friends into the garden and demanded to
know if they had ever seen plants so flourishing.

Olive, orange, and mulberry trees responded to Fitzwalter's
care and to a bountiful soil and a favorable growing season.
Fitzwalter was proud of his accomplishments. The Trustees sent
many plants for experimental purposes, and Fitzwalter planted
and cared for them all. "I have met with Some Cotton Seeds from
Guinea which from it I have Raised a Thousand plants som of
which Shott Eight foot in higth and The Second Season will come
to its Bringing Forth Fruits in Abundance so that I shall be Able
to send a Large Quantity of Cotton to the Trustees Use. . . ."

Joseph Fitzwalter thus proved himself to be perhaps the earliest Georgia cotton planter.

Then he came to his main interest. "As for the Kitchen Garden Every thing thrive as well as ever in Europ And As for Wheat, Barly, Rye, Oates, Tares, Beans, pease, Rye grass, Clover, Traifoil, Sinque foil, and Lucern Seeds, Never Seen finer than this Country produce," he declared roundly. Fitzwalter was evidently describing his planting in his own ground as well as the Trustees' garden. "Hemp and Flax will do as well here as in any part of Urope, Rice I have had very good Indian Corn, and pease in great plenty," he said proudly, showing that already he had grown some of the food which he knew that the colony needed.

Fitzwalter was well aware of the natural advantages of the colony. "In a Word I take it to be the promised land, Its Lands Rich and Fertile, Its Trees Large and good for Building both for Land & sea, Various Sorts of Gum and them as good as Comes from East Indies, Various Sorts of Druggs, flowering Shrubs and plants of Various Kinds, Fruits wild of Different Species and very Good, when Cultivated will be Much finer. Clay of Different Kindes both for the Moulder and potter, Mindes of Different Species, Stones of Various Colors and them Transparent, Fine Springs and Some of Them Minerall, fine Rivers and them plenty who Affords us Multitudes of Fish and the Best in the world Salmon Trouts, Sturgeons of which I Caught one weighed Upwards of Three Hundred weight, Mullets, Bass &c. Our woods Affords us great plenty of Dear and bear who Meat is extream good Turkeys in great plenty I have Shott Six of a Day and them very Large Some weighed Twenty Five pounds each. Wood Pidgeons Innumerable and of other Sorts of fowles Abundance to tedious to mention Our Rivers afford Us abundant of Water fowles as for Geese, Ducks, Mallard, Teal, and Widgeons, I have been one of the Four that have Shott Thirteen Dozen in one Day. . . ." No chamber of commerce in later days, extolling the beauties and advantages of the Georgia coast, has surpassed Fitzwalter.

He was also enthusiastic about Savannah: "I Thank God our Town is in very good Health and Increases Mightily, for that place which was Nothing But Pine Trees when We Came is become almost as Many Houses, and As [for] Williams Burg which is the Metropoliss of Virginia we Exceed them in the Number of Houses

though been Settled Near a Hundred Years, Though not our
Buildings Quite so Magnificent," he added honestly.[31]

However, he was too generous in his estimate of Savannah,
even though improvements could be noted. The previous year
sixty-four private houses, besides public buildings and huts, were
finished and nearly eighty more houses were in process of construction, all twenty-four by sixteen feet, built of framed timber,
covered with shingles and eventually to have brick chimneys.
There was a store house forty by twenty feet, built of sawed
timber six inches thick, two stories in height, and with a cellar;
another store house was built of split boards, thirty-six by twelve
feet in which were kept arms, provisions, ammunition, and tools
owned by the Trust. A log jail and a fort took care of certain needs
of the people, while a chapel thirty-six by twelve served other
needs. Public facilities included a crane for unloading boats and
an oven described by a visiting South Carolinian as "a glorious
large Oven which convinces all Travellers that there is no want
of good Bread. . . ."[32] Fitzwalter was truthful when he said
the buildings in Savannah were not quite so magnificent as those
in Williamsburg; they were not at all magnificent. Fitzwalter's
pride in his town is pleasing when contrasted with the opinions of
some of the other colonists. He knew that this young town and
colony afforded him opportunity. Evidently he contrasted his condition then with bitter experiences in his past.

Now came two points which troubled Fitzwalter. First, he
wanted the salary promised to him by the Trustees "and what
ever Your Honours thinks fitt for the Boy Goddard my prentice,"
for though he had been in the colony almost two years he had been
paid only about £10. Fitzwalter needed cash which he "Could
Convert to a good Use in Improving my Estate." The second point
was one not to be settled for some time. "Mr. Amatis hath been
hear and at Puries Burgh Since the Beging of September and is
not for planting of anything of Kitching Stuff att all in the Garden
which I always Aprehended was to be Carried on Both by Your
Honour and Trust and Likewise Botany But Mr. Amatis is More
for the Merchant than Any thing Else for Severall Hoggshead of
Rum and wine Barrels Flower hath Landed and sold here to my
knowledge and have Taken the Servants out of the garden both to
Crane them Upp and to Carry himself and goods Severall times to
Puries Burgh and was for Displacing me out of the Garden, who
has gone through the Heat Burden of All the Improments in it,

Mr. Causton out of his wise Judgement would not Adhear to
him. . . ."

Fitzwalter's indignation that Amatis should want to displace
him was evidence of a fundamental disagreement between them.
Late in 1734 Thomas Christie wrote to London that "Mr. Amatis
and Mr. Fitzwalter have had Some Differences together concerning their Authority wch we have had Difficulty to Reconcile—."
Christie remarked also that the garden had hitherto been of little
use to the town; people who had the most need of it had the least
benefit and it seemed rather a private than a public property.[33]
Here he touched on one of the fundamental differences between
Fitzwalter and Amatis. Amatis had sowed about a thousand mulberry trees, Christie continued; the older mulberries as well as
the other trees were pruned and flourishing.

Paul Amatis, who came over on the *Ann,* was brought by the
Trustees from Piedmont to introduce the culture of silk into
Georgia and to instruct the people in its production. Nothing was
said at the time about his being a gardener; Fitzwalter was the
only one of the *Ann's* passengers whose occupation was so listed.
Paul sent for his brother Nicholas and several other silk workers
from Piedmont. Their arrival in England, early in 1733, caused
Lord Percival to remark, "We build great expectations on these
two brothers." Nicholas and his party left England for Georgia
in April, 1733, on the *Peter and James,* Captain Cornish. With
Nicholas came Jacques Camuse, with his wife and three sons.
Paul Amatis discharged his brother in the summer of 1735, and
Nicholas left the colony. Paul was embroiled in unpleasantness
with Nicholas and the Camuses from the moment of their landing.[34] Paul Amatis was frequently embroiled; it was his temperament to be so. Only the fact that he stayed in Carolina, and
worked, until Georgia's mulberry trees were of sufficient size to
provide for the silkworms, precluded earlier clashes in the colony.
After he came to Georgia on September 8, 1734, he saw much of
which he disapproved. Most of all he disapproved of Fitzwalter.

He was obliged in spite of himself, Amatis said, to say that he
found the garden in disorder; since Oglethorpe's departure almost
nothing had been done. Sufficient servants were left with Fitzwalter to cut down trees, uproot stumps, burn over the whole, and
have all in readiness for the plants and trees from the Charles
Town garden, "but the bad management that has been shown
here, in a few words, the pleasure of hunting, fishing and other

pleasures, have employed the larger part of the servants, and ever since I arrived in this city they are employing nearly all the servants that were meant for the garden to be going after window panes, making of prisons, running after society, and other things for the service of the public."

Amatis was a resourceful man, though, he implied. He brought in other workmen so that his trees might be set out. In nearly half the garden he intended to set out thousands of mulberry trees as well as other plants, and in that half would be found not one stump, one root, or one tree formerly grown there. Even now pleasure could be taken in the garden by promenading its beautiful walks. He expected to go to Charles Town soon for a boatload of trees from the garden there. He would keep the principal plants in Charles Town until the Trustees made it clear if he or Fitzwalter was to be the master of the garden. Fitzwalter insisted that he was, and had insulted Amatis twice; which behavior, Amatis said, forced him to carry his complaints to Mr. Causton and other gentlemen.

Even while he somewhat grudgingly admitted that Fitzwalter behaved better toward him now, Amatis had a list of complaints against him, the chief of which was that Fitzwalter had given away plants from the garden without Amatis's consent. Only four servants were now assigned to the garden and they were often taken away for other work. He could never take any pleasure in the garden, Amatis said, unless the Trustees ordered him full power "to be the chief in every thing that concerns the garden, and that the said servants be entirely under my directions, and that no one be able to take any of the fruits of the said garden in the future without my consent and to my generosity, which I hope will be for the public in general as I have always accustomed it to be in the past. . . ." Perhaps it was this policy of Amatis's that caused Thomas Christie to say that the garden seemed more a private than a public concern.

The Trustees or Oglethorpe evidently instructed Fitzwalter or Amatis orally, and each seemingly understood that he was in charge of the garden. The written statements on Amatis's work place him in charge of silk production with no mention of the garden. Fitzwalter understood it thus. Amatis, having by Oglethorpe's order been in charge of the Charles Town garden, may have assumed that he would have a similar position in the Savannah garden. Amatis said later that Oglethorpe placed him in a position superior to Fitzwalter's.

Amatis related other trials. He "suffered here as a poor unfortunate this winter by reason of the great cold and frost which we have had here. I have implored Mr. Causton and the other gentlemen to have a little compassion for one of the first forty, by having a chimney in some place in order to protect me from the cold. . . ." But, he said, they sat by their good fires and forgot how cold Paul Amatis was.[35] Certainly he was colder than these Englishmen long inured at home to cold. He was far from his home, among foreigners whose ways were not his ways, nor ever could be. For what he insisted were his rights, he would assert himself and watch for encroachments creeping upon him. He did not mention that not everyone had chimneys yet; perhaps he was too cold to notice this and only saw with envy that some were warm while he was not.

The first chimney, finished in the autumn or early winter of 1733, was in the house assigned to Samuel Quincy, the minister.[36] However, there was a saying in Savannah later in the winter that if one saw a house with a chimney, it belonged to a widow. Oglethorpe ordered those built first and the widows' chimneys were a feature of the landscape. Samuel Eveleigh in the autumn of 1734 found that the brickmakers had on hand about 100,000 bricks and that workmen expected to have all the chimneys up by Christmas of that year.

Eveleigh took with him some liquorice and hop roots which he gave to Amatis for the garden. Eveleigh could not find that the coffee berries, date stones, or various other seeds which he sent had been planted, but the "Orange and Mulberry Trees, Sent from Town, look very well, and Mr. Amathist had Sowne all along the Fence next to the Town, above Six foot deep with white Mulberry Seeds, wch came up very thick, and doubt but there will be one hundred thousand Trees if not more."[37]

Between Fitzwalter and Amatis there was now a basic conflict, due in part to temperament, still more to conflicting or misunderstood instructions. The following spring Fitzwalter asked Oglethorpe to clarify matters. Amatis's business was quite different from his, Fitzwalter wrote, quite different from botany, "Nussarys," or kitchen gardening. Matters were now at such a pitch "that what ever I do; in his petts he Destroys," Fitzwalter said of Amatis, and "I hope your Honour and the Rest of the Honourable Trust will see me writed. . . ."[38]

Paul Amatis's "petts" were a little more serious than Fitzwalter's choice of words would indicate. He was in Charles Town during most of January and February, 1735, preparing to remove plants and trees, of which he thought he would have more than 100,000 for the Trustees' garden. He wrote that "I should like with all my heart that you had the sight of them. It is very certain that one has never seen só beautiful a collection of trees as you will have in your garden in Georgia." Because of lack of funds he could proceed no further with plans for the silk business, though he did mention plans for another experiment with silkworms. He had now entirely quit the Charles Town garden and intended to concentrate his attention on the Savannah garden during the time he remained there (he was threatening to return to London). His first object would be the proper disposal of the 30,000 plants which he would take to Savannah from the Charles Town garden.[39]

When Amatis came to Savannah in the latter part of February, he was accompanied by his brother Nicholas, and he brought with him what Fitzwalter termed "a Generall Remove of plants" and immediately began to set them out. By early March he had planted about 200 mulberry trees, 10,000 mulberry seedlings, 2,000 grapevines, twenty peach trees, twenty plum and twenty apple trees, forty fig trees, and had fifty large orange trees yet to plant. Though they had severe frosts in February, no great damage was done; the season was now fine "and all that I have planted att This Time and Transplanted Breaketh forth finly. . . ."

These particular days were marked with drama, and "pets." On Monday afternoon, March 3, the day after the Red String Plot, two of the Trust's servants were punished with whipping at the whipping post, upon which, according to Fitzwalter, Amatis threw "himself into a passion saying that it was not in any ones power to do Any thing to Them, and said further that he would go for England Directly and if any person had Any Grievances to Come to him, and he would Redress them which words was very wrong Spoke at any Time, Especially at a Time when we Expected those Servants to Rise with Others to head them and Two Cutt us off." When one of the servants was sent for from the garden to be questioned by the magistrates concerning the plot, Amatis "Damned Mr. Causton and Me in a Violent Manner and Further sd Mr. Causton had no Business to Examine them upon no Account whatsoever not I had no Bussiness in the Garden nor with any of the Servants, and That if I Came any more after that Time he would Shoot me, however I went as usually Early to place my Men to their Bussiness, and about Nine in the Morn Amatis and his Brother Came with a Gun they did not Shoot but Thretned me very much, but I was not to be frietned,

"I have Since asked Mr. Amatis his Resolution, and still he persists that I have no Bussiness at all in the Gardens, though placed there by your Honours and the Honnerable the Trust. . . ." Fitzwalter then took a step which enraged Amatis yet more: "This Day being the 10th Instant and a Grand Jury Called and Sitting for the Safety of ye province, I have Taken Care to Bin'd Amatiss over to the peace. . . ."

Amatis's conception of his duty may have been derived from Oglethorpe. He read a statement in court which he said was to defend his character against the wicked designs of Fitzwalter, who certainly had no other view in bringing him into court than to cover and hide Fitzwalter's mismanagement and great faults in relation to the Trustees' garden. Furthermore, Amatis continued, Fitzwalter would not believe that another superior to him was appointed by Mr. Oglethorpe to overlook his proceedings and everything relating to the garden. But this was true he insisted: four Georgians of distinction, and Governor Johnson of South Carolina, heard the orders given by Oglethorpe several times, all of which he had obeyed in the strictest manner. Fitzwalter had insulted him, acted contrary to his orders, given away plants and trees without his sanction or that of the Trustees'; he opposed Fitzwalter's having anything further to do with the garden. Until the Trustees could receive his complaint against Fitzwalter and about the removal of servants from the garden, Amatis would stay in Savannah "with no other View than to perform my Duty to them and take due care of their Interest which tis Evident I have more at heart than My Rival Mr. Fitzwalter."[40]

Letters revealing the differences between Fitzwalter and Amatis reached London. In April, 1735, the Earl of Egmont commented that "Amatis, our silk man, . . . wrote divers complaints against Fitzwalter, our gardener." The distinction between the duties of the two men was thus clear enough to one of the leading Trustees. Egmont, considering this letter and several others about the Red String Plot, decided, "All these things show the necessity of sending a Governor over."[41] A number of colonists, among them Amatis, agreed with the Earl that Georgia needed a governor, or a resident Trustee concerned with the government.

Fitzwalter's letters of January and March were answered on July 15. The Trustees were glad to know that everything thrived so well in the garden. Fitzwalter's account of the country and soil was very agreeable to them "but at the same time they observe by Your own Relation, that a great deal of time has been spent in Shooting, which they are sorry for, and therefore they recommend it to You to employ it for the future in a manner that will be more useful both to Your self and the Colony."

Apparently it was not fitting that the pleasures of exploring their new homeland or hunting and fishing, which would supplement a monotonous food supply, should be enjoyed by "the poor." The Trustees directed that Paul Amatis was to have the chief direction of the garden while he was in the colony, and Fitzwalter was to obey Amatis's orders. If Amatis came to England, then Fitzwalter should have the care of the garden under the direction of the magistrates. Only one bright spot was apparent for Fitzwalter in these terse words: "Mr. Causton must pay Mr. Fitzwalter the Gardiner his Salary, as it was fix'd by Mr. Oglethorpe."[42]

Amatis was greatly elated when he received the news that he was to have the chief management of the garden in addition to "your Design of raising Silk in the Colony, for which you was sent." The Trustees reproved him for opposing the removal of the Trust servants from the garden for questioning in connection with the Red String Plot, and spoke of his having behaved in an extraordinary manner when he was expected to give all due obedience to the magistrates. The servants for the garden were to work under Amatis's direction and were to be employed there and nowhere else. None of the produce of the garden must be sold; it must be delivered to Storekeeper Causton, except for such as Amatis wished to have for his own family. Fitzwalter was vindicated by the instructions that plants must be delivered, under Causton's directions, to those whose land was ready for them, and receipts taken for them. The Trustees favored Amatis over Fitzwalter. Amatis had sent silk, and the Trustees' "hearts are set upon every thing that will contribute to the raising of Silk in Georgia."[43]

Amatis was now exalted and Fitzwalter made subordinate to him. Both men had been sure of their ground when the argument began. Both seemed to base their positions on instructions from Oglethorpe, who must have given conflicting verbal orders in the colony. He was present at the Trustees' meeting when Fitzwalter's and Amatis's letters were considered, and his advice would certainly have been asked and probably followed.[44] The Trustees thus changed the status of Fitzwalter, enlarged Amatis's status to an unworkable degree, endangered silk production, and decreed the fate of the garden.

Amatis wrote several letters to the Trustees before he knew of their decision. He was harassed, he was persecuted, he had money troubles. He wrote at length about silk production, yet he did not neglect to give news of the garden. The servants employed there were too few; he warned the Trustees that he would have to hire labor. When he did the Trustees refused to pay the bills, and Amatis was reproved for drawing them; but happily he was in ignorance of this when he wrote, although he had already involved himself financially in the work which he had done for the Trustees. If he hired men, he said, the reason would be "that you may have a Garden Pleasant Beautifull as well as Rich in its Productions for the Benefit in Genl of the Freeholders who at the Same time have the Pleasure to walk there on Sundays & Holydays & there see ye Plants & Trees they may Expect as Soon as they Cleard a Sufficient Quantity of Land."[45]

The soil in the top of the garden was sandy and must be improved. There ought to be two men constantly to water the garden. "I doubt not but you know that to have Such Large Garden as ten Acres taken care off & Improv'd, There must be an Assiduous Care & Necessary Persons & Therefore it Requires Four Domestick Servants at Least for two years Longer, for there must be a great deal of work done there during that time, It will be a great work to Clear the Lower part wch is a Swamp." If the Trustees would send him young trees, plants, and especially grapevines, he would take special care of them and not do as Fitzwalter did who "made Presents to I know not who. . . ."

Amatis inveighed strongly in each letter against Fitzwalter and Causton. It was now, he said in June, "about Six Months Since Fitzwalter has done any Service in your Garden and I dare him to Shew that he has done the Value of Five Pounds Sterling Service there. I thought Considering his Pay, he might have Endeavoured to have done something for it[.]" Here Amatis's spite for Fitz-walter caught him in a falsehood. Causton mentioned in July plac-ing certain servants in the garden to work under Fitzwalter. Amatis continued, "Please to Consider the Pains I have taken & Still Continue to take but I am Sorry that I am Obliged to Ac-quaint you that if Mr. Fitzwalter still remains in the Garden after the many Insults I have Received from him, I will Leave off Acting there, after I have Recd your Honnrs Orders. . . . I re-main for the present in this Colony only as a bird upon the branch ready to fly away into the place where it shall find more repose."[46]

So transitory a state was changed, however, by the arrival on July 21 of the Trustees' letters enlarging Amatis's authority. He immediately began to make plans for several years ahead. It would be about two years before the mulberry trees would be at their best but even now "The Trees & Plants in your Garden En-crease prodigiously to which My Continual Care, Labour & Fa-tigue are not a little Contributing; I am there from Sun Rising to Sun Setting Meals Excepted I am no Free Mason, nor a Member of any Clubb, I frequent No Dancing; neither do I Encourage any Caballs."

Causton and Fitzwalter were both masons along with gardener John Brownjohn and Francis Percy, who was sometimes em-ployed in the Trustees' garden.[47] Amatis's statement, "I live a Solitary Life like a Monk, let others live as they Please. . . . if all men here, were like me, there would not be So Much Vanity, & So Great Poverty as there is," was not agreed to by Edward Jenkins, who said that he judged Amatis an improper person to have the care of Peter Tondee's two orphaned sons, "By his ill Conduct of taking a scandilous wench to himself instead of a wife." Neither did Jenkins judge Fitzwalter's care of young John Goddard proper, though he assigned no reasons.[48]

When Fitzwalter wrote to London in July, 1735, before he knew the Trustees' decision about the garden, he said, "This is to Acquaint Your Honnours That I am Disapointed by Mr. Amatis in Carrying on the Business your Honnour Ordered, I wrote to your Honnours about the same . . . But have had no Instructions from your Honnours I always Apprehend the Ground was for Carrying on Botany and Kitchen physick, as Baby Nussary of plants, As for the silk Business I Know nothing of But, I do Assure Your Honnors as for a Tree, plant, or Any other Vegetable Mr. Amatis is a Stranger as much as him that never Knew any thing of the art of Gardening. . . ."[49]

Fitzwalter's idea of the garden as a "baby Nussary of plants" exactly coincided with that of the Trustees. "The Trustees have always designed it as a Nursery for such Productions as it is in the Interest of the Province to Cultivate, such as Mulberries, Vines, Olives &c., which were to be delivered out to the People as they could get their Grounds ready to Receive them."[50] This view was not changed.

Fitzwalter had important personal news also. "I hope Your Honnours will not Take it Amiss of my Marriage in this province without first Having Your Honnours Consent, The 8th of Aprill last I was Married by Mr. Quincey to Tuscanies Eldest Daughter Neice to, Skee. . . ." Mr. and Mrs. Causton, Mr. and Mrs. John West, Mr. and Mrs. Montaigut and others attended the wedding; Tomochichi gave the bride away; the Upper and Lower Creeks expressed satisfaction at the marriage.[51] Tuscaney and Skee were the two of Tomochichi's men who were appointed captains of the two companies of Indian militia which Oglethorpe organized in 1733. Skee had already received considerable mention for his sometimes intemperate habits and his association with Joseph Watson. Tuscaney's standing was better; when the news of his death was sent to England, he was spoken of as Captain Tuscaney, the beloved Indian. Both men were dead when Fitzwalter's letter was written.[52]

Elisha Dobree, who enjoyed sending news of the colony to London, succinctly announced the marriage: "Mr. Fitzwalter your Gardner was this week married to an Indian woman & soon after took Mr. Johnson who was running away from this Province for fear of a Debt of £5 stg."[53] Samuel Quincy was censured for performing the marriage service, but Oglethorpe reported to London the next year, after asking John Wesley to inquire into the circumstances of the marriage, "With respect to his marrying an Englishman to an Indian woman unbaptized, he was advised to do so by most of the people then in Savannah, [and by what I found in conversing with them] the generality of the people thought they had done a very pretty thing in getting an Intermarriage."[54] Fitzwalter himself said, "It is to be hop'd That Time will wear her of the Savage way of Living."

Since his marriage the Indians wanted Fitzwalter to go into the

Creek Nation to trade with them; he asked the Trustees' advice about this, being unwilling to do anything without their instructions. He would like to have the Trustees' permission to return to England next January to settle his affairs; he would then "Spend the Residue of my Time in Georgia as Long as God shall think fitt to spare life. . . ." He apologized for not sending the journal they wanted: "I Should have sent my Journall by Mr. West, but the Business of the Day being tiresome and Rest at night Reviveing for the Next Day Employ is the only Reason I Could not finish Time Enough to Come by him, but hope That I Shall bring it myself with a great Deal of Satisfaction to your Honnours[.]"

He continued to take an optimistic view of the colony: "The Ground produces Beyond Every Ones Expectation and Every Body is very Industrious upon their Lotts Both Town & Country in Generall, Bread Kind their will be Raised in this Year more than the Inhabitants Can Use, I have seen all in Generall and do believe it to be so. . . ." True, the spring had been hot and dry but the weather now was seasonable and, after all, he said philosophically, "I Cannot find but people in England are Subject to Fevers either Spring or fall as well as here so that when the Appointed Time Comes we must Submitt to him that made all things [.]"[55]

This is the last of his three known letters. Not long after writing this one the Trustees' letter arrived with the news that Amatis was to be in charge of the garden and with the terse words in answer to his about the wonders of the Georgia coast. These answers apparently dried up Fitzwalter; his enthusiasm could not blossom in the cold of displeasure from London.

Fitzwalter did not mention an affair detailed in another of the letters John West took to London. Thomas Gapen, who reached the colony on August 29, 1733, wrote concerning an affront to his honor and pride. One of the most memorable days in the life of the young colony was in June, 1735, when Tomochichi distributed to the Indians presents sent from England. Great preparations were made; the most delicate diplomacy was involved in details which should enhance Tomochichi's standing as the friend of Englishmen and create and preserve amity among the Creeks by tangible evidence of the King's and the Trustees' spirit of benevolence and justice to all who were on their side.

On Sunday, June 8, a dress rehearsal was held in Johnson

Square; the militia was mustered there and Gapen, who said that he was appointed some days before to bear the colors, was in his place. "Gentlemen you may be assured that not a Town in America can produce a more Willinger and Steadfast people both to Serve the King and Colony, then here is among us, Ready and Willing to run upon all Alarms for the good and Safety of the Colony."

How rude then was the shock on Monday, the great day when the Creeks came for their presents. Another appointee also appeared to bear the colors, and though younger than Gapen, claimed the senior post. The culprit was Joseph Fitzwalter. This was a serious matter, with the militia already drawn up both to honor and impress the Creeks. "I was resolved to maintain [the senior post] . . . ," Gapen said firmly. To settle so serious a matter, "we agreed to meet the next morning and try it by Point of Sword, but Mr. Fitzwalter did not think proper to face me, being willing to Sleep in a whole Skin. . . ." On the standard post in Johnson Square, the town's informal newspaper, on June 10 Thomas Gapen posted Joseph Fitzwalter as a coward. Someone must have told Gapen that duels were not countenanced in the colony, for he finished his account of the affair with an apology: "this Gentlemen is the whole truth of the affair . . . and I most Humbly beg Pardon of the Honble Trusstees for breaking through any Law, which they have Appointed relating to Duels, and hope they will please to forgive my rashness [.]"

He hoped never to trouble the Trustees with any complaints, Gapen continued; after detailing several more, he said, "My whole Study being to Labour and Work for the forwarding of the Town and Colony." He was the public butcher. He wrote of work done and plans made, particularly of the need of pasture on which to turn fat cattle brought from Carolina until time for them to be killed. He knew of one such piece of land which had "a good Honey Suckle bottom with Plenty of fresh water in ponds" and there too "Hogs might be bred in great numbers and at Small charge, the Land bearing Mostly Oak and Hickery Trees, with abundance of Chinkampen trees, whose nuts are the most Delightful food that the Hogs will feed on in the woods, and grow fat thereupon. . . ."[56]

Sometime after the Trustees' letters were received Fitzwalter left the colony. If he made the trip to England for which he asked permission in his last letter, no record of it survives. He did go to South Carolina, though the date of his leaving the colony is uncertain. He is mentioned as being in Georgia in the latter part of July. He may have remained until after the autumn term of court. He recognized that his position in the garden was now untenable and so left, probably to hunt other work.[57]

When Charles Wesley returned to England in July, 1736, he gave the Trustees an account of the garden: there was a good store of mulberry trees but none asked for as yet by the planters; the garden abundantly furnished the people of Savannah with cucumbers, melons, and vegetables; but the nurseries of trees had been ill managed by the former gardener [Amatis], whom Oglethorpe removed and replaced with Francis Percy.[58]

After Oglethorpe arrived in February, 1736, he was in Savannah but a short time, with many details there and at Ebenezer claiming his attention before he went down to found Frederica. In that time he must have discharged Amatis. The latter was thought early in March to have gone to England, but he returned to Savannah in April. He "took a disgust and settled chiefly at Charlestown," according to one account, "where he died," in December, 1736. His wife, Catherine, was married by John Wesley to Thomas Neal on February 27, 1737, in Savannah. They were said to have lived in Charles Town but Neal, in the next month after the marriage, was improving lot number four, Jekyl Tything, Savannah, which belonged to his wife's son, Paul Amatis, a child then too young to sign his name on the property listings.[59]

A report on Amatis's death was made by Mrs. Joseph Stanley, one of the *Ann's* passengers and the public midwife at Savannah. She went back to England and talked to the Trustees in March, 1737. A story was current that Amatis burned all of his silkworms and the silk machine before his death because the magistrate (presumably Causton) would not allow him when ill to see a priest. This was false, Mrs. Stanley said. She was with Amatis when he died, and he made no such demand; his wife, who had been his maid-servant, turned over the eggs and machine to the magistrates.[60] From this account, the better of the two, it would seem that Amatis died in Savannah.

Francis Percy worked in the garden most of the year 1737. Causton mentioned receiving bamboo canes and seed for the garden from the Trustees and turning these over to Percy. No gardener except Percy is mentioned in a schedule of expenses that summer; his pay was one shilling, six pence a day.[61] "Your Public Garden at present has a Melancholy Aspect; continuing much in the same State as Mr. Anderson found it, or as it was left by Piercy when he went off;", William Stephens wrote, "without any cultivation since of Note; wch in a little time would make it desolate. . . ."[62] Percy had gone before Stephens first mentioned him. He was gone before John Wesley left Georgia on December 2, 1737, according to Wesley. Egmont summed up Wesley's conversation thus, "Percy, our gardener, had left it on some distaste with Mr. Causton and the garden now under no care and half the trees dead, &c."[63]

Fitzwalter returned to the garden the latter part of December or early in January, 1738. He must have worked furiously, for Stephens, after remarking on the melancholy state of the garden in December, could say in January, "I wrote you in my last there was no appearance of much care taken . . . Mr. Anderson (who has the Inspection) not much heeding it . . . but of late I observe a great alteration: one Fitzwalter (a Freeholer) who was formerly gardener under Amytis, with whom he could not agree, & therefore left it, & has lived a rambling life since; He has now been employed there about 3 or 4 weeks; with a few hands; and having lately some additional help, he has reduced it into a decent Order again: I presume by Mr. Anderson's Directions, who comes sometimes to visit it. . . ."[64]

Hugh Anderson had arrived in the colony in the summer of 1737. In May, 1736, he talked to the Earl of Egmont, who described him as "a decent, considerate, and very intelligent gentleman." His liberal education had not fitted him for any profession; family misfortunes and money losses reduced him "so that he has now but 200£, which being too little to live on, he is resolved to go to Georgia. . . ." Two hundred pounds, Egmont told him, would barely cover the cost of the journey to Georgia for twelve people (himself, wife, five children, a maid, and four menservants), build two houses, buy tools, and maintain his family possibly two years in case he should lose the planting season the first year or a blight of squirrels should destroy his crops. Squirrels had a bad reputation in Georgia; a colonist lamented that "ye Squerills destroy'd me, three thousand hills of patatoes. . . ."[65]

Egmont warned that Anderson must not expect, in case these misfortunes attended him in Georgia, to be fed from the Trustees' store; nor could Anderson's request for an advance of money be granted. Egmont's advice to take only 200 acres of land (this being at the usual rate in the grants of fifty acres for each man-servant or working man taken over) and then take a larger grant later if all went well, was accepted as practical by Anderson. He wished also to have a town lot in Savannah "by reason his children are young and many," Egmont said, "and his wife, who is grand-daughter to an Earl, has been tenderly brought up, and would require some society."

Hugh Anderson, gentleman, of Bridge Castle, Scotland, received his grants and an appointment with a sonorous title which at his own request carried no salary: Inspector of the Public Gardens and of the Mulberry Plantations in Georgia. The appointment was made, the Trustees said, because they had a good opinion of Mr. Anderson.[66] It is uncertain what the Trustees expected from this appointment. They were not pleased at that time with the results for the garden from Robert Millar's expedition; Amatis's and Fitzwalter's letters showed conflict in their aims. It is probable that with Anderson the friend of one Trustee, the interest of another bespoken in his behalf, and his wife the grand-daughter of an earl, the appointment was made to give a little more dignity to one who had seen better days and hoped yet to see them again. The Trustees were somewhat susceptible to the influence of earls, and of their descendants.

Shortly after his arrival Anderson thanked Egmont for credit obtained at the Trustees' store in Savannah for twelve bushels of corn and 200 pounds of meat for himself and each of his servants for a year, in case he needed it. He promised to use credit no more than was absolutely necessary. He expressed himself optimistically about the colony and had sent a memorial on the state of the garden to Adam Anderson, one of the Trustees. As for himself, his expectations were not high nor his views ambitious: "I in no ways Despair through the Blessing of God upon the means of Sobriety and Industry to live with Contentment my Self and get needfull Education to my Children, and as what time can be Spared from the necessary affairs of Life, will be Spent in the Study of Nature, and Improvements, what Discoveries I can make with Certainty in my progress this way I shall presume to Communicate to your Lop [Lordships]."[67]

The Trustees replied that they had no doubt that with Anderson's care and industry the garden might soon be brought to a state which would answer their expectations. They always planned it as a nursery for productions of interest to the colony, such as mulberries, grapevines, and olives, which were to be delivered out to the people as soon as their ground was ready. The Trustees still had this plan for the garden and gave Anderson suggestions and instructions for its development.[68]

Misfortunes crowded upon Anderson. William Stephens wrote in the summer of 1738 that Anderson "was pretty active for a Season, in directing what he thought needfull; I am far from thinking his discontinuance of it would have been voluntary; but (poor Man) he & all his Family have been very long (some Months) in a very weak & sick condition which yet so far continues as to call for the Prayers of the Church. . . ."[69] Anderson said later that "two of my Servants deserted to Carolina four dyed out of my family twelve continued Sick a long time my Self after Six months of Illness given over by Physicians and a Charge of Sick-bed expenses included in the former of above 50£ Str." He was by that time convinced that the colony could not continue on the present footing and that he and others should be "chargeable with blame but that We could not effect impossibilities." He had cleared, enclosed, and planted fifteen acres with corn, potatoes, peas, rice, cotton, tobacco, and a nursery of plants. On this and the maintenance of his family he spent £150 sterling; the returns amounted to £6 sterling. "God forbid I should lay down my Case as a means to judge oyrs by, I hope few have Shared so many misfortunes, but I may be bold to Say that every Person has sustained losses and that none can pretend by his improvements to defray the fifth part of his necessary expendings." It was probable that "the particular difficulties of my Cituation may necessitate me to Seek bread for my family & Children in Some other Corner of the World before Measures for retriving the State of this Collony can be taken by the board. . . ." Egmont, in a long comment on this letter, remarked that "the chief purpose whereof was to set forth the bad state of the colony, and to prepare us for his retiring to settle with his family in Carolina, as he did soon after."[70]

Even before Anderson's misfortunes piled so thickly upon him and his dislike of the Trustees' system grew, the garden must not have been one of his chief concerns, if Stephens's remark that "he comes sometimes to visit it"[71] can be taken literally. Fitzwalter could hardly have been closely supervised. Stephens speaks of him several months later as the principal gardener; he must have been responsible alone for the furtherance of the garden. Stephens took a walk in the garden on the afternoon of Tuesday, February 14, 1738, and was pleased to set down in his journal later that "I was very glad to see so good a Progress made in putting all in due order again, after the sad Confusion it had been lately in."[72]

Fitzwalter had to contend with intemperate weather that spring of 1738. March was at first warm and sunny. Then suddenly appeared an "extream Variation of Weather," first a gale, then "such a sudden and severe Frost as is but seldom seen in the depth of Winter in England, Water standing in Pans or Basons within Doors, being frozen entirely into a solid Lump of Ice." It was no wonder that Fitzwalter and others feared for their young plants. Yet a visitor from Charles Town in the middle of April found the grapevines and trees in the garden flourishing, though "Some few of the Oranges had met with the Tail of a Blight wch. Demolished numbers in this Province."[73]

This good news about the garden was welcomed when it reached London. The Trustees already knew that Fitzwalter had returned, for Captain William Thomson reported so when his ship, the *Two Brothers,* was in port in April. Egmont noted Captain Thomson's remarks that "through Mr. Anderson's care (inspector of the public garden) the same is putting again into order, and that Fitzwalter, formerly gardener, and who ran away to Carolina, is returned and employed therein."[74] The Trustees were always pleased to hear that anyone found South Carolina inferior to Georgia. Too few were of this opinion.

Captain Henry Daubuz sailed the *Georgia Pink* from the colony in March, and upon his arrival in England in June, told the Trustees that the garden was in a miserable condition, with such inferior soil that nothing would grow. Egmont added in some bewilderment: "Yet Mr. Jenys wrote us that our garden is in good order." Captain Daubuz's entire report was most unfavorable to conditions and people in Georgia.[75]

Fitzwalter had to see his plants contend not only with an unkind spring, but with a summer of great severity. "The Heat was so excessive," Stephens wrote in June, "that few People dared stir Abroad; the like not having been known before, since the first Comers settled (as they reported) so early in the year." A Carolina visitor provided a dramatic affirmation; he com-

plained of the heat after dinner one day in Savannah, sat down in
a chair, and died. Stephens late in August said, "The Heats were
now grown very sultry, and People begin to find the ill Effect of
them, several falling down frequently in Fevers, &c."[76]

Two substantial changes occurred in Fitzwalter's life in this
year 1738. He re-married. Molly, his Indian bride, the records
say, "ran from him."[77] Fitzwalter's second marriage was to
one of those Georgia widows who usually remarried quickly after
the first husband's death.

John and Penelope Wright with their children, John and Elizabeth, sailed on the *Ann*. John Wright was a vintner. Little is
heard of him after his arrival in Georgia. He was a member of
the first jury, empanelled in July, 1733. He had a license to
keep a public house which the Trustees revoked at one time because he refused to allow the rum in his house to be staved in
accordance with an order that all in the colony must be disposed of. Wright was mentioned with some astonishment by John
Brownfield, the registrar, because he was the only man of those
interviewed in the spring of 1737 who wanted to keep his swamp
lot, which was on the river below the Trustees' garden. Such lots
certainly were not in demand. They overflowed; labor required to
improve them was greater than most colonists could afford;
they could not be cultivated in accordance with the Trustees' requirements. It was only after slavery was introduced, giving an
impetus to the cultivation of rice, that part of this land became
valuable.[78]

John Wright died in December, 1737.[79] Fitzwalter married
Penelope Wright at some time before the following August. In
mentioning the marriage, William Stephens's remarks concerning Fitzwalter were most uncomplimentary. Commenting upon
Hugh Anderson's illness, Stephens remarked that the garden
was much neglected, and that the principal gardener under Anderson, "one Fitzwalter, a Freeholder of this Town, deserves
certainly the Character of an Idle Fellow; and as he could never
stick long to any thing commendable, he perseveres in the same
loose way of Life; wch I apprehend he'll not easily break from
now; having married the Widow of one Wright, who had a License for keeping a Public House, where he naturally takes most
delight."[80]

Stephens seems somewhat less than just in these remarks. He
had been in the colony less than a year; he had no personal

knowledge of Fitzwalter's earlier work in the garden, his knowledge of gardening, his progress under disadvantageous conditions.
Fitzwalter, by leaving the colony to seek work in the neighboring province when the situation with Amatis became untenable,
merited the discredit, by prevailing standards, of having run
away to Carolina. Stephens, to the end of his life, looked with a
prejudiced eye on public houses. He thought that trouble-makers
in the colony hatched most of their schemes in the public houses,
and he was never one to look with a kindly eye on tippling.

Still, Fitzwalter, however ardent the attachments influencing
his second marriage, lost nothing economically. In addition to the
possibly great attractions of Georgia widows, a man who married
one was apt to reap some benefit from her first husband's labors.
In Fitzwalter's case, the re-instated Wright public house license
was not to be regarded lightly. As poor as the colony was, some
money could be made in this business. The public house was an
anchor to windward and proved so shortly.

By the Trustees' directions those selling beer, small beer, ale,
wine, cider, or any liquors at retail in quantities under twenty
gallons were sutlers, who must be licensed by the Trustees. Sutlers could keep ordinaries and sell victuals and provisions to be
eaten on the premises but they could sell no drygoods or any articles usually kept in shops. After one of the *Ann's* passengers,
Richard Hodges, died in the summer of 1733, his wife was told
when she wanted a license to sell beer, that if she accepted this,
she must give up the shop which she ran. Only sutlers could vend
liquors and all who had such licenses were required to give accommodations to travellers.[81]

Thus Joseph and Penelope could have had some income from
the thirsty at home and travellers coming to Savannah. Whether
they kept an ordinary is not known. If Fitzwalter took most delight, to quote Stephens's gibe, in their public house, it was more
probably the sensible fostering of a little business from which
a livelihood could be eked, rather than the consumption of his
own stock, which no poor man could afford. There is no mention
anywhere that Fitzwalter embarked on so uneconomical a course.
Probably he made a genial host.

CHAPTER NINE

Thomas Christie, Recorder

$\mathbf{A}$NOTHER of the *Ann's* passengers involved in the 1738 events was Thomas Christie, who came over with commissions as conservator of the peace and recorder of the court at Savannah. The court's authority was vested in the bailiffs, or magistrates, and the recorder; the latter's duties were not specifically differentiated from those of the magistrates. Christie's verbal orders from Oglethorpe were to keep an exact journal of all proceedings in court and everything else worth notice, and a record of warrants and writs.[1] Christie himself spoke of "we" in the proceedings of the court and seemed to have assumed no prerogative not considered rightfully his. The Trustees spoke of him as a magistrate and reminded an objector to this point of view that they had always so considered Christie. Not until a new recorder was appointed after the upheaval in the magistracy were the duties of the office more carefully defined, as taking the minutes of the court and keeping the records, and the new officer told that the Trustees never intended the recorder to be considered as a magistrate.[2]

Christie was a thirty-two-year-old merchant when he sailed on the *Ann* from England with his seventeen-year-old servant, Robert Johnson. Christie's wife, Elizabeth, remained in England though a lot was granted to her in Savannah in 1736.[3] Christie's life seems to have proceeded evenly enough in the early years of the colony; his few letters are informative and interesting. Late in 1734 he spoke of having rheumatism in his right arm and side to such an extent that he was hampered in making up his court records and in writing letters, but that did not prevent him from making some discerning comments on the colony.

Because many people did not yet know the boundaries of their lands, Christie said, they neglected their fencing, and most of the crops sowed the previous summer were eaten by cows and horses trampling over them. Corn and other seeds left by Oglethorpe in the storehouse for the people were musty and damaged so that much planted never came up. "I think if I had not represented this you might have been too Severe in blaming your Peoples Neglect. And indeed we have Some people who never were Masters of any Land and whose heads are turn'd no ways but to the Ale house and others are So Idle to think of nothing but Selling & running away. . . . Its certain that people being baulked as I said before in the Cultivation of their Lands did mostly turn upon Building & Improving their Lotts in Town. So that there is few Town Lotts but what are built or are building, the Town is greatly Encreased So that Whereas at first I could hardly See any thing but Trees I can now Scarce see any Trees for Houses."

Some people were trying crops to find which might be best suited to the climate: fruit trees, grape vines, corn, and cotton. Others were trying to produce pitch and tar. But, Christie observed, it would be a considerable time before any of these could be brought to perfection, "and we Shall always be poor & needy till we are able to make Exports of our own. . . ." Savannah, he thought, might "easily be made a Mart between North America & England & England & the Antilles, & the Spanish West Indies, which might prove of prodigious Advantage to this Place and I dare Say when once the Lighthouse is Finished this Trade will Entroduce it Self but in the mean time it Seems to me nothing can keep us alive but the Building of a Church & other Publick Buildings, the Raising of our Fortifications, The Indian Trade & the Fresh Embarkations of Mon'd men. . . ."

Christie noted improvements in Savannah. "We have Finished the New Guard house mounted four peices on New Large Carriages handsomely painted besides five ps fixt in a Platform & designed for a Salute besides four others on ye old Carriages. . . . We have likewise Paled all the strand in and new built the Stairs down ye Bluff & paled it in. wch together wth the Chimneys being almost Finished gives a good Grace to the Place." Mr. Montaigut had opened his store next to Oglethorpe's Savannah house and sold goods for ready money; brick making progressed;

Christie himself had set up a brewhouse "wch Seems to be the only way to bring the people off from Drinking Spirituous Liquors," and he had introduced a fishing trade by which people were supplied with quantities of fish from the Savannah River. Finally, he wished Oglethorpe would find someone else to take the office of recorder, giving as his reason his affliction with rheumatism.[4]

Peter Gordon took those letters to England in the spring of 1735 and himself made a long list of complaints about the colony, one of which was that Christie sold rum.[5] Gordon was not the only one who so charged Christie. The Trustees, however much they disapproved of Gordon's own conduct, were quick to demand answers of his accusations. They reproved Christie for an "odd Paragraph" in his letter "about sending over Embarkations of Money'd Men. The Industry of the People in cultivating their Lands is what they are to depend on for their subsistance." People's industry in cultivation was "the best & indeed the only Method to make them happy, and procure them whatsoever they may really want, or will be necessary for them. . . ."[6] Earthly happiness and success in Georgia was to be secured by cultivating the lots assigned—swamp, pine barren, or good soil.

Christie denied the charge of selling rum, met other complaints in Gordon's letters, asked for a grant of 500 acres so he could live outside of Savannah, and requested again to be relieved of his office of recorder.[7] A man could not quit his office without permission from the Trustees, and this was not given. The tone of these two letters of Christie's is quite different from the tone of the one he had written the preceding December; sometimes a man who was reproved by the Trustees either stopped writing or thereafter told the Trustees largely what they wanted to hear.

Christie now had help in the recorder's office, for the Trustees sent over William Russell, a young man bound to Christie, who had arrived the preceding December on the *Prince of Wales*, Captain George Dunbar. Russell was later transferred to work on accounts in the Trustees' store and evidently rose steadily in the estimation of those with whom he was associated. Even Thomas Jones did not speak ill of him; "a sober youth," Jones said in 1740, "whom I employ in writing for me."[8] Russell was married in February, 1745, William Stephens remarked approvingly, "to a young Damosel of Modest Behaviour and a good Character, which is looked on among us as a good Fortune here." Russell held several offices and in 1752 was appointed a magistrate by the Trustees, an office which he did not accept.[9]

When William Stephens arrived in the colony in the autumn of 1737 he found the officers of the court not very enthusiastic about their duties. John Wesley and some of his friends had used court days to address the people on their rights as Englishmen, so that the magistrates and recorder "had been divers Times apprehensive of being mobb'd and turned off the Bench." Christie and Henry Parker expressed themselves plainly to Stephens concerning their troubles in office for which they had not been recompensed and on which they had to spend much time. Christie was then determined to quit his office but acceded to Stephens's request that he wait a while longer.[10]

In the midst of urging economy on the colony, the Trustees decided in the summer of 1737 to "show their Favour to the Town" as well as give "more Weight and Distinction to the Court" by having the magistrates wear gowns in court, "those for the Bailiffs be Purple edg'd with Furr, and that for the Recorder be black tufted." [11] Henry Parker saw the absurdity of his wearing a purple fur-edged gown to cover the worn and poor clothing to which his needy state had reduced him and asked Stephens how well this fine gown would fit his mean apparel. Conversation about the gowns, evidence of office which neither Causton nor Christie wanted, was so prolonged when the court met on November 22, 1737; that it did not begin official session until the next day. Stephens should not have been surprised that Christie showed so little enthusiasm for the gowns or that he again expressed his determination to quit his office as recorder which "took up almost his whole Time, for which he had no other Recompence than to bear the Brunt of all Clamour, and was esteemed . . . Mr. Causton's Tool;. . ." Not until court sat on January 9, 1738, were the gowns worn.[12]

Christie was evidently in some uncertainty as to his future course. Family affairs needed his attention in England, but he could not leave without permission lest he displease the Trustees. He considered leaving Georgia, taking up land in Carolina, and establishing a fishery there. However, he decided against this and, after his return from inspecting land in Carolina, decided to improve what he had in Georgia and live on it, renting his house in Savannah, and keeping only one room in town, "where he purposed to be in certain Days, for executing his office as a

Magistrate. . . ." His consideration of these different plans led
Stephens to say that he was "A Man of competent Knowledge in
many Things, but unstable in all his Ways." Stephens did not
mention (perhaps he was ignorant of the fact) that so late as
1737 Christie's farm lot of 45 acres had not been surveyed and
determined for him.[13]

Captain William Thomson, in England in the spring of 1738,
commended Christie to the Trustees as being very zealous for the
colony; but to offset this was the report from Georgia that Christie was "suspected" of having taken lands in Carolina.[14] Anyone
suspected of preferring Carolina to Georgia dropped in the Trustees' estimation. However, as an encouragement to him, if he continued in the office of recorder the Trustees allowed Christie the
use of two indentured servants maintained by the Trust. Christie
assigned these indentures to Patrick Graham. Stephens remarked
that it was "an artful Contrivance of making a Penny (as he had
many others). . . ." The fact that Christie had been also allowed
an entire family as servants may have indicated that he did not
need the labor of the two additional servants.[15]

In late 1737 only two magistrates were serving, Causton and
Henry Parker. The third, John Dearn, had died in July, 1737.
Little is known about Dearn who was spoken of by the Scots as
a man nearly seventy years old and "crazed both in Body and
Mind. . . ."[16] Oglethorpe while in England recommended Robert Gilbert, a tailor in Savannah, who was appointed to the office
of third magistrate on May 3, 1738. Gilbert and his family had
arrived in Georgia on May 16, 1733, at their own expense. He
went back to England for a time, and on his return to Georgia
early in 1737 the Trustees loaned him money for his passage.[17]

Gilbert seems to have lived a quiet life, though some unsavory
gossip was attached to his daughter Elizabeth (Betty), who married William Mears, a sawyer.[18] The Gilberts were staunch ad-
mirers of John Wesley. Early in 1738 after Wesley left the colony
news went around Savannah that Mrs. Mears had, before Wesley's
departure, confessed to him her marital infidelity and received
absolution from him. Charles Delamotte, the only one remaining
of the original group of four missionaries, was not dismayed at
the subsequent charges by some people that this absolution proved
Wesley's Romish tendencies. Instead he related the details to
Wesley. Betty's confession took place at a night meeting at the
minister's house. The next minister, William Norris, said the

people at these meetings made no contribution to religion but practiced such things as public confession, penance, and absolution and were believed to be leaning toward Popery.[19]

Robert Gilbert was sworn in as bailiff in Savannah on October 16, 1738, the day before Oglethorpe's speech which so upset the colony. Georgia never had a more reluctant official. His reluctance to assume office was a personal one; he could not read or write. Even before he took the oath of office, he protested against accepting the place: "he thought himself by no means capable of discharging the Duty of such an Officer; for as much as he could neither read, nor write his own Name; and was not willing therefore to bring himself into contempt among his Neighbours wth whom he now livd in peace and quiet. . . ." [20] The appointment was a cruel one for Gilbert. The report went back to the Trustees that "it was a surprise and a jest our making Gilbert the tailor a magistrate." Oglethorpe arrived in Savannah on October 10, six days before Gilbert was sworn in and surely long enough, even in the midst of all the business he must transact to effect the major changes about to occur in the colony, to have heard Gilbert's plea against taking office.[21]

After October 17, when Causton was deposed as first magistrate, Henry Parker and Gilbert were on the bench with Christie continuing as recorder.[22] Parker was given to bouts of drunkenness but was a man spoken of generously by his friends, who held for him an affectionate esteem; others said that he was a man of no education and "an *absolute* Slave to Liquor. . . ." [23] Gilbert's appointment did little towards solving the problem of creating a respectable bench. His reputation as a magistrate was that he was ready to join in doing his duty, but was incapable in many respects. He was so miserable in the office that he had a letter written to the Trustees asking to be discharged and sent a verbal message to England by a relative, to the effect that he believed it would kill him to continue as a magistrate. So fervent an appeal was heeded when the Trustees removed him from office in May, 1739, and appointed John Fallowfield magistrate. A few weeks later Thomas Jones, the new storekeeper, was made third bailiff. Gilbert was "removed as an Improper Person for executing that Office, the Trustees being also assured he accepted the Office with Reluctance."[24] Gilbert must have been a happy man when the news of his release reached the colony later that year. He had had enough of Georgia, and the next summer he and his wife went to settle in Pennsylvania, making the trip with George Whitefield. Stephens said of him at his removal that he was "a sober, quiet man, doing no Harm, nor much Good, . . . he has found a Place [in Georgia] where he could live and make money;. . ." [25] Tailors were few and needed in Georgia.

Christie survived as the only one of the original court not removed by these fluctuations in the magistracy, though he was affected by the changes in the temper of the colony after October, 1738. He was one of those who signed the representation in December of that year, as did Henry Parker and Robert Gilbert. The Trustees reproved the magistrates that they should so far forget their duty as to join in petitioning for change of land tenure and the introduction of slaves and by telling the Trustees that the colony could never succeed as then regulated. [26]

The year 1739 was a hard one in the colony. General uneasiness was evident in and around Savannah after the events of the preceding October; both the people in Georgia and the Trustees paid dearly for the Trustees' abrupt and sweeping changes promulgated in Oglethorpe's speech. William Stephens spoke of "this gloom," and summed up the general state of affairs early in 1739 when he remarked that since Oglethorpe's disclosure of "the miserable Circumstances the Colony was under; it cannot but be shocking to men of the best Dispositions, when Want stares us in the face, far more terrible than any Spanish Threats." The sudden closing of the Trustees' store disrupted the economic fabric of the town. Crops in the autumn of 1738 were poor, because of the drought and inferior or damaged seed supplied to the colonists. The early spring vegetables were menaced by cold worse than ever seen in Savannah before. Water standing outdoors froze two inches thick, and inside, where a fire burned all day, ink congealed in the standish and the chamber pot froze under the bed. [27]

Fortunately the weather did not continue so extreme. Other discomforts were longer lived. Stephens remarked that some, "who in these times of Difficulty, instead of uniting to allay the present Discomposures, have joynd in stirring up Discontents to that degree, yt I might as well hope to asswage the raging of the Sea, as the Madness of the People." The more he thought of the representation, the worse it seemed. The scarcity of provisions was growing every day and people were suspected of killing cattle in the woods for food. Several robberies were reported. [28]

The general unease was not lessened by the behavior of Thomas Jones. It is true that Jones, coming as he did to replace Causton as storekeeper and having authority to make the inventory, was not in the most enviable position. Friends of Causton resented his treatment, and also resented Jones's somewhat high-handed procedure in many matters. Jones was known to be close to Oglethorpe—exactly how close nobody knew. Many suspected that besides being the storekeeper, he was an informer to Oglethorpe and the Trustees. Jones himself said that he had powers to make himself feared.[29]

The dislike of the magistrates and Christie for Jones grew during the spring of 1739. Christie was affronted by Jones's rudeness to him and angrily expressed his resentment. Magistrates Henry Parker and Gilbert joined Christie in expressing to Stephens their growing animosity towards Thomas Jones, who, they said, treated them like servants, expecting them to come whenever he called them and to act as he dictated, yet never thinking sufficient deference was paid to him. Christie and Parker thought no deference was paid to them, that Jones's treatment of them was making the magistracy contemptible in the eyes of the people, and that his petty means of showing his resentment was irksome. Christie said that he would leave for England; Parker asserted that he would never again as a magistrate wait on Thomas Jones. Both declared themselves not obliged to do as Jones demanded.[30]

Jones regarded Parker as a friend of Thomas Causton and any friend of Causton's was opprobrious to Jones. Since he had left England when the full weight of the Trustees' disapproval bore upon Causton, with instructions to replace him as storekeeper and ferret out all manner of crimes, Jones could see Causton and his friends only in the harshest light. By the spring of 1739 Parker recognized that Jones was his inveterate enemy, determined to ruin his reputation with the Trustees.[31] Jones scattered epithets and threats around Savannah, which, being a gossipy place, repeated everything that he said. His lack of discretion was emphasized by his showing around town a letter in which he wrote to the Trustees a serious complaint concerning Parker's drunken action. Stephens, minimizing the affair, termed it a foolish frolic at Edward Jenkins's public house.[32]

When Jones's letter reached England, the Trustees did not pursue their usual course of returning complaints to the colony to be answered. They were ready to remove Gilbert as a magistrate at his own request. First, they moved Thomas Christie from the recordership up to the position of third bailiff. Shortly afterward they unanimously removed Henry Parker as first bailiff for drunkenness, degrading his office, and because as first magistrate Parker might have power to save Causton if the latter should be brought to trial in the colony—all suggestions made by Jones. Christie was then appointed first magistrate, John Fallowfield second magistrate, Thomas Jones third, and William Williamson recorder. That he had signed the representation of December, 1738, was given as one of the reasons for removing Parker. Yet Christie, who had also signed, was elevated to the office of first magistrate. Christie was also appointed to replace Parker as one of the commissioners for stating the public debt.[33] Thomas Jones was enjoined, in his office of third magistrate, to pay due respect to and consult with William Stephens and as a magistrate "as much as in You lyes encourage the other Magistrates to Act in Conjunction with You by an affable and courteous Behaviour, which is the most proper Endearment for producing the Respect due to such an Office."[34] This was but one of several injunctions to Jones to mind his manners.

Christie as first bailiff was to have a salary of £30 a year and an allowance of £24.6.8 yearly to clothe and maintain two servants. He was instructed to send copies of the court proceedings not already forwarded to the Trustees up to the time when Williamson was sworn in as recorder.[35] The Trustees' instructions to William Stephens said that Christie was to make up his court records and then Stephens was to deliver to him his constitution as first bailiff. This conditional phrasing was not employed in the letter to Christie, or to Oglethorpe informing him of these changes, or to Williamson.[36]

Captain William Thomson's ship, the *Two Brothers*, bearing these letters which were to cause so great a contention in the colony, came to anchor outside the bar at Tybee on October 7. Oglethorpe was in Savannah, having arrived on September 23 from his trip into the Indian country undertaken to assure the loyalty of the Creeks, Choctaws, and Chickasaws, in the event of war with Spain.[37] News of this war reached Savannah on September 8 by a sloop from Rhode Island. It was exciting and disturbing intelligence, with St. Augustine so close by. Other disquieting news was that of a Negro revolt in South Carolina,

known as the Stono Rebellion. Lieutenant Governor Bull asked
Oglethorpe's vigilance in intercepting any straggling Negroes
and Spaniards.[38]

War with Spain was proclaimed in solemn manner on October 3, 1739, in Savannah. The beat of drums called the people
together, the freeholders under arms. At noon the magistrates
in their gowns took their places on the bench. Oglethorpe arrived and took his place on the bench with the magistrates. The
militia, drawn up outside the building, then entered. Oglethorpe
assured the people of preparations for their protection against
the enemy and complimented them on their cheerfulness in the
face of danger. He told them of his plan to besiege St. Augustine
and was reported to have promised that if he did not take that
place he would leave his bones before its walls. Stephens then read
the declaration of war. This declaration was fixed to the door of
the building so that people might read at leisure of the dangers
which confronted them and exercise the vigilance requested by
South Carolina in looking out for runaway Negroes and lurking
Spaniards. When Oglethorpe left the building, five cannon were
fired and the militia "gave three handsome Vollies with their
small Arms, as it were in Defiance, without the Appearance of
any Dread of the Spaniards." [39] Georgia thus announced herself
at war with the Spanish.

Captain Thomson's ship brought letters from England four
days later. War with Spain took second place as the news spread
of the change in the magistracy. Stephens, always alert to savor
the temper of the people, thought they were disposed to be
pleased and to obey whatever orders the Trustees gave for the
government. Christie and Stephens had lately had some disagree-
ments on procedure, and Stephens now brought to bear all his
arguments against Christie as first magistrate. Stephens doubted
whether the court records, which he thought were confused, could
ever be brought into acceptable form. People who approved of
Christie's appointment as first magistrate Stephens scorned as
"that mischievous Assembly at Jenkins's . . . that Rump of an almost worn-out Party," referring partially to those who had signed
the representation of 1738, with whom Christie had associated
himself. This statement by Stephens was well calculated to rouse
the Trustees against Christie and would certainly disgust Oglethorpe, who was known to have hard feelings against all who
signed the representation. Stephens brought another charge

against Christie. The appointment was a little shocking because of Christie's "scandalous living in open Adultery with a Man's Wife (Richard Turner) who run away hence to the West Indies a while ago. . . ."[40]

Talk went around Savannah that some plan was on foot to change the Trustees' orders; that "some Craft was at the Bottom to destroy their Liberties;", and plans were made to put Christie on the bench by force if he could not be seated otherwise. Stephens's conferences with Oglethorpe resulted in the calling of all freeholders to attend court. Upon its convening on October 15, Stephens, by Oglethorpe's orders, delivered their constitutions as second and third magistrates to John Fallowfield and Thomas Jones, but also by Oglethorpe's order, withheld Christie's. The reason given was that Christie had not completed his court records. Oglethorpe further ordered that Parker continue as first bailiff and Christie as recorder until the Trustees' pleasure was known. Matters proceeded in an orderly fashion and no disturbance ensued that day.[41] At least three men must have been greatly disturbed. Parker, ignominiously dismissed by the Trustees, was made by Oglethorpe to retain his place. Christie, appointed to sit in Parker's place, was not allowed to occupy it. Thomas Jones, no doubt pleased at his honor and increase of power by accession to the magistracy, saw Parker, the man against whom he had written so plainly, retain a position superior to Jones's new office. It was the influence of Stephens rather than Jones which prevailed upon Oglethorpe.

In appointing William Williamson the recorder, the Trustees unknowingly named a man who no longer lived in Georgia. Williamson came from his new home in South Carolina, but his office was refused to him by Stephens until Christie made up his records. Christie said that his records were completed but that he would not deliver them to Stephens; he would give or send them himself to the Trustees. Williamson returned to Carolina, Oglethorpe later remarking disparagingly of him, "I found by his Conversation that he was very much of a Lawyer. . . ."[42]

The affair lingered in the colonists' minds, causing dissension and complaints to the Trustees that Stephens did not carry out their orders. It strengthened those who complained of how badly the colony was managed, and created new political alliances. Henry Parker seems to have taken little part in these; in his unenviable position of being thrust back into a position from which he had been dismissed and knowing himself to be the target of much talk in Savannah, he must have been humiliated and distressed. In his uneasy position, from which he might be dismissed again when the Trustees were heard from, he would not act except on such occasions as his presence was absolutely necessary as a magistrate.[43]

When Christie did deliver the sealed court records to Stephens in December for transmittal to the Trustees, Stephens still refused to give Christie his authorization as first magistrate, alleging that the records could not be complete and that his orders from Oglethorpe were that matters should remain as they were until the Trustees could be heard from. Stephens forwarded the court records to London in January.[44]

The year 1740 opened with Jones and Stephens in alliance, determined to keep Christie off the bench, and supporting Parker. Stephens acknowledged that Jones, "tho' upon a Pett at one time taken against him," might have written hard words against Parker, but Jones now knew Parker better. The truth came out, perhaps inadvertently, when Stephens remarked that Jones "is very sensible that upon Christies sitting the First on the Bench, such a Conjunction would ensue betwixt Two (right or wrong) yt. there would be no occasion of him for a Third." Jones would find himself lessened in power with Christie and Fallowfield together on the bench; it behooved him to support Parker at the expense of Christie and hope that the Trustees would follow Oglethorpe's disposition of the matter. Strong recommendations for Parker's continuance on the bench were sent to England by Oglethorpe to justify his changing the Trustees' orders. He stressed that Parker had left off drinking; Stephens and Jones, somewhat more tepidly but still surprisingly gracious for Jones, agreed with Oglethorpe. Jones worked in a slap at Christie which was to give the Trustees a reason, or perhaps an excuse, for subsequent action. Christie had granted Adrian Loyer a permit to go to Port Royal, South Carolina, after permission was refused by Parker.[45] Whether Christie knew of Parker's refusal is not indicated.

Shortly after the letters reached England in March, 1740, the Trustees suspended Christie as recorder, revoked Williamson's commission, and appointed John Pye to that office during Christie's suspension. They revoked Christie's appointment as first magistrate and re-appointed Henry Parker. The Trustees gave

Christie as their reasons for this action his granting the permit to Adrian Loyer and his not having made up his accounts with the store.[46] These changes were received in Savannah on June 6, 1740, and Henry Parker was again constituted first magistrate on August 15.[47] The uproar in court the following day, while not attributable to Parker's re-instatement, was an evidence of the low esteem into which the court in Georgia had fallen.[48]

Christie was gone from the colony before these events, however. He was gone before the Trustees' action and the letters written in England concerning it. Undoubtedly the arrival of Stephens's Journal with the first mention of Christie and Mrs. Turner, after Christie's commission as first magistrate was received in Georgia, had much to do with Christie's dismissal. Egmont summed up Stephens's remarks as "Mr. Christie gives offence, living in open adultery."[49]

When Thomas Christie's affair of the heart with Mrs. Richard Turner began is unknown. Neither is it clear to what extent political capital was made of it. Turner, a carpenter, and his wife arrived on December 16, 1733, on the *Savannah*, Captain Lionel Wood. Their son, apparently their only child, died two months after their arrival. Turner has already been mentioned in connection with the Mellichamp case. He was in other trouble, also. He could not be said to meet the Trustees' requirements for an industrious man; by the summer of 1738 he had planted but one acre of his five-acre lot. Because of his lack of enthusiasm for agricultural pursuits he was judged by Stephens "to be ranked among the least deserving. . . ." Turner left Georgia and his wife for the West Indies in 1739.[50]

Stephens's first mention of Christie's enchantment with Mrs. Turner came in the autumn of that year. The affair seems to have progressed, at least in Stephens's opinion, for he remarked a little later: "Mr. Christie not thinking it convenient (I suppose) to be observed going out, and coming in, so frequently to his Doxy, Mrs. Turner, at her House here, thought it best to remove to his Hut on the Lot, about two Miles off: So sent her with Bed and Bedding, &c. before, following her soon after."[51] Stephens could not let it alone, observing five days later in November, immediately before closing this installment of his Journal to send to England that Thomas Jones informed him "that the Report of Mr. Christie's Intention to quit the Colony, began to find a little more Credit than hitherto; and some People are inclined to believe it; as also that he would take his Beloved with him."[52]

Christie left Georgia in March, 1740, accompanied by Mrs. Turner and Mr. and Mrs. Theophilus Hetherington of Thunderbolt, who were going to Carolina to join their brother Joseph.[53] Thomas Jones, in a letter to a friend sent through the Trustees' office and left open so that it could be read, asserted that Christie absconded, and accused him of being heavily in debt and of other financial variations. Jones asserted that Christie brought a concubine with him from England and left her for Mrs. Turner.[54] The Trustees must have been astonished at this charge of concubinage on the *Ann,* a charge which does not seem very probable.

Christie went to Charles Town to wait for a ship for England. In Thomas Jones's opinion, he "lurked about Charles Town," and the report reached England that Christie was in Carolina with his mistress on his way to London.[55] He reached London in June and presented a long memorial to the Trustees supported by affidavits, concerning his ill treatment by Stephens and Jones, services he had performed and money owing to him, and asserting his ability to vindicate himself. That Mrs. Turner came over to England on the same ship with him was due, he said, to her employment as a servant by Mrs. Carteret of Frederica. He said that he avoided her company on the passage over.[56]

The commissioners for stating the public debt in Georgia, of whom Stephens and Thomas Jones were the majority members, had found Christie in debt to the Trustees to the amount of £30. Christie's accounts showed that the Trustees owed him £100. Jones ridiculed the idea that Christie was owed this money. However, the Trustees found Christie's accounts correct, and the balance he claimed was paid to him. At his request the Trustees leased to him a tract of approximately 200 acres on the Savannah River upon which he said he had spent £60 in improvements.[57]

Christie had several conversations with the Earl of Egmont concerning the needs and possibilities of the colony. He remarked that Thomas Jones "was a severe passionate man," but complimented Stephens. Dining by invitation at Egmont's home, Christie showed the Earl the manuscript of a pamphlet which he had lately finished and intended to print anonymously in answer to criticism of the colony in England. Christie's pamphlet was published in April, 1741; one printed in London that year entitled *A Description of Georgia, by a Gentleman Who Has Resided There Upwards of Seven Years, and was One of the First Settlers* is attributed to Christie.[58]

At Christie's request to be appointed naval officer at Savannah, the Trustees recommended him to the Commissioners of the Customs. They had some reservations among themselves, remembering "the frequent bad characters given of him by Col. Stephens," but it was an advantage to have some one able to give security in England, and so they recommended him.[59] Christie did not pursue the matter, however, for in the meantime he had heard that Thomas Jones had seized his house in the colony for debt, "wherefore he resolv'd never to return to Georgia whilst Jones remain'd there." He changed his mind, gave the security, and received the appointment from the Commissioners of the Customs in the summer of 1742. In August he went to bid Egmont good-bye. The opening sentence of his farewell letter to Trustee James Vernon is strikingly like the closing one of *A Description of Georgia*. "I am goeing into a Country wch. I Intend not as a Visit but an Abode for life. . . ."[60] His ending to the pamphlet is: "and am going there in order to spend the remainder of my life." Perhaps he did.

Christie arrived in Charles Town in November, 1742, and was expected soon in Savannah. A month passed and still he did not come. Stephens remarked that in Charles Town Christie "remains the same insignificant poor Man that he always was, and scarcely to be confided in by any body."[61] Christie had not always been a poor insignificant man in Georgia but Stephens had a fund of malice upon which to draw where Christie was concerned. After all, what could be expected of any one who preferred to remain in Charles Town when he could come to Georgia?

One reason for Stephens's disparagement may have been that Christie was known to have resumed his friendship with "the Scotch" from Georgia now living in Charles Town, people thoroughly hated and distrusted by Stephens. The following year Stephens had no more news of Christie to pass on to London than to send a copy of a letter from Christie and to remark that "he lives there [Charles Town] as a Clerk or Writer under some Persons to me unknown."[62]

What Thomas Christie did in Charles Town is not clear except that he was concerned in the writing of a pamphlet or book which was advertised in the autumn of 1743 as planned for publication in Charles Town, entitled *The Progress of Methodism in Bristol: Or the Methodists unmasked,* an appendix to which was "The Paper-Controversy between Mr. *Robert Williams,* supported by *Thomas Christie,* esq.; Recorder of *Savannah,* and the Rev. *Mr. Wesly,* supported only, by His Integrity and Assurance, &c, &c, &c." Robert Williams had left Georgia to live in Carolina, and returned from a trip to England in February, 1743.[63]

In 1750 the land which Christie leased from the Trustees was regarded as vacant and so was granted to another, Stephens and the new Board of Assistants in Georgia asserting that Christie had never come to take possession of it and that he was incapable of improving it, being in "miserable Circumstances" in Charles Town. In November, 1758, an effort was made by the grantee, Jonathan Bryan, to obtain the lot in Savannah originally granted to Christie, but consideration of this was postponed.[64]

Whether Thomas Christie returned to Georgia is not certain. A Thomas Christie, after nearly three years of residence in Georgia, petitioned for and received a grant of 350 acres of land in 1759, having then a wife and four slaves. He petitioned again in 1759 for an additional 100 acres, having then six Negroes, and his petition was granted.[65] If this was the same Christie, he would have been about fifty-six years of age, living in Georgia again, with his old enemies dead or long since returned to England, and Georgia itself under a form of government different from that he had known and shared in earlier days after he came on the *Ann.* He may after all have fulfilled the promise to himself to spend the remainder of his days in Georgia, but the identity of the Thomas Christie of 1759 has not been established as the one who came to Georgia on the *Ann* in 1733.

CHAPTER TEN

"Rejoicing Days" and Trade

DIVERSION and recreation are important in all societies and to all peoples. Often in new or isolated areas, such as Georgia was in the 1730's, recreation is of more importance than in older areas because life is rawer and has fewer established patterns. Recreational patterns are usually brought by settlers with them into a new area, and this was the case in Georgia. Public houses, where one could enjoy drink, food, and companionship, were central to eighteenth-century social life in England and in her American colonies. They soon grew up in Georgia.

Edward Jenkins's public house, until he moved to Carolina in September, 1740,[1] was a meeting place for friends, political factions, and gossipers who could learn the news at Jenkins's. Public houses existed before Jenkins established his and after he left the colony, but none was more popular in its day than his.

Anniversaries, or "rejoicing days," were celebrated with regularity in the colony. The festival of England's patron saint, St. George, April 23, was one of the more important days. The minimum observance of this day was the hoisting of the flag, but the ceremonies often expanded into a gala occasion. In 1738 the flag was run up; at noon the magistrates, officers of the militia, and inhabitants met at the guardhouse; eleven cannon boomed; wine glasses were raised to toast the King, the Royal Family, the Trustees, Oglethorpe, and the colony. The following year was a bad year in the colony and no public rejoicing seems to have taken place then or for the next two years. In 1742 Stephens observed that people seemed in a better temper towards each other that year. Most of the town assembled at noon to drink the King's

161

health; to cherish that good humor and promote the sorely needed unity, Stephens ordered five guns to be fired and produced wine for the toasts, "tho the small Estimate for rejoicing days would hardly allow it. And I was glad to see them all go off well pleased." In some years the celebrations were omitted, in order to save money, when Stephens said they were reduced to a lower state than they had ever known before.[2]

The anniversary of the King's accession to the throne on June 15 was observed. In 1737 the flag was hoisted, guns were fired, and the guard and all the officers enjoyed a barrel of beer. In some other years, the day was somewhat more elaborate, following much the same pattern as the celebration of St. George's Day. In 1744 it had perhaps its most elaborate celebration, combined with a militia muster. After the great guns were fired, nearly eighty militia gave three handsome volleys performed with lively spirit and greeted with applause by the inhabitants of Savannah. Afterwards, as they stood in ranks, the militia were regaled with two or three glasses of wine each, with which they toasted the King, the Royal Family, the Trustees, and Oglethorpe.[3] The King's coronation on October 11 and his birthday on October 30 were celebrated with toasts, firing of guns, and a church service.[4]

Oglethorpe's birthday was celebrated on December 21 for a number of years. The flag was hoisted, guns fired, and healths drunk. This birthday was celebrated with particular verve in 1737, when people met with the magistrates and military officers at the fort at noon to drink the health of the King, royal family, Trustees, and Oglethorpe after a discharge of thirteen guns. That evening "a handsome cold Entertainment was provided at a Tavern, by the Subscription of upwards of thirty, who (as many as could find them) brought Partners to dance; which they did and were merry."[5] Early in March when Savannah people heard from Carolina of Oglethorpe's safe arrival in England, a bonfire was lit and Causton gave a barrel of beer to add to the rejoicing. The birthday celebrations continued for some years later but perhaps none of them was enjoyed more than the one in 1734, to which people looked forward for weeks before the date.[6] This celebration may have been included in Elisha Dobree's disapproving comment, "Although we are a poor Colony we have had of Late great many marriages & Balls till 2 and 3 in the Morning an Excess wch in my humble Oppinion deserves no Encouragement or Countenance from Men in Power [.]"[7]

This business of dancing could bring no good, Dobree evidently thought. It led to a quarrel between the guard, with Tythingman Edward Bush in charge, and "Some Gentlemen who were dancing many blows were given, Dr Tailfer had like to have had his Arm Cut off by Bush wth his Dagger." Surely this was a sufficiently untoward state of affairs, but "The Intent of the Dancing was to Introduce Acting of Plays I am humbly of Oppinion we have Scenes of Poverty Eno in reality without Inventing ways to Divert our thoughts from business & the Care of providing food for our Families As to what I mentioned concerning the Play I beg my Name be Concealed I am no Enemy to the Gentlemen Concend tho I am to their Indiscretion & to their way of thinking—in Short we have too much of Publ: Entertainment. I wish Zeal was as warm agt Prophaness & Immorality as tis the reverse [.]"[8]

A good example of marriage gaiety in Savannah took place a year earlier, when four couples from Purrysburgh, South Carolina, which lacked a minister, came to Savannah for their weddings. The air in Georgia was sometimes considered to have a peculiar effect on women. The Purrysburgh correspondent thought this might be true of his town. "I am told that some of these Wives will hardly Stay the nine months out to Create a Progeny, whether by reason of the fruitfullness of the Air or of some Tryal of Skill beforehand I do not determine." On this occasion a procession came down the river, headed by the major of Purrysburg; Oglethorpe received them at the landing and ordered a hog killed for refreshments. Supplemented by generous portions of beer, wine, rum, and punch, everyone grew very happy and merrily danced the whole night through. The next morning when the newly married Purrysburgh couples and their attendants passed up the river in their boats, Savannah's great guns saluted them, roaring out the good wishes everyone had already expressed in words.[9] Savannah people had something to talk about for months afterward.

Feasting was considered proper at a wedding. When minister John Martin Bolzius at Ebenezer was married to a member of his congregation in 1735, Causton ordered one of the Trustees' steers to be killed and a hogshead of English beer sent up for the feast.[10] One wedding long remembered in Savannah occurred on New Year's Day, 1742, when James Anderson married Henry Parker's niece, described as an agreeable young girl. Anderson, a carpenter, had made money at his trade and saved it; when his wedding day arrived he was in a happy and generous mood, "distributing Knots and Favours among his Friends. . . ." In the evening he "made a Merriment at his house, upon bringing home his Bride. . . ."[11]

Beer was a most acceptable refreshment on rejoicing days and in ordinary life was considered indispensable. It formed part of the inducement to special public work. In 1739 the public squares and the common of Savannah were covered with a growth of "an offensive Weed, near as high as Man's Shoulders. . . ." People found it most unpleasant, and the growth was thought to harbor insects and vermin. Oglethorpe ordered that when the drum sounded at sunrise on October 17, the nearly 200 men and boys in town assemble and remove the weeds. Oglethorpe provided a cask of beer and one of bread at breakfast and the same in the evening when work stopped. The real reason for the day's work was probably to test if Oglethorpe would be obeyed when he set the task and for him to see the number of defenders Savannah might count upon. Another day's work, with the same refreshments, completed the cleaning.[12]

The festival of St. Andrew on November 30 was celebrated after the arrival in August, 1734, of the Scots, among them William and Hugh Stirling, Thomas and John Baillie, Andrew Grant, and Patrick Tailfer. Finding after a time that cultivation of their land would not support them, and never having wished to be far from Savannah, they moved to town. They formed a distinct and colorful group in the colony, joined in their opinions and social life by their countryman, Hugh Anderson, after his arrival. Samuel Eveleigh, on a visit to Savannah not long after the arrival of the Scots, was immediately struck by their appearance: "Seeing Some Gentlemen at a Distance with Laced Hatts on, I askt who they were, They told me they were Scotch Men; for that no other war laced Hatts (but the Gentn of that Nation) on that Bluff."[13]

In 1736 John Wesley preached a special sermon to twenty-one Scots and administered communion on St. Andrew's Day. Stephens joined with the Scots in the celebration of the first festival of St. Andrew after his arrival in the colony in 1737. He enjoyed himself at the public house on the evening of November 30 "where they were all in good Humour and cheerful." The following year Stephens aided the preparations for St. Andrew's

Day by ordering the flag to be displayed as a compliment to Scotland, eleven guns to be fired, and healths drunk. St. Andrew's Day in 1739 had an agreeable observance despite the recent declaration of war; "we passed it away inoffensively, with Chearfulness, without entering into any political Arguments, which could not well take Place at this Time. . . ." The Scots were gone from Georgia before the day came around again, but enough North Britons were left in Savannah to honor the day in 1742 by assembling in Johnson Square, playing cricket, and regaling themselves with a barrel of New York ale.[14]

When the Scots moved to town, Thomas Christie rented his house to the Stirlings. Christie's friendship with the Scots and his attendance on their meetings at Edward Jenkins's public house was one reason for Stephens's distrust of Christie. That "insolent Club . . . Tailfer and his Adherents" was among Stephens's mildest terms of opprobrium for the Scots. Stephens came to hate them, and with increased bitterness after the Scots, following their removal to Charles Town in the late summer of 1740, published *A True and Historical Narrative of the Colony of Georgia.* Stephens rose to a pitch of quivering indignation upon the publication of this work.[15] What the Scots wrote of Stephens was no stronger than what Stephens had written of them to the Trustees, but this did not seem to occur to him.

The Free and Accepted Order of Masons caused considerable comment in Savannah. Thomas Jones, detailing the activities of the Scots, remarked that they dressed gay, set up a Free Mason's club, a St. Andrew's club, and other tippling societies.[16] The order was probably organized on February 10, 1734, about six months before the Scots arrived in Georgia. The membership in Savannah was composed of others than the Scots. Elisha Dobree cited as an evidence of good character that "The Body of Free Masons have accepted me as a Brother," while Francis Percy wrote with some elation that "to morro I ham going to enter my Selfe in to ye noble and onarabil Sosiety of free masons by ye Carreckter I bare to brothers gardnars Mr brownciohn [Brownjohn] and fichwallter [Fitzwalter] and all ye hole Sosiety was fond of my Coming. . . ."[17]

The Masons were a large enough body in 1735 for comment to be made on a preponderance of its members on juries. Paul Amatis hinted that the reason some people did not have to pay fines for selling rum was because they were Masons. Amatis himself had paid such a fine and he asserted with some pride that he was not a Mason,[18] but Amatis was a lonely bickering man and he may have wished for the companionship such as the order afforded.

The Masons did not escape Robert Parker's waspish comments. "We have about 30 or 40 Free Masons they have fine Supper every Saturday Night & often 2 or 3 in the Week besides where such an expence can be born I am at a Loss to know, one Night amongst other Disorders they went to the Guard Cut the Capt down the Head & Disarm'd the rest carrying the arms away. Wn they came to reflect on't on the Morrow to make things up they Call'd a Lodge at Night & admitted Goff the Capt a Free Mason, so I suppose the thing Dropt. . . ."[19] The Masons' feasts were probably among those Peter Gordon inveighed against in his accounts of the colony to the Trustees in 1735. The Masons' critics may not have known that various lodges in England had given money for the impoverished families sent to Georgia.

The Masons' annual feast was an event of the summer. John Wesley preached the sermon on Friday, June 24, 1737, after which the feast was held, with Wesley as a guest. The company broke up in mid-afternoon, as Thomas Causton recorded in his journal.[20] Two years later, William Norris preached the sermon on Monday, June 25. "From Church they marched in solemn Order to Dinner at a publick House," William Stephens wrote; "the Warden Dr. Tailfer (who likes Pre-eminence as well as any Man) attended by four or five with Wands, and red Ribbands in their Bosoms, as Badges of their several Offices, took Places foremost; but the Train that followed in white Gloves and Aprons, amounted only to about Half a Dozen more; which some, who are apt to burlesque the Order, turned into Ridicule."[21]

Georgian Robert Hows, who was in London in June, 1739, gave the Earl of Egmont his own version of the Masons when he said "That the Free Mason Company having spent all their money is now broke up, and whilst they subsisted, they met every Saturday at the Tavern, & Revell'd there 'till 2 a clock next morning, when they would reel home."[22] Hows's gloomy story may have been true, for 1739 was not a favorable year in many ways for Georgians. Thomas Causton's eclipse after October, 1738, and the subsequent disfavor and suspicion which attached to him and to his friends may have been a factor in curtailing the Masons' activities. The loss of some of the most active members

when the Scots moved to Charles Town in 1740 hurt them. If the
activities of the lodge were in abeyance during these years, they
were soon resumed.

The first Christmas that William Stephens spent in Georgia,
1737, he observed that the colonists kept the Christmas holidays
but that "Feasting here was not yet in Fashion. . . ." Three years
before that, although Robert Parker had good beef, pork, cheese,
and flour, his servants asked for and were given leave on Christmas Eve to go hunting for the Christmas dinner. They returned
with "4½ Coople of Ducks 1 paire of Doves one Turkey and a
fine Buck together with a fine young Pig," which caused Parker to
comment, "We are not altogether destitute of Provissions when
we have time to seeke it Especially Turkeys & Venison Ducks &c
in plenty but very shy [.]" In 1736 John Wesley mentions a sermon and holy communion but no other celebration.[23] Only
brief glimpses of Christmas in the colony remain. Church services
were always held. In 1738, that upset time, when Stephens described Christmas as a festival without any feasting, there was
still a note of warmth and cheer during the holidays at Edward
Jenkins's public house, where cards, backgammon, and a friendly
companionship diverted those present.[24]

The Easter holidays were celebrated with some gaiety. Easter
Monday was a holiday when all business stopped in Savannah, and
it became a day when various sports were enjoyed. The cricket
game in Johnson Square brought out most of the inhabitants
either to play or to watch. Whitsun Monday and Tuesday also
were times for games before interested spectators.[25]

Another sport was considerably enjoyed by Savannah people
in June, 1740, though its initiation worried and puzzled Stephens. "An odd Humour," he termed this new diversion, horse
racing. The race was for about a quarter of a mile from the gate of
the Trustees' garden to the middle of Johnson Square. When
Stephens found that the races were promoted by Dr. Tailfer and
the Scots he could say nothing good of them; "it gave me a
Jealousy of some farther latent Design. . . ." Other people looked
on with pleasure, but Stephens and Thomas Jones viewed the
races with suspicion. They went to the public house where drinks
were served after the races and in a room adjoining that where
the public was served and gay talk bubbled of the races, the two
men over their wine listened with distrust to all that was said,
hearing no good of themselves or of the colony. The races were

continued the following day, and though Stephens thought the magistrates should stop them, they did not do so. But before a week had passed Stephens's worry was allayed, for the sponsors moved the races to the outskirts of Savannah.[26] Thomas Jones remarked in September that the Scots broke out in a rage when the Reverend George Whitefield found fault with their horse racing. Soon Whitefield was greatly concerned "that several Persons in this Town lived most scandalous Lives with their Whores," and at one term of court he "made an Oration, setting forth the Heinousness of such Crimes, in very pathetick terms."[27]

Some people always deplored other people's recreations. John Pye, mentioning the poverty of Savannah in 1743, disapproved of "Drinking and Gameing [which] Sett Bad examples to the poor People of the Town." Even stronger disapproval was expressed by John Dobell of two new magistrates, John Spencer and Charles Watson, whose time "has been spent in Carousing in Taverns, and Jaunting about from place to place, a Singing and Dancing. . . ."[28]

Hunting was an important recreation. Joseph Fitzwalter was not alone in writing of the game he saw, though none was so eloquent as he. One early visitor remarked on the deer on Tybee Island and on his subsequent trip from Savannah up to Purrysburg again saw deer as well as wild turkeys "and six Bears. . . ." He did better than that a little later for "I met with great plenty of Bears, Woolfs and Tygers. . . ." Deer often destroyed part of the crops, and in 1744 William Stephens suffered the loss of some hogs when bears ate them.[29]

The wood pigeons which Fitzwalter mentioned were doubtless what Stephens referred to as wild pigeons in 1744. He said that the rains ceased, and severe frost came, "which brought incredible numbers of wild Pigeons from the Northern Regions, to such a degree that the Trees of the woods were filled with them, which our people of all Ranks fed plentifully upon; everybody . . . that would make use of a Gun, taking as many as they pleased; like quails to the Israelites in the Wilderness. Some persons made Observations upon it, that the like happened in the year 1735, and never since, from whence they will prognosticate this to be a hard Winter, as that was."[30]

Most of the hunting was for additional food as well as pleasure. Little mention is made of hunting alligators, but they were there if anyone wished to pursue them. Philip Thicknesse was startled to count twenty basking on the shore of Hutchinson's Island opposite Savannah. That island continued for years to be infested with alligators and bears, both taking their toll of the stock there. Alligators were observed in the Savannah River as early as March 12, 1733, and sometimes were the cause of accidents or death. William Stephens wrote in 1742, "those voracious Creatures being too frequently lurking for their prey; and our young people nevertheless not deterrid from Bathing [in the river] almost daily." John Wesley mentioned bathing in the river but said nothing of alligators.[31]

Thomas Jones related with pride the hunting prowess of one member of his "family," as any household was called. Jones in 1740 had board and lodging at Mrs. Vanderplank's but shortly afterward took a house for himself and his family. Besides his indentured servants, two young men, William Russell and Francis Harris, composed this group. Harris came over at his own expense on Captain William Thomson's ship, the *Two Brothers*, arriving on October 15, 1738. In that disturbed time Harris, recommended to Jones by friends in England, was welcomed as a reliable person to work on the store's accounts. Jones said a little later, "I cannot find any one person whom I can confide in (excepting one Mr. Harris . . . who assists me in the Store). . . ."[32] Harris, according to Jones, was an expert fowler who seldom failed to bring in wild turkeys, curlews, rabbits, partridges, squirrels, ducks, and geese in season. He sometimes brought in venison, though Jones said the Indians were usually depended upon for venison and bear.[33]

One temporary resident in the colony greatly enjoyed an oystering party to which he was invited by Tomochichi and the Yamacraw Indians. At low tide Tomochichi's people would make a fire on one of the small islands in a salt creek where oysters abounded, leaving the fire to roast the oysters while the island was high and dry. Later they would collect roasted oysters in their canoes and feast upon them. The Englishman enjoyed Tomochichi as company and the oysters as food, and considered the feast a most agreeable occasion.[34]

Early Georgia residents were considerably restricted so far as merchants were concerned. At the founding of the colony the Trustees' store was the leading source of supply, and continued so until it was closed in 1738. Yet other stores were soon doing business in Savannah. The Trustees accepted with some eagerness in May, 1733, the proposal of John Tuckwell, of Wallingford, Berkshire, that the ironmonger firm of Pytt and Tuckwell should furnish the colony with its wares. Tuckwell gave in 1735 a large clock for the church valued at £21, though the church was not to be built for a number of years. In February, 1736, this firm's factor, John Brownfield, arrived in Savannah for business, though he had probably been in the colony earlier. Many items carried by Pytt and Tuckwell were purchased and used widely, such as iron pots, pothooks, spades, hoes, cane hooks, axes, hatchets, bullets, shot, tin lamps, lanterns, nails, guns, shovels, frying pans, and hinges. This firm enlarged its business to include clothing and other merchandise. Montaigut and Company, opened in 1734 and backed by the English shipping firm of Peter and J. C. Symond, sold bed cords, beef, cow bells, brown bread, ship's bread, butter, candles, cheese, corn, wheat, flour, gun powder, hats, hatchets, farm tools, grindstones, knives, leather for soling shoes, yard goods, pork, potatoes, rice, shoes, fishing hooks, needles, and undoubtedly other items.[35]

The Trustees' store bought some of its goods from these stores and from Abraham Minis and Company. The majority of provisions were purchased from importing vessels. Causton followed the precedent set by Oglethorpe, and bought from sloops, usually from New York but occasionally from Philadelphia. Scattering retail prices for the years 1735-1743 have been discovered for the Trustees' store, Montaigut and Company, Minis and Company, Nunez and Company, and Pytt and Tuckwell. There were other shops for which no record of prices exists.

The following are prices for provisions in Savannah:

	1735	1737-38	1740	1743
Fresh meat, per lb.	5-6d			
Beef, per lb.			1½-2½d	2d
Pork, per lb.			2-2½d	3d
Veal, per lb.			2½-3d	
Mutton, per lb.			4½-5d	
Butter	10d			11d
Cheese, per lb.				8d
Candles, per lb.	2-3d			
Brown sugar, per lb.				6d
Green tea, per lb.		5s 6d	5-7s	5s

Coffee, per lb.		18d	1s 4d
Chocolate, per lb.			4s
Beer, 4 doz., 2 bottles	£1.19.7		
20 doz., 8 bottles	9.16.4		
per qt.			6d
strong, 30 gal. barrel		20s	
Cider, per barrel		10s	
Madeira wine, per gal.		3s-3s 6d	5s
Wheat flour, per lb.		1d	
Indian wheat (corn), per bu.		10-18d	
Rice, per cwt.		3s 6d-5s	
Bread, per lb.	2-3s		

Peter Gordon complained in 1735 that the prices of provisions were very high in Savannah. In 1743 John Dobell also considered prices "at a pretty Dear rate." These comments are likely a result of the common human tendency to complain of high costs of living. Thomas Jones in 1740 took a different approach and implied that prices were reasonable. He said that small beer was brewed of molasses "quite cheap" and commented on the plentiful supply of wild game, vegetables, and fruits grown in the colony. He said there were available apples, muskmelons, watermelons, nectarines, and peaches (the most common fruit), "very good" grapes, pulse roots, potherbs, pease, beans, walnuts, chinquapins, chestnuts, hickory nuts, and ground nuts. The cheap "Indian wheat" he thought "very tasted" and nourishing. Since fire wood was "very reasonable" and Savannah had "exceeding fine water" everyone should be able to prepare his food easily and inexpensively. In fact, said Jones, "I have not seen any part of the world where Persons that would labor and used any Industry, might live more comfortably in." There were no taxes or public duties, everything being furnished by the Trustees.[36] Many in Georgia did not agree with this picture of ease, as has been made clear from the numerous complaints of a hard life already cited.

Scanty mention is made of house furnishings or clothing. Almost no furniture was offered for sale. Bed cords, which served the place of springs, cost 1s. 8d in 1737. When William Ewen bought an iron pot and a frying pan from Montaigut and Company in March, 1738, he paid 11s. 9½d for the pot and 3s for the frying pan. Pots varied in size and perhaps in quality for they

could be bought for 5s. 1½d up. Pytt and Tuckwell sold Roger
Lacy a lamp, probably of tin, in April, 1738, for 1s. In the Trustees' store at the time of taking inventory were 129 iron candlesticks and an iron "sticking" candlestick, presumably a pricket
type. Though no curtain rods were on hand to be sold (they were
probably made of wood) curtain rod hooks were in stock. The store
had a supply of pewter pots in quart, half-gallon, gallon, and other
sizes, a pewter funnel, a pewter chamber-pot, and sixteen and a
half dozen pewter spoons. Pewter had not yet replaced wooden
utensils, for there were listed wooden bowls, three dozen wooden
spoons, thirty-two hollow wooden trenchers, seven and a half
dozen flat trenchers, and one dozen round hollow trenchers.[37]
The only set of china mentioned was a tea-set consisting of twelve
cups and saucers, a basin, and a teapot, which Montaigut and Company sold to Thomas Causton for £1.6.0 in August, 1937.[38]

Little enough is known of the furnishings of the early homes.
When Thomas Christie planned to go to England, he sold some
of his furniture, "a few of his own old Goods of little Value;
such as two or three ordinary Chairs and Stools, a Table, one
Pewter Dish, a few common Dutch printed pictures coloured upon Paper, and the like. . . ." When William Bradley moved
from Georgia to Carolina in 1739, Stephens remarked that "the
common Talk of the People was, that some of his best and choicest
Goods were sent before; such as Scrutores, fine Tables and Chairs,
with other fashionable Furniture, which was mostly the Operation of an ingenious Workman, . . . [who] was employed many
Months on such Curiosities. . . ."[39]

Samuel Eveleigh on one of his visits to Savannah went a few
miles to visit Sir Francis Bathurst, but it was Sir Francis's house
itself and not the furnishings which engaged Eveleigh's attention. Sir Francis must have fallen on very sad times indeed
before he came to Georgia but he seems to have been a cheerful
person and made Eveleigh welcome. The clapboard house was
a small one, twenty feet long, twelve feet wide, divided into two
parts, one a bedroom, the other a dining room; it might be in
some measure watertight, Eveleigh said, but he was sure it could
not be wind-tight. However, on a morning in May it was pleasant
enough. Sir Francis was about to have breakfast when Eveleigh
arrived and the two men ate together fried catfish and perch,
caught the night before, and a piece of cold pork. Eveleigh
took with him two bottles of red wine and two of punch. The

latter they drank after breakfast when, comfortably full of catfish, they sat and talked of the colony, crops, and perhaps of the great world. In the last glass of punch, they toasted Sir Francis's cousin, Lord Bathurst, in England.[40]

Clothing to be purchased in the Trustees' or other stores was of the plainest variety with but a few exceptions. On November 1, 1737, Roger Lacy bought from Pytt and Tuckwell for £27.6.0 osnaburg, a pea jacket, fear-nothings, strouds, shirts, gartering, handkerchiefs, buckles (doubtless for his shoes), thread, knives, and a silk quilted petticoat.[41] Fear-nothings were garments made of a thick woolen material called fear-naught. Osnaburg was a kind of coarse cloth widely used for rough trousers, jackets, and sometimes for dresses; the Trustees' store had ten osnaburg frocks with red sleeves. Pytt and Tuckwell sold William Bradley 102 ells (45 inches) of "oznabrigs" for £44.5.0. Stroud was a coarse material used for blankets and sometimes clothing. It was included on almost every list of Indian presents.[42]

The Trustees' store had also two women's stuff gowns, one of linen, and ten long blue capes. Stuff (worsted), garlix, green serge, linsey, bunting, Scotch plaids, grograms, plains, flannel, flannel cambric, and linen could be purchased either by the yard or made into garments, some of these materials being used for both men and women. White, green, yellow, crimson, and citron ferret or ferreting (a narrow tape) was available for trimming and binding. Women's thread and worsted stockings were in stock. Twenty-two dozen men's and women's stockings were given for the colonists in 1736, valued in England at £21.17.0; there were mint short stockings for men, for women blue and green stockings with scarlet clocks and blue stockings with white clocks.[43] Glimpses of legs thus brightly clad, when a breeze on the bluff in Savannah swept women's long dresses around, must have added a pleasing color to the scene.

Thomas Causton bought two pairs of shoes from Montaigut and Company in September, 1737, for twelve shillings; John Desborough paid 13s 6d for three pairs of shoes the following year, while in March, 1738, Noble Jones bought one pair of "Negro" shoes for three shillings, another not described for four shillings, and four other pairs for six shillings each from Montaigut. The Trustees' store had in stock four pairs of girls' "callimance" shoes; callimance was a shiny woolen fabric so woven that checks showed on one side. At this store also were nineteen men's beaver hats; a man's hat could be bought from Montaigut for six shillings, sixpence.[44]

In 1735 each indentured servant sent by the Trustees had as his clothing allowance yearly six yards of linsey-woolsey for a frock and trousers; nine yards of osnaburg for a shirt, frock, and trousers; a pair of shoes from England; two pairs of country shoes; needles and thread—the value of the whole not to exceed twenty shillings sterling.[45]

Thomas Causton soon after his arrival wrote to his wife that he would need thread or cotton stockings and some checked or blue linen for waistcoats and trousers. John Pye, articled to the Trustees and engaged under Thomas Causton in the store in clerical work and accounting, was in Savannah less than a month in June, 1737, before he wrote back to England that he found his wages so small they would scarcely "find me in Shoes and Ozzenbrig Cloaths things are so dear. . . ." He wanted "some Dowlass & thin Cloathing. . . ." When Henry Parker was reported by Stephens to have clothes scarcely fit to wear on the magistrates' bench, the Trustees ordered that "Linen, and Woolen Cloth and Shoes and Stockings and other Cloathing to the Value of twenty Pounds be sent to him in consideration of his Services as second Bailiff of the Town of Savannah. . . ."[46] It was not unusual for colonists to ask friends or relatives in England to send them certain articles of clothing or other things they could not obtain in Georgia. Late in 1735 Oglethorpe, in the hurry of preparing to return to the colony, instructed Harman Verelst to execute several commissions for him: to buy four spirit levels and have his thermometer repaired at Mr. Scarlet's in Thrift Street, Soho. Verelst filled another request of Oglethorpe's: "As you desired I would send over a Reading Glass from Mr. Scarlet suitable to one about 50 years old, when I got the Thermomiter mended (which I have sent you). I bought not only a Reading Glass but a pair of Spectacles for the same Age to be used occasionally, as might best sute the sight or Convenience of the Reader."[47]

Perhaps the several peruke makers who came to the colony worked at their trades in the intervals of farming their land, if they could find those with money to pay them; for wigs were important articles of a man's attire. One of the captains in Oglethorpe's regiment at Frederica had to have his peruke sent out from London. Thomas Jones earned a sharp reproof from Colonel James Cochran of the regiment because of leaving off his wig. The Colonel told Jones "That I was very impudent to appear before him in that Dress, (I had a Velvet Cap, on, without a Wigg, being Warm Weather [.]" However, Cochran was angry at Jones because of a disagreement about matters at the Trustees' store.[48] What Jones said in reply he did not report to the Trustees.

The wig was so important an appurtenance that when anyone ran away or was wanted for misbehavior the newspaper advertisements mentioned the wig in the description of personal appearance. A servant who ran away from Georgia was advertised as "an Irishman, bred a Perukemaker and Barber, is of low stature, wore his own hair. . . ." In 1739 three of Robert Williams's indentured servants escaped from his plantation near Savannah in May and three more in June. One of them, a bricklayer by trade, about five feet, nine inches tall, was "a strong made Man, born in Wiltshire, talks broad, and when he went away wore his own short Hair with a white Cap: *Among his Comrades he was call'd Alderman.*" No mention is made of wigs in the descriptions of the other two, one of whom "did formerly belong to the Pilot Boats at *Pill* near Bristol," while the third of this group was "a lusty young Fellow . . . has a good fresh complexion, bred by trade a Taylor, but of late has been used to sawing, talks very much Welshly, and had on when he went away a coarse red Coat and Wastecoat, the Buttons and Button Holes of the Coat black."[49]

If advertisements can be believed, Charles Town furnished all that gentlemen could desire in the matter of head coverings. Hair for wig making was imported as well as ready made wigs, hair powder, wig ribbons, and cauls (the netted substructure of a wig), and wig bags.[50] If sometimes a man did not wish to wear a wig, he might wear a hair cap of linen, cotton, or wool over his short cut hair. Hats were apparently worn outdoors over hair caps and the absence of cap, hat, or wig was thought worthy of notice.[51]

The contrast between the economic status of the people of Georgia and their next-door neighbors in South Carolina is shown in the goods for sale in each. Charles Town merchants carried a varied range of goods from the widely used osnaburgs and garlix to silks, velvets, and many other luxury items. Hollands, Russia linens, cambric, lawns, "Chints and Callicoes of all sorts," India silk, Italian and British silk, linen sheeting, linen bedticks, gold and silver brocades, velvets of several sorts, silk and gold lace, and assorted buttons were offered for those who would make up their clothing or household linens. In finished items there were silk waistcoats worked with silver, quilted or hooped silk petticoats, plain and laced French and English belindas, India silk handkerchiefs, umbrellas, "table Linnen in setts & board cloths with or without napkins," worsted or silk hose for both sexes and all ages, leghorn hats, women's velvet hoods and caps, and scarlet mantles.[52]

A Charles Town jeweller imported from London "silver candlesticks, and snuffers, punch ladles, silver handle Knives and forks, and spoon handled forks, soop spoons, table and teaspoons, mens, womens and boys buckles, coffee and tea pots, milk pots and pepper boxes, sleeve buttons and thimbles, rings and ear-rings, of several fashions, with various other things too tedious to mention. . . ." Mahogany card tables, chests of drawers and chairs, "hard pewter dishes and plates and water ditto," came over in the same ship. Lewis Janvier, lately arrived from London in Charles Town, would sell all sorts of gold and silver work, "snuff-boxes, tooth pick cases, seizors cases, spunge boxes (to put spirits of Harts horn or Lavender in), needle cases, ink bottles, books for chains, tea and pap spoons, mens shoe and knee buckles, plain or wrought, stock buckles, clasps, plain and with joints, womens buckles, gold sleeve buttons, and gold rings of all sorts. . . ."[53] Such luxury goods were not yet available in Georgia.

In the summer of 1743 the *South-Carolina Gazette* observed plaintively in its news columns: "Tis thought, That if the Merchants at Home would send over here a large Quantity of *Scotch* Kenting for Pavillons, it will come to a good Market, there being at present a very great Demand for that Commodity, the Inhabitants being almost devoured by the Musquito's, for want thereof [.]" At least one merchant in Charles Town acted on this suggestion for well before the hot weather the next year he had for sale "silk gauze pavillions ready made. . . ."[54] If such protection against insects was available in Savannah, the records are silent.

Georgia was beginning to be a little self-conscious about that season in which William Stephens spoke of "the heats." South Carolina, being older, was even more so. Since Georgia had no newspaper as yet, she could not establish her case in the public print. The *South-Carolina Gazette* sometimes used its obituaries for remarking on the longevity of those deceased in a healthy climate. When an eminent merchant died, the editor commented that here was a man in his seventy-third year who had lived in Carolina nearly fifty-five years. His pall was supported by six ancient inhabitants of Charles Town hardly one of whom had seen less than forty years revolve since first arriving in the province, "and whose several Ages put together amounted to about 400 Years." It was indeed "A sufficient proof, this, that Carolina *is not* one of the *most unhealthy* Climates on Earth." Another prominent citizen died in his sleep, in his seventieth year, exactly sixty-one years to the day after he came to Carolina.[55]

Georgia's climate was similar to South Carolina's, but the harder life in the new colony was not so conducive to longevity. In Georgia, William Stephens in 1740 spoke of Joseph Stanley, one of the *Ann's* passengers, as being in his old age, superannuated, weak and past any labor. Stanley was then about fifty-three years old; but he had just left Georgia, which would tend to lower Stephens's estimation of his value. Down at Frederica, Dr. Thomas Hawkins reported that a woman there died not of any illness but of old age, for she was upwards of sixty years old.[56]

CHAPTER ELEVEN

Selected from the "First Forty," I

T HERE were a number of the first colonists who never occupied any official position in Georgia and about whom very little is known. All the first settlers were humble folk, of no great importance by the standards of the eighteenth century. Yet any knowledge of the *Ann's* passengers helps to measure the success of the Trustees' original purpose.

When Timothy Bowling, potash maker, came with the first colonists, he left his family behind him in England. His wife Elizabeth and eleven-year-old daughter Mary embarked on the *Susannah*, Captain Baillie, in May, 1733, and arrived in Savannah on September 23. They settled on lot number 35 granted to Bowling. Bowling died on November 5 of that year and Mrs. Bowling and Mary were left to make their way as best they could in the strange new country.[1]

Under Oglethorpe's plan of giving each of the widows one of the Irish transport servants to help cultivate her land, Robert Story was assigned to Mrs. Bowling. He was of little use to her as he died early in March, 1734, about two months after he arrived. Mrs. Bowling and Mary lived quietly but life could not have been easy for them.[2] Mrs. Bowling became indebted to the store in the amount of £15.7.1½ sterling before her house burned in a fire which started at John West's about three o'clock on the afternoon of April 2, 1741, and was spread rapidly by a high wind. In an hour it had burned five houses, numbered one through five in Tyrconnel Tything, Derby Ward. They were occupied by John West, James Wilson, James Burnside, Anthony

Camuse, and the Bowlings. The occupants could save only a few
of their household and personal possessions.[3]

The loss was not easy for any of the victims; for Mrs. Bowling it was disastrous. By the autumn of that year her health was
so bad that Mary became a full-time nurse for her mother. Mary
could thus earn no income, and the Bowlings were in actual want
by November when Mrs. Bowling petitioned the President and
Assistants, who allowed her twenty shillings. In April of the following year she petitioned again, saying she must perish of want
without some assistance. This time the Board allowed her ten
shillings for her immediate relief and delegated a member to
inquire into her condition. Once in 1743, twice in 1745, and once
in 1746 she petitioned for help and received twenty shillings each
time. She was in great want, weak and helpless, having lost the
use of her limbs. She also called attention to the condition of the
house she lived in, and the Board decided that it "should be
refitted so as to keep her from the Inclemency of the Weather."
She could do nothing about the house herself, since she was "in
a very deplorable Condition, being for some Time past supported
by the Charity of the Honourable Trustees. . . ."[4]

Fifteen months later in October, 1747, the house which a neighbor had allowed her to live in after her own burned was "entirely gone to Decay, no longer habitable"; the neighbor was
dead; Mrs. Bowling had been bedridden for some years. Upon
inspection the magistrates found conditions as Mrs. Bowling said,
and again promised to repair her house to keep her from the inclemency of the weather.[5]

For the next twelve years the Bowlings fade from the picture.
Undoubtedly Mrs. Bowling died in this period. In December,
1759, the governor of Georgia signed a grant to Mary Bowling for
a town and a garden lot in Savannah. In November, 1761, another
governor signed another grant to her of a town and farm lot in
Savannah.[6] One or both of these grants may have been a re-affirmation of the original grant to her father, Timothy. She certainly had one grant; she may have had two. In 1759, at the age
of about thirty-seven, when most of her life had been spent in dire
poverty Mary was sufficiently undefeated to want her lot or lots
and to make plans for her life.

Several of the first colonists break their obscurity only when
they signed the representation to the Trustees in December, 1738.
William and Charles Greenfield, William Calvert's nephews, each

signed with their mark, and little more is heard of them.[7] Nor is
any more heard of William Calvert, after he signed the representation.[8] Mrs. Calvert died in the prevailing illness in July, 1733,
and though Calvert had a lot granted to him in Savannah he
seems to have lived at Fort Argyle[9] before his life became ob-
scured.

The other member of the Greenfield family who came with
Calvert was his niece Sarah, aged sixteen years, who married
William Elbert in June, 1734.[10] Later Elbert wrote: "I Left my
Native Cuntrey, England Veary young staid sometime in Caro-
lina: from thence came to Georgia. in ye: yere 32 About two
months after ye: first setlers, some small time after married into
one of ye first forty fameleys Obtain,d a Lott of Esqr: Oglethorpe,
and Bult a house thereon Conformable to ye Honours Charter,
I servd: your Honours as Lieutenant at Fort: Argyle under Capt:
Jas: Mc:pherson, Better then two yeres, Commishon,d by ye:
Esqr: [Oglethorpe] After which servd: one yere as mesinger to
Chorls: Town in Carolina-"[11] Elbert was one of the unfortunate
possessors of a swamp lot and asked for a new grant of 500 acres,
"which i hope you will out of goodness gront: the fifty Acres of
Land allready gronted me: Being Land not posable to make
aney thing ofe from it: my forty five Acres being Low pine
Barren and scruby Bay Bushes: and my five Acres a Deep swamp
so deep yt a man must be up to his arm-pits in clearing it-"[12] A
request for so large a grant was refused, one reason probably
being that Elbert had signed the remonstrance of 1740, and William Stephens had nothing good to say of him as a result. Even
before he received the news, Elbert, his wife, and two daughters
had moved to Carolina. As with anyone leaving in 1742, their
"running away" was attributed to fear of the Spaniards, though
they had previously lived in Carolina. Legitimate business could
call people elsewhere but if they left in 1742, William Stephens
particularly frowned upon it. When the information was received
in London and was entered on "the list" it was with the impli-
cation of cowardice.[13]

After the deaths in December, 1733, of Henry Close and his
baby Georgia, Mrs. Close was married the next February to James
Smith who had come to the colony from Carolina. Mrs. Smith
lost another daughter, Anne, that April. Little is heard concerning
this family other than that Smith signed the representation in
1738. They left Georgia in 1740, arriving in England in May

on Captain Thomson's ship, the *Two Brothers*, which made a speedy passage from Georgia of only twenty-five days. Smith had inherited property in Scotland and received the Trustees' permission to sell his wife's lot in Savannah to apply the proceeds to the debts which encumbered the estate to which he had fallen heir. Georgia lot number forty granted originally to Henry Close was bought by Captain Thomson for £20.[14]

Elisha Dobree wrote somewhat mournfully in 1735 of several deaths among which were "Mr Cole one of ye first forty of wch Number remains alive 19 or twenty." Joseph Coles, or Cole, died on March 4 and his widow married Thomas Salter in September, 1736.[15] Salter, a brickmason and brick-maker, arrived by the *Savannah*, Captain Lionel Wood, coming at his own expense and bringing with him three men-servants.[16] Salter was evidently a man of considerable industry. As a brick mason he built some of the greatly needed chimneys in Savannah, and seeing the needs of the colony he signed the representation of December, 1738. He was a tythingman in 1739 and in 1741 was made a constable upon the recommendation of William Stephens, Salter "being very well approved of." He served in this office at least ten years, his salary being £2.10.0 a quarter, even though John Pye did speak of him once as being "much Disguised in Liquor." Salter was even mentioned as a remote possibility, with three other men, for the office of one of the President's Assistants. They were "diligent working people; but illiterate, and know very little beyond the use of their Tools; wherefore I humbly conceive yt in such a Station," William Stephens wrote, probably remembering Robert Gilbert, the reluctant magistrate, "they would rather expose their want of knowledge than contribute to our Consultations."[17]

Salter's standing in the colony is shown by his being chosen as one of five colonists to settle the problem about cattle ownership in 1744. Many cattle died in 1743 of an undiagnosed disease, thought to have been helped by a severe drought. Stephens spoke of the "Intemperate heats," and the want of wholesome water in the ponds for the cattle, "the Puddles that were to be found in the Swamps abounding with divers Amphibious and Noxious Animals."[18] Many cattle were lost because some people paid no attention to brands but took cattle which looked best to them when they needed meat. By October, 1744, losses had so mounted that the grand jury asked the magistrates to devise some remedy for the situation. The magistrates were at a loss but made a sug-

gestion novel in the colony—all the people interested in the state
of affairs should meet to consider what might be done.[19]

The meeting was held at the courthouse on November 2. A
numerous meeting, Stephens said, of all the people far and near
who were interested. Stephens scented danger, watching closely
that he might report to the Trustees in case the people assumed
too much power and attempted to establish rules. He was obviously distrustful, not believing in democratic processes in the
colony. The meeting nominated five men to present suggestions
to the court. This was unusual; nothing like it had ever occurred
in the colony. The committee (Thomas Salter, James Habersham,
William Woodrooffe, Peter Morelle, and William Ewen) prepared proposals and submitted them to Stephens to lay before
the President and Assistants. Stephens received them gingerly
lest, as he said, through want of caution they should take too
much upon them and exceed the power given to the Board.[20]
The President and Assistants judged the proposals abusive in
their meaning, and full of inconsistencies; the Board would not
sign such a paper, leading people into such schemes.[21]

If Salter had any political ambitions for himself, he kept quiet
about them. He seems only to have wanted to further his business,
in which he prospered. In 1741 he asked for and received a
grant of Dawbuss's Island, later called Salter's Island, and five
years later received permission to rent ten acres on Hutchinson's
Island, fronting Savannah. The clay there was of superior quality and the nearness to the town allowed him to deliver bricks at
seventeen shillings and six pence a thousand, about one-third less
than the usual price. This caused the Board to remark to the
Trustees, "We making no Doubt but that their Honours will encourage so good an Undertaking."[22]

When Elisha Dobree wrote of Joseph Cole's death, he recorded
that of another of the *Ann's* passengers, "29 March Mr Cooper
dyed this morning suddenly he was abroad two days agoe, there
was no body wth him wn he Expired."[23] Joseph Cooper, who
came as a "writer," or clerk and copyist, came alone but was
married at the time of his death. His widow rented her house in
June of that year to Henry Parker and returned to England.
She later became Mrs. Crowder and the yearly rent of £10.10.0[24]
owing to her was the subject of considerable correspondence before she finally vanishes from the records.

The first tragedy for the Robert Clark, or Clarke, family was

the loss of an infant son, James, on board the *Ann* before arrival in Georgia. Robert Clark died in April, 1734; his mother-
in-law who had arrived some months earlier, died on June 16.[25]
Mrs. Clark married Thomas Cross, a soldier in the Independent
Company, on June 29. The Crosses lived in and out of the colony,
probably in Carolina part of the time, which doubtless occasioned
the entry of "run away" for Cross, though he was in the colony
in the latter part of 1738 and signed the representation to the
Trustees. Mrs. Cross had been an adherent of John Wesley's, but
Charles Delamotte wrote of her as one of the "hirelings who
have gone from amongst us."[26] Mrs. Cross was in the colony
at Christmas of 1739, for on that day she put her two sons, Peter
and John, aged ten at that time, in the orphanage. The children
were returned to her the next June, and the family seems to have
lived in Georgia for some years.[27]

Richard and Mary Cannon arrived with their children Marmaduke and Clementine, after the youngest, James, had died on
the *Ann*. Another baby was born in July, 1733, but died in a
month, preceded by her mother.[28] The Mrs. Daniel Preston who
arrived on the *Georgia Pink* on August 29 of that year, and whose
opprobrious conduct immediately after landing has been recounted, even to her pregnancy in her plea for postponement of
her trial and admission to bail, became Richard Cannon's second
wife on October 14, one of her children dying shortly before
her marriage, another shortly afterward.[29]

Cannon was not a letter-writer who sent details of his troubles
to the Trustees and only slight references are made to him occasionally. Since no mention is made of his new wife, she must
have become a more peaceable person. Alice Riley, after her arrival with the Irish transports in January, 1734, was assigned to
him as a servant. She could not have remained with him long,
for she was William Wise's servant when she murdered him
in March.[30] Less than two years after Cannon married Mrs.
Preston he died on May 27, 1735. Elisha Dobree in mentioning
it, remarked, "At this time this place is very Sickly." Thomas
Causton wrote that summer, "The weather has been very hott,
and we have had very little Rain which will make a Thin
Harvest. . . . Some of Our People have been ill, chiefly with
Agues, Malignant Feavers, and some fluxes; I bless God, tho'
some have dyed, many more recover. . . ."[31]

Sometime after his father died, Marmaduke Cannon went to

work for Thomas Causton at his country home, Ockstead. When Marmaduke next appears in the records five years later William Stephens said, "The Boy was taken by Mr. Causton (with the Allowance and Approbation, it may be supposed, of his Brother Magistrates at that Time) into his House, with Intent to maintain him; for which undoubtedly his Master had Reason to expect some Service from him: This commenced several Years since, long before I saw Georgia in the Year 1736; at which Time I observed him there a lively Youth; from which Period, Mr. Causton then beginning his improvements at Ockstead, the Boy was sent thither, and there employed in hard Labour, as others were; where he has continued ever since, excepting when sent to Town on an Errand."

When Marmaduke came to Savannah on an errand this Wednesday, May 14, 1740, Stephens had him brought before the magistrates "that due Enquiry might be made concerning him, and the Way of Life he was in, many Stories, and uncertain Reports, often passing, which we wanted to get to the Bottom of. . . ." Savannah was at that time very conscious of its orphans, owing to George Whitefield and the powers which the Trustees had given him over the orphans in the colony. Causton had refused to give up Marmaduke to Whitefield, "though some others, who had equal Pretence, gave up theirs," Stephens remarked, "howsoever against their Inclination." He referred here to Henry Parker who reluctantly gave up the two Tondee orphan boys to Whitefield. Marmaduke unknowingly had become a minor phase of a political situation at this juncture. Stephens always placed Parker in the best possible light, but he must decry Causton since the latter was now so much in the Trustees' disfavor.

In any event, Marmaduke "now appeared much dejected, looked poorly, and in miserable Rags, weeping: Upon asking him whether or not he was misused, he seemed under a Terror, not daring to complain. . . ." Some of the bystanders said that Mrs. Causton "tyrannized over him with great Cruelty, whilst his Master gave little Heed to Things of that Kind." It made quite a scene, with Marmaduke thrust suddenly into the limelight. It was discovered he could hardly read his primer, though a big boy at least five feet tall. Neither had he done any guard-duty at Savannah; so Stephens sent him back to Causton with orders to report that night with his gun. The boy was a freeholder, having inherited his father's lot, and by Oglethorpe's order all orphan boys who were freeholders must be trained in guard-duty. Marmaduke returned that night with his gun "and did his Night's Duty with the rest very orderly."

The following day he returned, "declaring his Desire of leaving Mr. Causton and putting himself under Mr. Whitefield," where-upon Thomas Jones immediately sent for someone from the orphanage "to whom the Lad was delivered." So Marmaduke Cannon, his age given as sixteen years, entered the orphanage on May 15, 1740. There he remained until March, 1741, when he was placed out to Joseph Wardrope, a carpenter in Savannah.[32] Obscurity covers Marmaduke after this.

Though it is not unusual for girls to drop out of the records (some of them who came on the *Ann* cannot be traced), occasionally a welcome inadvertency brings some of them to light for a moment. Marmaduke's young sister, Clementine Cannon, vanished from the records except for one curious entry. When John Coates denied in the Charles Town newspaper that he knew anything about an appointment as trustee of Georgia orphans he said, "the only Case in which I was employ'd in relation to the Orphans was as *Coroner* in the suppos'd Murder of *Clementine Cannon*."[33] Extensive search of the records reveals nothing else about Clementine. There is no known reason why someone in Savannah would want to murder a poor orphan girl between four and eight years of age.

Clementine probably never knew John Coates. He arrived in December, 1733, on the *Savannah*, Captain Wood, became a constable and seems to have attended to his duties as officer of the guard and as constable properly. Coates became disaffected toward the colony, in part through his sympathy with Joseph Watson. When John Wesley left the colony on that December night in 1737, Coates was one of three men who went with him, causing Stephens to remark that Coates "run away with Mr. Wesley," and to be listed in England as "deserted to Carolina" and "run away."[34]

Early in 1739 Coates, stung by certain reports from Georgia, took space in the Charles Town newspaper to answer them. He was informed, he said, that at the court in Savannah he was charged with deserting the colony and was therefore discharged from the commission given him by Oglethorpe as constable of Heathcote Ward and also from being a trustee for the orphans. He answered this strongly: "I never understood or consider'd my self to have been enlisted as a Soldier, or under any Restraint than English Laws, Liberty and Property, and therefore think my self not liable to a charge of Desertion . . . ," especially as he stayed in Georgia longer than he had engaged himself to the Trustees to remain.[35]

Walter Fox came alone on the *Ann* and alone he seems to have remained. By the time he came to write his first letter to the Trustees he had several grievances. He was the gunner "in ye See Services," he said. He also looked after the crane during the first year, and "I used to goe in a boat Night & day where Ever his Honr Esqr Ogelthorp Orders was" though he never had any pay for it and "Rowing night & day is Very hard work. . . ." Oglethorpe told him, he reported, that he should have what he needed out of the Trustees' store, but he got little from the store. After Oglethorpe went to England Causton told Fox, evidently by Oglethorpe's orders, that he was to have eighteen pence every time he fired the gun upon the sailing of a vessel. Sometimes he had to wait three or four days for a ship to sail, not knowing when it would leave, and he had to fire the gun at the exact moment a vessel sailed. Thus he had "Lost a great deal of time. . . ." He also claimed compensation promised by Oglethorpe for his work on Savannah houses; but John Dearne and Noble Jones, who were supposed to settle these accounts, told Fox they could not pay him the £3 he claimed.[36]

However he went along peaceably doing his duty and by August, 1738, had cleared most of his five-acre lot but planted only one acre, a fact which was held somewhat against him when he signed the representation that December.[37] Two years later he wrote again that he was "Still Labouring under very narrow Circumstances. . . ." His house had burned, "Suposed to be Ocasioned by Lightining & lost all yt: I had in ye World Except ye Shirt I had on. . . ." Because of his various tribulations, "I hope yt: Your: Honrs: will consider my hard case & as theare hasss benn a great deal of money given for Charitable Uses & yt: I never received a farthing of it have always benn willing to Serve this Colony & have spent all most nine Years of ye Prime of my Years & by fair un proformed Promis have still Kept on But now if with out Assistance I must entierely be uncapible of ever doing for my Self Unless Your: Honrs: do grant ye Above Request. . . ."[38] Fox died on December 30, 1741, as a result of several days' illness "under a Complication of Distempers. . . ." as one of the oldest tythingmen and one of the First Forty settlers. Three minute guns were fired at his burial.[39]

Richard Hodges came over on the *Ann* with a dormant appointment to succeed William Waterland as second magistrate. However, Hodges died in July, 1733, and never became a magistrate. Mrs. Hodges kept a small shop to help support herself and the three girls, Elizabeth, Mary, and Sarah. In July, 1734, Mrs. Hodges was given a license by the Trustees to sell beer provided she gave up the shop. This license did not allow the selling of any distilled liquors; in fact it had been taken away from John Wright, one of the First Forty, for selling distilled liquors. The Trustees could not know when the license was granted that Mrs. Hodges had just been fined twenty shillings for retailing rum without a license.[40] The Trustees were very insistent, since Oglethorpe attributed the deaths of the first summer to rum drinking, that all rum found in the colony be staved; but convictions in the court were difficult and resulted mainly from pressure on the jury by Causton.[41]

When threats were made to sue Constable John Vanderplank in England for staving rum, the Trustees assured him that he should pay no attention. Nobody could give directions in Georgia but the Trustees, and they would support officials who obeyed them. Vanderplank was told in no uncertain terms to "stave all Rum and other distilled Liquors in Georgia; and if any Person shall resist or refuse to comply with these Instructions, you are to compel them to submit, and if you have occasion for any Force, the Trustees will give Directions for the Effectual supporting the Execution of their Orders."[42]

Mrs. Hodges's business as a sutler had some modest degree of prosperity, and she enlarged it to provide lodging as well as meals. She proved herself so good a hostess that at least one Carolina gentleman sent her his good wishes after he returned home.[43] Oglethorpe assigned her, as a widow, an Irish transport servant; but in less than three months he was convicted of theft and running away. Another servant who arrived in August, 1734, ran away three years later, "a white Woman Servant, about 16 Years of Age named *Ann Brown,* born in London and can talk a little French," she was described when a reward was offered for her in Charles Town.[44]

Mrs. Hodges, Samuel Mercer, and James Muir (another *Ann* passenger), the three people who had licenses from the Trustees, complained of Mrs. Penrose because she sold rum and punch and had no license even to keep a public house.[45] Mrs. Hodges had to look after her business and she was never one to take imposition from another person. Neither was Mrs. Penrose, for that matter. They were both forthright women who knew how to stand up for themselves.

Several changes occurred in Mrs. Hodges's life during 1734 and 1735. Her daughter Elizabeth married Richard Lobb in May, 1734. Lobb was an apothecary who came over at his own expense in February, 1734. Shortly after his marriage in May he killed a chicken and, for this breach of law and order, was fined double the value of the fowl. The next May he paid a fine of three shillings, four pence for "defamation." However, these were not serious offenses, and he did work. In two years he had fenced five of his acres, and cleared three and a half, which he planted in corn, making a crop of fifty-five bushels which was considered worthy of comment.[46]

Elizabeth Lobb died in August, 1735, after little more than a year of marriage, and her husband returned to England. Mrs. Hodges's second daughter, Mary, married to John Brownfield, died on the afternoon of March 24, 1738.[47] Thus of the original Hodges family of five who came on the *Ann* only the mother and daughter Sarah remained. Sarah was now about eight years old.

In 1735 Mrs. Hodges married Edward Townsend, who had arrived in February, 1734, from England or Carolina. Oglethorpe gave Townsend a grant of 100 acres at Tybee about which Townsend said, "is well known to be nothing but a sandy Soile: and Experiantley known yt: it yealds not sufficiant to answer ye: troble thare on Bestoed." This was at the time when Oglethorpe was settling colonists at points which he wanted to have manned. Townsend remembered that "at ye time I had ye. grant of ye said Land had ye: promiss from Esqr Olgethorpe of a twelve mo (nths) provisions for my self and famely: which as I married one of ye: [first] forty Widows: Consisted of five in famely: And was to a had all manner of work: tools for planta-tion work: but: never yet Reciv,d Either, for applying after was Refus'd by Mr: Causton Here, told me he did not know yt. i had Either Title to them or ye Land. . . ."[48]

Townsend had a license to keep a victualling house, and he and his wife must have pooled their resources and knowledge in this business. Townsend had to pay a fine of one shilling for assault in July, 1735. The following year his license to keep a victualling house was recalled.[49] Townsend continued to keep his public house despite the loss of his license. William Stephens looked on this house with some suspicion as he did all public houses. William Aglionby, "bred a Smatterer in the Law," lodged there. Stephens had no liking for anyone with a knowledge of the law coming to the colony, and considered Aglionby as "one of the greatest Mischiefmakers in the whole Town"; because of his legal knowledge he was frequently consulted by those formulating the representation of 1738.

Aglionby need have caused little concern; he died at Mrs. Townsend's house in August of that year. "He was of a good Family," Stephens said then, "and had the Appearance of some Education; but as he had a little Smattering of the Law, he made use of that Talent, in being a great Adviser among divers of our late Malecontents . . . as he was a great Devotee to Rum, it is said, that using it to Excess brought a Flux upon him, which after all Endeavours to the contrary, at length carried him off. . . ." George Whitefield visited Aglionby during his illness but made small headway with him. Two days before his death, Whitefield was attempting to extract a statement of his beliefs, but delirium ended the talk. Whitefield refused to perform the funeral service because Aglionby was not a believer, but "as soon as the Corpse was interred, before the Company dispersed, came to the Grave, and there made a very pathetick Exhortation to the People, to be stedfast to the Principles of Christianity, and careful not to be seduced into damnable Errors." Whitefield said that he believed the people "were thoroughly satisfied that I had done right."[50]

Early in 1738 Stephens said that Townsend, an industrious man in making money though his house was unlicensed, was now "a man of some Substance, has his House always well provided, with such Things as are inviting, which brings him Custom indeed more than enough." Townsend signed the representation in December, 1738. It was recorded in London that Townsend "deserted the Colony on shutting up the stores Dec. 1738." The list says "he run away Dec. 1738."[51] If he "run" he did not run far or long, for Mrs. Townsend wrote from Savannah the following spring and no mention is made of any absence. She still smouldered over her husband's losing his license and she could tell how it came about. She and her husband had their license renewed shortly before Oglethorpe's arrival in February, 1736, she said. Some time after this when a group of Indian traders were lodging at her house, Jacob Mathews, Mary Musgrove's second husband, came in with a halfbreed Indian and picked a quarrel with the traders, who sent for the guard. The traders and Townsend requested that the Indian should not be sent to the guardhouse. Mathews insisted, with a fine disregard for the principles of Indian amity which the traders and Townsend were endeavoring to preserve, that the Indian should be jailed and even took him to the guardhouse for the night. The next day Mathews told Oglethorpe that Townsend was responsible for this undiplomatic act. This was at a time when Oglethorpe needed all the friendship he could secure from the Indians and he was evidently angry at this breach of amity. He equally needed to retain Mary Musgrove Mathews as an interpreter and for her influence with the Indians, for she was related to some of the most influential Creeks.

Townsend offered to produce ten men to prove that the Indian's night in jail was none of his doing, but "Neither he or they Could be heard a Very *ood* way of administering Justice tho Common to us," said Mrs. Townsend. So "we Must Loos our Licanc Right or Rong to make Room for an Ierish Roge and an Enlish fool the one had not honesty enouf to live and the other not Sence." Soon after this, she continued, four constables came to read the act of Parliament about people who sold liquor without a license. But Townsend's license had not expired. He was informed that if he would ask pardon, all would be forgiven. But, protested Mrs. Townsend, they had done nothing to ask pardon for. Yet Oglethorpe would give them no satisfaction nor reason why their license should not be continued. Thus, she pointed out to the Trustees, there was no redress at law to maintain the rights of Englishmen in Georgia. Such rights guaranteed, said Mrs. Townsend, would probably have brought in enough settlers to remove the need of Parliamentary funds or a regiment to support Georgia.

As to the Townsends' dependence upon the Trustees' store, Mrs. Townsend said, "had that fatal Plas bin Shut four Years agoe it wod have done some littil good," for the store cut into the small dealers' business. Her husband was now not well and in part at least she attributed this to his hard work on the Tybee lighthouse. Even if sickness and want of employment "has broke his littil Substanc" now, before this "we have god be Praised

lived independant" and there was no doubt she intended to do
so again. Townsend had no land, she said, evidently not counting
the Tybee grant as worth anything. Her two small tracts were
too far apart to cultivate. Besides they were not large enough for
both livestock and grain, which were essential to life. Hence she
wanted a grant of 500 acres. Besides the land she asked for a
gift, or loan without interest, of £100 to adequately stock the proposed grant and set the Townsends up as planters.[52] There is
no record that the Trustees paid any attention to this letter.
They did mention another letter she wrote the following year,
which they said they deemed not worthy of an answer. When in
1742 Townsend applied to the President and Assistants for the
grant and wrote to London concerning it, it was refused.[53]

Townsend kept a boat which was employed by Oglethorpe and
was at the siege of St. Augustine in July, 1740. Mrs. Townsend,
in Stephens's eyes, committed the unpardonable sin of being in
active correspondence with the erstwhile Georgians who removed
to Charles Town and who wished to alter land tenures, have
Negro slaves, and make other changes in the colony. To further
these plans they were thought to be preparing an appeal to
England. It was very well known, Stephens said, how kind Oglethorpe had been to her family; and yet Mrs. Townsend reviled
her kind benefactor most ungratefully, taking unwarrantable
liberties with her tongue. Stephens blamed Mrs. Townsend that
her son-in-law, John Brownfield, had become disaffected toward
the colony.[54] It is noticeable in the colony that a man was never
thought capable of seeing wrongs for himself; he was always
said to have been influenced by some one—by Dr. Tailfer or the
Scots, by the Spaniards, by the people of Carolina, or by this or
that person in the colony.

Mrs. Townsend now joined the company of influencers, in
Stephens's opinion. She was duly entered in London on the List
as "A vile mouthed Malecontent. . . ." Worse was to come. Mrs.
Townsend "fled the Colony 21 July 1740 with her young daughter." and "Run away 29 July 1740 to Carolina & there died."[55]

This has all the appearance of a fitting end for one who would
run from Georgia to Carolina. The only trouble is that it is not
true. Mrs. Townsend did not flee to Carolina; she went to New
York. Several people left the colony at this time. The Spaniards
seemed nearer than ever. She and Sarah went on Captain Tingley's
cargo ship returning from selling provisions at Frederica. Among

the passengers he took north from Savannah was "last of all
(thank God) the eminent Mrs. Townsend. . . ," Stephens wrote
on July 20, 1740, "whose Tongue has been a Nuisance to the
Town ever since I knew it; taking her young Daughter with her
now, and had not Patience to wait her Husband's Return home
from the South. . . ."[56]

That winter of 1740-1741 was severe in Savannah and New
York. December brought the severest frost in the memory of any
Savannah inhabitant. Stephens made it his business to find out
from the master of a cargo sloop how people fared in New York,
and was cheered to learn of the extraordinary prices of flour
and bread: "Fire-Wood cost forty Shillings Sterling *per* Cord,"
with snow so deep that country roads were impassable, and great
numbers of ships locked in their harbors because of ice. "He told
us farther," Stephens said, "it was owing to the great Rigour of
the Season that our fugitive Wives, who went thither last Summer,
by their Husbands and other persuasions, on Pretence of Fear of
the *Spaniards,* had got experience enough, what was to be gained
by that Change of Places, and wished to be here again; so that
he thought we might expect them about the Time of Swallows
coming."[57]

Three of them did come shortly, laughed at by people in New
York because they were glad to return to the place they had so
criticized, Stephens said.[58] Mrs. Townsend was not one of the
three returned; it is doubtful if she was daunted by the weather,
however rigorous. In June a letter came from her by Captain
Tingley who, bound for Frederica with provisions for Oglethorpe's
regiment, was chased by a Spanish privateer until he put in at
Tybee. The news in this letter to her friends was that she had
heard that Georgia was about to become a royal province, King
George II being dissatisfied with the Trustees' management.
Stephens anxiously questioned Captain Tingley, who said that he
had heard this rumor in New York. It might even be, Stephens
decided, that "the noted Mrs. *Townshend"* had herself set this
rumor afloat in New York.[59] Greater evil against Georgia he
could hardly imagine.

Stephens remarked in August, 1742, on a common report that
Townsend with his wife and family "had stolen off to Chas. Town,
in the same manner as he [she?] had formerly eloped to New
York, and after a years Experiment returned with Shame." It
seems more probable that he wanted her to return with shame

than that she came back to Savannah with that emotion. Townsend was buried in Charles Town on August 26, 1748, his death attributed to yellow fever, said Mrs. Timothy Breed (the former Sarah Hodges). Mrs. Breed was applying for his land and that formerly given to her sister's husband, Richard Lobb, then dead also.[60] The absence of any mention of Mrs. Townsend by her daughter in 1759 leads to the supposition that she was dead then also.

━━

CHAPTER TWELVE

Selected from the "First Forty," II

━━

SEVERAL men who came on the *Ann* had little or nothing to say for themselves. They were not letter-writers, and the mention of them by others lacks the detail necessary for the story of their lives.

Thomas Pratt was one of these; he was twenty-one years of age and unmarried when he left England. He returned to England early in 1735 to recover his health and asked the Trustees to pay him rent for his Savannah house, then being used to house sick people. This request with another asking permission to sell his house and lands was denied by the Trustees because he had not asked permission to return to England. His grant was declared forfeited to the Trustees and was immediately granted to another.[1]

Francis Mugridge, who came with a dormant commission from the Trustees as a tythingman, spent but few years in Georgia. Once he appears in the records as having taken part in the Red String Plot, and once he caused Thomas Causton to remark in some exasperation, "'Tis true That Mugridge did some Silly Things, too bad to born with. . . ." Mugridge died, reportedly in debt, in July, 1735, when Savannah was reported to be very sickly.[2] That summer the Trustees sent over the first nurse, Mrs. Ann Bliss, a widow whose duty it was to assist the sick under the direction of the magistrates.[3]

James Carwell, or Carwells, was a peruke-maker before he and his wife came on the *Ann*. His earlier training as a sergeant in the army he employed in exercising the militia and as tythingman and constable. When the Spanish threat became evident in 1740, he responded to it by going down to Frederica to enlist under Oglethorpe for the siege of St. Augustine.[4]

Carwell has a most confused record in the List, with a character attributed to him in London which he seems not wholly to deserve and another man's appointment fastened upon him. His family affairs are confused, for his wife is said to have given birth to a daughter on June 12, 1733, who died in September, as did Mrs. Carwell, yet Mrs. Carwell is listed as having another child born to her in July, 1734, and dead in August.[5]

Carwell seems to have lived a quiet enough life, perhaps not prompt enough sometimes in paying his debts and perhaps with a fondness for the rum which other Savannah men found so refreshing, and with a bad recommendation as the keeper of an orphan. In January, 1737, Carwell was made keeper of the jail, often called the log house, in Savannah, a position which he held for slightly over two years before he was discharged. This job he found of some expense to himself in providing for the prisoners. To James Carwell is attributed incorrectly an appointment by Oglethorpe as provost marshal of Savannah and an appearance before the Trustees in London which he never made; he was confused with James Anderson whose history did include these events.[6]

Carwell suffered losses in the Spanish campaign for which he was not reimbursed, and by the latter part of 1741 he was "reduced to very low and melancholy Circumstances. . . ." In spirit, too, he was low, "my Hopes having been baffled by unperform'd Promises, and by nye nine Years of my time zealously expended here in public Service without a deserved reward." At the age of forty-four he felt "Stricken'd in Years,"[7] and so perhaps he was.

Another peruke-maker, James Muir, had but few more years in the colony than the first men in this group. Mrs. Muir died in July, 1733, and Muir remarried in December, 1734. Mary Woodman who came over as servant to a passenger on the *Savannah*, Captain Lionel Wood, arrived on December 16. Muir married her before she had been in the colony two weeks, having bought her indenture.[8] Muir must have attained some small degree of prosperity by the autumn of 1734, for Samuel Eveleigh, commenting upon Savannah's progress with its fourscore houses and forty more being built, remarked that Muir was then building a two-story house joining his former one.[9] Muir was one of the three people who had licenses to retail certain liquors and who joined Mrs. Hodges and Samuel Mercer in complaining of unlicensed dealers.[10]

Muir went into bankruptcy, probably in 1737, but was ready early the next year to begin making payments to his creditors. At the end of 1738 he signed the representation, having since his arrival cleared and planted three acres of his land.[11] Muir moved to South Carolina in 1739, where great sickness prevailed that summer. An illness described as a contagious, malignant fever, which occasioned numbers of deaths, was responsible for his death in September.[12]

John Gready was another of whom little is known. In the spring and summer of 1735, when Thomas Pratt's house was used for sick people, Gready was very ill.[13] At some time after his recovery he went to Carolina. In 1737 John Brownfield observed that one reason more land was not improved was that some lots were held by people who did not live in the colony. Among these were Gready and another of the *Ann's* passengers, James Wilson, who lived chiefly in Carolina. Gready returned to the colony and exchanged lots with Peter Baillou in 1743 before he disappears from the records.[14]

Not until 1740 does James Wilson's life emerge in any pattern. He assaulted the guard on duty in June, 1734, and was fined the following year for wilfully destroying some hogs, but such scattered mention does little to reveal his life. Wilson married in February, 1735, Mildred Moore, who with her father Robert, a cabinet maker, arrived on the *Georgia Pink,* Captain Henry Daubuz, in August, 1733. It is known that he lived part of the time in Carolina, but he was back in the colony in 1740[15] when William Stephens summed up Wilson's life in most uncomplimentary terms. Stephens could see only in the worst light anyone who signed the representations to be sent to England. Stephens tried to stem by his own indignation the rising tide in favor of change of land tenure, the introduction of slavery, and some voice of the people themselves in the determination of their government. Upon his arrival in Georgia Stephens had adopted the policy of inviting in a few people to a meal or for a dish of tea, but this had little effect in stemming the tide against the Trustees' ideas. Stephens himself was in a ticklish position because his son Thomas was one of the foremost advocates of change in the colony, never hesitating to explain to the Trustees, to Parliament, to anyone whom he could reach, what was wrong with the colony. Thomas Stephens has been ridiculed down through the years for his efforts and opinions. He was a brash young man, but courage was needed for what he did, and he must be credited with helping to bring about a change in Georgia.

Probably to no man in the colony could slavery have been more acceptable economically than to William Stephens, for none was more incommoded by indentured labor than he. All indentured servants did not bear bad characters, but inevitably some were of low habits and lazy. Stephens had his share of bad servants and his share of the inconvenience which resulted from the terms of indentures running out at the time when work in the fields was most needed. Often he was left with crops half planted or half harvested and no one to do the work, however much he may have endeavored to forestall this situation by trying to obtain new servants.

The Trustees maintained that if Negroes were allowed in the colony they would all desert to the Spaniards at St. Augustine and would constitute a threat. Stephens, employed by the Trustees, must not only abide by their views; he must actively sponsor them and thought he should heap scorn upon any who opposed those views. His service to the Trustees might have been more effective had he appraised the situation in Georgia more realistically. Yet the Trustees would not have this. Not long after he came, Stephens told of the growing desire for changed land tenure and was so frowned upon and so coldly answered[16] that he did not attempt it again. It is easy to say that Stephens should have altered his policy, but this might have brought dismissal by the Trustees. His service consisted mainly in bringing to bear whatever influence he could to induce people to accept the Trustees' views, summed up in the directions they gave to one colonist: "It is yours and every one's Duty in the Colony to Act in their proper Stations, and mind their own Business to raise a Maintenance for themselves and Familys; And by a peaceful and orderly Behaviour to be quiet with each other and enjoy the Fruits of their Labour with Comfort; Which will best conduce to their own Happiness and the favour of the Trustees."[17] Stephens's criticisms of the colonists must be read in the light of whether the person of whom he spoke—Mrs. Townsend, Dr. Tailfer and the Scots, Thomas Christie, James Wilson, or any colonist—had any connection with representations to the Trus-

tees or was known to favor change in Georgia. Those who favored
change, except Henry Parker, were always put in the worst light
to show to the Trustees that only the lower element would
align itself with that side against them.

James Wilson was shown in the worst light. "Always clamorous,
and complaining at he knows not what; and where any seditious
or turbulent Meetings have at any time happened," Stephens
said of Wilson, "he never failed to make one of them . . . a
noisy Zealot in promoting both these Demands on the Trustees,
newly framed, for Relief of Oppression . . . admitted into high
Favour with our Demagogues, as a Person fit for their Purposes,
how dark soever. . . ." Stephens was angered because Wilson refused to take a boat down to Frederica with letters for Oglethorpe
and could see in this only another of those dark purposes: "I had
pretty good Reason to believe (from what was told me) that his
falling off from the Agreement he had made, to go in this Boat
now sent, was owing to the Advice he had given him, by those
who took Pleasure in obstructing whatever I attempted, as far as
was in their Power, though but for a few Hours Duration, believing (not without Reason) that what information I sent to the
General would not be much in their Faviour." Stephens sometimes inadvertently betrayed his perception of others' opinion of
him as he did in this instance.

James Wilson was twenty-one years old when he left England
for Georgia and about twenty-nine when Stephens wrote of his
"idle and sottish Behaviour" though Wilson "values on the Title
of Freeholder, and being one of the first Forty . . . He is an able-
bodied, middle-aged Man; has a House built (as all the first Forty
were) by joint Labour; has a Wife and Children, whom he lam-
entably ill treated; till at length he was prevailed on, to let
them go, and live with her Relations in *Carolina,* who feeds and
cloathes them. . . ." But here was the point most calculated to affect the Trustees, who demanded that everyone cultivate his land
and avoid drinking rum: "Planting and clearing of Land, he
has an utter Aversion to; and likewise all Sorts of Labour, more
than what will supply him with little Food, but much Rum,
wherewith he is commonly drunk four Days, acquired by working two. . . ." Wilson evidently had no proper respect for Stephens or anyone else for he was "Insolent in his Behaviour, and
abusive in his Language, towards all in any Authority. . . ."[18] In
his comments on those who signed the remonstrance of Novem-

ber, 1740, Stephens could only say again of Wilson that he was "continually quarrelling—". Wilson must have been a vociferous man in defence of the changes which he thought the colony needed and which he must have lived to see.[19]

Daniel Thibaut, who came with his wife and two children, died in October, 1733, when he had been in the colony less than a year. Early in 1735 Mrs. Thibaut married John Sellier (Cellier), a Swiss brick-layer from Purrysburgh; and they resided on the lot in Savannah originally granted to Thibaut.[20]

Oglethorpe thought well enough of Sellier to make him a tythingman.[21] He settled down to become a citizen of the colony, the needs of which so impressed him that he signed the representation in 1738. In estimating the agricultural accomplishments of those who wanted slave labor, he was reported in London to have cleared two acres but to have fenced or cultivated none of his grant. That August Stephens reported Sellier as having planted four and a half acres of Thibaut's grant. Sellier also signed the remonstrance of November, 1740. Earlier that year Stephens praised his industry though deploring his judgment.[22]

Daniel Thibaut's son James, twelve when he came on the *Ann*, was by 1740 "grown a good hard Youth, and trained up to Labour by his Father-in-Law Sellier." The boy tried Whitefield's orphanage but returned home after about a month. Sellier himself came so much under Whitefield's influence that Stephens said he "is grown lately so signal a Convert, through the Power of the Word as delivered by Mr. Whitefield, that he has bid adieu to all worldy Care; and resolving from henceforth to be content with Food and Raiment for his Labour, has given himself up to Mr. Whitefield's entire Disposal for his Service, on the said Condition of being fed and cloathed for Life. . . . He is a strong, healthy Man, betwixt forty and fifty Years of Age; has left his Wife, &c. regardless of this Colony, to make one in building up the New Jerusalem: Young Tibeau, who left that Station which his Father-in Law has now taken, continues with his Mother; and it is to be hoped they will be able to plant their five-Acre Lot without him."[23]

It is not known how long Sellier continued at the orphanage or whether he ever intended so drastic a change in his life as Stephens indicated. He was brought into prominence in October, 1743, through an accident. William Ryley, a boy who came on the *Savannah*, Captain Wood, with his parents in December, 1733, and was orphaned as the result of the death of his father a month after his arrival and of his mother in 1734, was in the orphanage. At this time he was living in Savannah with Dr. Joseph Hunter, who came from England with Whitefield.[24] William "being in the Woods a Hunting as also happen'd to be John Seillier: The latter shot at the former, mistaking him for some wild beast, and lodg'd above 20 shots in his Body, at which said Seillier is exceedingly grieved Tis supposed that the Lad is not dangerously wounded." Another version says that Sellier and William were both shooting at the same squirrel and that Sellier's aim was so bad that William was dangerously injured.[25] Presumably William recovered. Sellier was in Savannah in 1754 and 1756.[26]

James Thibaut must have done well with his planting and earned for himself a good reputation. In 1752 when he applied to the President and Assistants for land he was "Mr James Thebault, who came to the Colony with the first Embarkation," and his petition for 300 acres of land on the south branch of the Little Ogeechee River was granted. "He had a Prospect of setling it advantageously for the Benefit of his encreasing young Family, by a Legacy, that was bequeathed him and lodged in the Bank of England."[27]

Less is known of John Sammes, or Samms, than of other men in this group. He came alone on the *Ann* and died in August, 1733. His wife evidently remained in England. She was given permission to sell her interest in the lot and was thought to have done so, but the rumor went around Savannah in 1737 that she was coming to claim it. Oglethorpe had already granted it to William Cooksey.[28] This lot, number nine, was perhaps the most variously lived upon of any of those granted to the first colonists. Lewis Bowen lived there in 1734 before his death. William Cooksey had it for a time, and then Elisha Dobree bought it. It was probably after Dobree went to Frederica that William Woodrooffee lived there.[29]

Joseph Stanley and his wife lost the servant they brought with them on the *Ann*, John Mackay, in the sickness of the first summer. They themselves seem to have weathered the trials of that time. Mrs. Stanley was the public midwife to whom the Trustees paid a crown for each woman whom she attended.[30] Early in 1735 she wrote her first letter to the Trustees in which she said that none of the fifty-nine women she had attended had been unsuccessful in childbirth. She also asked that the colonists be

warned against other women in Georgia who were calling themselves midwives, as one mother attended by such a person had
died. Mrs. Stanley wanted a servant sent to her husband and
asked that his sexton's fees be settled. Neither had she been sent
the £5 which Oglethorpe had promised her. She did not think
these requests too great, for the Trustees' tender behavior toward
Georgians made her sure they would consider her case with a
fatherly care.[31]

The following year Mrs. Stanley went to England, as the Earl
of Egmont recorded in his Diary: "She lately came over to lie in
herself, not caring to trust herself to the other midwives of Georgia." By the time she left the colony Mrs. Stanley had brought
into the world 128 children, forty of whom were then dead.[32]
It was evidently expected that she would return to Georgia to
resume her duties, but she did not.

Stanley remained in the colony and signed the representation
of 1738. He had by that time felled, cleared, and fenced four
acres of his land.[33] In the summer of 1740 he left in the same
group with Mrs. Townsend, on Captain Tingley's sloop bound
for New York. William Stephens, to show of how little account were those who would "run" from Georgia, described him
thus: "Joseph Stanley, a Freeholder superannuated, weak and
past any Labour; his Wife left him, and went to England three
Years since, and he now went to a Relation, who he expects will
keep him in his old Age; He never did any Thing towards
maintaining himself by Planting whilst here." The List also has
Stanley vanish from our knowledge in 1740 "being superannuated and past Labour."[34]

Stanley returned to the colony in January, 1744, and received
the Trustees' permission to transfer his Savannah garden and
farm lots to James Campbell in return for which Campbell would
pay him £8 sterling a year for life.[35] In August, 1753, Joseph
Stanley was granted 100 acres of land by the President and Assistants and in 1756 the governor signed a grant of 100 acres to
him, which was doubtless a re-affirmation of the 1753 grant.[36]

When apothecary George Symes came with his wife and daughter on the Ann, he held a dormant commission to succeed Peter
Gordon as first magistrate,[37] but never served in this office. After
almost two years in the colony Symes felt the need of a servant
and wrote to Oglethorpe, "I Disser a Small favor from your
honor if you please to Send Me one Man Sarvant or a boyer it

will be of a greate youce [use] to Me My Agge I have no more att
preasent But I Return you harty thinks for all favers I am in
good hlth att this time ixceapte My Rupter that will be on me
whill in this world." Being an apothecary was not lucrative in
Georgia. "I Cant Not gett aney Monny for all the Cores [cures]
that I have don."[38] This continued to trouble him. He wrote
later that year that Elisha Foster and John Coates, who had built
his house, were still demanding their money. But, he remarked,
"tis very hard that soe many Medicines of my own I brought out
of England which ye people have had of me att least fiveteene
pounds Sterling ye time I have been here."[39]

Mrs. Symes died in the summer of 1733 and Symes married in
March, 1735, Elizabeth Grey, who arrived the preceding August
as a servant of John Baillie, one of the Scots. About six weeks after
her arrival Elizabeth gave birth to a daughter who lived only a
few months. Elizabeth was discharged from Baillie's service before she married Symes. Elizabeth Symes died in June, 1737, "of
a violent Flux, wch she had laboured under above a month."
Symes died within the next few years.[40]

His daughter Anne, who came over with him, married one of
her fellow-passengers, Robert Johnson, who came as a seventeen-
year-old indented servant to Thomas Christie. He had a lot in
Savannah granted to him when the heads of families received their
grants in 1733. Johnson died in the summer of 1734; Anne married Morgan Davis the following spring and died four years
later.[41]

John and Elizabeth Penrose were among the first colonists said
falsely to have deserted the colony. Penrose was said in the List
to have "Run away to Carolina Aug. 1742." Of Mrs. Penrose,
it was reported that she "Went to Carolina for fear of the Spaniards. Quitted Sept. 1740."[42] It is doubtful if Mrs. Penrose was
afraid of the Spaniards or anyone else. Penrose was in the colony
long after this entry.

The Penroses were the despair and the envy of those others
who kept public houses in Savannah. They would sell liquor
without a license; but eventually, despite the reluctance of juries
to convict, they paid two fines and continued their business,
despite the rage of the licensed public-house keepers. Mrs. Penrose was reported guilty of keeping a bawdy house in 1736, but
no more is heard of this.[43] Penrose came over as one of the two
tythingmen and in this capacity was zealous at one time in catch-

ing and bringing to conviction sailors from a ship in port who were selling rum. This so pleased the Trustees that they decided Penrose must have a reward; their decision probably occasioned considerable mirth in Savannah.[44]

Mrs. Penrose was a somewhat rambunctious woman not to be tangled with lightly. Once she took into her employ a servant boy, John Godley, who was anxiously awaiting a ship to return to England. During this two-months period the magistrates could not persuade John to return to Joseph Hetherington, his master, at Thunderbolt. Hetherington said, "I believe he was Encouraged by Mother Penrose, for She kept him in her Employ the whole time; I am Sure nobody Elce wod give him Encouragement, and as for troubling my head with her, is what I did not Care for, She still remaining Conqueror Over the whole place. . . ."[45]

Peter Gordon took to London various complaints about the Penroses. Gordon himself complained that they were encouraged to sell rum publicly and in great quantity despite Penrose's having been fined twice in court, and he blamed Causton for taking his guests to this unlicensed public-house. Samuel Mercer, a licensed seller, said, "Mr. Penrose have Continued to Sell Rum and Other Liquors Ever Since the Esqr [Oglethorpe] Left this place without Licence he hath been fined a Second time for it but doth not minde it Any ways and Continues to do the Same as before and Says that he will So Continue on."[46]

Penrose, despite complaints against him, was given a license for his public house in December, 1736. Before that he had begun to run a boat between Savannah and Charles Town when any business was to be had and upon occasion to Frederica as well. This he continued for some years, often being sent express from Savannah to Charles Town or to Frederica. Many of the ships' stores had to be housed in Savannah and Penrose's boat was engaged in helping to transport them from the anchorage at Tybee to Savannah. After the regiment's arrival at Frederica, Penrose with his boat was more in demand; at one time in 1740 Penrose's long boat with its crew of three men was engaged by Oglethorpe for four months.[47]

The public house, in the meantime, continued to do well, and in 1739 Penrose and Edward Jenkins had more trade than any of the other licensed victualling houses.[48] Mrs. Penrose was responsible for the success of the business during her husband's absence with the boat, and she also kept a shop. Three other shop keepers had Oglethorpe's official sanction about 1739, which gave them advantages in the matter of credit and otherwise, yet they failed while Mrs. Penrose survived.[49]

The Penroses were both in favor of changes, and he signed the representation in 1738. He was marked up in England as having cleared and fenced no land. Penrose was the only one of the *Ann's* passengers who was listed as a husbandman, and he knew that the stretch of pine-land which fell to his share when grants were made was too poor to be worth planting. The only hope that he could see was to have a stock of cattle and turn the forty-five-acre tract into a cowpen for some time, for he was sure that it was not worth planting. In 1741 he asked for 500 acres on Hutchinson's Island but was refused on the ground that he had never been industrious in cultivating his original grant.[50]

After Edward Jenkins moved to Carolina in 1740,[51] the Penroses' public-house had less competition but, perhaps because of its popularity, it came to be viewed with deep suspicion by William Stephens, who thought that some of the schemes for new representations were projected by those who gathered there with Penrose's approval.[52] Stephens, having been down to Frederica, returned to Savannah after an absence of almost three weeks in September, 1740, to find that several women had gone away. He remarked, "It is said that the Fear of the Spaniards was what drove away these. . . ." Among those he mentioned were several who had left their husbands behind, "and Penrose's Wife went off in Defiance of hers; a notorious Termagant, whom I suppose he thinks himself well rid of, . . ." Stephens could not imagine any man not rejoicing when rid of a woman who favored representations; his sorry bit of gossip was duly entered in England as a fact concerning Mrs. Penrose: "Went to Carolina for fear of the Spaniards."[53] Mrs. Penrose probably was not away from Savannah very long, for the public house continued to operate despite Penrose's absences with his boat.

Peter Shepherd, the patroon of a trading boat from South Carolina and one of Penrose's lodgers in 1741, caught one of his Negro crew thieving, brought the man to his quarters at Penrose's, and punished him by lashing. The magistrates sent for Shepherd and Penrose, the latter averring that he was absent when the Negro was brought to his house. Shepherd had sent the Negro back on board his boat and said that he was unaware of offending against Georgia laws, thinking that only if the Negro was employed in town was he liable to seizure. So strict was the rule against slaves in the colony, that Negroes on board vessels were permitted only to come ashore to boil their kettles on the strand; if they came up into town, they were liable to seizure.[54]

This episode was not held against Penrose, for in 1742 his license was renewed, along with the licenses of three other keepers of public houses, Joseph Fitzwalter, Peter Morrell, and John Teesdale, no complaint having appeared against them.[55] That year Penrose was building a schooner in the Savannah River. The following year he borrowed £200 sterling from David Montaigut at ten per cent interest to complete and fit the vessel.

The sum was to be repaid in one year, and as security Penrose gave his bond and a bill of sale of the schooner. She was completed and taking on board a load of rice for New York when in February, 1744, Montaigut petitioned the President and Assistants to stop her from sailing on any voyage until the debt was paid or security given. Penrose offered as collateral security to mortgage his improved lot in Savannah which was then rented at £20 sterling a year. The Board decided that should they stop the vessel injury would be done to Penrose and the shipper of the cargo since Montaigut's money was not due until the following August. The vessel was allowed to sail as originally planned.[56] Savannah was quite proud of that schooner, built by William Seales, launched in the summer of 1743, and brought up to Savannah to be rigged. Computed to be about forty tons, she was the largest boat yet built on the river.[57]

Penrose sailed from Savannah on February 11 for New York with his cargo of rice. He returned on May 4 with a cargo of provisions consigned to Peter Baillou, one of the storekeepers. A few days later Penrose proceeded to Frederica with two Spanish deserters to be delivered to Captain William Horton by order of the President and Assistants.[58]

Penrose made a second voyage to New York, returning early in September, 1744; shortly after, he went on to Frederica again. Captain Patrick Mackay, roused to protect the interests of his wife's son, David Montaigut, followed Penrose to Frederica concerning the loan on the vessel which was due the preceding month. Perhaps Penrose lost the schooner; a vessel which seems to answer her description is mentioned a few months later as Montaigut's, and Penrose himself became the patroon of Montaigut's schooner.[59]

In 1747 Penrose asked the President and Assistants for a grant of 300 acres of land, comprising a small island of possibly 60 acres, where he built his schooner, and the remainder on near-by Whitemarsh Island. The Board granted it, "He being one of the first Settlers in this Colony, and having made considerable Improvements on his Town Lott in the Town and Township of Savannah And knowing him to be a very industrious Man Do Agree to his Petition hoping the Trustees will confirm the same." Penrose thus received the accolade: he was a very industrious man. Though confirmation of the grant in London is lacking, Penrose had the land and for years afterward grants on Whitemarsh Island were spoken of in relation to Penrose's. In 1754 he asked for and obtained a lot in the proposed new town of George Town.[60]

When complaints of David Cunningham, the pilot at Tybee, accumulated in 1750 to the point that his deficiencies were thought to be detrimental to the business of the port, he was displaced by the President and Assistants who named to the place "John Penrose, who appeared to be most capable of acting in that Station." The appointment, confirmed in London, gave Penrose a salary of £40 a year, with an additional sum limited to £10 yearly for one man and provisions.[61]

The vagaries of the Savannah River were commented upon wrathfully from time to time. Before David Cunningham was dismissed as pilot, James Habersham urged that the river be surveyed to determine the degree of Cunningham's fault. "But People were so prejudiced in Favour of the River," Habersham said, "that it was almost deemed Treason to contradict the received Opinion. Mr Cunningham was displaced, and Mr John Penrose was put in his Room. Since which, almost every Vessell has been run on Ground in going Down, that draws above Ten Feet." Ships of 200 tons or upwards had come up to Savannah, Habersham continued, but he knew of none of near that burden that had been carried down loaded without running aground, and this plainly was a hindrance to exportation. He and his partner Francis Harris shipped a cargo of rice the previous year and even though part of it was loaded at Cockspur Island below Savannah, yet the *Snow Mary* "met with Difficulty in going down, and was so often run on Ground, that it almost drove the Master mad. . . ." Only six days before he wrote, a large sloop freighted by Harris and Habersham, two thirds loaded was four times on ground on her way down the river between Savannah and Cockspur. An insupportable inconvenience, Habersham termed these conditions; the case was the same with every vessel of upwards of ten feet draught loaded at Savannah.[62]

Penrose held his place as pilot for four years and was then displaced in 1754 by the President and Assistants, after they received a petition from the merchants, mariners, and planters that he was deficient in his duty and that the port of Savannah suffered as a result. A few months later Penrose was granted the George Town lot by the same Board that displaced him as pilot, so his reputation cannot have suffered greatly. Penrose was dead by 1758.[63]

John Wright was another of the first colonists who fell afoul of the Trustees' orders concerning the sale of distilled liquors. He lost his license in 1734, and it was given to Mrs. Hodges, later Mrs. Townsend. Wright died in the latter part of 1737, and by the summer of 1738 his widow, Penelope, had married Joseph Fitzwalter. Wright must have recovered his public house license, or else he ran the place without a license for it seems to have been in operation at the time his widow remarried.[64]

John and Penelope Wright brought two children with them on the *Ann;* the elder, John Norton, was thirteen and his sister Elizabeth was eleven. John was an ambitious youth, who asked for a 500-acre grant at age twenty-three and held the offices of tythingman, jailer, and messenger to the President and Assistants before he was twenty-five. He was not quite satisfied, though he did his duty in his offices and received his salary. He wrote the Trustees, "I am not Easy the pepel Not Paying the Same Regard to Me as they Wold Provid'd I was Impowead by a Commission from Your Homours Seting forth the Power and Extent of each branch of Business by Reason A person who Receives his Commision here is Lyable to be Turn'd out Every Day he Lieves and Powerful Enemys Are Very Plenty in Savannah." He therefore asked for commissions from the Trustees as a better authority for his offices than appointment by the President and Assistants in Georgia. The next year Wright was deprived of his offices for a youthful prank which excited the town and for which he refused to ask pardon or admit any wrongdoing.[65]

In the meantime, Fitzwalter and his new wife Penelope fared

well enough. The year they were married, 1738, was a hard one in the colony, and Fitzwalter lost his place as the Trustees' gardener in October. Times were hard and uneasy that year and the next and this affected the business of Penelope's and his public house. After the arrival of Oglethorpe's regiment in May, public houses picked up some business from the officers and men when any of them were in Savannah. Fitzwalter did well enough at one time to buy £40 worth of wine from Colonel Cochran of the regiment. No complaint having been made against him, his license was renewed in 1742 along with the licenses of John Penrose, Peter Morrell, and John Teesdale.[66] Presumably Fitzwalter was occupied with this business and his own planting during these years, for little mention is found of him. He was one of twenty-five men who signed "A State of the Province of Georgia on November 10, 1740," written by William Stephens by order of the Trustees, in an attempt to answer the representations sent to England and criticism there concerning Georgia. Some of the remarks in this document concerning the agricultural possibilities of the colony were made in more detail by Fitzwalter before Stephens came to the colony.[67]

Whatever Fitzwalter's other concerns, he was still at heart a gardener. In the three years preceding December, 1741, his grapevines were among the most flourishing in the colony. Stephens, Causton, Noble Jones, and Henry Parker were among the eleven men whose vines were accounted best.[68] That year Stephens spoke kindly of Fitzwalter, as "being bred a Gardener, and having his Lot near Town converted into a Garden, and well fill'd with many valuable Things (besides for the Kitchen) various Kinds of Plants for Experiments, Vines, Mulberries, &c. . . ."[69] In the summer of 1741 Fitzwalter suddenly did battle for his plants.

Animals and geese commonly fed about the streets of Savannah and caused no special trouble until Robert Williams brought his goats to the colony in 1741. No sooner were the goats turned out to feed than people began to complain of their depredations on farm and garden lots. The "old He-Goat was so cunning," William Stephens remarked, "that by getting his Horns within the Pale of any close Fence, either by pulling, or thrusting, he would soon make Way for all his Tribe to follow. . . ." Soon the goats visited Fitzwalter's garden and ate the tops of all his cherished plants and "seriously defac'd" the whole garden. Fitzwalter exclaimed against these depredations but took no other action until the second visit of the goats when "he was so provoked, that . . . he slew the Leader, and openly declared in the Town what he had done."

Robert Williams soon returned from Carolina and swore revenge. Knowing that Fitzwalter had geese feeding about the streets of Savannah, Williams shot several of the first geese he met with. They were Mrs. Vanderplank's geese and Williams had to pay for them. This occasioned considerable merriment in Savannah. Some weeks later Fitzwalter, driving his geese before him as he sauntered peacefully home in the late summer afternoon, met Williams, who fired and killed one goose. The rest of the flock escaped in noise and confusion, while Fitzwalter was himself pursued by Williams with upraised cane and threats to serve Fitzwalter as he had already the dead goose. Fitzwalter swore out a warrant against Williams. When Williams refused to give surety for appearance at the next court to answer this and other charges but threatened to go to England instead, he was retained under guard in his house until he posted bail.[70]

Fitzwalter was appointed wharfinger and vendue master on December 31, 1741, by the President and Assistants.[71] Probably the work as wharfmaster and auctioneer was not too much to be combined easily with that of the public house. He continued to garden and at Stephens's invitation went with him and Samuel Mercer to spend a day and night at the Stephens plantation, Bewlie, on the Vernon River, where Stephens asked Fitzwalter's advice on planting grapevines, mulberries, and several varieties of fruit trees.[72]

Fitzwalter worked in the Trustees' garden again before his death for an unascertained period, replacing John Giovannoli as gardener.[73] It may have been during Fitzwalter's last period in the garden that additional land was cleared. The soil in the upper part of the garden was very poor, so the fourth part of the garden ("by a Steep declivity ending in a Boggy Swamp at bottom that was full of exceeding thick growing wood;") was cleared and trenched and proved to be a fertile addition.[74] Surely Fitzwalter had great satisfaction in working again with his "baby Nussary of plants" as he did when he first came to Georgia. Perhaps it was as well that his life ended before the day in 1755 when the garden ended its career as a public garden and its ten acres were granted to Georgia's first Royal governor.[75]

Time was running out for Joseph Fitzwalter, though. The last
year of his life was one of the hardest the colony had known,
for it was 1742 and the year of the Spanish invasion to the south
when Savannahians fled to the woods up the river in fear of the
enemy's approach. Food was scarce, times were hard, life was uncertain. A wave of that illness, usually spoken of as an epidemical
malignant fever, raged in Savannah in the latter part of that summer and caused a number of deaths. On October 14, the President
and Assistants, in view of the "helpless and distressed State
that Joseph Fitzwalter and his Family have been reduced to for a
long Time past" recommended that aid be given to them. On
Thursday morning, October 28, after an illness of several months,
Fitzwalter died.[76]

Mrs. Fitzwalter at her request in November, 1742, succeeded to
Fitzwalter's place as wharfinger, on the plea that she was left in low
circumstances and that her son, John Wright, could take proper
care of the wharf. But John's lack of success occasioned
many complaints.[77] Mrs. Fitzwalter suffered a shock in the spring
of 1743 from which she must have been long in recovering. On
Sunday afternoon, May 8, a violent thunderstorm burst over
Savannah. Mrs. Fitzwalter, her son John, and daughter Elizabeth
Wright were at home together when lightning struck the house,
shattered the plastering, and killed Elizabeth.[78]

By the latter part of 1748 Mrs. Fitzwalter's condition, reduced
when Joseph Fitzwalter died, was lower still. She had in the meantime had a lodger who provided a small addition to her income.
In 1744 Thomas Bosomworth, the minister, was well pleased
with his accommodations at Mrs. Fitzwalter's.[79] Four years later
the job of wharfinger had shrunk, since trade to Savannah had
decayed, until the small rates paid for wharfage were sufficient to
provide only scanty addition to Mrs. Fitzwalter's living. Now they
were stopped entirely by the Trustees' direction, "and the poor
Woman must inevitably be reduced to the utmost want and misery without the Charitable relief of the Trustees." The Board in
Georgia was prepared to render that aid and did, a few days
after writing their letter, "well knowing that thro old Age and Infirmities she is entirely uncapable of doing any Thing towards
her own Support. . . ." Mrs. Fitzwalter was allowed twenty shillings
quarterly until the Trustees' pleasure was known, the Board "not
being capable to go any farther having many other Demands of

the like Nature."[80] Mrs. Fitzwalter was about forty-nine years old, in the opinion of the time an old woman.[81]

In February, 1758, over nine years after that letter was written, the widow Penelope Fitzwalter sold her town and garden lots in Savannah to Dr. Lewis Johnston. On July 4, 1758, she had a grant to lot number 10 in Savannah signed by Governor Henry Ellis, an affirmation of an old grant.[82] Four years later, in 1762, twenty years after Joseph Fitzwalter had died and she had been said to be old and infirm, fourteen years after her old age and infirmities had been dwelt on, she was buying supplies at the store.[83] Somewhere along the way Penelope Fitzwalter took a new lease on life. She had, in common with some of the other women who were Georgia's first colonists, a certain toughness and stamina which, despite poverty, the death of two husbands and a daughter, illness and those disappointments in life which bear so hard upon women, enabled her to keep her head up and to pursue her course. The records are silent about Penelope Fitzwalter after this, as no William Stephens reported the goings and comings of the colony's humble folk henceforth. By 1762 she would have been sixty-three years old. She probably lived the rest of her life in Georgia.

Thomas Young, the wheelwright, was forty-five years old when he came on the *Ann* and in ten years he was spoken of as "the old Man"; in 1744 he was considered one of the most ancient inhabitants of Savannah. Young came from England alone, but he married in 1734 Mary, the widow of William Box. Box was a hatter who with his wife and two boys, James and Philip, arrived on the *Savannah*, Captain Wood, on December 16, 1733. The family settled at Abercorn and Box died the following April.[84] Mrs. Box wished to return to England after her husband's death but, as Thomas Causton wrote, "I promised her some assistance here, and did her some little Kindnesses: In a little time she altered her Mind and married Mr. Young the Wheelwright." It was indeed a little while, about three months, for the wedding took place in July, 1734. Young's family was further augmented by the arrival of his grandson, Thomas Egerton, on the *Prince of Wales*, Captain George Dunbar, in December of that year.[85]

Young had been almost two years in the colony when he made a report and a request to Oglethorpe, then in England: "I have Mounted all the Cannon and I have the Town Besness in Looking after the Street," he began cheerfully enough. He had no servant to look after his cultivating and extending his business as a wheelwright. Would the Trustees not take into consideration the public work he had done and "Allow Me Something Quarterly As What ye Honble Board Shall Think Proper I have Receve Nothing at all for all My Trouble and Care." Thomas Young was not the only colonist without an enduring enthusiasm for the Trustees' ideal of joint labor, and who did not think that being sent to Georgia and having provisions for a year or more, until crops could be made, formed sufficient recompense for labor. People who worked, wanted pay.

Young was one of those involved by Oglethorpe's promises which he did not make plain to Thomas Causton. Young wrote that because no written orders were left about materials for the house building he was behind in his own and the widows' houses he was working on.[86] Evidently receiving no reply to this, six months later he wrote to the Trustees, "I Should be Wary Ungrateful if I did Not Return My Great God, thanks, And your Honours for Sending me here to a Place Ware Noe Man Can Starve But to the Contrary Live in Plenty, if he Will Work as I doe, for I doe asure your Honours I work Dayly And, that Wary hard, and yett God, be pressed, have ad My health Ever Sence I have Been heer; And all the publick Work that his done for your honours his Done by Or My orders. . . ."

Young's responsibilities weighed upon him. God had blessed him with his wife and children, but they were "Every Year a further Charge," not that he complained about it. Then, "I have a Lott for to Improve, And, Another for my Grandson Thos Eggerton Whom his but a youth, Besides My home to take Care of Wich I May Build In time, Because tis My trade"; but he found it very hard to cultivate so much land without any help. "And his honor Esqr Eglethorpe, Before he Whent aWay. And Before I ad Soe Large a family, Did promise me that E Wold Lay before your honours My Case And that he Wold, Send me a Cople of Servants, In Order to Cultivate My Land; that as I Grow Old, I May Not Leave my family Destitute"; while he lived he intended to take care that they should have something after his death. "I Wold Not have Trubled Your Honours Eney More, But When Esqr Oglethorpe was hear E Made Me Wealright Wich Belongs to the train of Artilary Wich always ad Some

Small Salary, and Likewise the Care of the town And, Guns for Wich I have Ad, Noe Other gratuety But My Labour."[87]

Young was unusually busy shortly before this letter was written, for a great event took place in Savannah in June—the distribution of the Indian presents by Tomochichi. Much planning and exercise of diplomacy preceded this event. Thomas Young's part in this affair was to build an open shed on the western side of Johnson Square, with benches for the Indians and tables for the display of the presents. Surely he watched, as did most of Savannah, when the great day came. Colonel William Bull was there from Charles Town to lend his counsel and to participate in the events.

Nearly 200 men under arms, commanded by Noble Jones, and an additional company of about thirty under the command of Dr. Patrick Tailfer, gave the display and formality which accompanied such occasions. As the Indians came to the public landing, forty-seven cannon were fired; as they stepped ashore from the pettiaguas, Dr. Tailfer's company saluted them announcing that the magistrates were ready to receive them. The colonists, commanded by Noble Jones, with flags flying and drums beating, attended the Indians on the walk to Johnson Square; near the Square, some of the colonists filed off into other streets leading to the Square and drew up in two lines leading to the reception point. The Indians marched across the Square to be received by the magistrates, to be given Talks and to give Talks in return. The affair lasted several days. The hot June sun poured down as the Talks went on with the recital of events in their Nation and of parts played by their warriors. Finally the presents were distributed and Tomochichi's reputation was suitably enhanced. The Upper and Lower Creeks went home, and Thomas Young could take down his stand which had reverberated to the lofty words of whites and Indians alike.[88]

Young's plea for servants was heeded in London. Thomas Oakes, aged fifteen, bound himself to the Trustees for six years in 1735, and the Trustees assigned him to Young who was required to give a recognizance of £5 for performing the conditions of the indenture. Young Oakes arrived by the *Georgia Pink* in November, 1735. Young had other servants later, with the usual troubles of runaways.[89]

None occasioned as much correspondence as did Tommy Oakes.

In 1738 the boy's father, one of the King's coachmen, went to the Trustees with a complaint of the cruel usage which Thomas Young had given Tommy in Georgia. William Stephens was directed by the Trustees to obtain details of the treatment from Tommy and if the complaint were just, to have Young punished. The Trustees desired that all masters should be punished who used their indentured servants ill, "but particularly Mr Young for using this Lad ill who was a Servant assigned to him from them for better purposes, and as a matter of favour being bred to his Business; And therefore they think him a proper Example for Punishment." If Oakes wished to return to England, Stephens was authorized to vacate the boy's indenture and send him back.[90]

When William Stephens interviewed Oakes, the boy denied having sent any complaint to England; he suggested that this was the work of a woman who had left the colony. He was well used by Young, Tommy said; "he never failed by a Belly-ful of good Food, such as his Master himself eat; that he had Shirts and Cloathes as good as any in the Town of his Equals . . . but only wanted a better Coat for Sundays, which his Master had ordered to be provided for him: That he worked alike with a Grandson of his Master's at the Trade he was bound to, and that when his Master corrected him, it was just, and what he ought to expect for running away, which he had done more than once, but never would again; and was very well contented now. . . ."[91]

This was handsome of Tommy, but these fair promises were broken quickly. Before a month was gone, he ran away again, but not before he was given his new Sunday coat. He and Mrs. Brownjohn's servant boy ran away together, were taken at Fort Argyle in a few days, and were brought back together and committed to the jail for a brief stay.[92] In 1740 Tommy returned to England, Stephens predicting gloomily, "I fear he will be little comfort to his Father; but without good looking after, be in great danger of coming to shame, being prone to all Idleness."[93] Tommy Oakes saw a good deal of the colony on these run-away trips, the excitement of which must have greatly enlivened him. Young had taken another apprentice in 1739, sixteen-year-old John Peter Slechtermans, whose sister, eleven-year-old Juliana, was assigned to Young as a servant.[94]

In 1742 the Thomas Oakes business was repeated with Thomas Egerton, Young's grandson. Complaints were made by the boy's father in England to the Trustees that he was ill used and orders were sent from London for an investigation.[95] No one could say Thomas Egerton ran away or neglected his work. On the contrary, everyone spoke of him as a diligent, hardworking boy; but the magistrates found "that the old Man had been peevish towards him more than usual. . . ." However, what young Egerton disliked most was "that his Grandfather distinguish'd him from those Children which were his Wives, & he was not allow'd to fare as they did, either in Food or Raiment." Efforts at reconciliation proved vain, and the boy returned to England.[96] Whatever the degree of partiality, Young or his wife kept the Box boys in school; and their teacher, John Dobell, wrote approvingly of them the following year.[97]

Thomas Young signed the representation of 1738 with his mark and when William Stephens prepared "A State of the Province of Georgia" to counter it, Young signed that also.[98] When Penelope Fitzwalter's son, John Wright, was dismissed from the position of jail-keeper in 1744, Young, "One of the most antient Inhabitants and Freeholders of this Town and an industrious hard working Man" petitioned for the office and was given the appointment.[99] Young at the age of about fifty-seven might be considered ancient, but he had received the highest possible praise: he was industrious. Yet industry did not fit him to be a jail-keeper; prisoners escaped, as prisoners so often did in Savannah; and he was removed from the office in 1746.[100] With the office went his hope of a livelihood; a little over two weeks later he asked for relief, he having a large family of children and both he and his wife "being very infirm thro old Age and Sickness, wherein She now lies in a deplorable Condition. . . ." They were allotted as a temporary measure, four shillings a week.[101]

Four years later, in 1750, he was the late Thomas Young, and his widow, "absolutely incapable of subsisting herself and two Children without some Relief," was given an allowance of twenty shillings a quarter until the President and Assistants should have reason to recall it. Mary Young was still living in 1758.[102] Her boys, James and Philip Box, accumulated land by grant and purchase, owned slaves, and were substantial citizens in Georgia long after the Trustees gave up control of the colony.[103]

CHAPTER THIRTEEN

A House of Mercy

J OHN WARREN (or Warrin), a flax dresser, was thirty years old when he and his wife Elizabeth, twenty-seven, and family embarked on the *Ann*. The children were William, aged six; Richard, four; Elizabeth, three; and John, one and a half. The passenger list shows another boy, aged three weeks, not yet baptized. The christening of this boy, George Marinus Warren, on board the *Ann*, November 23, was celebrated by the passengers with a special supper, gift of the Trustees. Though alive at the time of landing, this child was dead at the end of the summer.[1]

The boy John died in June, 1733, the father died in August, and the boy William in September. When the guardhouse burned that summer, all of the Warren possessions stored there were lost. On his deathbed, John Warren had Oglethorpe's promise to send his family back to England. Mrs. Warren, herself ill from the prevailing flux and dazed by three deaths in rapid succession, well merited Oglethorpe's comment that she was an object of compassion. Richard, at the age of four or five years, was now the man of the family, and for him the house and the stock of cattle would be preserved.[2]

The children and their mother sailed back to England on the *Georgia Pink*, Captain Daubuz, in early September. The house which Richard would inherit was used for an infirmary. Jacques Camuse later occupied Richard's house, number 10, and as late as 1739 Oglethorpe concurred with Camuse, who was developing the silk business for the Trustees, in the opinion that the shortage of silk production that year was due to the mortality among the worms, they having become infected from the house where sick people had stayed, and that "occasioned a Sickness amongst the worms, which destroyed a great many."[3]

The passage to England was a long one; it took all winter. Towards the latter part of March, 1734, the vessel arrived in England.[4] Mrs. Warren went almost immediately to the Trustees. Her report on the colony pleased them, for she spoke well of the productivity of the land, of the lessening mortality after the people stopped drinking the river water (which she thought gave people the flux and from which she herself was suffering) and drank water from the well, where a pump was in place before she left. She had no criticism of her circumstances in the colony. Her garden lot of five acres, within half a mile of Savannah, she had used for her cows; on the forty-five-acre farm lot the timber was good and Oglethorpe promised to preserve it for Richard's use.

To the Trustees, Mrs. Warren and her two small children were something of a problem. They could not accede to Oglethorpe's request that the Trust help her, because its money could not be so spent in England. After consulting Captain Daubuz to verify her story, they took up a collection among themselves which provided the Warrens with eleven or twelve pounds. Captain Daubuz informed them that, presumably on the long passage to England, Mrs. Warren "had contracted herself to a seaman, who since his arrival is pressed on board a man-of-war now at Portsmouth. Upon which we told the woman we would get the man discharged and she should return to Georgia with him." She was ordered "to come from time to time to us till she shipped herself off."[5]

Mrs. Warren married the seaman, Jonathan (or James) Wood, about whose name some confusion at first existed, so that the Trustees had her married to another man, Johnathan Hood. They paid her £10 a year rent for Richard's house, which was used as an infirmary.[6]

On March 30, 1737, Mrs. Wood died in England. At the time of her death, her son Richard was at sea with his seaman stepfather and Elizabeth was in England. Richard returned to find that his mother was dead and that he now owned outright the house and fifty acres of land in Georgia.[7] After his wife's death Wood brought Richard and Elizabeth to the Trustees to be taken care of, saying that he would have nothing more to do with them. The Trustees shipped the children back to Georgia on the *Mary Ann,*

Captain Thomas Shubrick, bound for Charles Town in the summer of 1737.[8]

On the *Mary Ann* was a group of passengers for Georgia: William Stephens, coming out to be secretary for the affairs of the
Trust in Georgia, with five servants; Mrs. Samuel Smallwood
coming to join her husband at Frederica; two Trust servants; several recruits for the Independent Company, with their wives; and
the two youngest passengers, Richard, aged nine years, and Elizabeth, aged eight.[9] Not quite five months had passed since their
mother had died.

The children embarked at Gravesend on August 12, 1737.
The vessel sailed shortly after mid-day the following day, but
was delayed in the channel until August 24, by unfavorable wind
and weather.[10] England was soon behind them, America before
them, the second such passage for Richard and Elizabeth, and for
Richard the fourth time he had put to sea. "In our Passage divers
of our people, as well Sailors as Soldiers & Servants, fell ill of
Feavers, frequently 4 or 5 at a time; but tho' it pulled 'em down
very low," William Stephens wrote, "yet we lost none; & by the
help of a young Scotch Surgeon on board, bound for Carolina,
who could bleed & blister &c, they generally got on their legs
again in 7 or 8 days. . . ."[11]

Richard and Elizabeth reached Charles Town on October 20.
Stephens thought " 'Twas incumbent on me, wth as little loss of
time as possible, to get all ashore who were under my care . . . that
they might recover more Strength by the help of a little fresh
food for a few days . . . for wch purpose we got a little old
empty house, just capable of receiving them, & where they
might boyl their own Broth. . . ." No mention is made of the
children. It was not until October 27 that Stephens completed arrangements for passage to Georgia and the whole group went
on board the schooner where they spent the night. It sailed on
the twenty-eighth, arriving at Savannah on Tuesday morning, November 1.[12]

Two years, two months, and a little more than two weeks pass
before Richard and Elizabeth again appear in the records. What
arrangements were made for them before both were placed in
Bethesda Orphanage on January 18, 1740, are unknown. At
that time they had been under the care of Mrs. Sarah Goldwire,
who soon placed her own son, Nathaniel Polhill, in the orphanage.[13] William Stephens described John Goldwire's new wife as

having been "a widow with divers children which she had by her two former Husbands Polhill and Retford." Several Goldwire children were born also, who were "carried" to Carolina in 1742 when their parents "run away to Carolina Aug. 1742."[14]

The crowded condition of the household might account for the removal of Richard and Elizabeth Warren, but a more probable cause was George Whitefield's zeal for orphans. He gathered orphans wherever he found them, sometimes leaving controversies rolling in his wake.

Whitefield did not come to Georgia for the purpose of opening an orphanage. He came with an appointment from the Trustees as the minister at Frederica, amended even before he reached Georgia to include the church at Savannah also until a new minister there could be secured.[15] Whitefield brought with him James Habersham, from Yorkshire, and said frankly that both would "want many Necessaries, as to wearing apparel, &c." Except that Whitefield was given the watch which he asked for and Habersham received none, the Trustees gave them identical outfits, exactly as Whitefield requested. Each received six shirts, four pairs of stockings, two pairs of breeches, one waistcoat, a close coat, a great coat, one night gown, a wig, a hat, six handkerchiefs, four pairs of shoes, and six pairs of socks. Thus accoutered, they embarked on the *Whitaker,* one of the troop-ships bringing Oglethorpe's regiment, on December 19, 1737; they arrived in Savannah on May 7, 1738.[16]

Whitefield immediately began visiting and expounding in Savannah, seeking out people in their homes there as well as in the outlying settlements. In June he opened a girls' school in Savannah and planned for the education of the children in the nearby settlements. He visited the Germans at Ebenezer and the French at Hampstead and Highgate, paying John Dobell to teach the children there. Hampstead he resolved to visit once a week, for among the seven children in the settlement (the population included only four adults) he could see those who would prove useful members of the colony if a proper place was provided for their education and maintenance. "Nothing can effect this but an Orphan House," he decided, "which might be erected at *Savannah,* would some of those that are rich in this World's Good, contribute towards it."[17] The idea may have been in his mind before but it found expression that Friday, May 19.

By the early part of June, 1738, when Whitefield had been in the colony one month and three days, he knew that what he had most at heart was building an orphan-house, which he hoped to make arrangements for on his return to England. His idea received impetus on a visit to Ebenezer in July. He was greatly pleased with the order and industry of the place and, above all, with Bolzius's orphan-house and the regularity with which it was managed. In it were seventeen children and a widow. To its inmates he gave some of the stores he had for the poor in Georgia. Bolzius called the orphans about him, catechized them for Whitefield's benefit, exhorted them to give thanks to God for His good providence, prayed with them, made them pray after him, and had them sing a psalm. Then, Whitefield said, "the little Lambs came and shook me by the Hand one by one, and so we parted, and I scarce was ever better pleased in my Life."[18] Whitefield *must* have little lambs of his own.

Whitefield left Georgia in August for England and while there received a grant from the Trustees of 500 acres of land for the orphan-house, and collected about £1000 for the orphan-house in Georgia. He left England in August, 1739, with thirteen adults and three children, all coming as staff or inmates in the orphan-house. All reached Savannah on January 11, 1740.[19]

Whitefield now came with an appointment from the Trustees as the minister at Savannah, and thus displaced William Norris, who had held this appointment since his arrival in October, 1738. Norris was removed from Savannah to Frederica because Whitefield said he needed to be in Savannah to erect his orphan-house. Norris courteously turned over the Savannah church to Whitefield immediately. Had he been given to contention, Whitefield said of Norris, he might have disturbed Whitefield in his ministry.[20] Whitefield was even then, five days after his arrival, planning to leave again in about three months and was about to decide that it would be inconsistent for him to keep the parish under his care.[21]

But he would not leave until work was well under way on the orphan-house, which he planned to call Bethesda, "that is," he said, *"the House of Mercy.* For I hope many Acts of Mercy will be shown there, and that many will thereby be stirred up *to praise the Lord, as a* GOD *whose Mercy endureth for ever."* He could not wait for buildings to be built; he rented David Douglass's house in Savannah, described by William Stephens as much the largest on any private lot in town.[22]

Richard and Elizabeth Warren were charter members of the orphanage, entering it on January 18, 1740. Richard's name heads the list of boys and Elizabeth's the list of girls.[23] There was no one to controvert Whitefield's taking Richard and Elizabeth; they were bound to no one by ties of blood and abiding love. They were made to order for him, with their tenuous hold on any certainty in life.

Here they would have, for the first time since the summer of 1733, a settled existence. Here they were, or would shortly be, with some of the children who came on the *Ann*: Marmaduke Cannon; John and Peter Clark; temporarily Richard and Frances Milledge; Mary, Lucy, and Catherine Mouse; Peter and Charles Tondee; and others.[24] Whitefield took not only orphans but children whose families could not maintain them, a fact which probably accounts for Nathaniel Polhill's admittance and certainly for the Mouse children's. The children were assured of food, clothes, and schooling. While the orphanage was in Savannah, many of the Savannah children went to day school with the resident children. Whitefield had a varied assortment of charges and he remarked concerning them, "Most of the orphans were in poor case; and three or four almost eat up with lice."[25]

Richard and Elizabeth could scarcely have been greeted by the welcome song, since they were such early arrivals. They must, though, have sung it to others who came:

> Welcome, dear Brethren, whom we love,
>   Bethesda this we call.
> A House of Mercy may it prove
>   To you, to us, to all.
>
> What tho' our Parents dear are dead,
>   Yet our Great God provides:
> Our Bodies here are clothed and fed;
>   Our Souls have Christian Guides.[26]

Richard and Elizabeth would surely have taken part in the funeral that occurred on March 11, less than two months after their arrival. That day "a furious Wind from the North-West blowed all this Day, and so piercing cold, that no Day in the past Winter exceeded it. . . ." In the evening of the same day an old woman of Whitefield's household was buried. Despite the piercing cold, thirty or forty boys and girls from the orphanage walked solemnly in pairs, singing psalms, to the courthouse, where church

was held. The children headed the procession; then came Whitefield; next was the corpse carried by six men, and finally a number of other people. Whitefield read the prayers and preached
on the text "Watch and pray"; then the procession moved to
the cemetery, where Whitefield gave an exhortation and the
corpse was interred.[27]

On January 30, 1740, Whitefield marked the sites for the
Bethesda buildings. Building began in March. The orphanage
was "scituated upon a high Bluff, with a pleasant Prospect before
it," the *South-Carolina Gazette* reported; "it is to be 60 Feet long,
and 40 Feet wide, with a Yard and Garden before and behind.
The Foundation is to be Brick, and is to be sunk 4 Feet within
and rais'd 3 Feet above the Ground, which is intended for a
Kitchen Cellar, &c. The House is to be two Stories with a Hipp
Roof, the first 10 and 2nd 9 Feet high there will be 20 commodi-
ous rooms, behind which will be a Still House, and two other
Houses, the one for an Infirmary, and the other for the Cotton
Manufacture which he intends to prosecute with all possible
Expedition: He has called the Place BETHESDA the *House of
Mercy. . . .*"[28]

In the latter part of July, William Stephens found that "The
principal House was a grand Edifice . . . they were in such For-
wardness, as to be ready for raising the Roof this week . . . and the
Rooms of both Lower and upper Story are of good Height: As we
approach it, are six good handsome Edifices, three of each Side,
for the following Purposes, viz. a Work-house for Women and
Children, opposite an Infirmary of like Dimensions; next a
Kitchen, opposite to it another of the same Size, for Washing,
Brewing, &c. the other two I was not yet informed what Uses
they were designed for."

The buildings were not completed when the removal day came.
On November 3, 1740, everyone moved from the house in Savannah to the new site. Some went in wagons with the baggage, some
on horseback, some on foot. It was quite a caravan, for the numbers were probably substantially the same as those six weeks
earlier when "the family" consisted of 146 persons: 60 people
including hired servants, 61 orphans and other children, and an
additional 25 miscellaneous workmen.[29]

Whitefield was absent when the move to Bethesda took place,
for he left on August 19 to make again what William Stephens
usually referred to as "a progress" to the northern colonies. During

Whitefield's absences, the Reverend Mr. Barber acted as superintendent of spiritual affairs, while James Habersham was the schoolmaster.[30] Habersham had come over to Georgia with Whitefield and was much under Whitefield's influence. His enthusiasm for Whitefield led him at one time into excesses which drew reproof from the Trustees.

Christopher Orton, the new minister for Savannah, arrived in December, 1741. He "has behav'd unexceptionably well to all; & done the Duties of his Office with great Decorum & Diligence: but were he an Angel from Heaven; the Distractions about Religion," said William Stephens, "which our Methodists have been so zealously fomenting, would stirr 'em up to oppose him; unless his Doctrine squared with those Enthusiastic & uncharitable Notions, which they have imbibed." Orton, only twenty-four years old when he left England and ordained but a few days before sailing, was in the colony less than two months when he underwent, as Stephens said, "such vile treatment . . . from those Christians: (A Name which they affect to be called by, but allow it to none but themselves, as being most assuredly in the Number of the Elect.)" Orton himself spoke of the "late Unchristian, & rude Behaviour of some of the Chief of the Dissenting Party (or Methodist) here towds. me . . . ," but this was mild compared to what the Bethesda people and their friends said of him, a strict Church of England man. Orton thought that the Methodists were mistaken; of the children sent to the orphanage "many of them suffer'd (as I have been credibly informed) in their Bodies by hard Usage, & In their principles & manners by the mistaken Doctrines of their Teachers. . . ."[31]

The result of Orton's being so vigorously and scathingly denounced by Habersham and Barber was that the magistrates, to protect Orton in the future, issued warrants against Barber and Habersham. They were heard in a scene of considerable excitement and religious argument, offered bail which they refused, sent to jail, tried a week later, found guilty by the jury on two presentments, fined five marks each, and required to find sureties for their good behavior for a year.[32]

The Trustees sharply reproved Habersham; they were "concerned to find, that you, who have such a Trust as the Care of the Orphans (committed to you by Mr. Whitefield) have been guilty of a Misdeamnour, which called for the Cognizance of, and Punishment by a Court of Justice. Your going with Mr.

Barber, Hunter and others to the late Revd. Mr. Orton, forcing him into Disputes on Points of Religion, and then treating him with Scurrility, because he differ'd from your Sentiments; Your denouncing Damnation against him for preaching false Doctrine, tho' you never heard him, charging him with being no Christian, and not understanding the Articles of the Church of England, and asking him how he dared to preach without being call'd to it by the Holy Spirit, was a Behaviour unjustifiable in every Light. It could only tend to inflame the Minds of the People, and lay a Foundation for perpetual Discord in a Place," the Trustees said, remembering John Wesley, "which had been too much disturb'd and harrass'd with it before. It was indecent with regard to him as the Establish'd Minister of the Town, whose Conduct was unexceptionable. It was indecent with regard to the Trustees, who thought him a proper Person for that Employment: And it was inconsistent with that Meekness and Charity, which Christianity so strongly inculcates." The Trustees were, they said, resolved to support fully the Act of Toleration which though it provided "that all Dissenters from the Church of England shall be undisturbed and protected in their Worship; it does not entitle them to offer insults to others; The Law is open to those who receive them, and the Magistrates have ample Power to protect all Persons from them; The Trustees do therefore require & expect from you, that hereafter you carefully avoid raising any Contentions upon Points of Religion, or giving any Disturbance to the Minister of the Church of England, or others, who are equally intitled with yourself to the Protection of the Act of Toleration."

Nor was this all. "The Trustees cannot but be apprehensive, that those, who are possess'd with such fiery Zeal, are improper Ones to have the Care of Children, who had better have no Education, than such as will render them unfit for Society, and destroy in them the Seeds of Humanity."[33]

Orton was dead before the end of his first year in the colony,[34] leaving his friends gentle memories.

The Warren children were probably too young to be touched by these controversies but they participated in an event occurring less than two weeks after Barber and Habersham's trial. The magistrates had some time before received instructions from the Trustees to visit Bethesda and now resolved to do so, William Stephens going with them. Habersham or Barber had declared that Bethesda would submit to no visitation, since they considered

Whitefield's regime to be subject to no control in the colony. Habersham greeted the visitors when they arrived at Bethesda with this statement, but was persuaded by Stephens to allow the visit then rather than to have the magistrates institute legal proceedings. The magistrates talked to each one of the colony's orphans, about a dozen boys and only two girls, of whom Elizabeth Warren was one. The children were called into a room privately, with none of the Bethesda staff present, and questioned concerning their food, clothing, and general conditions, which none complained of. The magistrates thought that some of the boys, fourteen and fifteen years old, could be placed out to earn their own livings, and some but not all of the boys agreed, a course which Stephens thought "preferable to learning Latin. . . ." No effort was made by the magistrates to talk to any but Georgia children; about forty others were in the orphanage, Stephens thought, boys and girls of varying ages whom Whitefield "had gathered together from divers parts, and Countries," some of them orphans, some committed by their parents to be brought up there. The magistrates left with every one apparently in good humor, "but all were not a like pleased, to See such a Seminary rising in an utter Aversion to the Church of England."[35]

Richard and Elizabeth could not have been unaware of an unfortunate occurrence before these last events. This arose because "one of the Orphan Boys, under the care of Mr. *Whitefield*, had been treated with unwarrantable Correction, by Mr. *Barber*, the Presbyterian there. . . ." The boy, after a beating, ran away from Bethesda to Henry Parker, the nearest magistrate, at his home on the Isle of Hope. Though no names are mentioned in the account, this boy must have been Charles Tondee, then eleven, who had been in Parker's care before Whitefield began gathering up the orphans. Parker had been reluctant to release him to Whitefield. Parker, being unwell at the time, delayed several days to bring Charles before the magistrates. Then "the Boy being now present, and stripp'd, it is yet too visible from Scars and Wounds not yet healed, that great Cruelty had been used: It was not denied that the Boy was made naked to the Waist, after the Manner of common Malefactors, and lashed with five strong Twigs tied together, as long as they would hold, whereby his whole Back, Shoulders, Loins, Flank and Belly, were in a dreadful Condition. The Cause of this Severity, as alleged by the Boy, was, that he had wrote a Letter some Time before, to Mr. *Parker*, therein then complaining of severe Usage; which Mr. *Parker* now owned he received, but did not take great Notice of it, thinking it the common Case of many School-Boys under the Chastisement of the Rod. . . ." The letter was the cause of the beating; Charles was told that the punishment would be repeated unless he wrote again to Parker and retracted all that he had said, "which the Anguish he was under forced him to promise; but he made his Escape as aforesaid." Barber, before the magistrates, offered "nothing in his own Vindication, only that he thought himself the proper Judge, without Controul, in what Manner to govern the Boys that he had the Care of," and questioned the power of the Trustees to interrogate him or act in the matter, to which the magistrates replied that they would convince him of that power, as they would visit Bethesda and inquire into whatever they found amiss or seemed contrary to the intentions of the Trustees under their grant to Whitefield, this power having already been given to them as magistrates by the Trustees. Thereupon Charles was removed from Bethesda and placed out to Thomas Bailey, a Savannah blacksmith. The Trustees told Whitefield in no uncertain terms that he had no authority to take Charles from Parker and must return him.[36]

Richard and Elizabeth Warren, and the other children at Bethesda, were under what seems now a rigorous discipline. Whitefield said of himself, "I can truly say I was froward from my Mother's Womb . . ."; perhaps he thought all other children, from so immature a stage, were equally so, and that they shared with him the sins which he zestfully detailed: "I was so brutish as to hate Instruction . . . I soon gave pregnant Proofs of an Impudent Temper . . . Lying, filthy Talking, and foolish Jesting I was very much addicted to, even when very young . . . Sometimes I used to curse, if not swear . . . and have more than once spent Money I took in the House, in buying Fruits, Tarts, &c. to satisfy my sensual Appetite. . . . Cards, and reading Romances, were my Heart's Delight. . . . Often have I joined with others in playing roguish Tricks. . . . It would be endless to recount the Sins and Offences of my younger Days."[37]

So dramatic a sinner, knowing such evil ways, was well fitted to recognize sin in others and prescribe a remedy. On the ship during his first trip to Georgia, he had the opportunity. He wrote confidently: "Had a good Instance of the Benefit of breaking Childrens Wills betimes. Last Night, going between Decks, as

I do every Night, to Visit the Sick, and examine my People, I asked one of the Women to bid her little Boy, that stood by her, say his Prayers; She answer'd, his elder Sister would, but she could not make him. Upon this, I bid the Child kneel down before me, but he would not, till I took hold of his Feet, and forc'd him down. I then bid him say the Lord's Prayer, being informed by his Mother, he could say it if he would; but he obstinately refused, till at last, after I had given him several Blows, he said his Prayers as well as I could expect. I gave him some Figs for a Reward, and lo! this same Child, tho' not above four Years of Age, came to-night upon Deck, when the other Children came to say their Prayers to my Friend H. and he burst out into a Flood of Tears, and would not go away till he had said his too.

"I mention this as a Proof of the Necessity of early Correction. Children are sensible of it sooner than Parents imagine; and if they would but have the Resolution to break their Wills thoroughly when young, the Work of Conversion would be much easier and they would not be so troubled with perverse Children when they are old."[38]

In 1739 before Whitefield opened the orphanage, he brought with him from England two children of a friend. In them he observed a remarkable alteration after they were committed to his care. They were a boy and girl a little more than three years old, yet they could read in their primer and sing hymns very prettily, for he had them "under careful Discipline. They are both generally employ'd either in Working or Reading, and are taught to make Work their Diversion.—The little Boy picks Pease, and the little Girl sews with her Needle.—The Proficiency they have made gives me great Satisfaction, and I hope is an Earnest of the Improvement that will be seen in the poor Children that are shortly to be committed to my Care."[39]

Before the permanent orphanage buildings were ready, discipline was well established among Whitefield's charges. The family arose at five o'clock in the morning. The children first prayed for fifteen minutes, while the members of the staff exhorted them concerning their prayers, emphasizing their need of conversion and changed hearts. At six o'clock all went to church where a psalm was sung and the lesson was expounded by Whitefield or the person in charge during his absence. At seven all returned to the house, sang a hymn and said prayers before breakfast. The children usually sang a hymn before and after each meal, as well as saying grace. During breakfast the work of the day was discussed; the children were appointed to their tasks for the ensuing hours and often were questioned and exhorted.

From eight until ten the children worked; some cleaned the house, fetched water, cut wood, etc.; some worked with a tailor who lived in the house; others worked with carpenters and shoemakers. One worked with the apothecary. Others worked in the storeroom and kitchen, at sewing, knitting, carding, spinning, and picking cotton and wool. Any boy who showed by his spiritual progress and natural abilities an aptitude for the ministry was to be given some training for that profession.

At ten o'clock all went to school. The children were taught in school to read the Bible, which the master explained to them, singing and praying with them as seemed expedient. At noon dinner was served. At the conclusion of this meal and before two o'clock every child was given useful employment, "but no time is allowed for Idleness or play, which are Satans darling hours to tempt Children to all manner of wickedness as Lying, Cursing, Swearing, Uncleanness, etc. So that tho we are about 70 in Family, yet we hear no more noise than if it was a private House."

From two to four, the children went to school again; from four to six, again to work. At six o'clock they ate supper, when the master or mistress attended to help them, watch over their words and actions, and sing with them. At seven o'clock children and staff went to church again. At eight o'clock Savannah people often dropped in to hear Whitefield examine and instruct the children in a question-and-answer period. His main responsibility in this hour Whitefield conceived to be to ground the children in the belief of original sin, to make them sensible of what was termed their damnable state by nature, and the absolute necessity of a change being wrought by God in their souls before they could be in a state to be saved or have any right to call themselves Christians. For this purpose they were all ordered to memorize the articles of sin, free will, and identification.

At nine o'clock, the children went upstairs to bed. Some of the staff sang and prayed again with the children, and a private prayer period for each child by the bedside was enforced, someone giving instruction in prayer as in the morning, "and at ten o'Clock all the Family goes to Rest, unless any one or more chooses to sit up an hour or two for their private Devotion, or Meditatiòn, or Conference."

On Sundays all went to church four times, the hours spent in work on week-days being on this day spent in church. Thus, the Bethesda staff could say proudly, their and the children's time was all laid out in the service of God, the variety of which was a sufficient relaxation to a well-disposed mind, and obviated the pretenses for what "is called Innocent (tho in Reality damnable) Recreations."[40]

This account of the activities at the orphanage troubled the Earl of Egmont and caused him to write: "Not a moment of innocent recreation tho necessary to the health & strengthening of growing children is allow'd in the whole day, but much publick and private prayer with frequent singing of Psalms & Hymns (some of which their own immediate invention) required. The whole discipline appears to be too strict."[41]

In the earliest months of the orphanage, the children were chiefly employed in picking and carding cotton, and Whitefield's plans for the children's work were so large that he planned to take all the cotton, hemp, and flax produced in the colony and begin weaving. He shortly reported to the Trustees that spinning was going well. He was emphatically forbidden by the Trustees to continue. Parliament and the English public had always been of the opinion that the colonies should only raise products for manufacturing in England and not carry on manufactures themselves; the Trustees "are determined that no Looms should be set up in the Orphan House, or in any Part of the Colony." Whitefield explained that he intended to weave cotton only for the use of the colony, and he continued the loom for Bethesda's use only.[42]

To the staff at Bethesda, wondrous events seemed to take place at times. Habersham, superintendent of outward affairs at Bethesda, described a time when he spoke to the children. "I felt the Lord powerfully on my own Soul, and it seem'd to reach the Children, and put them under a visible Concern." Some of the children "were talking among themselves about Eternity; and they cried so much to *Jesus of Nazareth* that the Family soon heard them. We all went, and wept over 25 or 30 dear Lambs, upon their Knees before God, some pleading Promises, and others calling upon Jesus. O, how did my hard Heart rejoice!

Blessed be God, many of them seem to retain their Convictions, and all are serious."[43]

Barber, superintendent of spiritual affairs, was even more explicit: "Never, no never did my Eyes see such a Sight, nor my Ears hear such a Sound, as in the Day past; . . . It was nothing less strange and wonderful than a great Number of little Children in your Orphan-House crying out after the Lord . . . several of the biggest Boys of your dear Family were awakened, and still remain under deep Convictions." The larger boys were divided into two bands and allowed "two or three Hours every Day to spend in Reading, Praying, and Singing Hymns by themselves. They have been heard to pray very earnestly: I heard at one Time particularly some of them greatly affected. . . ." The younger boys, among whom Richard Warren was classed, caught the fervor. One day while they were in the school picking cotton, Barber related, one of them said to another, " *'If we do not believe in the Lord Jesus Christ, we shall all go to Hell*; and added, *that the children of God, prayed to God.* Immediately, the Boy to whom he spake, fell down upon his Knees and began to pray; and then another, till they were all on their Knees together praying. . . . Providence so order'd it, that some of the Family heard them, and 'twas not long before the whole Family was gathered round them. Oh how did the awful and pleasing Sight strike us, and melt us into a Flood of Tears! . . . The dear little Lambs continued crying out with the trembling Jaylor,'*What must we do to be saved?'* They prayed, 'Lord God Almighty have Compassion upon us, prick us to the Heart, and pluck us as Firebrands out of the Burning; and, O Lord Jesus Christ, thou Son of *David,* have Mercy upon us, have Mercy upon us; . . . O Lord, take away our hard stony Hearts, and give us Hearts of Flesh. . . . O give us broken and contrite Hearts. O Lord, let our Sins be a heavy Burden upon our Backs, and let us find no Rest till we find Rest in thee!' And Oh, how did the dear little Souls plead with God! . . . They continued thus crying after the Lord an Hour or Two; and not only what I *say,* but what I *felt,* convinced me that the Lord was present with us. And he that has wounded, I hope, will ere long heal their poor Souls."[44]

If the two superintendents could write letters to Whitefield, so too could the orphans, though perhaps with a little prodding. The letters were published to show the work done at Bethesda.

A girl about ten years of age wrote: "I Have found great Concern about my poor Soul since your leaving us, God has shown me more and more of the Hardness and Wretchedness of my Wicked Heart, . . . O! it fills me with Wonder and Amazement to think God has not cut me off long ago and sent me to Hell, for I am sure I have deserved it. . . ."[45]

A boy of the same age was sure that the Lord had begun a good work in his soul even though "The Devil goes about like a rorring Lion seeking whom he may devour." He hoped "that my Convictions may never wear of: that I may never return with the Dog to his Vomet, and with Sowe that was washed to her Wallowing in the Mire." Still another ten-year-old hoped that "God will be pleas'd every Day more and more to make me sensible of the Vileness of my sinfull Heart. . . . I hope the Lord will be pleased to pitty me a sinful Creature. . . ."[46]

"W. . .m B. . .y," who was William Bradley, aged twelve, knew that "the Devil has told me how that it is Time enough to begin when I am upon my Death-bed. No, no; Now is the accepted Time, now is the Day of Salvation. . . . I have been sinning against Thee ever since I came from my Mother's Womb. O Lord, do not quench the smoking Flax, and break the bruised Reed, untel thou send forth Judgement unto Victory!"[47]

"J. . .n R. . .y," aged about twelve, who was John Riley, said frankly that "The Lord hath been pleased to shew me what a damned State I am in." It was a wonder "that the Lord hath not sent me to Hell long ago. . . ." But there was now a stirring among the dry bones and John could only hope that "the Lord will no more suffer me to go on in mine own Security, but rouse me out of my Spiritual Lethargy. I hope the Lord has not given me over to a reprobate Mind."[48]

Lachlan Mackintosh, aged about fourteen, was almost cheerful: "The Spirit of the Lord, I hope is beginning to blow among the dry Bones here. The House was never since I came thither liklier to answer the end of its Institution than now: Little Boys and little Girles, at this and that Corner crying unto the Lord, that he would have Mercy upon them. . . ."[49]

Richard Warren and his sister Elizabeth must also have cried unto the Lord. Richard wrote one of the letters when he was about thirteen:

Bethesda, March 24, 1740-41.

Dear and Honoured Sir,

This is to let you know tha I am in good Health, as I hope you are. Since you have gone, the Lord has been amongst us again. I hope I shall remember it all the Days of my Life. I have rebelled against the Lord all the Days of my Life; but the Lord has been gracious to me, and provided both for my Soul and Body in a plentious Manner by you. O that the Lord would give me a thanful Heart! The Lord has been pleased to give me Conviction, and let me see the Wickedness of my Heart. And the Devil tells me that it is Time enough to repent when I am a Man; But the Lord shews me it is the Devil that tels me so. O pray that the Lord may carry on my Convictions tel they end in a sound Convertion. . . . Dear Sir, I pray the Lord will bless what you are gone about, and return you in the Fulness of the Blessing of the Gospel of Peace to us again. I pray the Lord may reward you for your Works of Faith and Labour of Love to us. I desire you, if you be pleased, to send us all a Line or two. I desire you would remember me at the Thron of Grace. This is from your unworthy Boy,

R____d W_____n[50]

As for Elizabeth, she wrote no letter. However, Barber reported on her parenthetically in writing of two young men employed at Bethesda. He said, "I hope and trust [they] have been savingly converted since you left us, and also Eli. W...n; ...."[51]

Only three of the girls in Bethesda had their letters published in the little volume, and upon two of these their young companions must have looked with some envy, if so base a feeling was allowed at Bethesda. One of these was Ann Clark, who was fourteen years old when she entered Bethesda on February 11, 1740. Ann had arrived in Georgia with her family in August, 1733. She became an orphan soon after her arrival, her mother dying in less than a month, her father in December of that year. She lived with several Georgia families before going to Bethesda.[52] Ann had a trip to England and back, going with Whitefield as a companion to a younger girl who had been at Bethesda but who was being returned to her parents. Prior to the trip, Ann became the legal ward of Whitefield.[53]

Ann's letter to Whitefield from Bethesda revealed a certain spiritual drama of which she was conscious at the age of fourteen: "Blessed be God, I have had great Manifestations of his Love to my Soul in your Absence, but now he is pleased to withdraw himself from me, and I walk in Darkness and can see no Light."

However, she did not despair for "there hath been a Stirring amongst the dry Bones."[54]

Romance came to Bethesda when one of the girls, Mary Bolton, one of two sisters from Philadelphia, married schoolmaster James Habersham in December, 1740.[55] The other little girls must have thought that none among them could equal Elizabeth Pitts. Elizabeth was from Boston; she came to Bethesda on December 13, 1740. When she wrote her letter she was fifteen to seventeen years old. Elizabeth felt herself distinguished by a weight of sin: "O! I am the worst, the ungratefullest of all Sinners upon Earth. . . ." But Elizabeth's fortunes were not for long to coincide with those of the children at Bethesda. Her happy fate stands upon the records; she left Bethesda in July, 1742, "Married to a considerable person in S. Carolina."[56] It must have been almost more than the other little girls could bear. Cinderella, though the children were probably not allowed to know anything of her frivolous legend, could not equal Elizabeth Pitts, married to a considerable person and in South Carolina at that.

Doubtless it was while the Bethesda children were in Carolina that Miss Pitts had her exceptional opportunity. Richard and Elizabeth Warren and all of the children would remember for years the time they refugeed. Anyone who leaves the familiar, ahead of an invading army, has thereafter a hoard of strange memories. Sadness felt by their elders cannot be shared by children at such a time and so most of those at Bethesda must have been concerned largely with the adventure. To Richard and Elizabeth, the move must have been but another of the quirks of fate by which they had often been picked up and put down first in one place, then in another.

James Habersham removed everyone from Bethesda to Hugh Bryan's plantation in South Carolina as soon as he had news of the Spaniards coming into the harbor at St. Simons. If the Spaniards defeated Oglethorpe's forces, they would surely proceed to Savannah. By land or water, Bethesda would be along their way. Habersham took his charges off as quickly as he could to the Bryan plantation in the summer of 1742. Bethesda was used in their absence by other refugees, women and children coming from Darien and the neighborhood where the fighting was to occur.[57]

The children were back at Bethesda by the first part of August.[58] In their absence much had happened. Oglethorpe was victorious over the Spaniards. People who had fled were returning. The alarm in Savannah at the possibility of invasion was succeeded by sorrow as many families lost one or more members in a spreading illness. The heat was extraordinary that summer; even those who were left of the people who came on the *Ann* remembered nothing like it since they had lived in the colony. The illness was accounted a "Malignant Feaver of the worst sort, and near Epidemical. . . ." Scarcely had the children returned to Bethesda when many of them were "falling down a pace in the same Distemper. . . ."[59]

Several years pass before anything more is known of Richard and Elizabeth Warren. On August 22, 1744, Richard left Bethesda, placed out to James Habersham,[60] now of the mercantile firm of Harris and Habersham in Savannah. Richard and Elizabeth thus were separated. Elizabeth remained at Bethesda until January, 1746, when she was placed out in the service of one of the magistrates in Savannah.[61] Here she vanishes from the records.

Fourteen years later, in April, 1760, Governor Henry Ellis received a petition from Richard Warren, then married and with one child, who "had been brought up in the Province," for 200 acres of land on the south branch of the Little Ogeechee River. On the governor's council then were Noble Jones, who had come with him on the *Ann*, and James Habersham. Richard had not previously had a grant and his petition was acceded to. Two years later Governor Wright signed a grant for Richard of 200 acres, which may have been the same grant.[62] Richard Warren died in 1763, probably in November, of unannounced causes.[63]

One orphan, William Little (or Littel), was so situated that not even George Whitefield, eager as he was to take all orphans into Bethesda, could think it right to remove him. William Little, Sr., a flax dresser thirty-one years of age, and his wife Elizabeth, also thirty-one, brought their five-year-old daughter Mary and two-year-old son William on the *Ann*. William, Sr., and Mary died during the first July, that time of death and sorrow for so many of the original Georgians. The widowed Elizabeth married John West, whose wife and child had died in July, the next month and died herself in September.[64] The loss of two wives and a child must have left West dazed and uncertain. He was hardly able to take care of the young William Little. However, William had so endeared himself to Mrs. Samuel Parker, who came on the *Ann* with him and was later Mrs. Samuel Mercer, that she took him as one of her own.[65]

Oglethorpe solved the problem of orphans as best he could by appointing trustees to oversee them in whatever homes they could be placed and allowing food and clothing for each from the Trustees' store. The Trustees agreed that "The Orphans, who have no other means of supporting themselves, and have no Friends to take care of them, are by the Trustees Orders to be put on the Store, till they are of Age to be put out apprentices; They must be sure to be put out Apprentices as soon as conveniently may be."[66] If the house of the orphan's father could be rented, the income was to go to the child's support.

Edward Jenkins, a trustee for the orphans, reported on William Little with considerable satisfaction: "Mr West have agreed that we should have Little Child under our Care & agrees to Give twelve pounds pr Year for ye Childs House the Child Lives with Mrs Mercer which from ye Mothers Death have Taken a Great Deal of Care of, . . ."[67] However, a story went back to England that William was being defrauded by John West. This story probably originated from the fact that West lived in the Little house. William's grandfather, William Little in England, was aroused and complained to the Trustees that "John West keeps possession of the House belonging to the late William Littel, to the prejudice of William Littel the Infant." Instructions went to Savannah that the infant "who is kept out of his freehold and house at Savannah, that he should have all the justice the law can allow."[68]

The grandfather wished that Samuel Mercer (or Marcer) should be the child's legal guardian. Since his father's house belonged by entail to William, the rent from it must in the first place be applied to the maintenance of the infant, and residue to the improvement of the place during William's minority. It was ordered that the child must be kept at Mrs. Parker's.[69] Since Samuel Mercer married Mrs. Parker in Georgia before these letters were written in England, William's guardianship and his love and care were concentrated under one roof. Mercer became the legal guardian of the infant William Little. Edward Jenkins could say with pleasure, "Mr. Littles Child with Mrs. Mercer they are very kind to ye Child."[70]

William had no recorded history in the next few years. His business was that of any other small boy of his age, to grow and flourish. Because he did so in fortunate surroundings, no one mentioned him. William reappears in the records when George Whitefield arrived in the colony in 1740 to establish his orphanage. Whitefield, the magistrates, and William Stephens met to discuss the orphans in the colony. Whitefield was sure that the Trustees' deed gave him authority to take in all orphans who were or had been chargeable to the Trust, regardless of their present circumstances. Others disagreed with him, "having shewn an Unwillingness to deliver up those who were now grown up pretty well in Years, and therefore capable of doing them good Service, especially as the planting Season was coming on. . . ." But there was the deed, which as interpreted by the enthusiastic Whitefield, seemed to say that he had power to take any orphan from anywhere in Georgia. Even Whitefield agreed that he had no reason or power to take William Little, orphan though he was. William was the only exception, and with good reason, for "Samuel Mercer (Constable) . . . has taken the same care of him as of a Son; and from a Cow and Calf which the Child had at his Parents Death, he has seen them so well looked after, that from the Increase which he has in a few Years past, probably before he comes to Man's Estate (and he is not yet more than eight or nine Years old) he may be looked on as a Man of good Substance to begin the World, and make no contemptible Freeholder: This, therefore, all agreed to be a singular Case, and fit to remain as it was."[71]

Three and a half years later William was doing well in school. About twenty-five children went to the school in Savannah taught by John Dobell; about ten of these could write. Dobell was especially pleased with the writing of five of them: Peter Morel's son John; William Woodroofe's son William; the Box boys, Phillip and James; and "William Little, an Orphan, wth. Mr. Marcer Aged 12 Years." A sample of William's and the other boys' writing was sent by Dobell to England for the Trustees to see how well they did.[72]

This is all that the records reveal about William Little and his life until in 1759, at the age of about twenty-eight, he asked for a grant of one hundred acres of land, "setting forth that he was brought up from an Infant in the Province had had no Land granted him therein and was desirous to obtain Land for Cultivation. . . ."[73] Only by inference from the life and status of the Parker-Mercer families can it be determined that William probably spent a satisfactory, if uneventful, youth and young manhood. With his petition for land, William Little vanishes from the records.

Samuel Parker came over on the *Ann* with an appointment as one of the two constables. He was ill in the spring after his arrival, Oglethorpe said, with consumption contracted before he left England.[74] The name of Samuel Parker is among the list of the first jurors on July 28, 1733, but this must be Samuel Parker, Jr., for the father is said to have died eight days earlier.[75] It was only a few months after her husband's death that Jane Parker took into her own family of two boys, Samuel and Thomas, the orphaned child William Little, a notable act of love and generosity for one worn from her husband's long illness and death and anxious for the future of herself and her own boys.

Jane Parker was re-married in May, 1734, to widower Samuel Mercer.[76] Mercer and his first wife arrived in the colony on August 29, 1733. Mercer was among that group described as fifty able men least encumbered with families, which included Henry Parker and William Brownjohn, whom the Trustees decided in May, 1733, to send as quickly as possible to reinforce the original settlers. Some of the new arrivals died soon after landing, among them Samuel Mercer's wife Anne.[77] Mercer brought no children to Georgia, but upon his re-marriage he acquired a family of the two Parker boys and William Little.

Mercer was a tanner by trade, evidently an enterprising person, resolved not to trust to only one source for income. He obtained from Oglethorpe a license to sell liquor—not distilled liquor— and was at what he described as "a great Charge in Building and making Roome for Lodging and Getting a great many other things on purpose to Carry on the Buissness in a Handsome and Desent way to Entertain travilers in a handsome manner." He did not avail himself of the license until Christmas, 1734, and by the spring of 1735 he saw the likelihood of his success diminishing and so gave up his license. He would not sell illicitly as other people did. Mercer would probably have been astonished to read in a book published about Georgia that year that no victualler or alehouse keeper could give any credit;[78] all of them did give credit and everybody knew it.

Mercer was worried at that time because his forty-five-acre farm lot was not yet run out by Noble Jones, the surveyor. This, said Mercer, "is very hard upon a great many people for Several peo-

ples five Acre Lotts Lays So much Covered with watter and in
Such Swampy Wett ground that it is Impossible for them to be
Cleared as Yett to be fitt for any person to gett their Bread
on." Here were people who because they did not have land
fit to cultivate were forced to do any kind of work they could find
in town, "to keep them from Starving which is very great
hardships to them and makes them very uneasey." He had
waited a long time, he told the Trustees, "Expecting to See Some
Alteration for the Better but found none but Every thing to go
worse and worse." It was not that he did not like Georgia; he did:
"I Like it Exceeding well and hope Throug god Almightys
Blessing and the great Care that your Honnours hath for this
place to See this Collony in a florishing Condition as any part of
America."[79]

However, Mercer was never one to be idle and bemoan his
lot; he took what he had and did the best he could with it. He
managed so well on his five-acre garden lot that his work was
noted in London, despite his misfortunes in 1736 when deer destroyed three acres of peas and when he broke his leg in September taking some cattle down the bluff at Savannah.[80] Throughout
the years Mercer's knowledge of cattle was called into use many
times in the colony until William Stephens remarked in 1743 that
Mercer was looked on as the most skillful man among them
about cattle.[81]

Mercer's capabilities were greater than his opportunities on
the land he had; he wanted earth where he could grow crops or
where he could pasture cattle. His dissatisfaction with the
colony led him to make a brief trip to South Carolina in the latter
part of 1737, accompanied by William Brownjohn, to look for
better land. He was at a dead-end of discouragement with Georgia
at that time, outdone with the system of land tenure and doubtful about the future of the colony.[82] He was to have his hunger
for land assuaged when in 1738 Oglethorpe arranged for him to
have 300 acres on the south side of the Vernon River.[83] Soon
after, William Stephens selected 500 acres of land nearby for his
grant; Stephens and Mercer rode out to the mouth of the Vernon River to meet Oglethorpe, who arrived by boat, and after
Stephens's selection was made, Oglethorpe ordered food and wine
brought ashore where they picnicked. Stephens's and Mercer's
tracts were immediately south of the lower boundary of Whitefield's grant for Bethesda.[84]

Mercer was already spoken of favorably for his planting[85] but further commendation was to come. After Oglethorpe's speech in October, 1738, which so drastically changed affairs in the colony, Oglethorpe made Mercer second constable, "a Man in all Appearance very well qualified for that Office," as Stephens observed.[86] His new office did not prevent Mercer and his stepson Samuel Parker from signing the representation of December, 1738, advocating changes in land tenure and the admission of slave labor. In London, where the records of the signers were searched, the only thing found against Mercer was that he had made some protests in court in 1737. This was enough to list him as a "rioter" in court. Yet London could not deny him the high praise of being an "industrious man."[87] William Stephens, who made harsh comments on those who signed, did not visit his indignation upon Mercer. Instead, he consulted Mercer about improvements on the land, for his "Judgement in many Things relating to Improvements, I approved of very well," and was pleased that Mercer was to be "my next Neighbour, being assured in myself, that he would not be idle. . . ."[88]

From May 30, 1739, until that autumn Mercer was the only constable. Then Oglethorpe appointed Robert Potter to that office also. Potter, who came over on the *Georgia Pink* with Mercer, was given the office because he was an industrious man who had not signed the representation. In 1736 he had cleared his five-acre lot and that year produced on it seventy bushels of corn; one year he made £5 sterling from the sale of his mulberry leaves. In England someone thought that his "petty employment" as a constable ruined his industry.[89] Yet Potter had already discovered that he could not support himself by his land alone. He went on a voyage as a crewman on Caleb Davis's privateer in January and February, 1740.[90] Upon his return he went to South Carolina as an overseer, but was back in Savannah as a corpse to be buried on the evening of March 12, 1740.[91]

When Lieutenant William Horton went to England in 1740 to raise recruits for Oglethorpe's regiment, he answered many questions from the Trustees about the colony. One opinion that he gave them was that Mercer "is a Man of good sense, and fit as any he knew to be made a Magistrate." This opinion was reinforced by Stephens's remark that Mercer was "a man of Spirit . . . a more diligent Officer in that Post I never knew in Savannah." Mercer was busy with his usual duties of cultivation and as constable was on an unofficial committee with Henry Parker and Thomas Jones, which worked with Stephens on selecting and correlating information with which the Trustees hoped to combat the representation of 1738 and other bad reports of Georgia which had reached England. Despite the fact that they signed the representation, both Mercer and his step-son, Sam Parker, were among the small group signing "A State of the Province of Georgia" when it was finished in November, 1740.[92]

In 1741 when Georgia was divided into counties and William Stephens was made president of the county of Savannah, Mercer was appointed by the Trustees as the fourth of the Assistants, the others being the magistrates Henry Parker, Thomas Jones, and John Fallowfield. Mercer's salary in this office was £20 a year. This new government was publicly announced and inaugurated in Savannah on October 7, 1741.[93] The first meeting of the President and Assistants was held on October 12; Mercer was present and continued faithful in his attendance. He continued also to hold the office of constable.[94]

The summer of 1742 was a difficult period in the colony. For Mercer the time was one of trouble both in his family and in his public duties as Assistant and constable. Mrs. Mercer's son, Sam Parker, had died in 1741, diminishing still further the remaining number of the *Ann's* passengers. Sam's wife died in August, 1742. Mrs. Mercer is said to have died at the same time but this entry in the List is obviously incorrect, a confusion of Mrs. Mercer with Sam Parker's wife, since William Stephens, mentioning that sickness prevailed most grievously in the summer of 1742, wrote that another person died on August 7, "a young hail woman, in the prime of her years, and Widow to Sam. Parker (Smith) that died about a year since."[95] However, Mrs. Jane Parker Mercer may well have died about this time, for no further mention is found of her in the records. Thus knowledge of the two *Ann* passengers in the Mercer household ends. Mercer had a wife, unidentified as to name, in 1743. In 1755 he had a third wife.[96] Jane Parker Mercer had died sometime between 1742 and 1755.

Mercer himself continued as an Assistant throughout the exciting times of the War of Jenkins' Ear and thereafter. In 1747 he became third Assistant when Patrick Graham and James Habersham were appointed as fourth and fifth Assistants.[97] In 1750 the other Assistants took umbrage at Mercer's ill conduct of reading, sleeping, and otherwise ignoring the proceedings during Board meetings. A difference of opinion between Mercer and other Assistants was probably responsible for his actions. The Trustees first suspended and then removed Mercer. He henceforth refused to reply to communications from London about official duties and evidently was glad to be rid of them.[98] He remained in the colony and prospered. He was considered for appointment to Governor John Reynolds's council in 1755, but was not given the position. However, in 1756 he was elected to the Commons House of Assembly of the colony and by this time owned 900 acres of land and eighteen Negro slaves.[99] Many who came on the *Ann* would have envied his worldly success had they still been alive to know of it. Most of them were not.

Thomas Parker, Mercer's step-son and the remaining member of the *Ann's* passengers in the Parker family, was under nine years of age when he left England. Nothing is heard of Thomas for a number of years. In 1750 he went to Jamaica on Captain Caleb Davis's schooner. In 1753 he petitioned the President and Assistants, as "a Resident in the Colony from her first Settlement," and not possessed of any land in his own right, for a tract supposed to contain between 200 and 300 acres on the eastern end of Hutchinson's Island, which was granted to him. This land, however, did not meet his requirements; he resigned it in 1755 and obtained another grant of 300 acres on an island bounded by the Little Ogeechee and Vernon rivers.[100] Here he vanishes from the records.

Another orphan, John Goddard, was not so lucky in his foster parents as William Little, and less is known about him. James Goddard, thirty-eight-year-old carpenter and joiner, and his wife Elizabeth, forty-two, came on the *Ann* with a daughter Elizabeth, aged five, and a son John, aged nine.[101] That first summer bore hard on the Goddard family. James Goddard is said to have died on July 1, but it seems that he was alive on the thanksgiving and first court day on July 7. On that day he and Thomas Milledge, the two chief carpenters, offered in the name of themselves and their helpers to take the nineteen lots not yet built on so that the twenty-one houses already built could be used by those less able to help themselves. Goddard, Milledge, and some of their helpers died before they could fulfill this promise.

Sometime in July James Goddard died, and his wife followed him on the twenty-eighth.[102] Oglethorpe disposed of the two children as best he could, placing Elizabeth with James Carwell and his wife, and John as apprentice to Joseph Fitzwalter the gardener.[103] John was thus the first apprentice to work in the Trustees' garden.

Edward Jenkins, as a trustee for the orphans, was continually concerned about the children whose welfare he oversaw. "What Gives me the Greatest uneasiness Concerning the Orphants is—", he wrote in 1735, "That they are not Taken as Good Care of as I woud wish Altho we see ym often and is not Backward of telling any one yt abueses them, I am sorry I cant help but say the wimen Turn out but very Badly, which makes the orphants lives miserable. . . ."[104] Jenkins was no better satisfied later in the year. Elizabeth did not fare well with the Carwells. Mrs. Carwell is said to have died in September, 1733, but her death date may be confused with that of her baby, also named Margaret. However, Carwell had a wife in 1735, for Jenkins said that Elizabeth was "with Mr. Carwell & proves an unlucky child, I fear ye ill Conduct of the Master & Mistrise is two much ye Cause. . . ."[105] John was apprentice to Fitzwalter certainly until some time in 1735, perhaps longer. In that year Jenkins disapproved of the arrangement, remarking tersely, "Goddard son with mr Fithwater its to be Doubted will be ruined—we would be glad to have your order to remove him."[106]

In June, 1734, Jenkins rented the Goddard house, which John would inherit, to Thomas Christie for £18 a year. In the List Elizabeth and John are entered as servants to Christie. In 1737 the thirteen-year-old John was living with Christie. The rent from the property would, as in similar instances of orphans' property, have gone to the support of the children; but Christie seems to have been dilatory about payment.[107] Elizabeth was not mentioned with John in 1737 as living at Thomas Christie's. Edward Jenkins's remark about her in 1735, that she was an unlucky child, is the last mention of her in the records.

There are unfilled gaps in the story of John's life. Presumably he went to Carolina and was the boy advertised for in the newspaper of that province in 1742, "John Goddard, aged about 18 Years, pretty tall and thin, wearing a new Oznaburg Trowsers and check'd Shirt, Apprentice to *Nathaniel Ford.* shipwright, having about three Years yet to serve, hath absented himself from his Master several Months, and now intends to go off in some Vessel: This is to desire all Masters of Vessels not to carry off the said Apprentice, and all other Persons are likewise desired not to trust or entertain him, on pain of being prosecuted by the aforesaid   Nathaniel Ford.''[108]

John was back in Georgia by the spring of 1743 or earlier. William Stephens wrote of him in uncomplimentary terms because he sold his lot in Savannah. Stephens greatly disliked what he called "trafficking for Lotts in this Town & exchanging with one another. . . ." A number of people wanted to exchange their lots to secure one better suited to their needs or desires. This could be done only after the Trustees' approval, which was usually granted.

John Teasdale and his wife Elizabeth, widow of Will Cross, were keeping "a publick House by Licence," Stephens wrote, "which she understands the Management of well; & acting in a double Capacity, 'tis believed they get Money apace; but with a View of making more Speed, his Aim has been for a while past to get a Lott fronting the River, where all Comers might readily find Entertainment as soon as ashore." John Goddard had inherited from his father lot number one, Wilmington Tything, Derby Ward, in many people's opinion the best lot in town. Teasdale thought this lot was exactly situated for his public house.

As Stephens tells the story, John Goddard was "a most profligate extravagant young Man . . . seldome to be seen at Savannah, but mostly on the Ramble; engaging frequently in various Employments, & as frequently when weary of one, getting into another . . . It may be suppos'd a Person endued with so vicious a Habit, needed not much Perswasion to part with his Lott, & thereby become Master of such a Sum of Money as he knew not the Value of: accordingly a Bargain was struck up betwixt Teasdale & him for £25 to make Sale of the Lott; . . . & if I am rightly inform'd (as I think I am) in very few Days he had not a Penny left of it. I should hardly think it worth while to use many Words about it now; but let such a Wretch suffer for his Folly; were it not my Duty to represent it fully; that the Trustees may thereby see how this Itch prevails of buying and selling before and [any?] Leave from their Honours. . . ."

When Stephens's letter reached London, the Earl of Egmont noted John Goddard as "a proffligate young man." No one in England or Savannah seemed to have thought that a youth of eighteen or nineteen who had been reared an orphan needed good business advice instead of condemnation. The lot was probably worth considerably more than the price paid by Teasdale. There is no record that the Trustees confirmed this sale. At this time Goddard was employed on Noble Jones's guard boat at Skidaway Narrows, where he evidently remained for several years before he fades from the records for good.[109]

CHAPTER FOURTEEN

John Milledge — From Orphan to Principal Inhabitant

JOHN MILLEDGE was eleven years old when he left England on the *Ann* for the colony of Georgia.[1] Responsibilities such as few boys of his age have to bear w to devolve upon him shortly. He met them bravely and wi his years, beginning early to show the qualities tha later one of the most respected and trusted m ia. In a colony where reputations were eph n was written of Milledge in the availa ough, particularly since the wri s chided even from London ory is known only in c jor portions are m a child to rev other col John Mi shows acco

Thomas M barked on the With them were one and a half; Sarah, un John's older brother Thomas, ngland as did his sister Mary. An ned in connection with Mary was pre r.[2] Only seven men of the *Ann's* passengers Thomas Milledge and but two as old. Only one o Warren, brought as many children.[3]

Thomas Milledge was a carpenter nd joiner. He and James

Goddard were spoken of as the two chief carpenters in Georgia.[4] No skill was more necessary in a new colony than was carpentry. Thomas must have worked hard on building those first houses but he was already ill on July 28, 1733. Because of this his son John had an experience unusual for a boy of eleven. He served on the first jury of freeholders for which the names survive. Both he and Sam Parker, sixteen then, must have been chosen to represent their fathers, one about to die, the other dead.[5]

During the great illness of that first summer Thomas Milledge died on July 29. In his firm conviction that all of the illness that summer was caused by drinking rum, Oglethorpe easily attributed Thomas's death to this cause. Oglethorpe added that Thomas left a widow and five children, the eldest but eleven years old and "the Widow just ready to lye in of another." The new baby, Aaron, was already born when Oglethorpe wrote this letter; he arrived on August 9, a few days after his father's death, and died on October 3.[6]

Here then were young John and his mother, their father and husband dead, and four other children to care for while Elizabeth Milledge herself was recovering from the baby's birth and under a weight of sorrow and anxiety for the future. Young John shared in experiences that summer which should not be the portion of any boy of his years. Already the process of maturing must have been beginning.

They had the house, by the Trustees' system of land tenure belonging to the oldest son in England, though Elizabeth Milledge had her widow's rights. They were assured of subsistence from the Trustees' store for the time being. They had a cow, received in that distribution of milch cows given by friends of the colony in South Carolina, unless that animal had strayed away to the woods as so many cows did in the colony. Mrs. Milledge would have shared in the distribution of bricks sent from England by the Trustees and used for chimneys for the widows' houses. She had also one of the Irish transport servants which Oglethorpe gave to each of the widows to help cultivate their lands and maintain their families. The servant could have been of little help, for he died in little more than a month after being assigned to the Milledges.[7]

John's second year in the colony brought other profound changes in his life: his mother died on June 2, 1734; he went to England.[8] The records do not indicate if he went before or after his mother's death or what the reasons for this trip were, though they probably concerned the ownership of the property his father had left in Georgia. One possibility is that Oglethorpe may have taken John when, with Tomochichi and his party, he returned to England. The records do not indicate that this did or did not happen.[9] If John went with Oglethorpe, he left before his mother died. Probably only the greatest necessity would have forced John to leave the younger children. But if he left while his mother was still alive he would not have had the care of the children to concern him so greatly. John still stands today in the List with the notation, "quitted, ret. Engl," one of the incomplete entries which make this source of information so questionable about many early Georgians.

On October 7, 1734, the Common Council of the Trustees, Oglethorpe being present, ordered that Thomas Milledge, son of Thomas Milledge deceased, might have license to lease his house and lot to his brother John Milledge, "that he may be enabled to take care of his two Sisters and Younger Brother in Georgia." Thomas had already consented to this arrangement, to be in force until John came of age.[10] Mention of James, the youngest member of the family, was omitted in the Trustees' reference to one brother only. The List says that James died on November 4, 1734, but he may have already been dead.[11] Passage was ordered by the Trustees for John Milledge and one servant. The Milledge family, like several others sailing at that time, were to be maintained on the Trust account for one year.[12] John Milledge was sure of the house and land, sure of staple provisions for a year, and had an indentured servant allowed him by the Trustees to help him cultivate his land—he had a fair beginning for the care of his family. Oglethorpe was probably responsible for these arrangements. Ordinarily the Trustees would not have given an indentured servant to so young a boy, but all the Milledge children would have been provisioned by the Trustees until they were old enough to be apprenticed. Instead, "John Milledge must be look'd on as a Freeman, and must not be apprentic'd out to any other Person."[13]

John and his indentured servant, John Shears, embarked at Gravesend on October 31, 1734, on the *Prince of Wales*, Captain George Dunbar. On board the ship were a party of fifty-seven Salzburgers, twenty-two British passengers, and Tomochichi and his party. Tomochichi had seen London and London had seen him. Sir Francis Bathurst and his family were on board, coming out to settle in Georgia. Peter Gordon, then the first magistrate in Savannah, and his wife were returning from a trip to London.[14]

The party spent Christmas of 1734 on board the *Prince of Wales,* landing on December 28. The passage of fifty days was considered expeditious, as it was "but thirty-nine days between land and land."[15] What tales the Milledge children must have had to tell each other! John may have learned of the death of both his mother and James. He must answer as best he could the tumbling questions from Richard and the two girls, hear what they had done, where they had stayed, who took care of them while he was gone, and many other things. At thirteen years of age John was the sole source of security for his younger brother and sisters. He must have felt then that fierce protectiveness which he was soon to display. Four Milledges were dead; four remained. He accepted the responsibility for the three younger lives.

General oversight of orphans in the colony was entrusted in the early years to "three of our Best Persons appointed for that purpose." These men, their number later increased to four, were appointed by Oglethorpe or the magistrates as trustees for the orphans; they must inform the Trustees' storekeeper of the orphans' needs, see "that their Nurses or Masters be kind to them & Carefull of them . . . ," that their effects were not embezzled, and that improvements were made on their lots. These trustees acted under and were responsible to the magistrates. The requisite number was seldom filled and most of the work fell upon the man so often referred to, Edward Jenkins, who took his responsibilities to the orphans seriously.[16]

Jenkins said of the Milledge children in 1735, "John Millidge have got him up a hut by ye help of Mr. Young and some of his Neighbours. He desired we woud. let his Brother and sisters live with him as we have Consented to, But I fear its two young a family to do well, if they do not we will part ym."[17] It was indeed a young family but apparently not too young to do well, judging by later events. The threat of separation and the precarious conditions under which some orphans had to live when placed in homes spurred John to keep the children together. They would have lived in primitive conditions in the hut which

Thomas Young, one of the *Ann's* passengers, and other neighbors helped John to build. Huts were the lowest scale of housing in the colony. Yet huts were in common usage. John wanted shelter for his family, and the quickest way to get it was to build a hut, without a framework, of round poles and split boards. The Milledge house was rented to Robert Parker and his new wife for £14 a year.[18] The cultivation of John's land may have been seriously retarded by the death by drowning of his indentured servant, John Shears, in June, 1735. But plant and cultivate he must; the Trustees gave renewed emphasis to it that year. John must have managed; at least there is no criticism of him and but the barest mention in the next few years.[19]

Oglethorpe arrived in the colony for the third time in September, 1738. Because of the pressure of his military duties in the southern part of the colony he was in Savannah infrequently. He probably saw the Milledges and heard the story of their progress. At least once, probably in 1739, he gave John work by assigning to him the care of some of the Trust's oxen. In this connection John was spoken of in complimentary terms by William Stephens: "John Mellidge, a young Fellow, Son to one of them that came first over; who being a diligent Youth, the General had, among other Marks of his Favour, given him this farther Encouragement. . . ." More important than having the care of the oxen was the fact that John had won the accolade: he was a diligent youth. Oglethorpe gave John the remainder of the time of John Stout, an indentured Palatine servant, in April, 1740.[20] This servant was to help in cultivating the land and so provide a living for the family. The Milledges were doing nicely, despite their youth.

On January 11, 1740, George Whitefield arrived for the second time in the colony. He yearned for orphans and could not wait for the buildings of Bethesda to be completed. He rented the David Douglass house in Savannah as a temporary orphanage and went about scooping up orphans wherever he found them. He wrote happily, "I have taken in many Children & am now taking in fresh ones dayly."[21] On January 19, 1740, scarcely more than a week after Whitefield arrived, he removed Richard, aged thirteen, and Frances, aged twelve, from John Milledge's care and took them into the orphanage in Savannah.[22]

Whitefield met with the magistrates to discuss the orphans on February 1 and on February 8. When men argued against

Whitefield's taking away the orphans living with them whose
work was now beginning to pay for some of their keep, as in
the case of the Tondee boys with Henry Parker, Whitefield produced his deed from the Trustees and the magistrates were
silenced. By the Trustees' own words Whitefield was to erect and
maintain "an House for the receiving as many such Children as
now are and hereafter shall be left Orphans in the Colony of
Georgia. . . ."[23] No one could deny that the Milledge children
were orphans. They fitted the Trustees' sweeping orders exactly. It seemed to Whitefield that he had a better right to orphans and their work than any private person, even their brother
John Milledge. Whitefield obviously thought that only in the orphan-house were there means for orphans' spiritual growth. So
Whitefield removed Richard and Frances Milledge to his
own care and away from John's.

Thomas Jones informed Oglethorpe of Whitefield's action concerning the Milledge children. Jones explained the situation concerning the orphans generally and the Milledges in particular
to Oglethorpe, whose opinion was: "As for Milledge's Brother
and Sister I think yr. representation is very just, that the taking
them away to the Orphan house will break up a family, which
is in a likely way of living comfortably. Mr Whitefields design is
for the good of ye people and the Glory of God, and I dare
say, when he considers this he will be very well satisfied with
the Boy and Girls' returng: to their Brother John Milledge,
since they can assist him, and you may allow them upon my account the Provisions they used to have upon the Orphan account."

Oglethorpe had, he continued, examined Whitefield's grant; he
told William Seward, one of Whitefield's co-workers, that the
terms could not be meant as Whitefield interpreted them. "It is
most certain that Orphans are human Creatures & neither Cattel
nor any other kind of Chattels, therefore cannot be granted," he
said. He explained the laws of England relating to orphans and
concluded that "the Effects and persons of Orphans are as much
under the Protection of the Laws, as those of any other of His
Majesty's Subjects."[24]

Thus Oglethorpe in assuming the responsibility for the cost of
the Milledge children's food deprived Whitefield of a possible
argument that they might not have enough at home. Oglethorpe
sent Stephens a copy of the letter and after it was received,

John Milledge "was advised" to wait upon Whitefield and ask for the children's return home. This he did on March 25. "Mr. Whitefield gave him for Answer, his Brother and Sister were at their proper Home already, and he knew of no other Home they had to go to. . . ." Furthermore, Whitefield said, "you can tell General Oglethorpe I said so."[25]

Deep anger must have stirred John when Whitefield made that reply. How dared a stranger come here and tell him the children had no home except that orphanage? He had made a home for them. He would make it again. He must have felt help-less, as a boy would when suddenly he knows the world is for grown-ups and his own strength too small to pit against it. Neither Oglethorpe's views nor John's interview moved White-field. But John was determined to have the children again.

Late in March the rumor went around Savannah that White-field was going on one of his preaching and money raising tours. Whitefield preached his farewell sermon on Sunday, March 30. It would be some months, he said, before he returned. Early on Wednesday morning, April 2, accompanied by Seward and James Habersham, he went on board his sloop to sail north to Pennsyl-vania.[26]

A week later John Milledge removed his sister and brother from the orphanage. John must have had help from adults. White-field was later sure of it. Richard and Frances Milledge had been under Whitefield's care a little less than three months; none of the other orphans at that time were there for so short a time.[27]

Whitefield's prestige suffered by the removal of the Milledge children. He blamed Oglethorpe and wrote to the Trustees that "the General does by no means act as He ought to. . . . He mentioned nothing of taking away the two Children but since my departure. He has removed them I think after a very improper manner. I am verily persuaded the petition sent by John Milledge is only a Contrivance of the General. For He has got one Sister near 18 or 19 Years old that lives in his house, & can suf-ficiently do his busyness, He being but a single man—Besides I know the produce of all his land will not maintain the Chil-dren, & therefore they must be supported either by the Trustees or the General." It seems never to have occurred to Whitefield that John might love the children, as individuals and as mem-bers of his family.

If children were to be taken by force out of the orphan-house,

he would as soon throw away the money as expend it on so precarious a foundation, Whitefield said. "The Colony will never succeed, if such Arbitrary power be allowed of. Here are now
two Children taken away, but what provision is made for their
better parts, nay even for their bodies for any considerable time?
And how can I venture to put Children out Apprentices, if
they are every day liable to be removed in such an Arbitrary
manner? . . . I shall send a Copy of this . . . to the General & let
him make what Apology he pleases. I Honour him as my Su-
periour, but wherever he acts inconsistently with his Duty, I
shall think it my duty to inform him of it, with the meekness
& resolution that becomes a Minister of Jesus Xt."[28]

The Earl of Egmont in London termed this a harsh letter
against Oglethorpe for interfering in the orphans' affairs.[29] There
were those in Savannah who considered Whitefield as arbitrary
as he accused Oglethorpe of being. They saw enough of the
resolution he mentioned but little of the meekness. However, the
Milledge children remained at home with John and Sarah, while
letters crossed the Atlantic about them during the summer of
1740. Soon after Whitefield returned to Savannah early in June[30]
he called upon Thomas Jones, whom he blamed for taking the
children from the orphanage. Such action, Whitefield said, might
destroy the Trustees' deed to him. Stephens said that Jones "al-
ledged the General's positive Orders to him, to do what he did:
But that availed little with Mr. Whitefield, who said he was resolved to write thereupon to the Trust."

Stephens, making it plain that he was no party to the contro-
versy over the Milledge children, set down in his Journal an account of the affair. "Mellidge, a Freeholder here, and one of the
first forty, at his Death left several Orphans, whom the General (then only Mr. Oglethorpe) shewed particular Marks of his
Favour to, for their Father's Sake, whom he looked on as a
valuable Man; and in the Process of a few Years, the eldest Boy
proving to be an active, diligent, and well-grown Youth, he was
become serviceable, in many Cases, to his good Patron, and employed by him variously, as Occasion required: The eldest Sister
began now likewise to be capable of managing the House at home,
and guiding the young Family: Whereupon the General last
Spring encouraged them to begin, and try what they could do
about Planting, intending seemingly thereby to shew, what might
be expected of Boys, if encouraged and well looked after. About

that Time it happened, that Mr. Whitefield came, with the Power which the Trust had granted him, for taking the Orphans under his Care; among whom the Younger of these two Brothers (Mellidge) was taken by him for one, leaving the Elder at home; who complained, that his Brother being taken from them at this Time, when he could be of so much Use; it would be a Means of breaking up a Family that were now come to the Point of shifting for themselves: Which agreeing exactly with the General's Thoughts (then at Frederica) he sent Orders to Mr. Jones, to take the young lad home to the Family, which now would be no Charge to the Publick. . . ."[31]

If Whitefield expected the Trustees to confirm or support his position, he was disappointed. He and John Wesley before him in the colony showed a peculiar tactlessness at times, the results of which in wounded sensibilities, consequent criticism, and enmity they lumped together as persecution of those who did the Lord's work. They were singularly graceless in some respects. It was not to be forgiven, Trustee Edward Digby said, that Whitefield "should write so sawcily to his superiors," and Egmont remarked of Whitefield, "I was willing to excuse the fool the best I could, . . . I knew not how to excuse his want of respect for the Trustees, but by urging his youth, unexperience, un-mannerly education, and indiscreet Zeal. . . . I acknowledged him an Enthusiast, but Enthusiasts are ever sincere, tho often dangerously mistaken. . . . Therefore I was willing to think the best of him. . . ." Egmont had remarked earlier, "there is no knowing how to manage enthusiasts who take it into their heads that everything which comes uppermost is the immediate impulse of the spirit of God."[32]

Whatever their personal opinions, the Trustees at several meetings gave careful thought to Whitefield's letters. They had to answer him on a number of other points but told him that he had strangely interpreted his power over orphans and had exercised a power which no one could give him. They agreed with Oglethorpe's letter to Thomas Jones concerning the Milledge children, and sent instructions to the magistrates to preclude a recurrence of this procedure. These instructions clarifying the position of the orphans Whitefield seems to have accepted when he met with the magistrates later in the year, though to the Trustees he did not deviate from his position that the removal of the Milledge children was arbitrary and inconsistent with his grant.[33] In any event John Milledge's position as head of his family was now secure again.

John was on his way to becoming a man of affairs in the colony. He took his place with much older men in November, 1740, when he signed "A State of the Province of Georgia," that document for which the Trustees asked to help refute criticism of the colony and support their claims before Parliament. John was appointed a tythingman in Savannah in the autumn of 1741 and so began his experience in public office.[34] That year too he was employed by Oglethorpe's order in overseeing Trust servants who were clearing a tract of ninety acres about a mile from Savannah which the Trustees intended to have cultivated. Oglethorpe on one of his trips to Savannah in the spring of 1740 gave orders for work on this land, which was later planted in rice. Thomas Jones, making the only complaint recorded concerning John, said the "Youth" did not keep an accurate record of the servants' work and hours which he was to render to Jones. The servants were seen in town at their usual hours of labor when John's records showed them at work; "I found, upon Enquiry," Jones wrote, "that Millage had been prevaild with to connive at their not working. . . ." Whether John was lax or not, Jones's complaint to Oglethorpe concerning him apparently resulted only in inconvenience for Jones.[35]

England was now at war with Spain, the war being proclaimed in Savannah on October 3, 1739.[36] In the spring and summer of 1740 the impact of war was severe on the colony. John, if he was not concerned with some other service, had increased guard duty as a tythingman of Savannah. The war rendered watchfulness more necessary than ever. Oglethorpe had ordered that each orphan who inherited property from his dead father must, if he was capable of using a gun, be given one and trained to use it both to help in guard duty and to learn to defend his property; "such of them as I allowed of," Stephens said, "were delighted at it."[37] John certainly had a gun and knew how to use it.

In the autumn of 1740, before John became a tythingman, Oglethorpe instituted a system by which Stephens, as commander of the militia, would appoint nine freeholders of Savannah with a constable or tythingman who were willing to engage for six months. Two of them were required always to be ready with their horses and to set out immediately upon any alarm to range through the country. No one knew whether the Spaniards might slip up into those long stretches of woods back of Savannah and descend upon the town, or whether the Indians in alliance with the Spaniards might surprise Savannah people. Horses were provided for these men and an allowance of twenty shillings a month made to the constable or tythingman and ten shillings per month to the other men. About the same time Oglethorpe ordered a small force of rangers to be raised and stationed at Fort Argyle, each of whom was to be given fifty acres of land for planting, presumably in the vicinity of the fort.[38]

Evidently early in 1742, since William Stephens in April speaks of the appointment as lately made, John Milledge was appointed by Oglethorpe to the command at Fort Argyle as quartermaster, with six men under him, all mounted as rangers on horses of their own. John did not have a horse and was to pay for one out of his quartermaster's pay.[39] He was then about twenty-one years of age, but he must have seemed older than his years because of the responsibilities he had had. Perhaps boys matured earlier in the colony; one of them wrote back to England from Georgia that "Sixteen is looked upon as one & twenty in England," and that "every Coat & Wast coat I have is so much too little for me, that it will not button within 4 inches, & I am grown tall, & tan'd wth ye Sun, so yt no body guesses me to be under 20 years of age."[40]

A duty often devolving upon John personally was that of assuring communications between Frederica, Darien, and Savannah. Often Savannah people had not known what was happening to the southward, what the Spaniards were up to, nor what precautions they must take. Rumors abounded in Savannah, particularly in the summer of 1742 when the colony was invaded by the enemy. Great pressure was exerted on William Stephens as President by the people for various safety measures. Unable to obtain what he considered sufficient information to justify the exodus up the river and reluctant to permit it, in July Stephens sent John and another man by way of Fort Argyle to Darien and Frederica to learn what the situation was. John was gone a week and brought back an account from Oglethorpe of his success (the defeat of the Spanish at Bloody Marsh) which was greatly encouraging.[41]

John had written orders from Oglethorpe to gather all the horses and men he could in and around Savannah to take down to Oglethorpe. Few were left, most of the available young men having already joined Oglethorpe. Stephens said that the new levies "seem'd like the last Gleanings; Scarce any body being left but Masters of Families; most of whose Wives and Children were sent out of the way at the first alarm."[42]

Finally came the good news of the flight of the enemy and with it a consequent lessening of anxiety at Savannah.[43] But times were still unsettled. The Spanish might yet attack Savannah. Fort Argyle was an outpost where men would guard against the menace of surprise attacks and keep communications open. The garrison there was increased later that year to twenty men, with John in command. Except for Fort Augusta which had twenty men and officers, Fort Argyle was the only one of the four small forts with so large a garrison. The forts were located on the passages by which communications could be kept open through the colony and with Carolina.[44]

Men in these forts did not lead quiet lives; they must be continually alert to the threat of marauding Indians or Spaniards. The colony was shocked in November, 1742, by a tragedy at one of the forts, Mount Venture. In the absence of William Francis, the commanding officer, the Yamassee Indians attacked the fort, butchered Mrs. Francis and her child, murdered some of the men, and burned the fort. These deaths and the fact that the destruction of the fort opened a passage into the upper Indian settlements greatly alarmed the colony.[45]

Alarms continued at irregular intervals. In February, 1743 another raiding party of Indians crossed the Altamaha River going north. John Milledge, with the fate of Mount Venture in mind, informed Savannah of this unwelcome intrusion and said that all the rangers below Savannah were in pursuit, while the men under his command patrolled the long stretches of forest. Serious fears were entertained of another Spanish invasion in the spring of 1743, and Oglethorpe made an attempt against St. Augustine in March of that year, but nothing decisive resulted.[46] The *South-Carolina Gazette* remarked ironically and with considerable truth that Oglethorpe returned to Frederica on April 1 "from his Expedition (as it was called) against St. *Augustine* last Month; so that having only with the *Indians,* knock'd a few People on the Head about the Country, and *alarmed* the *Spaniards,* we find he did not stay long *endeavoring to excite the*

Enemy by all possible Means to Sallies, in order to bring the Place to a Condition of being surpriz'd."[47]

The Spaniards continued their annoyances. In late April or early May, 1743, John informed Stephens of their latest stratagem. A Spanish privateer off St. Simons bar, flying the English colors, fired a gun signalling for a pilot to come off. Too late the pilot and his men found the truth and neither boat nor men returned. As the spring and summer season of 1743 came on, increased fears were felt that another invasion was to be attempted; people were afraid that the Spaniards had captured this pilot with intent to force him into showing them the intricacies of the Georgia coast.[48]

John went back and forth from Fort Argyle to Savannah, Darien, and Frederica as necessity demanded. He often brought letters to Savannah, sometimes from an English ship which did not touch at Savannah.[49] Captain William Horton, left in charge on St. Simons after Oglethorpe went back to England in the summer of 1743, feared an invasion in 1744 and warned Savannah and Charles Town by letters carried by John riding as rapidly as horses could carry him. After the summer of 1744 ended, the Spanish alarms lessened. John was more at Fort Argyle and less often in Savannah. Though he and his rangers must still guard the passes, they also had such domestic duties as lending assistance with cattle run away to the woods.[50]

Several changes took place in John Milledge's life. His sister Sarah married Nicholas Rigby on January 4, 1743, the ceremony performed by the French minister from Purrysburg. Sarah's lot granted to her by Oglethorpe about two years previously gave the couple a place to live. Rigby apparently had no grant of his own. Rigby (or Rigbye as the name is sometimes spelled) who came over to Georgia in late 1737 on the same ship with Thomas Stephens,[51] was at the time of his marriage, clerk, or copyist to William Stephens.

Thomas Stephens is partly responsible for the unfortunate comment concerning Rigby in the List: "Rigby, als. Platrier, Jo.— Servt to Will. Stephens, Esq. . . . He took the name of Platrier to prevent being stopt from going by his creditors." Thomas Stephens wrote from Charles Town that some of the people and servants who came with him were reluctant to go on to Georgia after hearing stories to its disadvantage from a passenger on the ship in which he was joined by Rigby, whom Stephens called John Rigby alias Platrier. "It seems he's kin to Capt. Rigby yt commands ye Normington & was one of his Mates[.] I find yt he's a Sailor & acted as such aboard ye Minerva." Rigby thus presents varied talents—a sailor, a clerk, and later a school teacher. He spoke French fluently, was married by the French minister, and in 1743 with a number of French and German residents of Georgia signed a petition to Oglethorpe in support of the Reverend Henry Chiffelle, the French minister at Purrysburg, who preached to this group in Georgia.[52]

William Stephens spoke of Rigby early in 1742 as "a late servant of mine." Evidently by that time Rigby had worked out his indenture and was free to choose his employment. The previous autumn he had acted as clerk to the President and Assistants, being paid £4.10 for forty-five days of work. His duties as clerk to William Stephens grew heavier as time went on.[53] Not long after his marriage Rigby was nominated by the President and Assistants to succeed the former clerk of the Board and was appointed to this office by the Trustees early in 1744. He continued in this office for a number of years and in 1749 was also made secretary for Indian affairs by the Trustees.[54] The duties of this job were clerical, consisting largely of making out licenses when the Indian traders came down to Savannah to have them renewed.

Rigby and Stephens had an astonishing experience one March morning in 1744. Mrs. Camuse, who was employed by the Trustees in the silk business, came to see Stephens in a rather agitated state of mind. In her more positive moments, Mrs. Camuse never lacked drama, certainly not that morning. She strode to and fro, she clapped her hands, she clenched her fists, she poured out words over the two men. She spoke, or ejaculated, in French. Since Rigby spoke that language and Stephens did not, it fell to Rigby to try to appease her. Mrs. Camuse no sooner found herself answered in French, which she habitually spoke, than she switched to Italian, which neither man could speak. At intervals they caught the names of the Trustees, the President and Assistants, Stephens, the clerk at the Trustees' store, "and after half an hour thus spent to give Vent to her Passion," Stephens said, "she threw herself out of doors; leaving me not one Jot more knowing what she wanted than when she began." But there had to be some explanation of the reproaches which Mrs. Camuse hurled at the two men; "we had great reasons to apprehend there was some Sore fretting within her," Stephens said. When Stephens inquired he discovered that a board was left off the house where the silkworms lived and Mrs. Camuse reigned as their goddess.[55]

Rigby held his offices for some years and in 1750, when James Habersham succeeded Stephens as secretary for the affairs of the Trust in Georgia, Rigby was by order of the Trustees continued as clerk with a salary of £25 a year. However, Rigby was accused of neglect of duty, "but having a tender regard to his Family here," the Board delayed action for some time and then finally dismissed him.[56] Rigby protested his removal to the Trustees, remarking "that Things have made quite a different Appearance than what they formerly did, and as farr as I conceive, have carried the Face more of an Arbitrary Government than a Civil One, by the Influence some Persons have had over Coll: Stephens, who, I can't help saying, has given the Reins out of his Hands. I need not inform you that I have for several Months lain under a Suspension, for Reasons best known to themselves. But I defy the World to lay any particular Charge against Me, so as to occasion a Discharge of my Employments. But how can Publick Business be well carried on, when private Peaks place themselves in the Way; and Discords arising among the Heads of a Place."[57]

Throughout the years of her married life Sarah Milledge Rigby is little heard of. Her husband was dead by 1760, when she is spoken of as Sarah Rigby, widow. She evidently took passage for England with her daughters in July of that year but the details of her trip are not known, nor the reason for her going. Sarah Milledge Rigby died in Savannah in 1766, about forty-three years old.[58]

No matter what interests John Milledge had in mind or was engaged in, he always wanted more land. The new Board of President and Assistants had not been functioning a month when in December, 1741, Milledge and John Norton Wright, who came together on the *Ann,* each asked for 500 acres of land on Whitmarsh Island. The Board refused their requests, "They being both young Men and having no visible Substance wherewith to cultivate the Same at present, we apprehend they would be better employ'd in cultivating the Lands belonging to their Town Lotts yet while until they had acquired a better Competency for such an undertaking."[59]

Three years later John petitioned again for 500 acres on the north side of the Ogeechee River. The Board postponed

consideration of the petition until John should come to town from
Fort Argyle. In the latter part of January, 1745, he brought his
boat for provisions for the garrison at the fort. He appeared before the Board and explained that during the time he had commanded the garrison at Fort Argyle, he had made considerable improvements on some land about a mile below the fort, on
the north side of the Ogeechee, and as he wished to continue the
improvements he would be glad to have a grant of the tract. The
Board, "knowing him to have always been an industrious young
Man. . . ," was inclinable to approve the petition. Yet since John
had his father's original town lot and fifty-acre grant, the Board
would not grant the land until the approval of the Trustees
had been received. John was assured that he would not be mo-
lested on the land he had already worked until the Trustees
were heard from.[60]

The Trustees' decision did not arrive for some time. Much
mail between Georgia and England was lost because of the
war with Spain. Late in 1743, the Trustees sent Captain Andrew
Breading, of the ship *Britannia* captured by the Spaniards and
taken to France, to Audierne to recover mail from the colony.
Though some mail trickled through to England, every ship was
taken except one man-of-war, by which William Stephens sent
letters and papers from February through December, 1745. The
Trustees wrote in the summer of 1746 that except for one short
letter from Stephens, they had received none of later date than
April, 1745, and asked for copies of all others he had sent. When
Stephens and his clerk, Nicholas Rigby, finished copying these
papers to send, "God forbid such another Task should fall to
my lot," Stephens said wanly.

John's petition for land probably went by the *Nassau*, Captain Wilson, but she was lost, "& considering the Risque they all
run on their Passage 'tis no Wonder," Stephens said. He sent
copies of this correspondence by the *Rising Sun*, Captain Serjeant,
but she was lost also. The petition would have been sent again in
that great batch of mail of which Stephens must send copies.
Even when that reached Charles Town, difficulties were encountered in transmission and the letters were eventually sent in
care of a cadet from Oglethorpe's regiment who was returning
to England on a man-of-war.[61]

John's petition eventually arrived in London. It was considered
by the Trustees on December 29, 1746, and denied on February

16, 1747. The President and Assistants had not represented to the Trustees John's substance nor his ability to cultivate the tract he wanted; his town lot in Savannah was entirely neglected. If it was found that, independent of his military command, he had sufficient means to cultivate 500 acres, the Trustees would have no objection to making the grant provided that John would relinquish his town lot in Savannah.

In August, 1747, when John was in Savannah he was told of this decision and that he might have such part of the Ogeechee tract as the Board thought he could cultivate if he would surrender the Savannah property. John's indignation livens the dry record. The expense of improving and building on the Ogeechee tract had been nearly £300 sterling, John told the Board; he had on it a considerable stock of horses and black cattle; it would ruin him to move them. And besides, as the lot in Savannah "was the first Lands that ever he was possessed of, he absolutely refused to surrender the Same." The Board decided it could not grant him any of the Ogeechee lands without incurring the displeasure of the Trustees.[62] However disappointing this was to John Milledge, he would bide his time. He must often have had to work and wait; he could do so again.

In 1742 the Trustees gave some thought to the possibility of admitting slaves in the colony. They tacitly acknowledged that certain of their most cherished schemes would not work. They no longer fought the admission of rum but repealed the act which by its various provisions, including the free navigation of the Savannah River, had brought them into bitter and expensive disputes with South Carolina. Land tenures were liberalized and it seemed that the people who had for some years borne such severe criticism from the Trustees, Oglethorpe, and Stephens because they wanted these changes were about to be justified in their opinions. On the question of the admission of Negroes, the Trustees shied away, however. In 1746 they sternly reproved those colonists who still saw the need of slave labor; they warned Stephens "to discourage the same, and to convince the People that their own Industry will prove much more usefull to them; And that if they were once permitted to have Slaves they would soon become such themselves, by being Debtors to the Negro Merchants." This theory was one long held by Oglethorpe, who evidently thought that no man in the colony had sufficient business acumen to prevent his own ruin by debt for slaves. In the strong-

est terms the Trustees informed the President and Assistants in
March, 1748, that the Trustees were resolved "never to permit
the Introduction of Negroes into the Colony of Georgia," and
if people still persisted in the opinion that they could not succeed without Negroes, "it would be of service to the Colony as
well as themselves for them to retire into any other Province,
where they will be freely allow'd the Use of Negroes."[63]

In London, the governors of the colony might thus unequivo-
cally state their orders. The time had passed when they would
be obeyed in Georgia. New people were moving into the colony
who would not heed them. Both old and new settlers were harassed by a shortage of labor and could not see why slaves should
not be allowed in Georgia as they were in South Carolina. The
times were running against the Trustees, who could no longer
speak with authority of what they would "never" do.

The Trustees had often spoken of the danger of admitting
slaves in a frontier colony, so close to the Spaniards at St. Augustine. Now that peace had come some of this danger might be presumed to have vanished. Still larger loomed the fact that Georgia had to support herself. Because of the war the Trustees
asked for no grant from Parliament for three years, though a grant
was made early in 1749.[64] Georgia had to be settled further,
and the settlement must be partly by colonists coming in from
other provinces, instead of being entirely by settlers sent from
Europe, and she had to develop her resources in the neighborhood of provinces with a slave-holding economy.

In May, 1748, the President and Assistants informed the Trustees that slaves had been introduced into Georgia, despite all
efforts at prevention. Some of the slaves were seized, but a vigorous execution of the act against the importation of slaves might
dispeople Georgia "and occasion Numbers to leave the Colony
and Settle in Caroline as several have lately done. . . ." To lose
colonists now to Carolina, after all the Trustees' efforts, was
more than could be borne. The labor situation was poor in the extreme, planters "being destitute of Labourers to go on with their
Plantations and seem resolved to leave the Colony," and "the
working hands remaining here are so inconsiderable a number
that little can be done the want of which must soon drive
those few that remain on their Lands to the necessity of leaving
the same to seek their livelihood elsewhere if not timely prevented by a supply of useful laborious hands." Do not think we

Georgia Lakes, Rivers and Water Resources

► Lakes   ► Georgia Map Of   ► Georgia Mountains   ► Georgia Parks

Georgia Rivers Shown on the Map: Alapaha River, Altamaha River, Brier Creek, Broad River, Canoche River, Chattahoochee River, Etowah River, Flint River, Ochlockonee River, Ocmulgee River, Oconee River, Ogeechee River, Ohoopee River, Oostanaula River, Satilla River, Savannah River, St. Marys River and Withlacoochee River.

Georgia Lakes Shown on the Map: Allatoona Lake, Blue Ridge Lake, Hartwell Lake, J. Strom Thurmond Reservoir, Jackson Lake, Lake Blackshear, Lake Burton, Lake Oconee, Lake Seminole, Lake Sidney Lanier, Lake Sinclair, Russell Lake, Walter F. George Reservoir, Weiss Lake and West Point Lake.

The United States Geological Survey has a number of stream gages located throughout Georgia. These estimate stream levels, discharges and record them over time. This data is published on the web and many stations allow users to plot custom graphs. Get updated Georgia river and stream levels from USGS here.

Georgia Stream and River Level Alerts

The United States Geological Survey has a system that will send you an email message when flood levels are reached on any steam with USGS gaging equipment that you have selected. Sign up here to recieve Georgia stream and river level alerts.

Georgia Water Publications

The United States Geological Survey has a number of publications related to water use and water resources in Georgia. View the water resource publications for Georgia here.

Find it on Geology.com

| | Search |

More from Geology.com

100+ Gems - Photos of over 100 beautiful gems ranging from the popular to the obscure.

Dowsing is a method used to find underground water that is rejected by most geologists.

Alberta
Cab

Surrounded By
Nature. Unplug
Rel

Georgia Precipitation Ma

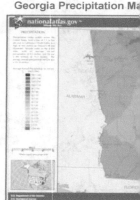

The National Atlas Project has precipit states that you can view online or print show the average annual precipitation View and print an Georgia precipitation prepared by the PRISM Climate Group United States Geological Survey.

Georgia Elevation Map

Elevation
7500-9000 Ft.
6000-7500 Ft.
4500-6000 Ft.
3000-4500 Ft.
1800-3000 Ft.
1200-1800 Ft.
600-1200 Ft.
300-600 Ft.
150-300 Ft.
0-150 Ft.

join with discontented people, the Board begged the Trustees, "but the real circumstances of the Colony are such that 'twould be an unpardonable Crime if we failed to represent to their Honours what We think ourselves in Conscience and Duty bound to do."[65]

Instead of vigorous protests and directions to end all slavery in Georgia, the Trustees directed a meeting to be held in Savannah to debate the best method of admitting Negroes. The unanimous opinion of those at the meeting was that the introduction of Negroes under certain regulations would make Georgia in a few years as flourishing as any province in America. The resolutions were signed by Noble Jones, Francis Harris, Isaac Young, William Ewen, James Habersham, John Martin Bolzius, the President and Assistants, and some less important colonists. Appropriate action followed in England in 1749, 1750, and 1751 for the repeal of the act against the importation of Negroes and a new act permitting their use. With this change and the broadening of land tenure to absolute inheritance in 1750, the Trustees were indeed enlarging the colony and giving up their earlier ideas.[66]

John Milledge signed his name to a second paper to the Trustees in October, 1749, when the limitations and restrictions best suited to the use of Negroes in Georgia were debated by some of the principal inhabitants at the Trustees' request.[67] John was the right age to profit by these changes in the colony, being about twenty-nine years old, and he must have seized every advantage afforded for his future.

In August, 1749, Savannah was in a greater uproar than the town had ever known before, stirred up by Mary Musgrove Bosomworth and her husband Thomas. The Bosomworths induced a number of Creek chiefs and their warriors to come to Savannah to demonstrate in support of Mary's claim to certain lands in the colony. About 100 chiefs were said to have come, and their behavior was anything but reassuring to the white inhabitants. The militia was called out, commanded by Noble Jones; it was supplemented by a party of mounted young men from Savannah and the out-lying plantations, "Headed by Quarter-Master John Milledge, which made a good appearance."

After various entertainments were provided for Chieftain Malatchee and his men, it looked as though matters would come to a peaceful conclusion, and the militia was discharged. Trouble flared anew when the report went around Savannah that William Stephens's head was cut off. Drum beats sounded through Savannah streets as a great number of Indians appeared. The President and Assistants ran out to the Square, unarmed, and stopped the Indians. "Our Inhabitants were so enraged, that it was with the greatest difficulty, they could be prevented firing on them and had not the Members of this Board Stood before the Indians, 'till they were induced to disperse, it was feared the Consequence would have been fatal."

The chiefs proposed to retire to Stephens's house and discuss matters over a friendly glass of wine, but they had scarcely reached the front steps when Mary Bosomworth "like a Mad and Frantick Woman came running in among them, endeavouring all she could to irretate the Indians afresh," threatening the lives of some of the magistrates and the destruction of the colony by the Indians under her influence. Upon her being removed and confined in a private house the Indians began to subside. The militia continued under arms and John's troop of horse "came to a resolution and offered their Service, which was kindly accepted, that though they were on their own expence, they would be on constant Duty Day and Night, 'till these Indians should depart from hence, and that Six of their Troop should every Night duly Patroll round and through the Streets of this Town."[68]

Subsequent conferences with the Indians cooled them. On Sunday afternoon the chiefs and some of the party, with Stephens and some members of the Board, walked out to the spring as a pleasant diversion; John's troop of horse accompanied them on foot. In hopes of getting the Indians out of Savannah, it was decided to give them presents. The troop of horse escorted the Indians to the building used both for a courthouse and a church on August 16, 1749, for the presents. "Malatchee appeared so angry as to foam at his Mouth," to the astonishment of the spectators, yet on the whole matters went well enough. Presents were given and Malatchee was amiable enough, after the four-hour meeting, to desire that the members of the Board would attend him and the other chiefs at a tavern. With them went the faithful troop of horse, "who have Shewn themselves on this occasion very alert and ready."

Another scene took place at the tavern. While Malatchee was in the friendliest humor and protesting affection for the English,

Mary Bosomworth rushed in upon them "in the most violent out-ragious and unseemly manner, that a Woman Spirited up with Liquor, Drunk with passion, and disappointed in her Views could be guilty of." Though she was civilly treated, her rage seemed to increase and must have been unbearable when she, who de-clared herself Empress and Queen of both the Upper and Lower Creeks, was advised to pursue so undramatic and innocent a program as going home and going to bed. She was incensed; speaking in the Creek tongue to Malatchee, she aroused him. The party at the tavern was now treated to the spectacle of Malat-chee "foaming at the Mouth, like a Mad Beast; [he] called on his People and said, tye her as soon as they would, He would untie her."

The peace officers removed her to a private room in the guard house, for temporary confinement. Most of the other chiefs con-veyed privately to the Board their dislike of this scene and of Malatchee's behavior, but one slipped out to the house where his men lodged and ordered them to arm themselves. When Captain Noble Jones sent some of his militia to tell these Indians that they must lay down their arms immediately, they obeyed. That night was an uneasy one. John's guard of horse were on duty all night, and most of Savannah's men kept their arms at hand.

As affairs quietened, the Board, wishing "to express some pe-culiar Mark of esteem" to the members of the troop of horse which John commanded, invited them to "a plain Dinner." It was not until the Royal governors came that "elegant" dinners were held. The plain dinner was given on Friday, August 18, and was attended also by some of the Indian chiefs. The occasion proved to be a felicitous one, and the Indians announced that they would go home the following day.[69]

Never could unwelcome guests have been more heartily speeded on their way, even to being supplied with provisions for their homeward journey. Some of them returned the following Wednesday, August 23, to say that inclement weather had forced them to camp twelve miles away (when Savannahians thought that by that time they were well over the Ogeechee River and on their way home) and now they needed more provisions, "which it was thought prudent to let them have."

It was probably at this pause in their homeward journey that the Indians committed depredations on John's plantation on the

Ogeechee. Malatchee and his people in the presence of some of
John's servants killed six of John's steers, "besides other Damages
done in and about his House." Though others suffered from damage and stealing, the Board thought that Malatchee intended revenge against John, "who was remarkably active in discounte-
nancing their Behaviour" in Savannah. But the only suggestion
the Board could make was that Patrick Graham, when he distributed presents to the Indians again, should keep back some intended for Malatchee and his party, to the amount of the damage
they had done.[70]

John could well join others in signing a petition telling the
Trustees that the depredations of straggling, thieving Indians
were becoming almost intolerable. Some settlements were lately
deserted as a result. The petitioners asked for a troop of rangers
and one other scout boat to help control the nuisance.[71]

The Trustees gave an unqualified refusal to the plan of withholding from Malatchee and his party some of the Indian presents,
because of the damage the Indians had done to the Milledge plantation and one other. In the Trustees' opinion withholding the
presents would incite the Indians to still further mischief. Give
the Indians notice, however, when presents were distributed
again, the Trustees said, that if they committed such mischief
to the person or property of any inhabitant in the future, those
responsible would receive no presents.[72]

When John presented a petition for land to the President and
Assistants in October, 1750, he was met with warm approval.
Some years ago, John said, he had made considerable improvements on a tract on the Great Ogeechee when he commanded Fort
Argyle on that river, but now that the provincial troops were
disbanded, that tract was no longer convenient for him and since
he "conceives it to be high Time to make a Settlement for his
future Welfare," he asked for a tract of 400 acres on the south
side of the Little Ogeechee. The Board "having for some Time
past observed, that this good natur'd Young Man has been employing his Strength and Industry rather for the Service of others,
than for himself, could not but approve of his Design of making a
Settlement, therefore granted his Request; and they cannot omit
observing that He has at all Times appeared peculiarly Active to
serve the Colony, whenever required, especially in all Disturbances with the Indians, being a good Horseman and well ac-

quainted with the Woods." Such a compliment from the Board was rare and showed the measure of esteem in which John was held. This grant was later spoken of as being 500 acres.[73]

John Milledge was by 1750 what was known as a principal inhabitant, a term having no official significance but one which clearly indicated a person of more than average importance. In July, 1750, John joined the President and Assistants and other Georgians in a representation to the Trustees declaring their alarm at and disapproval of the rumored annexation of Georgia to South Carolina after the expiration of the Trustees' charter.[74] In December, 1750, John was elected as one of the four representatives from Savannah to the assembly which the Trustees called into being to allow the people to advise, though not to legislate, in government.[75]

John seems to have kept the tract on the Great Ogeechee, or obtained another, for his land there is mentioned in connection with the boundaries of other plantations. He increased his holdings in the succeeding years. When in 1757 he asked for one tract of 160 acres adjoining his land on the Great Ogeechee, he had then a wife, three children, and five slaves. Land was granted on the basis of the number of people, white and Negro, in a family. This land was granted to him as were also other tracts and he later by grant or purchase owned land on Skidaway Island and elsewhere. By February, 1762, when he petitioned again for land, he had twenty-three Negroes. John Milledge, with these and his diversified land holdings, was now a substantial man in the province.[76]

John Milledge continued to be a "leading inhabitant" of the colony after it passed under the control of the King. He was captain of a company of rangers until the rangers were disbanded in the mid-1760's, and consequently involved in Indian diplomacy and military activity. He served in the Commons House of Assembly for a number of years and was a vestryman and church warden for Christ Church Parish after the colony was divided into parishes. He acquired more land and slaves, once the plantation pattern had become established in Georgia, until he was a man of considerable economic substance. He died in 1781 in the midst of the American War for Independence. His son of the same name was prominent in Georgia during the Revolutionary period and served as governor from 1802 until 1806. The name is perpetuated by Georgia's ante-bellum seat of government, Milledgeville.

CHAPTER FIFTEEN

Noble Jones — From Carpenter to Principal Inhabitant

AMONG the heads of families who came on the *Ann*, Noble Jones was probably the most versatile. He lived long enough to prove his versatility. Many of the other men did not. Jones was thirty-two years of age when he sailed in November, 1732, and his wife Sarah was the same age. His son Noble Wimberly was ten years old and his daughter Mary three. Noble brought with him two servants, Thomas Ellis aged seventeen, and Mary Cormock (Cornock or Charnock) aged eleven. Before he sailed, Jones was commissioned by the Trustees one of the eight conservators to keep the peace in the new town of Savannah. The Trustees made out a dormant commission for Jones as court recorder in case Thomas Christie should need to be replaced, but Jones never became recorder.[1]

Jones was entered as a carpenter on the passenger list of the *Ann*, though Thomas Milledge and John Goddard were spoken of as the two chief carpenters and Oglethorpe mentioned Milledge as "our best Carpenter." These men died during the great illness in the summer of 1733 when their knowledge of building was sorely needed, and Jones must have exercised his own skill in helping to provide the necessary housing. He was temporarily deflected from work during the great illness, for Oglethorpe remarked that Jones looked after the sick since Dr. Cox's death. Apparently he continued these ministrations until he himself became ill.[2] What medical training Jones had is not known. Perhaps he was at heart a physician who, with no formal training, was able to help others in times of illness. A pamphlet in his handwriting still exists in which are copied a number of prescriptions,[3] and these he must have used often when he was called upon in the colony.

Neither is it known what surveying experience Jones had had in England, but this was a skill badly needed in the colony. Jones evidently began his duties as the colony's surveyor in 1733 through a verbal agreement with Oglethorpe, whom he had known in England. When the Salzburgers arrived early in 1734 Jones accompanied Commissary Baron Von Reck on an exploratory trip to determine the course of streams in the vicinity of the land the Salzburgers would occupy. To Von Reck, Jones was *a* surveyor; to the Trustees he was *the* public surveyor appointed by Oglethorpe or *the* surveyor of Georgia.[4] The Trustees instructed Jones to keep them informed of the land he ran out, of the number of acres cleared on each lot, what crops were planted on each, and how they were cultivated.[5] Had Jones complied strictly with these orders he would have done little else, for this would have required constant inspection of planted land after the initial survey. Surveying in itself was arduous enough. When each new group of colonists arrived, Jones must survey their home lots, garden lots, and farm lots. Grants of more than fifty acres were usually in one unit. Of the fifty-acre grants, the home lot was surveyed first, the garden lot as soon as possible, while the farm lot was usually last. Once the Trustees told Jones to set out forthwith the town and garden lots for certain new colonists, and the farm lots when he conveniently could. This was probably standard practice.[6]

The Trustees prodded all officials in the colony to send regular journals of their activities to London. From Jones they wanted the plans of the land run out and what he was doing day by day. Numerous instructions were sent to Thomas Causton to be relayed to Surveyor Jones: set out a certain lot and send a description of it; measure out the lands for the Salzburgers and others from a certain grant; continue setting out the lands in the regular manner ordered by Oglethorpe. If any disputes arose among the people on Skidaway Island about the limits of their lands, Jones must settle them. August Gottlieb Spangenburg was coming over with ten male servants to take possession of 500 acres granted to Count Zinzendorf. Jones must run out this 500 acres on the north side of the Ogeechee and 200 acres adjoining to be reserved for the Count's servants when their times of indenture expired. Mark out instantly Spangenburg's town, garden, and farm lots;

if the servants should stand idle for want of having land to work, "it would be an unpardonable fault in Mr. Jones."[7]

Causton assured the Trustees that Jones would soon run out the land granted; Sir Francis Bathurst wrote that Jones had surveyed his land near Savannah;[8] but criticism mounted as rapidly as approbation. Thomas Christie remarked in the winter of 1734 that people would not fence until they knew their boundaries, and so most of the crops planted in the summer were eaten by horses and cows roaming at large. When Peter Gordon took to London in the spring of 1735 the colonists' complaints, several against Jones were included. One of the grievances that people labored under, Gordon told the Trustees, was that notwithstanding their repeated applications to the surveyor, their lands were not run out and as a result they were obliged to live in town at great expense as provisions were extraordinarily dear. Many people, because Jones did not run out their lots, were almost ruined and had no way of supporting themselves but by pawning their wearing apparel. Thus, Gordon added, people had their minds "entirely weakened and unbent, from the pursuits of labor and industry."[9]

This complaint may be traced largely to Robert Parker, Jr., who averred that Causton and Jones had solidly opposed his settling on the land he wanted, and that he could not get his land run out though he had offered Jones five guineas above the usual fee for surveying. He figured that he had lost £150 "by the Negligence of Mr. Jones" and expected the Trustees to reimburse him.[10]

The Trustees distrusted Gordon because he had left the colony without their permission but were quick to take up his complaints. The very thought that some men in the colony of Georgia longed to cultivate their land and were unable to because Jones had not ascertained the bounds, was not one they could bear with equanimity. They immediately sent the complaints against Jones to Causton to be answered. They informed Jones of the charges made against him and said that if the complaints were true, he was guilty of unaccountable negligence which had resulted in very bad consequences. They required his answer to the complaints, which must be shown to the persons making them.[11]

Jones's reply was largely concerned with the Parkers, father and son, their vacillations about the land they would settle on, and his endeavors to persuade them that they could not settle wherever they wished without a grant. He well remembered how angry Oglethorpe had been with him for believing the elder Parker without Oglethorpe's written order. Jones and Causton had a difficult time with the Parkers. The Parkers had a difficult time with themselves and with everyone else; they were egotistical men in a constant state of friction, convinced that they were above any rules ordered by the Trustees. As for the younger Parker's assertion that Jones was the cause of his losing money by not running out his land, Jones could show that Parker had town and garden lots, both his own and those of Mrs. Sale whom he had married. The garden lots could and should be cultivated for Parker's benefit and to employ the servants he acquired by his marriage to William Sale's widow. Jones said he had run out most of the land to which people had any title, "and hope 'ere long to finish which I had Done before Now had I Not had ye Misfortune, of Being Weak handed, Occassioned by ye Sickness & Death of Servants."[12]

To Oglethorpe, Jones wrote in more detail about his activities, and remarked mildly, "I Continue to Go on (as Nigh as I am Capable) by the Same Rules as Yr Honour was Pleas'd to Prescribe, Tho' I have Mett with Some Difficultys.

"I have had Some trouble with the two Mr Parkers the particulars of which I have Sent to The Honble the Trustees I have Done My Endeavour to Stick Close to the Instructions I Rec'd from Yr Honour."

Trouble with servants had retarded Jones's work. One had died after a long illness. Two others had been ill and, as soon as they were well, robbed Jones and other people and then ran away. Both were recaptured; one was now kept with a chain on his leg to prevent his running away again. Jones employed a man named Ford to help him, but "what he did for me cost me above three times what I had for it, If I cou'd Get a Sufficient Number of Servants I dont Doubt doing well. . . ."

News had come to the colony that Peter Gordon sold his "prospect of Savannah" to the Trustees for £100 (actually the price was sixteen guineas). When Jones reflected that Gordon took Jones's own plats to make that map, he told Oglethorpe, "I always thought him a Man of More Honour than to Enfringe So much on any Mans Right." Jones resolved to be cautious about putting any more plats in the register book, for others had ready access to it and might follow Gordon's example.[13]

Jones had been given other appointments by Oglethorpe besides that of surveyor. One was as ranger with police powers to prevent indiscriminate cutting of timber, particularly cypress and live oak. In this position Jones encountered difficulties when Oglethorpe gave verbal permission to individuals to cut trees but neglected to inform Jones, thus bringing criticism of the latter and arousing discontent among the colonists. Jones after being told by several people that they had permission from Oglethorpe to cut trees to make canoes, told Oglethorpe, "I should be Glad If Yr Honr wou'd favour Me with an Account of as many of those Orders as Yr Honour Shall think fitt to Grant."

Anyone cutting timber must have a license from Jones and he posted notices at various places warning of prosecution for infringement of the rule. He was particularly severe in his notice concerning the neighborhood of the spring in Savannah: "If any person Shall presume on Any Pretence to Cut Down Deface or Destroy any Tree or Shrub any where About the Spring or Make any fires there or Make it a place to wash Cloaths they will have their Tubs Potts &c broke & be Also Prosecuted for the Same." This regulation about timber cutting brought Jones into more unfavorable contact with the Parkers, for the senior Parker kept a sawmill.[14]

As a ranger, Jones must also investigate rumors of marauders coming into the colony. Before writing to Oglethorpe in July, 1735, he went twice to the unsettled southernmost parts of the colony. The first time was after an alarm, and he took the scout boat and about fifty men. The second time was in January, 1735, with Captain George Dunbar, whose ship the *Prince of Wales* was at Savannah, and with eleven white men and four Indians. The immediate reason for this trip was that a body of Spanish Indians had come up from the south, crossed the Ogeechee, and killed some Euchees. In case of accident, Jones was to succeed Dunbar as leader. The expedition inspected the islands and coastline but found no marauders, only evidences of recent fires on Sapelo Island.[15]

Jones, when he wrote to Oglethorpe on July 6, 1735, was to set off the next day to investigate another report that Yamassee Indians were skulking near Fort Argyle and were believed to have killed some of Tomochichi's people. Jones always thought it was his duty as ranger "to be the first out on those Occasions," and to "See If we Can Come up with those Strollers who Come to

Spy & Disturb our Peace." August Spangenberg would go with him, and Jones would run out Count Zinzendorf's grant before he returned to Savannah.

This letter revealed another duty given Jones by Oglethorpe, that of acting as agent or attorney for Tomochichi and his people. Jones was to protect their interests whenever anyone might steal their cattle, cut their timber, or oppress them in any other fashion. Jones noted, "I do Any Business for 'em that they Desire." One piece of business was Tomochichi's bread-and-butter letter to the Trustees after his return home from England in December, 1734. Jones said it was "a letter of thanks (which I writt from Tomochichi's words) to The Honble Trustees for the many favours they had bestow'd upon him."[16] Of the passage home, Tomochichi said, the Indians "were Very kindly Used by the Capt which we shall Endeavour to Return by our love as well to ye Captain as to all the white people who Now Are or Shall hereafter be known to Us." Tomochichi's people had delivered lately some skins to Causton "which they desire Your Honours to Accept as a token of there Gratitude & love, they are Sensible that Your Honours have Much better things but as they are few in Number hope the Skins will be Acceptable." It was a nicely balanced and dignified letter containing the latest news, a little gossip, expressions of appreciation, and notice of a present sent.[17]

The years 1735 and 1736 were busy ones for Noble Jones. Complaints still went to London about him and were noted by the Trustees. Here he and others had been two years in the colony without seeing their forty-five-acre farm lots despite appeals to Jones and Causton, Thomas Gapen wrote, hinting darkly that everything went by favor. The Trustees again ordered that Jones report to them persons settled on granted lands and to what extent the lands were cultivated.[18] They ordered the purchase of "two Circumferenters and a Spirit Level" for the surveyor and ordered that £10 sterling be given to Jones and John Vanderplank for their services as constables. Jones also received the year's allowance of staple provisions for himself and family issued by the Trustees for the magistrates, constables, and tythingmen in consideration of the time they spent in public service.[19]

Jones had the 2500 acres to lay out for the Salzburgers in the spring of 1735. This occupied him for some time and considerable correspondence developed about it. Von Reck protested to the Trustees when he found that each man was to pay Jones five shil-

lings sterling for his survey; nothing had been said previously
about this payment. But the Trustees upheld Jones, saying that
he was entitled to his fees, set by Oglethorpe as low as possible.[20]
Jones insisted that fees were set too low by Oglethorpe to allow
him to hire any help in surveying. When he hired Ford to survey
the farm lots belonging to some of the Savannah people, Ford's
pay was more than Jones received for surveying the entire township.[21] Though no one commented on it, the lowness of surveying fees was obviously one reason that surveying went so slowly.
If Jones surveyed in or near Savannah, the Salzburgers wanted
him; if he was at their settlement or elsewhere, Savannah people
clamored for him. Whatever he did, someone was dissatisfied.

In June, 1736, Oglethorpe appointed Jones as one of several
men to acquaint Indian traders with the details of the Trustees'
act for maintaining peace with the Indians.[22] A few days later
Oglethorpe directed Jones to survey and lay out a town to be
called Augusta, at whatever point Roger Lacy, appointed to enforce the Indian act, should designate as most convenient on the
Savannah River. Oglethorpe ordered a square in the center of
the town with public lots on each side, totaling not less than
four acres. The main streets were to be at least twenty-five yards
wide, and there was to be a 600-acre common. Originally forty
house lots of one acre each in town were to be laid out. House lots
must be built on within a year and a half, and could be granted
only to people who held grants of 500 acres outside the town.
Farm lots of fifty acres each were also to be laid out adjoining the
town. Jones was directed to mark out 500-acre lots for certain
men, most of them Indian traders, including Cornelius Docherty
(or Dougherty). The fifty-acre lots were to be granted to such
persons as Roger Lacy approved. Augusta was to be under the
same regulations as the remainder of the colony.[23]

Roger Lacy, of Thunderbolt, was ordered by Oglethorpe in
June, 1736, to send a constable and men to enforce the Trustees'
act for maintaining peace with the Indians and to take into
custody any traders not licensed by Georgia. This brought down
upon Georgia protests from South Carolina, whose traders had
long been in the Creek and Cherokee nations. Carolina's Assembly
thought the Trustees' act should extend to traders who went
from Georgia and not to others. The Trustees' law contravened
Carolina regulations about traders, and Carolina refused to have

her traders subject to Georgia law.[24] Lacy seized traders and their goods in the Cherokee Nation who were not licensed by Georgia. The Carolina Assembly sent a committee to Oglethorpe to work out some peaceable procedure until the King's pleasure could be known. After this conference Oglethorpe gave instructions not to molest traders with licenses from Carolina in the Cherokee or Creek areas, until the matter could be settled in England.[25]

Because of these happenings, the Spanish alarm, and want of provisions, Lacy did not go to the site of the new town until the following spring. Augusta, named for a Royal Princess, was to be situated in an old Indian field on a bluff about thirty feet above the Savannah River, some 150 miles upriver from Savannah. On May 19, 1737, Lacy set out with about twenty men, arriving at the site on May 29. Seven more men followed him on June 28.[26] Jones did not go with Lacy; he was busy setting out the glebe land at the request of John Wesley and doing several other things. He must have left for Augusta early in June, leaving Thomas Ellis, the indentured servant who came with him on the Ann, to do some necessary surveying in and about Savannah and to serve in his place as officer of the guard.[27] The garrison boat, arriving in Savannah on June 19 for provisions, brought news from Lacy that land had been cleared for the fort at Augusta. The fort was already begun and was almost finished by the latter part of that year.[28]

Jones was back in Savannah early in July in a dissatisfied state of mind. He and Causton had probably not then become as friendly as they were to be later, for the latter recorded their conversation in the brisk, impersonal style in his journal. Jones came to Causton and asked for an advance of money, insisting that Oglethorpe had ordered him to be paid for the lands he had surveyed. Causton said he could not comply with Jones's request, but that if Jones would turn in a list of people who had not paid him, he could be given credit for this amount in the store. But he must bring a certificate from every person whose lands were run out, because Oglethorpe intended that each person should pay for his own survey. Causton reminded Jones that his helpers had been paid and victualled and his family supported, so that there was little prospect of anything being due him, unless he could obtain the Trustees' approval of his demands. Jones recounted various difficulties in surveying for which he received no

pay. Causton advised Jones to return his plans and endeavor
to remove people's complaints, which he believed to be generally
just.[29]

Jones was in and around Savannah for the remainder of July.
Another surveyor named Ross, about whom little is known, was
delegated to set out more of the Salzburgers' land. As the weather
was so hot, he promised to start in September so as not to injure
his health.[30] An assistant in surveying is listed in the Trustees'
estimate of expenses in the summer, to work in the newer part
of the colony south of Savannah. A new colonist sailing in November, 1737, John Amory, was recommended to the Trustees as
a surveyor. They suggested to Causton that Amory might help in
pushing the needed work.[31] The Trustees were at last beginning
to understand that Jones could not do all the necessary surveying.
Oglethorpe, then in England, undoubtedly gave the information
that the Trustees used when they wrote of their satisfaction that
Jones had provided himself with helpers to carry on the necessary
surveying. They hoped he would run out all lands, "that those,
who have made his Neglect of doing it a Pretence for their
Idleness, may be left without Excuse if they continue in it."[32]

William Stephens arrived in Savannah on November 1, 1737,
and about three weeks later began an acquaintanceship with
Noble Jones. Stephens was instructed to send "a just Report of the
Surveyor's Negligence & who among the People there are capable
of taking that Business upon them." He was to call upon the
various officers, to make up their accounts and send them quarterly to the Trustees. He was to send an account of the magistrates
and other officers, "their Diligence or Carelessness, Abilities
&c, without Fear, Affection or Partiality. . . ."[33]

By the middle of January, Stephens was ready to report to the
Trustees on Jones. "I ought (in pursuance of my Instructions)
not to let this letter go without giving you some acct of your
Surveyor Jones; whose Character is of so mixed a nature,"
Stephens wrote, "yt 'tis not easy to hit it right in all its parts: for
twere doing him wrong, not to allow him some degrees of
Worth on several occasions; and (as I am told) a competent
share of knowledge of Geometry: Nevertheless 'twould be Injustice to the Trust, not to say yt he has certainly been negligent
in his Duty of running out Lands; which has occasioned many to
complain, who have thereby been under disappointments; &
sometimes Losses in mistaking land, & cultivating what afterwards

they found not to be their own; for wch. they could find no recompense. To 'speak my thoughts freely of him; I take him to be an indolent man, as well in relation to publick work, as to private Oeconomy; wch is sufficiently visible from the manner his Family lives in, & the very mean appearance he makes in his Garb: I have never yet seen any of his Plans, & the Trust (I fear) not many."

John Amory might take Jones's place, Stephens wrote, yet "I should think it not advisable immediately to remove Jones; for this reason: whatever has yet been done, he is Master of; & out of that Heap, probably some Good may with care be collected: but in case he found himself at once dismissed; I know not how far a vindictive temper might prompt him to be wicked enough to destroy whatever he has (such a thing I once heard whisperd) & that must certainly produce the utmost confusion, to begin all again. Besides, in some discourse I had with Mr. Amery, I found he should not think it worth his pains, to work on that Affair at so low a rate, as he understood Jones was to be allowed."[34]

Stephens said he had met Jones three times, as surveyor on November 24 and January 14 and on December 15 as a constable. Stephens was at Thomas Causton's home in Savannah with the magistrates when Jones and John Fallowfield dropped in and a conference was held about the apportionment of the work of four constables between these two men. One constable, John Vanderplank, had lately died, and another, John Coates, removed to South Carolina. Stephens had remarked earlier that he had to send for Jones, who was out of town about twelve miles upon some land where he was beginning an improvement, and that Jones was seldom in Savannah.[35] Stephens's personal acquaintanceship with Jones was thus slight, but Jones had already become what he was to remain to Stephens—something of an enigma.

Stephens reported to the Trustees complaints about Jones. Stephens found a mistake which he thought Jones had made. John Amory told him on January 23 that his land was not run out though he had been in the colony since before Christmas (December 21, to be exact). In January Jones was busy running out some of the Trust lands to be worked by the German servants who had arrived on December 20, 1737. William Bradley, sent over to cultivate some of the Trust lands in Georgia, was unhappy in the arrangements made for him and complained bitterly to Stephens of both Jones and Causton. Causton said that Bradley wanted more

Trust farms set out, though not twenty acres of the first one was cultivated and that Jones did everything Bradley required, leaving the latter without an excuse to delay his cultivation.[36]

Stephens saw little of Jones in 1738. In the spring fear of the Spanish brought the two constables, Jones and Fallowfield, in from their plantations to inspect arms. It was decided to have a muster to see how many men would respond to the drum beat. About eighty men responded with their arms and were reviewed on April 10; others were too far away on their farm or garden lots, for it was the planting season, to hear the drum.[37]

In March, 1738, the Trustees resolved to make inquiries into the conduct of Noble Jones, the surveyor, along with the other inquiries which have been mentioned above. They were not pleased with the report which Charles Wesley brought them in December, 1736, nor with other reports about Jones. Stephens's letter of January 19, reaching them in April, could not have helped Jones.[38] On October 17 Oglethorpe made his speech relating to what was termed Causton's mismanagement of affairs and the changes about to take place. Causton was dismissed as magistrate and storekeeper; Noble Jones was dismissed as surveyor and suspended as constable.[39]

Noble Jones was granted lot number forty-one in Savannah, but evidently had no great liking for life in town. It must have been in 1736 or 1737 that he began to cultivate a tract which he held by lease some ten or twelve miles from Savannah. This tract was on the Isle of Hope, described by Stephens as "a Peninsula, cut off from the Main with a very little Isthmus, which by a short Fence makes the Island an entire Possession" to its three inhabitants —Noble Jones, Henry Parker, and John Fallowfield. "It is equally divided betwixt them, which they hold by Lease (or Expectation of such) from the Trust, having occupied it two or three Years, and made considerable Improvements: The Isle of Skeedoway lies without it, and betwixt them is the Way all Boats must pass to and fro betwixt us and the South." Thomas Causton described Jones's plantation in 1741 as consisting of "what very Justly (when finished) may be called a good house with Convenient Out-Houses for Servants, Cattle &c he has also fenced and brought into tillage about 14 acres of land, he appears very industrious, the land is the best kind [this Noble Jones would later dispute], and has produced very well, . . . "[40] Jones's property, Wormsloe, is still occupied by his descendants today.

There was much passing by Wormsloe as a result of its location. Boats usually stopped in the vicinity waiting for the tide to pass through Skidaway Narrows; to save time, men rode horseback out to the Jones plantation to take a boat from Savannah to Frederica. Mail arriving from England for Frederica was frequently sent to Jones to be put aboard a boat to the south. Stephens felt uneasy about what went on at such places, which he usually referred to as distant plantations, following the upheaval in the latter part of 1738. Early in January, 1739, he said that several people rode out on Sunday to Causton's, Fallowfield's, and Jones's, where Stephens "presumed some further Consultations were to be held towards supporting that Spirit of Faction, which began to wax cold again and decline."[41] There is no evidence that Jones supported any faction against the Trustees; he signed "A State of the Province of Georgia," prepared by Stephens for the Trustees in November, 1740.[42]

In February, 1739, Jones and John Burnside captured three deserters from Oglethorpe's regiment stationed on St. Simons Island. These three men, already advertised for, were unable to make their final escape through unfamiliar and heavily wooded country, and being almost starved succumbed readily to capture.[43] This was not the first time that men fleeing from capture had stumbled into the Jones plantation and been captured.[44] In December, 1739, a small schooner "lurking" in Ossabaw Sound was suspected of spying for the Spaniards at St. Augustine. Her master and crew were ordered ashore at the Jones plantation where the magistrates, Henry Parker and Thomas Jones, examined them and found that the vessel, though loaded with Spanish contraband, was owned by the firm of Woodward and Flower of Port Royal, South Carolina.[45]

In the worsening situation with the Spaniards, the strategic situation of Jones's land was one factor in Oglethorpe's ordering a watch house, or small fort, to be erected there in 1739, which Noble Jones was paid £40 for building. The Scots remarked sarcastically of this fort, "a Timber building called *Jones's Fort;* which serves for *two* Uses, namely, to support Mr. *Noble Jones,* who is Commander of it, and to prevent the poor People of *Frederica* from getting to any other Place, where they might be able to support themselves."[46] Jones contributed considerably more to Oglethorpe's war effort than keeping the people at Frederica. He carried messages, received visitors at his plantation going to or from Frederica, did investigations and scouting work, and other things which Oglethorpe directed. He also held a lieutenant's commission in the South Carolina regiment enlisted briefly to help Oglethorpe.[47] Stephens several times remarked on this enlisting. In the latter part of April he said that "Enlisting of Men was now the principal Affair in hand; which had so drained the Town that it was hard to find a Man more to enter," though only about thirty Georgians enlisted in the Carolina force.[48]

Oglethorpe's attempt to take St. Augustine in June and July, 1740, was unsuccessful. On August 11 Noble Jones arrived in Savannah from Frederica to raise ten men for a guard and scout boat, which Jones was to command under the direction of Stephens. Stephens was pleased with this measure of protection. Jones brought with him from Frederica nearly thirty men from Savannah who had enlisted for four months in the Carolina regiment and whose time was now nearly expired. Oglethorpe, suspecting that if these men went to Charles Town they might not return to Georgia, ordered Jones to go to Charles Town, obtain the men's pay, and pay them off in Savannah. Jones went to Charles Town for this purpose on November 21 and returned to Savannah on December 19.[49]

In the meantime Jones must procure a boat for the guard service at Skidaway Narrows and enlist his men, which he did shortly. Stephens planned to go south to see Oglethorpe and warned Jones that upon his return from Frederica he would expect to find Jones's boat and men at their proper station, "and therefore recommended to him to use all possible Diligence in so necessary a Piece of Service; which he promised." Jones received Stephens at his plantation a few days later and took him to the watchhouse which Stephens said was in pretty good order and with a little more money spent on it would be very useful for defense and offense. On his return in September, Stephens found the guard-boat at its proper station at Skidaway Narrows, "and it was a Satisfaction to me to find the Orders I left with Noble Jones . . . so well observed. . . ."[50]

Stephens was not always so pleased with Jones, of whom he seems to have been continually suspicious. Stephens said in October that Jones "had been loitering about this Town and Neighborhood for several Days past; and some of his Men likewise had been seen idling and drinking here, in some private Corners.

. . . " To make matters worse in Stephens's opinion, Jones was that day at Ockstead with Thomas Causton. Stephens wrote Jones a letter "reprimanding him for so great Neglect of his Duty; requiring him, on Sight thereof to repair to his proper Charge"; and told him that if he did the like again it should be reported to General Oglethorpe, who would probably appoint one more diligent in his place.[51]

Stephens did not say that great sorrow recently had fallen to Causton and that Jones was trying to help as a friend, leaving the command of his boat to another that day. To Stephens it was enough that Jones had visited Causton, still under the Trustees' disapproval. Jones frequently had business in Savannah about his boat and supplies; and, when Stephens was informed of and consulted about this, he did not accuse Jones of "loitering" nor his men of "lurking" in town. Certainly he did not in the next few days when Jones consulted him and obtained a small swivel gun for his boat, ammunition, and more muskets. A Spanish privateer was thought to be on the coast, and more precautions must be taken. Jones and his men had no trouble with the privateer, but off the coast of South Carolina she chased and fired on a small schooner hired by Major Heron, of Oglethorpe's regiment, to take provisions and recruits from Charles Town to Frederica.[52]

Reports of the Spanish privateer's activities continued to arrive; so in February, 1741, Jones's boat was fitted with what Stephens described as "one of our smartest Pieces of Cannon, carrying a four Pound Ball," a further defense for the Narrows. While the privateer ignored Georgia for the fatter prizes of Carolina shipping, alarms continued. In the latter part of March a party of Spanish Indians pillaged Mark Carr's plantation in the southern part of the colony,[53] and warnings went out for all to be on the alert for these marauders.

At this time, when it was most needed, the lighthouse at Tybee displayed its customary recurring signs of decrepitude. Stephens and Thomas Jones went down to Tybee to see if it was possible to keep the lighthouse from falling down (no more was hoped for). They took with them Joseph Wardrope, a master carpenter in Savannah, and Noble Jones. Stephens judged Noble Jones "a good Mechanick, having pretty good Skill in Architecture, as well as been conversant in the Manner of Scaffolding, in Use at the publick Work about Westminster-Abbey. . . ."[54] The Tybee beacon was not an inspiring sight. Wardrope could see no hope for it, but Jones thought it could be repaired. His opinion was concurred in by Thomas Sumner, sent by Oglethorpe from Frederica to confer about the beacon.⁵⁵ The lighthouse soon settled the argument by falling down. The *South-Carolina Gazette* in reporting its fall said, "this fine Piece of Workmanship, so beneficial to all those who fall in with the Coast of *South-Carolina* and *Georgia,* was erected at the beginning of the year 1736, and cost upwards of 1500 l. *Sterling*; It's Fall is entirely owing to the want of Covering; the Frame being expos'd was quite rotted. This was many times represented to the *ruling Powers* in *Georgia,* but to no Purpose, altho they were told it could have been Weather-boarded for 100 l. *Sterling,* which in all Probability would have made it stand for *Twenty* or *Thirty* Years longer— *What better can be expected* from THOSE *who Regard* their own PASSIONS and *private* INTEREST more *than the GOOD of their Country and Fellow Subjects.*" Work was begun on a new lighthouse that same year in the autumn.⁵⁶

Jones and his guard boat were more directly under Oglethorpe's orders from the spring of 1741. Though Stephens could speak in June of giving Jones "a sharp reprimand," the time when he felt himself entitled to do so was now passing. It was by Oglethorpe's orders that Jones, during the remainder of 1741, made his frequent trips back and forth from the Narrows or Savannah to Frederica.⁵⁷

Early in 1741 when the Trustees decided to divide Georgia into two counties, they told Stephens to have a map made of the northern part of the colony and asked Oglethorpe to have one made of the southern part. In September Stephens signed an agreement with Joseph Avery to make the map.⁵⁸ In November Oglethorpe indicated his disapproval of the map-making project for fear that the map might fall into the hands of the Spaniards and prove of value to them. Neither did he altogether approve of Stephens's choice of Joseph Avery to make it. Oglethorpe thought Noble Jones had plans of the whole country sufficient for the purpose. "To which last I have only this to say; that I never yet saw one of them," Stephens wrote, "nor do I expect that I ever shall; nor have I heard of any person that ever did see such works of his; tho in so long time as he was Employed, it may reasonably be supposed, that he has some Sketches of divers parts here and there run out by him, which nevertheless we may wait for years yet to come, of seeing reduced yet by him into a Compleat plan (if ever). . . ." Stephens said further, "I have good Reason to believe that these objections made against Averys work, are rather Noble Jones's own, than the Generals. with Intent to defeat any Attempt that may be made by another, which probably may eclipse what he has never brought to perfection."[59]

Jones was in Frederica with Oglethorpe for a longer period early in 1742 but returned in late February to his plantation to plant his land, while the guard-boat returned by Oglethorpe's order to Frederica.[60] Jones now had under his command at Skidaway Narrows a second and smaller boat, commanded at one time by Thomas Upton, later by Moses Nunez, and still later by Upton again.[61] The need was greater than ever now to watch the Narrows and identify each boat that passed, lest the Spaniards slip up the coast. Jones was back and forth several times between this post and Frederica on Oglethorpe's commands.

In June Jones went by Oglethorpe's order to inspect Tybee lighthouse. The *South-Carolina Gazette* now said that the lighthouse "is now rebuilt in a most magnificent Manner" to the great benefit of those who sailed the coast. Oglethorpe thought of fortifying Tybee against attack and stationing some men there who would be under Jones's command from the Narrows.[62] Apparently this was not done. Oglethorpe had every reason in June to expect an invasion of Georgia from St. Augustine and was preparing his defense. He was not surprised when Spanish ships appeared off St. Simons Island on June 22; instead he was ready for them.[63]

Noble Jones's movements cannot be traced clearly in the next few months. He was in Savannah on June 18 and 19 and had started his guardboat with Thomas Jones as a passenger to Frederica when he met Oglethorpe's secretary, Francis Moore, who had left Frederica on June 25 with an express to Charles Town to inform the government there of the Spaniards' arrival and attack. Upon Thomas Jones's insistence the guard-boat returned to its station and Thomas Jones to Savannah, "leaving Noble Jones to look narrowly about him, and take due care if any discovery could be made by him of the Enemies farther Designs."[64]

Noble Jones soon went to Frederica with the rangers and Indians and was mentioned by Oglethorpe as having participated in the Battle of Bloody Marsh. On August 23 Noble Jones, Captain Kent, and others, long looked for, returned to Savannah. They had much news to relate and brought a letter from Oglethorpe telling that the Spaniards had left Frederica and retired to St. Augustine.[65]

Oglethorpe followed the Spaniards into their own territory in the last of February, 1743, to prevent another anticipated invasion of Georgia. Oglethorpe's forces consisted of varied elements, including a number of small craft of which one was Noble Jones's guard-boat with Jones in command.[66] He returned from the St. John's River to Savannah on March 27 as Captain Noble Jones, "lately so entitled by the General," as Stephens said. Jones may have made another trip down to Frederica in June; the guard-boat went down and doubtless he did also. If so, this was probably the last time he saw Oglethorpe, who left Georgia in July, leaving Captain William Horton in command at Frederica.[67]

Jones's life began to change, imperceptibly at first, in 1743. He still commanded the guard-boat and the smaller boat of which Thomas Upton was in charge. The guard-boat continued to make trips to Frederica with mail for Captain William Horton and others but less frequently than before Oglethorpe left. Often mail to or for Frederica was given to Jones to be held until a boat passed and took on letters. Occasionally the guard-boat must be on the lookout for run-away servants; once officers in Savannah had to search for deserters from the crew of the boat; and in September Captain Horton asked Jones to keep an especially strict watch for a party of Yamassee Indians.[68]

Jones made two trips, each of several weeks, down to Frederica that autumn, returning from the second on November 19. Stephens thought that the second trip had something to do with Thomas Causton and his affairs, for Stephens had observed the increasing friendship between Causton and Jones.[69]

The fact that Causton went down to see Oglethorpe in Jones's boat early in 1742, just after Jones had returned from Frederica, aroused Stephens's curiosity. In the autumn Stephens became convinced that the friendship between Noble Jones and Thomas Causton boded no good for the colony. He knew that Jones and Causton met with William Ewen and William Woodrooffe, both of whom had signed remonstrances, and Stephens thought that another was under way.[70] Jones and Causton had not signed the former petitions to England and it seems clear now that Jones was endeavoring to help Causton in his tangled store accounts.

Thomas Jones, whose business it was to settle Causton's accounts at the store, spent a good bit of time with Causton in early 1743.

Sometimes Noble Jones joined them. Stephens several times commented on this and seemed to resent their meeting together without his being invited. Stephens could not understand why anyone would be intimate with Causton, a man under a cloud of the Trustees' displeasure. Causton still had friends, or adherents as Stephens termed them, and might yet cause trouble.[71] In this whole matter Stephens showed a petty suspicion, while Noble Jones was trying to help a friend in trouble. Perhaps Stephens could not understand this.

As president of the County of Savannah and later as president of the Colony of Georgia, Stephens filled his position conscientiously, and he never forgot the Trustees' original instructions to report to London in detail events in the colony. He fulfilled this obligation faithfully. He watched for threats to his office and to the Trustees. He watched so diligently that sometimes he suspected unduly. Yet he protected himself by recording alliances which he noticed, in case something might come of them later.

In the spring of 1743 Stephens felt the pressure brought by Causton to have Thomas Jones settle Causton's account and to have the President and Assistants to acquit him or bring a charge against him, which both Causton and Noble Jones insisted was Oglethorpe's desire when they saw him at Frederica. Noble Jones, Stephens observed, was present to discover what happened in all controversies. Causton, with his friend Noble Jones, insisted that Stephens and Henry Parker sign a statement that they found nothing amiss in Causton's accounts, but Stephens and Parker sidestepped a clearcut decision and sent a report of the investigations to the Trustees for a final determination. Naturally Jones and Causton did not like this. Jones and Causton were together for a week in Savannah that August. This aroused Stephens's suspicions. He thought it strange that "they spent a good part of their time chearfully, and one night in Dancing &c with such as they made choice of." He could only say that "Such uncommon Merrymaking among us was a matter of Speculation . . . but whatever was at the Bottom, I gave my Self little thought about it."[72] Obviously he puzzled and worried about it a great deal.

Stephens did not know, or did not say so if he did, when he continued to wonder why Causton and Jones were together, that they were helping John Dobell, the register, untangle the entries in the register book. The two men, one who had been a magistrate and the other surveyor, knew the people and their land as did no others. When Dobell sent the information the Trustees wanted, he said, "that tis so full as it is . . . is owing to the great Assistance I have received from Mr. Thomas Causton and Capt. Noble Jones, which they favoured me with, with much readiness and did not spare to Assist me by night as well as by Day. . . ."[73]

Jones's work with his guard-boat continued for the next two years on the same course already related, except for one incident in the summer of 1744. England was now at war with France. Down at Frederica Captain William Horton read to the troops and inhabitants His Majesty's declaration of war. Captain Jones, not having a copy of the official declaration, devised a form which carried an explanation of the causes of the war and read it to his crew at the Narrows. Guns were fired across the water, and Captain Jones and his guard-boat crew were at war with France. Savannah was slightly later than Jones. Drum-beat called the people together on the afternoon of July 23; seventy able men appeared with arms. The war was published, the people shouted, three volleys were fired, and toasts to the health of King George II and to success to his arms were drunk from a cask of beer.[74]

In the latter part of 1744 Jones was appointed by the Trustees along with Patrick Graham, and schoolmaster John Dobell, to examine and certify receipts for expenditures of public funds in Georgia. Except for his appointment as constable, Oglethorpe had given Jones his previous appointments, and Oglethorpe may have been responsible for this appointment. The auditors met upon call from Stephens when the accounts were ready, and several meetings were usually necessary before the accounts could be forwarded to London.[75]

Six years passed before Jones received another appointment from the Trustees; he was made one of the Assistants to the President in the summer of 1750. The following year he was appointed register of the colony. The Trustees said that "having heard a good character of Mr. Noble Jones, [we] have appointed him an Assistant."[76] This was a far cry from the day in 1738 when he was dismissed from one office and suspended from another. Jones had proved himself, if ever he needed to do so.

In 1750 the Trustees sent an appointment for James Habersham and Pickering Robinson, who was about to embark for Georgia, to make a survey of the colony, with particulars of the towns and settlements and details of the development of the silk industry. In case Habersham could not undertake to make the report, the Trustees suggested it be done by Jones, "as they have a good Opinion of Mr. Noble Jones, who must be well acquainted with every Part of the Province. . . ." Less than a month before this letter was written in England, the President and Assistants had themselves suggested that Jones, "the most intelligent, and the only Surveyor of those Times now remaining," be the one to give the account of the inhabitants for which the Trustees had asked earlier. Unfortunately Jones "is now, and has been some time very ill."[77]

Jones took office as an Assistant on November 9, 1750, attending his first Board meeting on the 14th, and remained thereafter a faithful member of that body. He was sworn in on January 10, 1751, with Pickering Robinson, to make the survey desired by the Trustees.[78]

It was in 1751 when the first General Assembly of Georgia, authorized by the Trustees, met in Savannah on January 9. Henry Parker, the vice-president, addressed the Assembly, explaining the reasons for calling it.[79] On Sunday, January 20, the Board (Henry Parker, Patrick Graham, James Habersham, and Noble Jones) and the Assembly attended church together, where minister Bartholomew Zouberbuhler at the request of Henry Parker, took cognizance of the occasion and preached a sermon his congregation thought appropriate. After church, the Board, the minister, and some others dined with the members of the Assembly, at the request of its speaker, Francis Harris, "who gave a handsome entertainment."[80]

Jones, Graham, and Habersham must each have observed what was called "some disagreeable Humours" among the Assembly members. As would be expected, the President and Assistants, still bound to the Trustees, often took a different viewpoint from the Assembly, trying to establish itself as a legislative body. The Trustees had never intended to give legislative powers to the Assembly, only advisory powers. The President and Assistants insisted on remaining at all the Assembly sessions to keep control, to the irritation of the Assemblymen. However, the President and Assistants tried through personal hospitality to maintain good relations with Assemblymen.[81]

Some warm debates marked the closing sessions in which the Board endeavored, as it said, to show an open and easy behavior. When the Assembly said that its business was finished and requested to be dissolved, the Board reminded it of other business yet undone. Since the Board could not bring the Assembly to its way of thinking on several points, it finally agreed to dissolution on the morning of February 8, 1751.[82]

Among the recommendations of the Assembly was one relating to regulation of the militia by the appointment of proper officers to command, exercise, and train it. In April the Board decided that men possessed of 300 or more acres of land should, if properly accoutered, constitute the horse troops, and those having less land, the foot. For the territory near Savannah, Noble Jones was made senior captain of the troop of horse, and Newdigate Stephens, William Stephens's son, lieutenant. Francis Harris was made captain of the Foot Company of Savannah; Isaac Young, lieutenant, and Noble Wimberly Jones, ensign.[83]

The Trustees declared themselves impatient to know how the Assembly proceeded. Before their letter could reach Georgia, President Parker and the Assistants wrote several letters concerning the session and sent over eleven representations and an address from the Assembly to the Trustees. The Trustees expressed themselves as well satisfied with the conduct of the Assembly and approved some of the representations. They disapproved the request that the Assembly's by-laws should be in force until disapproved by the Trustees, and also disapproved the suggestion for a court of equity in Savannah to which people might appeal from the verdicts of the town court. They thought "such a court would prove of bad Consequence, as it would tend to the Encouragement of vexatious Suits, and must detain the Inhabitants too long from the Business of their Planting."[84]

Jones and Pickering Robinson were now beginning to make their reports to the Trustees on the state of the colony, reports delayed the previous autumn by Jones's illness. Robinson became so busy with his work at the filature that much of the work on the survey fell upon Jones. By the end of the year the part of the report about Savannah was sent to London. Robinson planned to leave the colony, but Jones told the Trustees that he was willing to proceed as they wished.[85] Jones was a busy man; the minutes and correspondence of the Board show the amount of business coming before the members at their frequent meetings. Jones's son, Noble Wimberly, who had come on the *Ann*, was so gravely ill in the spring of 1751 that it was thought he could not

NOBLE JONES—FROM CARPENTER TO PRINCIPAL INHABITANT   289

live.[86] Jones managed to attend most of the Board meetings, despite the care of his son and the consequent anxiety.

He was present on June 10 to receive his commission as captain to command the militia. The following day a general militia muster for Savannah and its environs was held. The horse and foot, well armed and accoutered, consisting of about 200 men, made a pretty appearance the Board thought. The Cherokees were threatening trouble which the Board thought might come to an open rupture, and the muster was held to assess the strength of that part of the colony.[87] The anticipated Indian trouble, though it caused the Board anxiety, did not become serious.

In June the sound of shots in the night alarmed Savannah people. The deep-lying uneasiness at the thought of Indian troubles must have sprung up instantly. Jones and Habersham went immediately in the direction of the shots, meeting on their way the officer of the guard, his usual six men augmented to twelve. They found one of the neighboring Indians shot and stabbed in the breast. Despite Jones's quickly-applied remedies, the man died before daylight. A wounded Cherokee was found by Francis Harris and his militiamen. Threats were made by some of the Indians to burn the others, but the Board managed in the next day or so to pacify those swearing vengeance. Jones, as a captain of the militia, was out several times with a mounted party on this alarm and on another shortly afterward when Cherokees entered Newington, a settlement about four miles west of Savannah, and committed several depredations.[88]

In 1751 the Trustees made Henry Parker president of Georgia (Stephens had retired because of ill health) and added to the Assistants Francis Harris and Pickering Robinson. The additions to the Board were a welcome relief since affairs rested heavily on too few men. Habersham had commented several times that the Assistants were too few to conduct the public business. "Mr Parker and Mr Jones are both Men of Sense and Probity," he wrote, "and perhaps know more of the Original People and Settlements of the Colony, than any in it, but neither of them like Writing." Habersham's duties as secretary and as an Assistant had become so heavy that his own business suffered, but "I know not what Remedy to propose, as we have so few People capable to transacting publick affairs, and indeed of giving up their Time for the small Salarys the Trustees do, or I fear can allow—" The Trustees said of the salaries of the Assistants which were £20 each, and of others, that they "are not proportioned to the Nature of the Offices, but to the Abilities of the Trust."[89]

The Trustees surrendered their charter on June 24, 1752, and recited the history of their endeavors for the colony. They had spent the sum of £130,000 granted by Parliament for Georgia, and were concerned lest "Your Majesty's wise and just Design of forming a Barrier for the Southern Provinces of North America will be Overturn'd;" and stressed the necessity of a continued civil government in the transition period.[90]

On November 24, 1752, in Savannah, "in the most publick and solemn Manner," Georgia was publicly proclaimed a royal province. Jones, with the President and other Assistants, wrote that the inhabitants of Savannah expressed "the greatest Satisfaction and Joy . . . for His Majesties most gracious and Paternal Regard for them," and for the fact that they were under the immediate care of the Board of Trade in England. By direction of the Board of Trade, the men in office in Georgia were to continue the civil, ecclesiastical, or military government until further notice. President Patrick Graham (Henry Parker had died in the summer) and Assistants James Habersham, Noble Jones, Pickering Robinson, and Francis Harris therefore continued in office.[91]

The first royal governor, Captain John Reynolds, Royal Navy, was appointed the following year but did not arrive at Savannah until the afternoon of October 29, 1754. The demonstrations of hearty welcome caused Reynolds to write to England that "the People appear'd extremely well pleased on that occasion."[92]

Jones attended the last meeting of the President and Assistants on Wednesday, October 30, when the members waited on Governor Reynolds, who produced his commission as governor, took the necessary oaths, and became the first governor of Georgia.[93] This ended the first epoch in Georgia's history, which Noble Jones, alone of these gentlemen in Savannah, had seen inaugurated twenty years before.

Governor Reynolds went immediately into a meeting of his council, of which the ex-President and Assistants all became members. Jones and the other councilors took the oath of office on October 31. At the termination of the meeting the drum beat sounded and the King's commission appointing John Reynolds captain-general, vice-admiral, and governor of His Majesty's province of Georgia was published to the militia and inhabitants of Savannah.[94]

Noble Jones in his twenty years in Georgia had seen many of his fellow passengers on the *Ann* die, leave in disgust, or live in frustration and disappointment in Georgia. He had seen the hard work, the heartbreak, the fear of the Spanish, and all the troubles of that first twenty years. He was made of tougher fiber than most of the *Ann's* passengers, or was luckier—perhaps both. He had lived through it all, with his share of troubles and criticism, and was now one of the more important men in the colony. His was a success story that few of his fellow passengers were left to observe.

In the twenty years he was yet to live in Georgia Jones would be of increasing importance. He acquired more lands and slaves. He remained on the Governor's Council until his death, except when suspended by Governor Reynolds, 1755-58. In 1754, he was appointed by Governor Reynolds to be one of the two judges of the highest court in Georgia. He retained this office until his death except for a suspension by Governor Reynolds. Reynolds was so unpopular in Georgia that suspensions by him certainly did Jones's reputation no harm. He was given frequent commissions for special jobs by the Assembly and became the commanding officer of the first regiment of the militia. In 1760 Jones became treasurer of the colony. He was a vestryman of Christ Church Parish and a local leader in the Savannah area. In the growing troubles between Georgians and the British government, Jones was a loyal backer of Governor Wright in his support of British authority, while his son, Noble Wimberly, was a leader in the opposition party. Noble Jones died in Savannah on November 2, 1775, before he had to make a decision to support Georgia or Britain. Jones had lived in Georgia for forty-three years and was presumably the last surviving head of a family that came on the *Ann*.[95]

Epilogue

T HIS is the picture, so far as the records of the time indicate, of the colonists who came to Georgia on the *Ann*, and of many others with whom they came in contact during Georgia's first twenty years. There is no intention to prove that the Trustees were wise or foolish, successful or otherwise in their announced aims and their regulations for Georgia. Rather, this account has sought merely to show through a picture of life in the infant colony some results of the aims and regulations of the Trustees.

The first and most obvious fact about life in Georgia in its first twenty years is that it was very hard. It could not have been otherwise. Frontier conditions are always hard, raw, and close to nature. Life had been hard in all the colonies settled before Georgia. The presence of the Spanish in Florida made for more strain than if a friendly people had been located there. The fact that so many of the colonists had had discouraging business experiences before they came to Georgia undoubtedly made life seem harder to them and achievement more difficult than it might have to people made hopeful by former success. People who had been artisans and tradesmen found the exertion of taming a wild unsettled country—clearing and planting land, building houses— much harder physically and psychologically than the activities of their former life.

These facts, together with the change in climate, undoubtedly help to explain why so many of the colonists died or left in the first few years. The change was literally too great. Some people realized this and left Georgia. Other colonists stayed in Georgia and killed themselves with hard work for which they got little in return. The case of the settlers on Cockspur Island is a case in point. Insistence in the early years that a colonist improve his original grant, regardless of its inferiority for cultivation, sent several colonists to early graves or out of Georgia as disillusioned people. Yet those who left were all set down in the list in London as "quitted" or "gone to Carolina," and made to seem unappreciative of the bounty of the Trustees. Since the Trustees were kind and humanitarian gentlemen they must not have realized the magnitude of the settlers' problems. Perhaps it was asking too much of eighteenth-century London gentlemen to see the real problems of the poor American frontiersmen. Certainly the Trustees did not really understand the difficulties involved, despite letters and visits of colonists to them.

Frontiers are always the most fluid area of society, where many experiments are tried, and discarded when they are found not to be satisfactory. The frontiersman is a kind of pragmatist with little patience with theoretical restraints which do not work in his particular case. From the days of Jamestown, English colonists in North America had continually illustrated this fact. Yet the Trustees seem not to have realized this. Though in the end they did change or abolish many of their early regulations, much of the change came too late to help the earliest colonists. Most of the real changes came after Georgia had already succeeded in establishing itself upon a permanent basis. The Trustees were so concerned with their philanthropic and economic experiment that they never seemed to take into account adequately the human element in Georgia.

Certainly the Trustees had noble motives; they gave long hours and much money to the experiment. But they did not realize that independence was necessary for the colonists if they were to succeed, that changes would gradually become essential—and inevitable—, and that it was important that they should know how the colonists felt on things vital to Georgians. Though the Trustees continually complained that they did not know enough of what happened in Georgia, it is possible to argue that they did not seem to want to know of happenings or ideas there that did not fit their own ideas of what should happen. William Stephens and others learned that opinions contrary to the Trustees' beliefs did not set well in London. The reaction to remonstrances and representations sent over by the colonists illustrates that the Trustees did not care for the opinions of the colonists as to what was best for Georgia. Had complaints been listened to sympathetically things might have been vastly different in early Georgia. Probably the colonists would have had a different feeling towards the Trustees from what most of them had by 1752.

Something else that probably the Trustees did not realize or would not admit was that in reality the colonists who stuck it out in Georgia were stronger, in body and character and spirit, than the Trustees who sent them. These stout people fought at once an uncooperative environment, the Spanish, and the Trustees' regulations, and won in the end. Most of the original prohibitions of the Trustees were gradually modified until they were gone at the end of the period. The Spanish were frightened into returning to St. Augustine and leaving Georgians to themselves after 1743. And gradually, as in the other colonies settled before Georgia, those who remained adjusted to the environment. They bent the Trustees' theory to the practical needs of Georgia. The tough survived; the weak died or left. William Stephens often speaks of youths or young men reared in Georgia as inured to hard labor. The hard work of the early colonists was necessary to bring an easier and better life later. Few of the early settlers lived to enjoy a better life. Most of them met an early death the reward of most real pioneers.

APPENDIX

LIST OF PASSENGERS ON THE *ANN*

Name	Age	Occupation and Family Connection	Savannah Lot No.	Official Position in Georgia	Disposition by 1754
Amatis, Paul		Italian silk man		Gardener and silk care	Dead, Dec., 1736
Bowling, Timothy	38	Potash maker	35		Dead, Nov. 5, 1733
Calvert, Mary	42	Wife of William			Dead, July 4, 1733
Calvert, William	44	Trader in goods	77		No record after 1738
Cameron, John (Richard)	35	Servant to Francis Scott			To S.C.
Cannon, Clementine	3	Daughter to Richard			Supposedly murdered (?)
Cannon, James	7 mo.	Son to Richard			Dead, on *Ann*, Nov. 26, 1732
Cannon, Marmaduke	9	Son to Richard			No record after 1741
Cannon, Mary	33	Wife to Richard			Dead, July 22, 1733
Cannon, Richard	36	Calendar & carpenter	5		Dead, 1735
Carwell, James	35	Peruke maker	4	Keeper of workhouse	No record after 1741
Carwell, Margaret	32	Wife to James			Dead, Sept. 7, 1733
Causton, Thomas	40	Calico printer	24	Bailiff, public storekeeper	Dead, 1746
Christie, Thomas	32	Merchant	19	Bailiff, recorder	In S.C. (?)
Clark, Charles	11	Son to Robert			Dead, no date
Clark, James	9 mo.	Son to Robert			Dead on *Ann*, Dec. 22, 1732
Clark, John	4	Son to Robert			No record after 1740
Clark, Judith	24	Wife to Robert			Perhaps in Georgia
Clark, Peter	3	Son to Robert			No record after 1740
Clark, Robert	37	Tailor	37		Dead, April 18, 1734
Close, Ann	2	Daughter to Henry			Dead, April 2, 1734
Close, Hanna	32	Wife to Henry			To Scotland, May, 1740

Name	Age	Occupation and Family Connection	Savannah Lot No.	Official Position in Georgia	Disposition by 1754
Close, Henry	42	Clothworker	40		Dead, Dec. 14, 1733
Coles, Anna	32	Wife to Joseph			Apparently still in Ga.
Coles, Anna	13	Daughter to Joseph			" " " "
Coles, Joseph	28	Miller and baker	27		Dead, Mar. 4, 1734/5
Cooper, Joseph	37	Writer	20		Dead, March 29, 1735
Cormock, Mary	11	Servant to Noble Jones			No record
Cox, Eunice	3	Daughter to William			To England, 1734
Cox, Frances	35	Wife to William			To England, 1734
Cox, William	41	Surgeon	6		Dead, April 6, 1733
Cox, William	12	Son to William			To England, 1734
Ellis, Thomas	17	Servant to Noble Jones	55		No record after 1738
Fitzwalter, Joseph	31	Gardener	8	Constable, public gardener	Dead, Oct. 28, 1742
Fox, Walter	35	Turner	2	Port gunner, tything man	Dead, Dec. 30, 1741
Goddard, Elizabeth	42	Wife to James			Dead, July 28, 1733
Goddard, Elizabeth	5	Daughter to James			No record after 1735
Goddard, James	35	Carpenter and joiner	1		Dead, July, 1733
Goddard, John	9	Son to James			No record after 1743
Gordon, Katherine	28	Wife to Peter			To England
Gordon, Peter	34	Upholsterer	23	Bailiff	To England, April, 1738
Gready, John	22	Farmer	3		Apparently in S. C.
Greenfield, Charles	16	Nephew to Wm. Calvert			No record after 1738
Greenfield, Sarah	16	Niece to Wm. Calvert			Apparently to S. C.
Greenfield, William	19	Nephew to Wm. Calvert			No record after 1738
Hicks, Mary		Servant to Richard Cannon			No record after 1733
Hodges, Elizabeth	16	Daughter to Richard			Dead, Aug. 4, 1735
Hodges, Mary	42	Wife to Richard	17		Apparently in Georgia
Hodges, Mary	18	Daughter to Richard			Dead, March 24, 1738
Hodges, Richard	50	Basketmaker	17	Bailiff	Dead, July 20, 1733
Hodges, Sarah	5	Daughter to Richard			Apparently in Georgia
Hughes, Elizabeth	22	Wife to Joseph			Dead, June 5, 1740
Hughes, Joseph	28	Cider trade, understands writing and accounts	16	Storekeeper to Trust	Dead, Sept. 30, 1733

Name	Age	Occupation and Family Connection	Savannah Lot No.	Official Position in Georgia	Disposition by 1754
Johnson, Robert	17	Servant to Thos. Christie			Dead, July 23, 1734
Jones, Mary	3	Daughter to Noble			In Georgia
Jones, Noble	32	Carpenter	41	Surveyor, constable, guard boat commander, register, capt. of militia	In Georgia
Jones, Noble W.	10	Son to Noble	46		In Georgia
Jones, Sarah	32	Wife to Noble			Probably dead, 1752
Little, Elizabeth	31	Wife to William			Dead, Sept. 26, 1733
Little, Mary	5	Daughter to William			Dead, July 12, 1733
Little, William	31	Understands flax and hemp	37		Dead, July 12, 1733
Little, William	2	Son to William			In Georgia
Lloyd, Henry	21	Servant to William Cox	171		No record after 1739
Mackay, John	25	Servant to Joseph Stanley			Dead, July 25, 1733
Milledge, Elizabeth	40	Wife to Thomas			Dead, June 2, 1734
Milledge, Frances	5	Daughter to Thomas			Probably in Georgia
Milledge, James	2	Son to Thomas			Dead, Nov. 4, 1734
Milledge, John	11	Son to Thomas	91	Tythingman, commander at Fort Argyle	Still in Georgia
Milledge, Richard	8	Son to Thomas			No record after 1740
Milledge, Sarah	9	Daughter to Thomas			In Georgia
Milledge, Thomas	42	Carpenter and joiner	36		Dead, July 29, 1733
Mugridge, Francis	39	Sawyer	12		Dead, July 1, 1735
Muir, Ellen	38	Wife to James			Dead, July 10, 1733
Muir, James	38	Peruke maker	18		To S.C., 1739, died there
Muir, John	2	Son to James			To S.C.
Overend, Joshua	40	Mercer	11		Dead, June, 1733
Parker, Jane	36	Wife to Samuel	38		Dead, 1742 (?)
Parker, Samuel	33	Heelmaker, understands carpentering	38	Constable	Dead, July 20, 1733
Parker, Samuel, Jr.	16	Son to Samuel	93	Blacksmith	Dead, 1741
Parker, Thomas	9	Son to Samuel			In Georgia
Penrose, Elizabeth	46	Wife to John			Apparently in Georgia
Penrose, John	35	Husbandman	15	Pilot at Tybee	In Georgia
Pratt, Thomas	21		33		To England, April, 1735
Sammes, John	42	Cordwainer	9		Dead, Aug. 21, 1733

Name	Age	Occupation and Family Connection	Savannah Lot No.	Official Position in Georgia	Disposition by 1754
Satchfield, Elizabeth	24	Servant to James Muir			No record
Scott, Francis	40	Reduced military officer			Dead, Jan. 2, 1734
Stanley, Elizabeth	35	Wife to Joseph		Public midwife	To England, Oct., 1736
Stanley, Joseph	45	Stockingmaker, can draw and reel silk		Sexton	Apparently still in Georgia
Symes, Ann	21	Daughter to George			Dead, 1739
Symes, George	55	Apothecary	7	Magistrate (?)	Dead, by 1740
Symes, Sarah	52	Wife to George			Dead, July 21, 1733
Thibaut, Daniel	50	Understands vines	39		Dead, Oct. 24, 1733
Thibaut, Diana	7	Daughter to Daniel			Dead, no date
Thibaut, James	12	Son to Daniel			In Georgia
Thibaut, Mary	40	Wife to Daniel	39		Apparently in Georgia
Wallis, Elizabeth	19	Servant to Wm. Calvert			Dead, no date
Warren, Elizabeth	27	Wife to John			Dead, March 30, 1737, in England
Warren, Elizabeth	3	Daughter to John			No record after 1746
Warren, Georgius Marinus	3 wks.	Son to John			No record. Apparently dead.
Warren, John	34	Flax and hemp dresser	10		Dead, Aug. 11, 1733
Warren, John	2	Son to John			Dead, June 12, 1733
Warren, Richard	4	Son to John			In Georgia
Warren, William	6	Son to John			Dead, Sept. 5, 1733
Waterland, William	44	Mercer	34	Bailiff	To S.C., 1734
Wellen, Elias Ann	18	Servant to Joseph Coles			To England
West, Elizabeth	33	Wife to John			Dead, July 1, 1733
West, John	33	Smith	31	Bailiff	Dead, 1739
West, Richard	5	Son to John			Dead, July 31, 1733
Wilson, James	21	Sawyer	32		No record after 1740
Wright, Elizabeth	11	Daughter to John			Dead, May 8, 1743
Wright, John	33	Vintner	30		Dead, Dec., 1737
Wright, John Norton	13	Son to John		Tythingman, jailor, messenger to President and Assistants	No record after 1742
Wright, Penelope	33	Wife to John		Wharfinger	In Georgia
Young, Thomas	45	Wheelwright	26		Dead, by 1750

RECAPITULATION

All passengers

Dead*	60
No record	19
To S.C.	7
To Britain	10
Alive in Ga.	11
Probably in Ga.	9
Total	114

*1 to S.C. and died there
 1 to Britain and died there
 1 no record, apparently dead

Heads of Families

Dead*	27
No record	3
To S.C.	3
In Georgia	2
Probably in Ga.	2
To Britain	2
Total	39

Date of Deaths

1732	2
1733	26
1734	6
1735	5
1736	1
1737	2
1738	1
1739	3
1740	2
No date	4

Wives of Heads of Families

Dead*	13
To Britain	5
In Georgia	1
Probably in Ga.	5
No wife came with	15
Total	39

*1 dead in England

Notes

CHAPTER I

1. *Daily Advertiser* (London), October 16, 1732.

2. Benjamin Martyn, *An Account Shewing the Progress of the Colony of Georgia in America from its First Establishment* (London, 1741), reprinted in Allen D. Candler and Lucian Lamar Knight, eds., *The Colonial Records of the State of Georgia* (26 Vols., Atlanta, 1904-1916. Vols. 20, 27-39, in manuscript at Georgia Department of Archives and History, Atlanta), III, 378-79 (Hereafter cited as *CRG* or MS. CRG); I, 83; II, 7; *The South Carolina Gazette* (Charles Town), Jan. 13, 1732/3; Historical Manuscripts Commission, *Diary of John Percival, First Earl of Egmont* (3 vols., London, 1920-1923), I, 295. (Hereafter cited as *Egmont Diary*.)

3. Martyn in *CRG*, III, 378; Oglethorpe to Dean George Berkeley, May, 1732, in Benjamin Rand, *Berkeley and Percival* (Cambridge, 1914), 277-79. For inception of the colony see *Egmont Diary*, I *passim*; W. L. Grant and James Munro, eds., *Acts of the Privy Council of England, Colonial Series* (6 vols., London, 1908-1912), III, 299-305; *Some Account of the Designs of the Trustees for Establishing the Colony of Georgia in America* [London, 1732?]; *CRG*, I, 65-80; II, 3-10.

4. *Gentleman's Magazine* (London), Oct., 1732, p. 1029.

5. E. Merton Coulter and Albert B. Saye, eds., *A List of the Early Settlers of Georgia* (Athens, 1949), *passim* (Hereafter cited as *LES*.); *CRG*, II, 7; *Daily Advertiser*, Nov. 7, 1732.

6. *Daily Advertiser*, Nov. 13, 1732; *Egmont Diary*, I, 295; *CRG*, I, 84-85; III, 379; MS. CRG, XXXII, 49-50; *LES*, 23.

7. *CRG*, I, 85-86; MS. CRG, XXXII, 44; Account of Thomas Christie in Robert G. McPherson, "The Voyage of the *Anne*—A Daily Record," in *Georgia Historical Quarterly*, XLIV (June, 1960), 222. (Hereafter cited as *GHQ*.)

8. Egmont Papers, Phillipps Collection, University of Georgia Library, No. 14207, pp. 61-63.

9. *CRG*, I, 85-86; III, 379; *GHQ*, XLIV, 222.

10. *Egmont Diary*, I, 295-96; *CRG*, I, 80; II, 8; Benjamin Martyn to Governor Robert Johnson, Oct. 18, 1732, MS. CRG, XXIX, 1-2; Horatio Walpole to Johnson, Nov. 5, 1732, Egmont Papers, 14207, pp. 53-54; Duke of Newcastle to colonial governors, Nov. 8, 1732, *ibid.*, 55; Lords of Admiralty to naval vessels on Virginia and Carolina coast, Nov. 10, 1732, *ibid.*, 59.

11. *Egmont Diary*, I, 295-96.
12. *Ibid.*, 288.
13. Oglethorpe to Trustees, Nov. 18, 1732, Egmont Papers, 14200, p. 5; *Daily Advertiser,* Nov. 21, 1732; *GHQ,* XLIV, 223.
14. Oglethorpe to Trustees, Nov. 18, 1732, Egmont Papers, 14200, p. 5; Wm. Brownjohn and Thos. Gapen to Trustees, June 18, 1733, *ibid.,* 89; Harman Verelst to Thomas Causton, Aug. 7, 1735, and June 17, 1736, MS. CRG, XXIX, 150, 279-80; *GHQ,* XLIV, 223, 225-26.
15. *CRG,* I, 83-86; III, 10-11, 21-22, *passim*; *Egmont Diary,* I, 295, *passim,* for gifts to colonists.
16. Charter Party, Nov. 6, 1732, MS. CRG, XXXII, 43-49; *CRG,* II, 14.
17. *Ibid.; CRG,* III, 16.
18. MS. CRG, XXXII, 45; *CRG,* II, 127-28.
19. Harman Verelst to William Jeffrys, May 13, 1735, MS. CRG, XXIX, 94-95; XXXII, 43-49; *CRG,* III, 409; *GHQ,* 225-29.
20. Oglethorpe to Trustees, Jan. 13, 1732/3, Egmont Papers, 14200, p. 13; Thomas Causton to his wife, March 12, 1732/3, *ibid.,* 56; *GHQ,* 223-29.
21. *South-Carolina Gazette,* March 24, 1732/3; *CRG,* III, 380, 405; I, 102; *Egmont Diary,* I, 399; Oglethorpe to Trustees, Jan. 13, 1732/3, Egmont Papers, 14200, p. 13; *GHQ,* 223-29.

22. Oglethorpe to Trustees, Jan. 13, 1732/3, Egmont Papers, 14200, p. 13; Governor Robert Johnson to Oglethorpe, Sept. 28, 1732, *ibid.,* 2; Benjamin Martyn to Robert Johnson, Jan. 24, 1732/3, MS. CRG, XXIX, 3-4; *S. C. Gazette,* Jan. 20, 1732/3; March 31, 1733.
23. Oglethorpe to Trustees, Jan. 13, 1732/3, Egmont Papers, 14200, p. 13; Benjamin Martyn to Gov. Johnson, Sept. 18, 1732, MS. CRG, XXIX, 1; *S. C. Gazette,* March 31, 1733.
24. Oglethorpe to Trustees, Feb. 10, 1732/3, *CRG,* III, 380; William Kilbury to Francis Harbin, Feb. 6, 1732/3, Egmont Papers, 14200, p. 29; *S. C. Gazette,* March 31, 1733.
25. Thomas Causton to his wife, March 12, 1732/3, Egmont Papers, 14200, p. 53.
26. Benjamin Martyn to Robert Johnson, Jan. 1, 1732/3, MS. CRG, XXIX, 4.
27. Governor Johnson to Oglethorpe, Jan. 26, 1732/3, Egmont Papers, 14200, pp. 21, 25-26; Johnson to Martyn, Feb. 12, 1732/3, *ibid.,* 37-39; *CRG,* III, 380-81.
28. *S. C. Gazette,* March 31, 1733.
29. *Ibid.;* Thomas Causton to his wife, March 12, 1732/3, Egmont Papers, 14200, p. 53; Oglethorpe to Trustees, Feb. 10, 1732/3, *CRG,* III, 380; *ibid.,* 90.

CHAPTER II

1. Thomas Causton to his wife, March 12, 1732/3, Egmont Papers, 14200, p. 53; Oglethorpe to Trustees, Feb. 20, 1732/3, *CRG,* III, 381; Francis Moore, *A Voyage to Georgia Begun in the Year 1735* (London, 1744), 39.
2. *S. C. Gazette,* March 31, 1733.
3. Oglethorpe to Trustees, Feb. 10, 1732/3, *CRG,* III, 380.
4. *Ibid.;* Benjamin Martyn to Governor Robert Johnson, Jan. 24, 1732/3, MS. CRG, XXIX, 3.
5. *S. C. Gazette,* March 31, 1733; Oglethorpe to Trustees, Feb. 10, 1732/3, *CRG,* III, 380.

6. Benjamin Martyn to Robert Johnson, Oct. 18, 1732, MS. CRG, XXIX, 1-2.
7. *S. C. Gazette,* March 31 1733; Oglethorpe to Trustees, Feb. 10, 1732/3, *CRG,* III, 380; Thomas Causton to his wife, March 12, 1732/3, Egmont Papers, 14200, p. 55.
8. Patrick Tailfer and others, *A True and Historical Narrative of the Colony of Georgia* (Charles-Town, 1741), 104.
9. *S. C. Gazette,* March 31, 1733; Francis Moore, *A Voyage to Georgia,* 28-29; Thomas Causton to his wife, March 12, 1732/3, Egmont Papers,

14200, p. 55; Oglethorpe, "A State of the Colony of Georgia," *ibid.*, 516-17; *GHQ*, XLIV, 224.

10. *S. C. Gazette*, March 31, Aug. 25, 1733; Oglethorpe to Trustees, Aug. 12, 1733, Egmont Papers, 14200, p. 106; Oglethorpe to Trustees, about Dec., 1733, *ibid.*, 125; *CRG*, III, 65-69, 90-91; *LES*, 36, No. 1018; 18, No. 514; 26, No. 735.

11. Thomas Causton to his wife, March 12, 1732/3, Egmont Papers, 14200, p. 55; *S. C. Gazette*, March 31, 1733.

12. Oglethorpe to Trustees, March 12, 1732/3, Egmont Papers, 14200, p. 46.

13. Account of Samuel Eveleigh, *S. C. Gazette*, March 24, 1732/3, reprinted in *CRG*, III, 406.

14. *S. C. Gazette*, April 21, 1733; Oglethorpe to Trustees, about Dec., 1733, Egmont Papers, 14200, pp. 125-26; Samuel Eveleigh to Trustees, May 18, 1733, *ibid.*, 69.

15. Thomas Causton to his wife, March 12, 1732/3, Egmont Papers, 14200, p. 55; Oglethorpe to Trustees, about Dec., 1733, *ibid.*, 128; Oglethorpe to Trustees, June 9, 1733, *ibid.*, 81.

16. Francis Moore, *A Voyage to Georgia*, 23.

17. Oglethorpe to Trustees, June 9, 1733, Egmont Papers, 14200, p. 81.

18. *Ibid.*; Oglethorpe to Trustees, March 12, 1732/3, *ibid.*, 45; Samuel Eveleigh to Trustees, April 6, 1733, *ibid.*, 61.

19. Thomas Causton to his wife, March 12, 1732/3, Egmont Papers, 14200, p. 55; Samuel Eveleigh to Trustees, April 6, 1733, *ibid.*, 61; Samuel Eveleigh in *S. C. Gazette*, March 24, 1732/3, reprinted in *CRG*, III, 405-07.

20. *Ibid.*

21. Oglethorpe to Trustees, March 12, May 14, Sept. 17, about Dec., 1732/3, Egmont Papers, 14200, pp. 45, 65, 115, 126, 129, 130.

22. Benjamin Martyn to Oglethorpe, March 31, May 11, 1733; March 25, 1734, MS. CRG, XXIX, 13, 25-26, 47; Oglethorpe to Trustees, about Dec., 1733, Egmont Papers, 14200, p. 129; *Egmont Diary*, I, 387.

23. Harman Verelst to Thomas Causton, Dec. 12, 1734, MS. CRG, XXIX, 75-76.

24. *Egmont Diary*, II, 41-43.

25. Thomas Causton to his wife, March 12, 1732/3, Egmont Papers, 14200, p. 56.

26. Benjamin Martyn to Robert Johnson, Oct. 18, 1732, MS. CRG, XXIX, 2; Robert Johnson to Benjamin Martyn, Feb. 12, 1732/3, Egmont Papers, 14200, pp. 37-39.

27. *S. C. Gazette*, April 7, 1733; Oglethorpe to Trustees, May 14, 1733, Egmont Papers, 14200, p. 66.

28. F. W. Hodge, ed., *Handbook of American Indians North of Mexico* (2 vols., Washington, 1907-1910), II, 776, 986; J. R. Swanton, *Early History of the Creek Indians and Their Neighbors* (Smithsonian Institution, Bureau of American Ethnology, Bulletin 73, Washington, 1922), 108-09; Thomas Causton to his wife, March 12, 1732/3, Egmont Papers, 14200, pp. 53-54.

29. *Ibid.*

30. Oglethorpe to Trustees, June 9, 1733, *ibid.*, 86.

31. *Gentleman's Magazine*, April 1, 1733, p. 213; June, 1733, p. 329; *CRG*, III, 381-82; Oglethorpe to Trustees, March 12, May 14, June 9, about Dec., 1732/3, Egmont Papers, 14200, pp. 45-46, 65, 81-82, 125; Samuel Eveleigh to Trustees, April 6, 1733, *ibid.*, 61.

32. *S. C. Gazette*, May 12, 1733; Oglethorpe to Trustees, May 14, 1733, Egmont Papers, 14200, p. 65.

33. "State of the Colony of Georgia," Egmont Papers, 14200, p. 515; Oglethorpe to Trustees, June 9, about Dec., 1733, *ibid.*, 82, 129; *S. C. Gazette*, June 2, 1733; Feb. 23, 1733/4; *CRG*, II, 44; MS. CRG, XXXII, 178-84, 296-99; Force Transcripts, Georgia Indian Records, 1753-1825, Library of Congress (for copy of treaty); *Egmont Diary*, I, 402.

34. *S. C. Gazette*, June 2, 1733; *CRG*, III, 91; MS. CRG, XXXII, 175-78, 184-95.

35. Oglethorpe to Trustees, Aug. 12, 1733, Egmont Papers, 14200, pp. 105-08.
36. *CRG*, I, 83; II, 11; III, 379; MS. CRG, XXXII, 22-38; *Egmont Diary*, I, 295; *S. C. Gazette*, Aug. 25, 1733; Oglethorpe to Trustees, Aug. 12, 1733, Egmont Papers, 14200, p. 108.
37. *Egmont Diary*, I, 295; *CRG*, II, 11.
38. *S. C. Gazette*, Aug. 25, 1733; *Gentleman's Magazine*, Nov., 1733, p. 609; Oglethorpe to Trustees, Aug. 12, 1733, Egmont Papers, 14200, p. 108; proceedings of the court at Savannah, *ibid.*, 101-03.
39. Thomas Causton to his wife, March 12, 1732/3, Egmont Papers, 14200, p. 54.
40. Oglethorpe to Trustees, May 14, 1733, *ibid.*, 65; *CRG*, II, 465-66; Benjamin Martyn to William Stephens, July 17, 1745, MS. CRG, XXXI, 16; *LES*, 11, No. 288-91, *ibid.*, 69, No. 263.
41. *Egmont Diary*, I, 364, 372, 388, 389; *S. C. Gazette*, May 5, 1733; *Daily Advertiser*, June 15, 1733; *LES*, 23, No. 654.
42. *LES* shows birth date of another child, Elias Clark, earlier on March 13, 1733, but as the parents did not arrive until August, 1733, an error seems evident. *LES*, 10, No. 241-43; 68, No. 221, 233; *CRG*, III, 91.
43. *LES*, 18, No. 514, 515-17; 9, No. 220; *S. C. Gazette*, Aug. 25, 1733; Oglethorpe to Trustees, Aug. 12, 1733, Egmont Papers, 14200, p. 108.
44. *LES*, 30, No. 871-74; 57, No. 1610-12.

45. *Ibid.*, 23, No. 670; 26, No. 730; 33, No. 940; 36, No. 1018; 39, No. 1120; 45, No. 1299; 55-56, No. 1585-1589; *Egmont Diary*, II, 69.
46. *LES*, 5, No. 117; 9, No. 220; 10, No. 260; 52, No. 1504; 67, No. 195; 68, No. 233.
47. *Egmont Diary*, II, 70, 72; Patrick Mackay to Oglethorpe, Nov. 20, 1734; MS. CRG, XX, 59.
48. Oglethorpe to Trustees, May 14, 1733, Egmont Papers, 14200, p. 66.
49. *S. C. Gazette*, June 30, 1733; Oglethorpe to Trustees, Aug. 12, about Dec., 1733, Egmont Papers, 14200, pp. 105, 126.
50. Oglethorpe to Trustees, Aug. 12, 1733, Egmont Papers, 14200, p. 105.
51. Oglethorpe to Trustees, Nov. 15, 1733, *ibid.*, 121.
52. *Egmont Diary*, I, 451.
53. Oglethorpe to Trustees, Aug. 12, 1733, Egmont Papers, 14200, p. 106.
54. *S. C. Gazette*, Aug. 25, 1733.
55. *Egmont Diary*, I, 451.
56. Oglethorpe to Trustees, Aug. 12, 1733, Egmont Papers, 14200, p. 106.
57. *Ibid.*, 106-07.
58. *Ibid.*; Oglethorpe to Trustees, about Dec., 1733, *ibid.*, 126; Feb. 12, 1742, *CRG*, XXIII, 486-87.
59. Oglethorpe to Trustees, Sept. 17, about Dec., 1733, Egmont Papers, 14200, pp. 114, 128; *Egmont Diary*, II, 36-37, 70.
60. Tailfer and others, *True and Historical Narrative*, 105-06.
61. Isaac Chardon to Harman Verelst, Jan. 17, 1733/4, Egmont Papers, 14200, p. 137.

CHAPTER III

1. *CRG*, I, 90; MS. CRG, XXXII, 217; *S. C. Gazette*, Feb. 24, April 7, 1732/3; *Daily Advertiser*, June 26, 1733; Thomas Causton to his wife, March 12, 1732/3, Egmont Papers, 14200, p. 55.
2. Passenger list, Egmont Papers, 14207, p. 63; *CRG*, I, 90; *LES*, 54, No. 1533-34. Date of arrival of *Volant* passengers is given in *LES* erroneously as of those on the *Ann.*
3. *LES*, 54, No. 1533-34; 20, No. 546; 17, No. 472; 26, No. 732; Oglethorpe

to Trustees, Aug. 12, 1733, Egmont Papers, 14200, p. 105; *S. C. Gazette*, June 30, 1733.
4. *Egmont Diary*, I, 306-477 *passim*.
5. *S. C. Gazette*, June 2, 1733; *CRG*, I, 97-98; II, 8, 17; III, 22; MS. CRG, XXIX, 7, 8; XXXII, 5-21; *Egmont Diary*, I, 306, 310; *LES*, 97, No. 1100.
6. *S. C. Gazette*, May 12, June 2, 1733; Oglethorpe to Trustees, May 14, and about Dec., 1733, Egmont Papers, 14200, pp. 65, 130; *Gentleman's Magazine*, July 1733, p. 384.

7. *LES*, 99, No. 1183-85; 69, No. 260.
8. *LES*, 64, No. 115-17; 67, No. 191, 199; 72, No. 358; 75, No. 447; 78, No. 533, 537, 540; 79, No. 544; 81, No. 617-20; 88, No. 798, 801; 91, No. 942; 92, No. 970; 96, No. 1094; 98, No. 1156; 99, No. 1172; 101, No. 1247; *CRG*, II, 14-15; 24, 35, 36, 41; MS. CRG, XXIX, 5, 14; XXXII, 142-44.
9. *CRG*, II, 14-15; MS. CRG, XXXII, 70-83.
10. *CRG*, II, 25, 35; *Egmont Diary*, I, 305, 379.
11. *CRG*, I, 110; II, 25; Martyn to Oglethorpe, April 11, 1733, MS. CRG, XXIX, 21; Oglethorpe to Trustees, Aug. 12, 1733, Egmont Papers, 14200, p. 107; *LES*, 78, No. 534; *S. C. Gazette*, June 16, Aug. 11, 1733; *Daily Advertiser*, April 20, 21, 1733.
12. *CRG*, I, 87, 92, 110; II, 19, 25; MS. CRG, XXXII, 217; *LES*, 35, No. 1010; 42, No. 1193; *Egmont Diary*, I, 297, 302-03, 336.
13. *CRG*, I, 93; II, 25; *Egmont Diary*, I, 305, 309, 345; Martyn to Oglethorpe, Jan. 24, April 4, 1732/3, MS. CRG, XXIX, 6, 17; Oglethorpe to Trustees, Aug. 12, 1733, Egmont Papers, 14200, p. 107.
14. *CRG*, I, 102-03, 110, 164; II, 18, 63-64; Martyn to Oglethorpe, Feb. 21, 1732/3, MS. CRG, XXIX, 10; *ibid.*, XXXII, 97-100; *LES*, 92, No. 962; *Egmont Diary*, I, 313, 336; II, 54.
15. *LES*, 1, No. 18; 16, No. 437-41; 17, No. 473; 23, No. 660; 24, No. 678; 67, No. 190; 73, No. 385-87; *CRG*, I, 105-06; II, 22, 24; MS. CRG, XXXII, 104, 215; Martyn to Oglethorpe, March 31, 1733, *ibid.*, XXIX, 13; *S. C. Gazette*, Aug. 4, 1733.
16. *CRG*, III, 381; MS. CRG, XXXII, 217; *LES*, I, No. 21; 8, No. 202-06.
17. *CRG*, I, 120, 122-23, 127; II, 35; *Egmont Diary*, I, 379; Martyn to Oglethorpe, June 15, 1733, MS. CRG, XXIX, 29; XXXII, 217; *Daily Advertiser*, June 16, 1733.
18. *Egmont Diary*, I, 383; Martyn to Oglethorpe, June 13, 1733, MS. CRG, XXIX, 28.
19. *CRG*, I, 126; II, 38; III, 59; Martyn to Oglethorpe, June 15, 1733, MS. CRG, XXIX, 30; *Egmont Diary*, I, 383-84.
20. *CRG*, III, 58, 61.
21. *CRG*, I, 126; II, 38; Martyn to Oglethorpe, June 15, 1733, MS. CRG, XXIX, 30; XXXII, 128-30.
22. *Daily Advertiser*, June 16, 1733; Wm. Brownjohn and Thos. Gapen to Trustees, June 18, 1733, Egmont Papers, 14200, pp. 89-90; *Egmont Diary*, I, 387.
23. *Daily Advertiser*, June 21-25, 1733; *LES*, 21, No. 590; 41, No. 1179; Oglethorpe to Trustees, Sept. 17, 1733, Egmont Papers, 14200, p. 113.
24. *CRG*, IV, 78, 423; *LES*, 2, No. 44; 4, No. 105; 13, No. 357-61; 39, No. 1106; Oglethorpe to Trustees, Sept. 17, 1733, Egmont Papers, 14200, p. 115; Causton Journal, *ibid.*, 14203, pp. 31, 40.
25. *LES*, 7, No. 185; 10 No. 241; 17, No. 479; 19, No. 526-30.
26. *Ibid.*, 6, No. 149-51; 57, No. 1618; Verelst to Oglethorpe, n. d. (probably soon after Nov. 17, 1733), MS. CRG, XXIX, 188; *CRG*, IV, 54, 63-64, 84-85, 103-05, 107-08, 184.
27. *LES*, 3, No. 61; 9, No. 236; 12, No. 313; 13, No. 335, 337; 14, No. 386; 25, No. 728; 30, No. 875; 39, No. 1108; 41, No. 1174; 48, No. 1381; 55, No. 1579; 57, No. 1632.
28. *Ibid.*, 5, No. 115; 12, No. 310; 36, No. 1031; 39, No. 1125.
29. *Ibid.*, 5, No. 115; Thomas Christie to Oglethorpe, Dec. 14, 1734, MS. CRG, XX, 88-89.
30. *LES*, 40, No. 1140-42; 92, No. 964.
31. *Daily Advertiser*, June 21-22, Nov. 22, 1733; *CRG*, I, 111; III, 22-23; Martyn to Oglethorpe, May 11, 1733, MS. CRG, XXIX, 26.
32. Martyn to Oglethorpe, May 11, 1733, MS. CRG, XXIX, 26; Causton to his wife, March 12, 1732/3, Egmont Papers, 14200, pp. 55-56; *LES*, 5, No. 118-19; 9, No. 222-23; 24, No. 685.
33. *CRG*, II, 33; MS. CRG, XXXII, 127-38; Martyn to Oglethorpe, May 11, 1733, *ibid.*, XXIX, 25; *LES*,

72, No. 349; 80, No. 573-78; 101, No.
1255; *Egmont Diary*, I, 377.
34. *Daily Advertiser*, Nov. 22, 1733.
35. *Egmont Diary*, I, 372-74, 376.
36. *CRG*, I, 134-35; II, 43; III, 383;
Martyn to Oglethorpe, May 11, June
13, and Sept. 12, 1733, MS. CRG,
XXIX, 24, 28, 31-33; *S. C. Gazette*,
Aug. 25, 1733; *Egmont Diary*, I,
398.
37. *CRG*, I, 127-39, 141; *Egmont Diary*,
I, 384, 389, 391.

38. *Daily Advertiser*, July 11, Aug. 17,
Nov. 10, 1733.
39. *CRG*, III, 383.
40. *CRG*, I, 143; III, 58, 59; Martyn to
Oglethorpe, Sept. 12, 26, 1733, MS.
CRG, XXIX, 31-32, 34; XXXII, 217.
41. *Daily Advertiser*, Sept. 24, 27, 29,
Oct. 1, 3, 5, 6, 8, 1733; Causton to
Trustees, Jan. 1733/4, Egmont Papers, 14200, p. 141; Hector Beaufain
to Mr. Simond, Jan. 23, 1733/4,
ibid., 149.

CHAPTER IV

1. Francis Moore, *Voyage to Georgia*,
29; Eveleigh to Oglethorpe, Oct. 19,
1734, MS. CRG, XX, 646.
2. *S. C. Gazette*, June 30, July 7, 1733;
Avery to Trustees, Oct. 27, 1742,
CRG, XXIII, 413.
3. Oglethorpe to Trustees, Aug. 12,
1733, Egmont Papers, 14200, p. 107.
4. Oglethorpe to Trustees, Sept. 17,
1733, *ibid.*, 113.
5. *Ibid.*, 113-14.
6. *S. C. Gazette*, Feb. 23, 1733/4; Oglethorpe, "State of the Colony of
Georgia," Egmont Papers, 14200, p.
513; *CRG*, II, 87; *Egmont Diary*, II,
147; Wesley's account is in Egmont
Papers, 14203, p. 91.
7. Oglethorpe, "State of Colony," Egmont Papers, 14200, p. 516; Causton Journal, *ibid.*, 14203, 25-26;
CRG, IV, 511, 522; Thomas Broughton to Causton, April 28, 1735, MS.
CRG, XX, 282.
8. *LES*, 14, No. 393-94; 15, No. 533; 52,
No. 1495.
9. *CRG*, II, 44, 45; MS. CRG, XXXII,
159-60, 204; Tailfer and others,
True and Historical Narrative, 109.
10. Oglethorpe to Trustees, about Dec.,
1773, Egmont Papers, 14200, pp.
126-27; Peter Flower to ____, Jan. 7,
1733/4, *ibid.*, 133; Wesley's account,
ibid., 14203, p. 90; Martyn, "An Account," in *CRG*, III, 382; Francis
Moore, *Voyage to Georgia*, 32; Abercorn settlers, *LES*, 2, No. 35; 5, No.
120; 6, No. 156; 11, No. 305; 12, No.
315; 25, No. 705; Highgate settlers,
ibid., 9, No. 233; 14, No. 387; 15,

No. 419; 19, No. 524; 45, No. 1282;
29, No. 835; 36, No. 1037.
11. Oglethorpe, "State of Colony," Egmont Papers, 14200, pp. 513-14.
12. John Brownfield to Trustees, May
17, 1737, *CRG*, XXI, 466.
13. Oglethorpe to Trustees, Aug. 12,
1733, Egmont Papers, 14200, p. 107;
Oglethorpe, "State of Colony," *ibid.*,
513.
14. *A New Voyage to Georgia*, by a
Young Gentleman, p. 3; Oglethorpe
to Trustees, Sept. 17, 1733, Egmont
Papers, 14200, p. 114; Peter Flower
to ____, Jan. 7, 1733/4, *ibid.*, 133;
Oglethorpe, "State of Colony," *ibid.*,
515.
15. Martyn to P. G. F. de Reck, July 13,
1737, MS. CRG, XXIX, 401.
16. *CRG*, IV, 411; *LES*, 3, No. 71; 4,
No. 105; 7, No. 185; 12, No. 310; 23,
No. 661-62; 25, No. 728; 30, No.
875; 40, No. 1140; 55, No. 1579.
17. Pensyre to Oglethorpe, Jan. 5,
1734/5, MS. CRG, XX, 99-103.
18. *LES*, 92, No. 963-64; 40, No. 1140.
19. Oglethorpe to Trustees, Aug. 12,
Sept. 17, 1733, Egmont Papers, 14200,
pp. 108, 114.
20. Tailfer and others, *True and Historical Narrative*, 110.
21. Hector Beaufain to Mr. Simond,
Jan. 23, 1733/4, Egmont Papers,
14200, p. 150; Peter Flower to ____,
Jan. 7, 1733/4, *ibid.*, 133; Oglethorpe
to Trustees, about Dec., 1733, *ibid.*,
128; Isaac Chardon to Verelst, Jan.
17, 1733/4, *ibid.*, 137-38; Oglethorpe,
"State of Colony," *ibid.*, 515; William Stephens to Verelst, Aug. 6,

1741, *CRG*, XXIII, 86-87; *Egmont Diary*, II, 54; Francis Moore, *Voyage to Georgia*, 18; *S. C. Gazette*, April 20, 1734.

22. Elisha Dobree to Trustees, Jan. 27, 1734/5, MS. CRG, XX, 175.

23. Anon. to "My Lord," June 5, 1735, *ibid.*, 370; Paul Amatis to Trustees, June 30, 1735, *ibid.*, 416; Peter Gordon to Trustees, May 7, 1735, *ibid.*, 492-93.

24. Causton to Trustees, Sept. 8, 1734, *ibid.*, 297-98.

25. Eveleigh to Verelst, March 24, 1735/6, *CRG*, XXI, 116-17; Causton to Trustees, Nov. 26, 1736, *ibid.*, 274; Francis Moore, *Voyage to Georgia*, 17-18; *Egmont Diary*, II, 358.

26. William Stephens to Verelst, Aug. 6, 1741, *CRG*, XXIII, 86-87; Oglethorpe, "State of Colony," Egmont Papers, 14200, p. 515; Tailfer and others, *True and Historical Narrative*, 36, 47; *S. C. Gazette*, Aug. 29, 1741.

27. Wesley's account, Egmont Papers, 14203, p. 91.

28. Oglethorpe to Trustees, Aug. 12, 1733, Egmont Papers, 14200, p. 107.

29. Oglethorpe, "State of Colony," *ibid.*, 513; Martyn to Oglethorpe, March 27, 1734, MS. CRG, XXIX, 49; *CRG*, I, 141, 200, 201; III, 32, 74; *LES*, 9, No. 232; 12, No. 307; 14, No. 402; 61, No. 13; 18, No. 483; 26, No. 742; 30, No. 548; 36, No. 1048; 49, No. 1406; 50, No. 1452; 55, No. 1582; 57, No. 1614.

30. *S. C. Gazette*, Aug. 3, 1734; Thomas Gapen to Trustees, June 15, 1735, MS. CRG, XX, 400; Eveleigh to Oglethorpe, Nov. 7, 1734, *ibid.*, 43.

31. W. J. Dalmas to Oglethorpe, Aug. 23, 1734, MS. CRG, XX, 12-13.

32. George White, *Historical Collections of Georgia*, 335; *LES*, 36-37, No. 1048-54; 49, No. 1406-07; 96, No. 1089; Force Transcripts, Library of Congress, MS. Council Journals, Jan. 8, 1751, p. 86; Frances Smith to James Vernon, July 20, 1735, *CRG*, XXI, 180.

33. Martyn to Causton, July 27, Oct. 28, 1734, MS. CRG, XXIX, 61, 67.

34. *CRG*, II, 75; George Dunbar to Oglethorpe, Jan. 23, 1734/5, MS. CRG, XX, 158-62.

35. Thomas Mouse to Oglethorpe, Jan. 23, 1734/5, MS. CRG, XX, 168-70.

36. Causton to Trustees, Sept. 8, 1735; *ibid.*, 297-98; Causton to Trustees, Nov. 26, 1736, *CRG*, XXI, 274; Verelst to Causton, Dec. 14, 1737, MS. CRG, XXIX, 487; Verelst to William Stephens, Dec. 14, 1737, *ibid.*, 488; *LES*, 50-51, No. 1452; 55, No. 1582.

37. Philip Thicknesse to his mother, Nov. 3, 1736, *CRG*, XXI, 256; Dalmas to Oglethorpe, Aug. 23, 1734, MS. CRG, XX, 12; Dalmas to James Vernon, Jan. 24, 1734/5, *ibid.*, 171.

38. Causton to Oglethorpe, July 7, 1735, MS. CRG, XX, 219; Elisha Dobree to Verelst, March 28, July 8, 1735, *ibid.*, 327, 655; *S. C. Gazette*, April 20, 1734; Francis Moore, *Voyage to Georgia*, 41.

39. Causton's Journal, Egmont Papers, 14203, p. 59.

40. Wesley's account, *ibid.*, 90.

41. Oglethorpe to Trustees, Dec. 29, 1739, *CRG*, XXII, Part II, 290-92; II, 328.

42. Ewen to Trustees, Dec. 4, 1740, *CRG*, XXII, Part II, 455-58.

43. "A True Acct. of the Inhabitants in the Village on the Island of Skidaway in the Province of Georgia from their first Settling there on 16 January 1733 [O. S.] to the present time. As also the present State and Condition of that Village." Signed by Wm. Ewen and Thos. Mouse. Written about Feb., 1740/1. Egmont Papers, 14205, pp. 276-79; *Egmont Diary*, III, 223.

44. George White, *Historical Collections of Georgia*, 335.

45. Wm. Norris to Verelst, Dec. 12, 1738, *CRG*, XXII, Part I, 355; Isaac Young to Trustees, March 29, 1738, *ibid.*, 112-14; II, 158; Verelst to Oglethorpe, June 17, 1736, MS. CRG, XXIX, 278; XXXII, 480, 515; *LES*, 6, No. 142; 65, No. 139-40.

46. Coulter, *Journal of William Stephens, 1741-1743*, pp. 117, 121, 132; *CRG*, V, 631-32, 655-56.

47. Lucy Mouse to Trustees, May 15, 1747, *CRG*, I, 505; IV, 520-21.
48. Martyn to Stephens, March 10, 1747/8, MS. CRG, XXXI, 174-75; Stephens to Verelst, Aug. 18, 1748, *CRG*, XXV, 319-20; XXVII, 211; X, 282, 605-06, 667, 751; "Salaries and Expenses from Christmas to Lady Day 1751," in Georgia Records Miscellaneous 1732-1796, Force Transcripts, Library of Congress.
49. *CRG*, I, 21, 67, 69, 77-79; *Egmont Diary*, I, 287-89, 303.
50. *Egmont Diary*, I, 282-83, 286, 327-28; *Daily Advertiser*, July 22, 1732.
51. *CRG*, I, 93, 129, 137-40; *Egmont Diary*, I, 305, 378; Martyn to Oglethorpe, Jan. 24, May 11, 1732/3, MS. CRG, XXIX, 6, 24; XXXII, 220-24.
52. *Egmont Diary*, I, 402; *St. James Evening Post*, Nov. 6, 1733, quoted in *S. C. Gazette*, Feb. 23, 1733/4; *Daily Advertiser*, Dec. 13, 26, 1733; Jan. 2, 1733/4.
53. *CRG*, I, 152; Martyn to Oglethorpe, Nov. 22, 1733, MS. CRG, XXIX, 41; XXXII, 218; *Daily Advertiser*, Jan. 11, 1733/4; *An Extract from the Journals of Mr. Commissary Von Reck, Who Conducted the First Transport of Saltzburghers to Georgia; and of the Reverend Mr. Bolzius, One of Their Ministers* (London, 1734), 1, 8; *S. C. Gazette*, March 9, 1733/4. LES gives forty-six Salzburgers.
54. *Journals of Von Reck and Bolzius*, 11, 31; Oglethorpe to Trustees, April 2, 1724, Egmont Papers, 14200, p. 169.
55. *Journals of Von Reck and Bolzius*, 12, 32.
56. *Ibid.*, 12-14, 32.
57. *Ibid.*, 33, 40-41, 63.
58. *Ibid.*, 12-18, 23-24; *S. C. Gazette*, March 23, 1733/4.
59. *Journals of Von Reck and Bolzius*, 20-24, 50-60.
60. *Ibid.*, 22-26, 61-71.
61. *Ibid.*, 69.
62. *S. C. Gazette*, March 13, 1735/6; Oglethorpe to Trustees, Feb. 13, 1735/6, *CRG*, XXI, 453; Martyn to Oglethorpe, June 10, 1736, MS. CRG, XXIX, 261.
63. *S. C. Gazette*, Aug. 10, 1734; *CRG*, II, 111; Von Reck to James Vernon, June 24, 1736, *CRG*, XXI, 172-75; Eveleigh to Verelst, Oct. 16, 1736, *ibid.*, 212.

CHAPTER V

1. Oglethorpe to Trustees, June 9, 1733, Egmont Papers, 14200, p. 83.
2. *S. C. Gazette*, June 16, July 14, 1733; Johnson to Martyn, July 28, 1733, Egmont Papers, 14200, p. 93; Johnston to ———, July 27, 1733, *ibid.*, 97.
3. Oglethorpe to Trustees, Aug. 12, Sept. 17, 1733, Egmont Papers, 14200, pp. 107, 114.
4. Oglethorpe to Trustees, Nov. 15, about Dec., 1733, *ibid.*, 121, 130; *Egmont Diary*, II, 3.
5. Isaac Chardon to Trustees, March 14, 1733/4, Egmont Papers, 14200, p. 165; Oglethorpe to Trustees, April 2, 1734, *ibid.*, 169; *S.-C. Gazette*, March 23, March 30, May 11, Sept. 14, 1733/4; *Egmont Diary*, II, 112.
6. Causton to Trustees, March 10, Nov. 26, 1735/6, *CRG*, XXI, 125, 271; John Brownfield to Verelst, Feb. 11, 1735/6, *ibid.*, 112; Nathaniel Polhill to Thomas Towers, Feb. 12, 1735/36, *ibid.*, 93-94; *S.-C. Gazette*, March 13, Oct. 23, Nov. 6, 1735/6; *John Wesley's Journal*, III, 32.
7. *S. C. Gazette*, Oct. 5, 1738; Oglethorpe to Duke of Newcastle, Sept. 13, 1738, MS. CRG, XXXV, 163; Oglethorpe to Trustees, Sept. 13, 1738, *CRG*, XXII, Part II, 249; *CRG*, IV, 206; V, 86; G. Burridge to Thomas Winnington (?), Sept. 21, 1738, *Notes and Queries*, Third Series, X (whole vol. XXXIV), (London, July 28, 1866), 63-64.
8. Stephens to Verelst, July 18, 1743, *CRG*, XXIV, 60, 78-80; *S. C. Gazette*, July 25, Oct. 17, 1743.

9. Martyn to Thomas Hawkins, May 10, 1743, MS. CRG, XXX, 304; Oglethorpe was given powers to grant licenses to leave the colony, *CRG*, II, 9, 120; MS. CRG, XXXII, 21-22; to administer oaths, *CRG*, II, 11, 125; MS. CRG, XXXII, 35-38, 428-31; *Egmont Diary*, II, 197; to direct granting of lands in trust and to lay out lands granted by the Trustees, *CRG*, II, 9-10; MS. CRG XXXII, 17-21; *Egmont Diary*, II, 194; to appoint commanders for and to command the militia, *CRG*, I, 87, 228; MS. CRG, XXXII, 41-43, 383-85; *Egmont Diary*, I, 298; to license persons to trade with the Indians, *CRG*, II, 120; MS. CRG, XXXII, 406-07; *Egmont Diary*, II, 195-96; to install people in office, *Egmont Diary*, I, 295.

10. Martyn to John Vanderplank, July 27, 1734, MS. CRG, XXIX, 58; Martyn to Count Zinzendorf, Sept. 23, 1737, *ibid.*, 450.

11. Verelst to Stephens, Dec. 17, 1740, *ibid.*, XXX, 304.

12. *Egmont Diary*, II, 309-35.

13. Verelst to Oglethorpe, Nov. 24, 1736, MS. CRG, XXIX, 322-23; *Egmont Diary*, II, 309, 335, 368, 393, 424; *CRG*, II, 190-92.

14. Martyn to Causton, Aug. 3, 1737, MS. CRG, XXIX, 407-08; Verelst to Causton, Aug. 11, 1737, *ibid.*, 422-23; Stephens to Trustees, Oct. 26, 1737, *CRG*, XXI, 512; IV, 7, 11; Stephens to Verelst, Dec. 10, 1737, *CRG*, XXII, Part I, 27; IV, 55, 382; II, 307; A. S. Salley, Jr., ed., *Death Notices in the South-Carolina Gazette, 1732-1755* (Columbia, 1917), 25.

15. Martyn to Oglethorpe, June 15, Nov. 22, 1733, MS. CRG, XXIX, 30, 40.

16. *LES*, 9, No. 221-23; 24, No. 685; Causton to his wife, March 12, 1732/3, Egmont Papers, 14200, pp. 53-61.

17. *CRG*, II, 11; MS. CRG, XXXII, 28-33.

18. *CRG*, II, 439; Causton to his wife, March 12, 1732/3, Egmont Papers, 14200, pp. 53-54; Causton's petition

19. Causton's petition, Egmont Papers, 14204, p. 172.

20. *Ibid.*

21. *Ibid.*, 174-76.

22. *LES*, 56, No. 1593; J. Burnside to Trustees, Jan. 16, 1734/5, MS. CRG, XX, 128; *S. C. Gazette*, Nov. 16, 1734.

23. *Ibid.*, Aug. 25, 1733.

24. *Egmont Diary*, II, 36-37; *CRG*, II, 65.

25. *CRG*, II, 72-73; Martyn to Causton, Oct. 28, 1734, MS. CRG, XXIX, 69; Capt. George Dunbar to Trustees, Nov. 5, 1734, *ibid.*, XX, 11; John Vat to Henry Newman, n. d. (late 1734 or early 1735), *ibid.*, 267.

26. Patrick Houstoun, Patrick Tailfer, and Andrew Grant to Gordon, Jan. 21, 1734/5, MS. CRG, XX, 494-96; Houstoun to Gordon, March 1, 1734/5, *ibid.*, 592-600; Robt. Parker, Jr., to Gordon, March 2, 1734/5, *ibid.* 332-34; Samuel Quincy to Gordon, March 3, 1734/5, *ibid.*, 600-03; Joseph Watson to Gordon, March 10, 1734/5, *ibid.*, 603-05; John West to Gordon, March 10, 1734/5, *ibid.*, 605-06; Susan Bowling to Gordon, March 20, 1734/5, *ibid.*, 335-37; Thomas Christie to Trustees, March 19, 1734/5, *ibid.*, 626; *CRG*, II, 102.

27. Causton to Trustees, April 2, 1735; MS. CRG, XX, 576-77.

28. *Egmont Diary*, II, 169; *CRG*, II, 102.

29. *CRG*, I, 236; II, 209; Gordon to Trustees, May 7, 1735, MS. CRG, XX, 489-94; *Egmont Diary*, II, 201.

30. Verelst to Causton, May 15, July 18, 1735, MS. CRG, XXIX, 103-04, 142-43; Verelst to Bailiffs and Recorder of Savannah, May 15, 1735, *ibid.*, 105, 111, 116-17.

31. *CRG*, II, 11.

32. Patrick Houstoun to Peter Gordon, March 3, 1734/5, MS. CRG, XX, 599; Causton's Journal, Egmont Papers, 14203, p. 47; *LES*, 26, No. 730; 51, No. 1478-81; 70, No. 290; 77, No. 487-88.

33. Symes to Oglethorpe, Jan. 2, ____ 19, 1734/5, MS. CRG, XX, 97, 451-52.

34. *LES*, 23, No. 670; 47, No. 1342; Causton to Trustees, Jan., 1733/4, Egmont Papers, 14200, p. 141; *CRG*, II, 73, 120, 123; MS. CRG, XXXII, 263-64, 385-87.

35. See *CRG*, I and II, *passim; Egmont Diary*, II, *passim;* especially *Egmont Diary*, II, 313, 317, 414, 451-52.

36. *Ibid.*

37. *Ibid.; CRG*, IV, *passim; Egmont Diary*, II, 195.

38. *Egmont Diary*, II, 513-14; III, 134.

39. *Egmont Diary*, II, 195.

40. West to Oglethorpe, Dec. 20, 1734, MS. CRG, XX, 95; *LES*, 30, No. 872; 25, No. 704; 57, No. 1610.

41. West to Oglethorpe, Oct. 12, 1734, MS. CRG, XX, 30-31.

42. Martyn to Causton, Oct. 28, 1734, *ibid.*, XXIX, 69.

43. Martyn to Causton, Jan. 25, 1734/5, *ibid.*, 80-81; Verelst to Bailiffs and Recorder of Savannah, May 15, 1735, *ibid.*, 114; West to Oglethorpe, April 18, 1735, *ibid.*, XX, 280-81; Elisha Dobree to Martyn, July 9, 1735, *ibid.*, 379.

44. *Egmont Diary*, II, 195.

45. *Ibid.*, 404-05, 491; *CRG*, II, 130, 198, 246; MS. CRG, XXXII, 440-52, 469, 472; Verelst (?) to Oglethorpe, n. d. (Nov., 1735), MS. CRG, XXIX, 179-80; Verelst to Oglethorpe, Nov. 26, 1735, *ibid.*, 198; West to Verelst, March 17, 1735/6, *CRG*, XXI, 118-19; John Brownfield to Verelst (?), March 18, 1735/6, *ibid.*, 106-07.

46. Causton's Journal, Egmont Papers, 14203, p. 24; *LES*, 101, No. 1249; Verelst to Causton, Nov. 5, 1737, MS. CRG, XXIX, 476-77; Causton to Trustees, March 1, 1737/8, *CRG*, XXII, Part I, 108-09; West to Trustees, Aug. 28, 1738, *ibid.*, 244-45; Verelst to Oglethorpe, Aug. 11, 1738, MS. CRG, XXX, 5; Verelst to Stephens, Aug. 11, 1738, *ibid.*, 9.

47. *CRG*, IV, 198, 209.

48. West to Verelst, Feb. 5, 1738/9, *CRG*, XXII, Part II, 39-40.

49. *CRG*, II, 283, 328; IV, 377; *Egmont Diary*, III, 65; Martyn to West, July 11, 1739, MS. CRG, XXX, 94.

50. *CRG*, IV, 588-89; *LES*, 25, No. 704.

CHAPTER VI

1. Tailfer and others, *True and Historical Narrative*, 30n; Oglethorpe to Trustees, about Dec., 1733, Egmont Papers, 14200, pp. 127-28; Causton to Trustees, Jan., 1733/4, *ibid.*, 141.

2. Oglethorpe to Trustees, April 2, 1734, Egmont Papers, 14200, p. 170; Eveleigh to Oglethorpe, Oct. 19, 1734, *ibid.*, 268.

3. Wise to _____, April 14, 1733, Rawlinson MSS. D839, f. 155, Bodleian Library, Oxford University (Library of Congress transcript).

4. *Egmont Diary*, I, 384.

5. Martyn to Oglethorpe, Sept. 26, Oct. 18, 1733, MS. CRG, XXIX, 35-36, 38-39; *CRG*, I, 141.

6. Christie to Oglethorpe, July 31, 1735, MS. CRG, XX, 229.

7. Fitzwalter to Oglethorpe, Jan. 16, 1734/5, *ibid.*, 112; Oglethorpe to Trustees, about Dec., 1733, Egmont Papers, 14200, p. 127; Oglethorpe, "State of the Colony," *ibid.*, 514-15.

8. *LES*, 95, No. 1045-46; 101, No. 1255, 1257-58; Christie to Oglethorpe, Dec. 14, 1734, MS. CRG, XX, 89-90.

9. Christie to Oglethorpe, March 19, 1734/5, MS. CRG, XX, 626.

10. Jenkins to Oglethorpe, Jan. 20, 1734/5, *ibid.*, 151-53; Causton to Trustees, July 25, 1735, *ibid*, 225; Martyn to Causton, March 17, 1734/5, *ibid.*, XXIX, 87; *CRG*, II, 90.

11. Patrick Houstoun to Gordon, March 1, 1734/5, MS. CRG, XX, 599; Causton to Trustees, March 10, 1734 (O. S.), *ibid.*, 560-65; Christie to Trustees, March 19, 1734/5, *ibid.*, 621-26; Samuel Quincy to Gordon, March 3, 1734/5, *ibid.*, 600-02; Sir Francis Bathurst to Trustees, March, 1735, *ibid.*, 526; Causton to Oglethorpe, incorrectly dated Jan. 16, 1734 (O. S.), *ibid.*, 639; Samuel Quincy to Verelst, Aug. 28, 1735, *ibid.*, 293; *LES*, 69-70, Nos. 262, 274; 78, Nos. 538, 539; *Egmont Diary*, II, 172.

12. *Egmont Diary*, II, 313, 317-18.
13. Oglethorpe to Trustees, Feb. 26, 1733/4, Egmont Papers, 14200, 161-62.
14. Causton to Trustees, March 24, 1734 (O. S.), MS. CRG, XX, 548-49.
15. *Ibid.*, 548-53; Eveleigh to Oglethorpe, Oct. 19, 1734, *ibid.*, 643.
16. Causton to Trustees, March 24, 1734 (O. S.), *ibid.*, 553.
17. *Ibid*, 546, 554.
18. Watson to Gordon, March 10, 1734/5, *ibid.*, 603-05.
19. *CRG*, I, 207; *Egmont Diary*, II, 367-68.
20. *CRG*, II, 90; Martyn to Causton, March 17, 1734/5, MS. CRG, XXIX, 86; XXXII, 267-70; *Egmont Diary*, II, 160.
21. Verelst to Bailiffs and Recorder of Savannah, May 15, 1735, MS. CRG, XXIX, 110.
22. Tailfer and others, *True and Historical Narrative*, 34-35; Causton to Trustees, July 25, 1738, *CRG*, XXII, Part I, 207-08.
23. *CRG*, II, 90; Oglethorpe to Trustees, Dec. 29, 1739, *ibid.*, XXII, Part II, 291; Martyn to Causton, March 17, 1734/5, MS. CRG, XXIX, 86; Creek Indian Talk, July 3, 1736, Egmont Papers, 14202, pp. 49-52.
24. *Egmont Diary*, II, 367-68, 375; *CRG*, I, 277; W. L. Grant and James Munro, eds., *Acts of the Privy Council, Colonial Series* (6 vols., London, 1906-1912), III, 562-63.
25. *CRG*, IV, 22; *Egmont Diary*, II, 379-410 *passim*, 487.
26. *CRG*, I, 424-26; V, 706-07; Verelst to Stephens, Sept. 14, 1743; MS. CRG, XXX, 565-66; Martyn to Stephens, Feb. 11, 1743 (O. S.), *ibid.*, 581.
27. *CRG*, VI, 96-102; Coulter, ed., *Journal of William Stephens, 1743-1745*, pp. 83, 87.
28. Coulter, *Journal of William Stephens, 1743-1745*, pp. 92-93, 95-96.
29. *Ibid.*, 135; *CRG*, VI, 110-11; Stephens to Martyn, Aug. 29, 1744, *ibid.*, XXIV, 295-96; Verelst to Stephens, March 7, 1744 (O. S.), MS. CRG, XXX, 615-16.
30. Coulter, *Journal of Williams Stephens, 1743-1745*, pp. 191-92.

31. *CRG*, VI, 96-97; Bonds, Bills of Sales, Etc., 1755-1762, Book 9, pp. 16-18, Ga. Dept. of Archives and History.
32. *CRG*, VII, 823; Estates, Inventories, 1754-1771, Book F, p. 69, Ga. Dept. of Archives and History.
33. *CRG*, I, 235, 241; Martyn to Quincy, Oct. 10, 1735, MS. CRG, XXIX, 165; Verelst to Oglethorpe, Dec. 6, 1735, *ibid.*, 202-03; *Egmont Diary*, II, 209.
34. *CRG*, I, 234-35; 241, 245; MS. CRG, XXXII, 434-35; *Egmont Diary*, II, 211, 214, 221.
35. *Egmont Diary*, II, 196, 200; Nehemiah Curnock, ed., *The Journal of the Rev. John Wesley*, ... (8 vols., London, 1910-1916), I, 109.
36. *Egmont Diary*, II, 200; Ingham's Journal of his Voyage to Georgia, Egmont Papers, 14201, pp. 423-24; Luke Tyerman, *The Oxford Methodists*: . . . (New York, 1873), 63.
37. Curnock, *Wesley's Journal*, I, 146-47, 176-77.
38. *Ibid.*, 237-39, 297-98.
39. *Ibid.*, 197-205; *Egmont Diary*, II, 370.
40. Curnock, *Wesley's Journal*, I, 234-35.
41. *Ibid.*, 251-55, 307-13.
42. *Ibid.*, 313-14.
43. *Ibid.*, *passim*, especially 287-91, 327.
44. Causton to Trustees, July 25, 1738, *CRG*, XXII, Pt. I, 204.
45. Curnock, *Wesley's Journal*, I, 347-53.
46. Causton's Journal, Egmont Papers, 14203, pp. 9, 20-23, 32, 39-40.
47. *Ibid.*, 41, 51-52; Wesley to Causton, July 5, 1737, *CRG*, IV, 15-16.
48. Curnock, *Wesley's Journal*, I, 364-66, 376; *S. C. Gazette*, Jan. 2, 1737/8.
49. Curnock, *Wesley's Journal*, I, 377-78.
50. *Ibid.*, 378-79.
51. *CRG*, IV, 14; Stephens to Trustees, Dec. 20, 1737, *ibid.*, XXII, Pt. I, 34; Delamotte to Wesley, Feb. 23, 1737/8, Egmont Papers, 14203, pp. 106-09.
52. *CRG*, I, 303; Verelst to Wesley, Dec. 14, 1737, MS. CRG, XXIX, 492; *Egmont Diary*, II, 450-51.
53. Curnock, *Wesley's Journal*, I, 381-95, 398-400; *CRG*, IV, 40.

54. Curnock, *Wesley's Journal*, I, 400; *CRG*, IV, 40-42.
55. Curnock, *Wesley's Journal*, I, 409-

13, 421-22; *S. C. Gazette*, Jan. 2, 1737/8.
56. Curnock, *Wesley's Journal*, I, 422.

CHAPTER VII

1. *Egmont Diary*, II, 466-68, 313.
2. *Ibid.*, 481.
3. *Ibid.*, 499; *CRG*, IV, 18-19.
4. *CRG*, II, 56; Martyn to Oglethorpe, March 25, 1734, MS. CRG, XXIX, 48; *Egmont Diary*, II, 22-23, 32, 41, 55.
5. Martyn to Causton, July 27, Oct. 28, 1734, MS. CRG, XXIX, 61-62, 67-68; Verelst to Causton, Dec. 13, 1734, *ibid.*, 76-77; Verelst to Isaac Chardon, Sept. 25, 1735, *ibid.*, 167-77; Chardon to Oglethorpe, Nov. 4, 1734, MS. CRG, XX, 40; Oglethorpe to Trustees, Nov. 15, about Dec., 1733, Egmont Papers, 14200, 121, 129.
6. *CRG*, II, 113-14; *Egmont Diary*, II, 186, 188-89.
7. *Egmont Diary*, II, 278.
8. Martyn to Oglethorpe, April 1, June 10, 1736, MS. CRG, XXIX, 234-37, 265-67; Verelst to Causton, April 2, 1736, *ibid.*, 242-43; *Egmont Diary*, II, 252, 279.
9. *Egmont Diary*, II, 295, 302; Causton to Trustees, July 22, 1736, *CRG*, XXI, 190.
10. *Egmont Diary*, II, 302.
11. *Ibid.*, 278-80, 291; Martyn to Oglethorpe, June 10, 1736, MS. CRG, XXIX, 267-69; Verelst to Oglethorpe, Aug. 9, 28, Oct. 22, Nov. 24, 1736, *ibid.*, 298, 309-12, 320, 322-23; *S. C. Gazette*, Sept. 25, 1736.
12. *Egmont Diary*, II, 468, 472-82.
13. Causton to Trustees, Nov. 26, 1736, *CRG*, XXI, 272-73.
14. Causton to Trustees, Dec. 14, 1736, *ibid.*, 287-88; Martyn to Causton, March 7, 1736/7, MS. CRG, XXIX, 343; *Egmont Diary*, II, 358.
15. *Egmont Diary*, II, 411-12.
16. *Ibid.*, 396, 398, 411-12.
17. Causton to Trustees, April 25, 1737, *CRG*, XXI, 401.
18. Causton to Trustees, March 24, 1736/7, *ibid.*, 383.

19. *CRG*, I, 19, 24-25, 288; Martyn to Lt. Gov. Thomas Broughton (S. C.), Jan. 2, 1735/6, MS. CRG, XXIX, 208-09; *Egmont Diary*, II, 410.
20. Verelst to Causton, Aug. 11, 1737, MS. CRG, XXIX, 427-28; *Egmont Diary*, II, 428.
21. Causton to Trustees, Jan. 16, Feb. 24, March 24, 1736/7, *CRG*, XXI, 305-06, 312, 386-87; Paul Jenys to Trustees, May 20, 1737, *ibid.*, 431; John Brownfield to Trustees, May 17, 1737, *ibid.*, 470.
22. John Brownfield to Trustees, May 2, 1737, *ibid.*, 413-17; *Egmont Diary*, II, 421.
23. *Egmont Diary*, II, 460-63; *CRG*, II, 221-24; Verelst to Causton, Jan. 11, Feb. 17, 1736/7, MS. CRG, XXIX, 498-501.
24. *Egmont Diary*, II, 472-74; *CRG*, II, 226-27; MS. CRG, XXXII, 601; *S. C. Gazette*, Sept. 14, 1738.
25. *Egmont Diary*, II, 474.
26. *Ibid.*, 475, 482.
27. *Ibid.*, 482-86, 491; *CRG*, II, 231, 238.
28. *Egmont Diary*, II, 485; *CRG*, II, 239; V, 137; MS. CRG, XXXII, 601-03.
29. Tailfer and others, *True and Historical Narrative*, 73.
30. *CRG*, II, 237; Verelst to Parker, n. d., MS. CRG, XXIX, 515-17; Verelst to Stephens, May 20, 1738, *ibid.*, 518-19; Verelst to Causton, May 19, 1738, *ibid.*, 525-27.
31. *Egmont Diary*, II, 488; Verelst to Causton, May 19, 1738, MS. CRG, XXIX, 522-23.
32. *Egmont Diary*, II, 490, 500-01, 506.
33. *CRG*, IV, 226-27; Causton petition, Egmont Papers, 14204, p. 184.
34. *CRG*, I, 321-25; II, 247; MS. CRG, XXXIII, 3-4; *Egmont Diary*, II, 491, 494-95.
35. *CRG*, IV, 206, 208, 212-13; Egmont Papers, 14203, 254-86.
36. *CRG*, IV, 213.
37. *Egmont Diary*, II, 516-17; III, 4.

38. Norris to Verelst, Oct. 19, 1738, *CRG*, XXII, Pt. I, 289-90; IV, 212; *Egmont Diary*, III, 37.
39. *CRG*, IV, 213-14.
40. *Ibid.*, 214.
41. Oglethorpe to Trustees, Oct. 19, 1738, *CRG*, XXII, Pt. I, 281-88; Stephens to Trustees, Nov. 21, 1738, *ibid.*, 320-21; Thomas Jones to Verelst, Nov. 12, 1738, *ibid.*, 302; IV, 221-23, 233, 250-51, 260.
42. Causton to Trustees, Jan. 14, Feb. 11, Nov. 22, 1738/9, *CRG*, XXII, Pt. II, 20-34, 59-75, 270-71; Causton petition, Nov. 22, 1739, Egmont Papers, 14204, pp. 171-95.
43. *CRG*, IV, 217.
44. *Ibid.*, 217-18.
45. *Ibid.*, 224.
46. Stephens to Trustees, Jan. 2, 1738/9, *CRG*, XXII, Pt. I, 366; IV, 242, 246-47, 251-53.
47. *Egmont Diary*, II, 491-92, 501; Causton to Trustees, May 26, 1738, *CRG*, XXII, Pt. I, 153-58; Verelst to Oglethorpe, June 14, 1738, MS. CRG, XXIX, 560; *S. C. Gazette*, Sept. 21, 1738.
48. Tailfer and others, *True and Historical Narrative*, 50; Stephens to Trustees, Jan. 2, 1738/9, *CRG*, XXII, Pt. I, 367.
49. *CRG*, III, 422-26.
50. *CRG*, IV, 243-44.

51. *CRG*, II, 30, 32; MS. CRG, XXXII, 115-26.
52. *CRG*, IV, 245, 274; Stephens to Trustees, Jan. 2, 1738/9, XXII, Pt. I, 365, 369.
53. Oglethorpe to Trustees, Jan. 16, 1738/9, Egmont Papers, 14203, pp. 376-77; Oglethorpe to Trustees, March 12, 1738/9, *CRG*, XXII, Pt. II, 111-12.
54. *CRG*, I, 351; V, 76; Martyn to Magistrates of Savannah, June 20, 1739, III, 431-32; MS. CRG, XXXIII, 38-40; *Egmont Diary*, III, 70-71.
55. *CRG*, IV, 255-56, 260-61, 263, 306-07, 309-10; *Egmont Diary*, III, 39.
56. *Egmont Diary*, III, 54, 57, 66.
57. *Ibid.*, 94, 132; *CRG*, IV, 360, 384-87, 393, 405.
58. *Egmont Diary*, III, 131; Egmont Papers, 14204, pp. 171-95; 14205, pp. 327-65; *CRG*, IV, 609, 617, 650, 660; *LES*, 9, No. 221-22.
59. Coulter, *Journal of William Stephens, 1741-43*, 53-54, 74, 132, 148, 153-54, 156-57, 161, 187-88, 192-93, 198.
60. *CRG*, XXIV, 16-19.
61. *Ibid.*, 230, 233-34; Coulter, *Journal of William Stephens, 1743-45*, 36, 56-57, 59.
62. *CRG*, II, 438-42, 450-51, 460-61.
63. *CRG*, XXV, 8, 86-87, 93-94.

CHAPTER VIII

1. MS. CRG, XXXII, 26-27, 31-33, 38.
2. *Ibid.*, 23, 25; Verelst to Bailiffs and Recorder of Savannah, May 15, 1735, *ibid.*, XXIX, 116-17; Martyn, "An Account . . ." *CRG*, III, 379; Oglethorpe to Trustees, about Dec., 1733, Egmont Papers, 14200, p. 129; Oglethorpe, State of Colony, *ibid.*, 517-18.
3. Oglethorpe to Trustees, about Dec., 1733, Egmont Papers, 14200, p. 129; Moore, *A Voyage to Georgia*, 26; Eveleigh to Oglethorpe, Oct. 19, 1734, MS. CRG, XX, 641-42.
4. *Egmont Diary*, III, 120; *CRG*, IV, 61.
5. Oglethorpe, State of Colony, Egmont Papers, 14200, pp. 516-18.

6. *CRG*, II, 95; *LES*, 88, No. 813-20; 69, No. 265, 269.
7. Augustine to John Brownfield, June 13, 1735, MS. CRG, XX, 213; Samuel Quincy to Henry Newman, July 4, 1735, *ibid.*, 207.
8. Causton to Trustees, July 25, Sept. 8, 1735, *ibid.*, 223-25, 298; Christie to Oglethorpe, July 31, 1735, *ibid.*, 230; *S. C. Gazette*, July 5, 19, Aug. 2, 23, Sept. 27, Oct. 11, 1735.
9. Wm. Mellichamp to Trustees, Sept. 8, 1735, *CRG*, XXI, 15.
10. *S. C. Gazette*, July 17, Aug. 7, 1736.
11. *Ibid.*, Aug. 21, 1736.
12. *LES*, 56, No. 1594; 57, No. 1632-33; Causton to Trustees, Nov. 20, 1735, *CRG*, XXI, 57-58.

13. Christie to Oglethorpe, July 31, 1735, MS. CRG, XX, 229.
14. Parker to Trustees, n. d., *ibid.*, 480.
15. Wm. Gough to Oglethorpe, Nov. 13, 1736, *CRG*, XXI, 247-55.
16. Verelst to Bailiffs and Recorder of Savannah, May 15, 1735, MS. CRG, XXIX, 109-10; *Egmont Diary*, II, 172.
17. Causton to Trustees, Nov. 20, 1735, *CRG*, XXI, 56.
18. Martyn, "An Account . . . ," *CRG*, III, 382; *ibid.*, 86.
19. Estimate of the Charges Necessary for Defending Carolina, March, 1735, Egmont Papers, 14207, p. 340; Philip Alexander Bruce, *Economic History of Virginia in the Seventeenth Century* (New York, 1895), I, 51-52, 239-45.
20. *CRG*, I, 72; II, 5-6; III, 51-52; MS. CRG, XXXII, 1-5, 144.
21. Houstoun to Oglethorpe, Dec. 21, 1732, Jan. 25, 1732/3, Egmont Papers, 14200, pp. 9, 17; Mr. Cochrane to Philip Millar, Sept. 11, 1733, *ibid.*, 109-10; *Egmont Diary*, II, 32; Francis Moore, *A Voyage to Georgia*, 31.
22. *CRG*, II, 59-61; MS. CRG, XXXII, 225-32; *Egmont Diary*, II, 32, 37; Oglethorpe to Sir Hans Sloane, Sept. 19, 1733, British Museum, Sloane MSS, 4053, f. 53, Library of Congress Transcripts.
23. *CRG*, II, 174; V, 63, 65-66; Millar to Trustees, May 26, 1738, *ibid.*, XXII, Pt. I, 150-52; Martyn to Andrew Millar, Aug. 23, 1738, MS. CRG, XXX, 26; XXXII, 489-94; *Egmont Diary*, II, 288-89, 306, 503, 506.
24. *S. C. Gazette*, May 19, 1733; Eveleigh to Trustees, May 18, 1733, Egmont Papers, 14200, p. 69.
25. Oglethorpe to Trustees, Nov. 15, 1733, Egmont Papers, 14200, p. 121; Eveleigh to Oglethorpe, Aug. 12, 1734, MS. CRG, XX, 6-7.
26. *S.-C. Gazette*, March 24, 1732/3.
27. *Egmont Diary*, II, 69; Oglethorpe to Trustees, March 12, 1732/3, Egmont Papers, 14200, p. 45.

28. *Von Reck Journal*, 13.
29. Oglethorpe, State of Colony, Egmont Papers, 14200, pp. 511-12.
30. Oglethorpe to Trustees, about Dec., 1733, *ibid.*, 128.
31. Fitzwalter to Oglethorpe, Jan. 16, 1734/5, MS. CRG, XX, 110-14.
32. Oglethorpe, State of Colony, Egmont Papers, 14200, p. 511; Isaac Chardon to Verelst, Jan. 17, 1733/4, *ibid.*, 137.
33. Christie to Oglethorpe, Dec. 14, 1734, MS. CRG, XX, 87.
34. *CRG*, I, 80, 100; II, 20-27; Martyn, "An Account . . . ," III, 379; passenger list, *GHQ*, XXXI, 283; Oglethorpe to Trustees, Nov. 18, 1732, Egmont Papers, 14200, p. 5; Martyn to Oglethorpe, March 31, April 4, MS. CRG, XXIX, 13, 16-17; XXXII, 215, 217; Paul Amatis to Trustees, Aug. 15, 1735, *ibid.*, XX, 288-89; *LES*, 1, No. 21; *Egmont Diary*, I, 309, 327, 336, 339, 340, 344-45, 347.
35. Amatis to Oglethorpe, n. d., MS. CRG, XX, 142-48; John Lyndall to Oglethorpe, Oct. 29, 1734, *ibid.*, 33-34.
36. Isaac Chardon to Verelst, Jan. 17, 1733/4, Egmont Papers, 14200, p. 137.
37. Eveleigh to Oglethorpe, Oct. 19, 1734, MS. CRG, XX, 641, 643.
38. Fitzwalter to Oglethorpe, March 10, 1734/5, *ibid.*, 250-53.
39. Amatis to Trustees, Jan. 12, 1734/5, *ibid.*, 120-22.
40. Amatis' statement read in court, Savannah, April 5, 1735, *ibid.*, 342-43.
41. *Egmont Diary*, II, 172.
42. Martyn to Fitzwalter, May 15, 1735, MS. CRG, XXIX, 127-28; Verelst to Bailiffs and Recorder of Savannah, May 15, 1735, *ibid.*, 111.
43. Martyn to Amatis, May 15, 1735, *ibid.*, 128-30.
44. *Egmont Diary*, II, 172.
45. *CRG*, II, 116, 121; Verelst to Amatis, Sept. 6, 1735, MS. CRG, XXIX, 164; Verelst to Causton, Dec. 3, 1735, *ibid.*, 202; Isaac Chardon to

Trustees, Dec. 2, 1735, *CRG*, XXI, 60-61; Amatis to Trustees, July 24, 1735, MS. CRG, XX, 382.

46. Amatis to Trustees, June 30, July 5, 1735, MS. CRG, XX, 416, 453-56; Causton to Trustees, July 25, 1735, *ibid.*, 226.

47. Francis Percy to Oglethorpe, Feb. 16, 1734/5, *ibid.*, 238.

48. Amatis to Trustees, July 24, 1735, *ibid.*, 383; Edward Jenkins and John Dearne to Oglethorpe, n. d. (received in London, June 18, 1735), *ibid.*, 629.

49. Fitzwalter to Oglethorpe, July 5, 1735, *ibid.*, 457-59.

50. Martyn to Hugh Anderson, May 18, 1738, MS. CRG, XXIX, 508; *CRG*, IV, 510, 515; *ibid.*, Supplement, 98.

51. Fitzwalter to Oglethorpe, July 5, 1735, MS. CRG, XX, 457-59.

52. Oglethorpe to Trustees, June 9, 1733, Egmont Papers, 14200, pp. 81-82; Causton to Trustees, Jan. 16, 1734/5, MS. CRG, XX, 636. (This letter as it stands is a mixture of two letters; some of the events mentioned occurred later than the date given.)

53. Dobree to Trustees, March 28, 1755, MS. CRG, XX, 327.

54. Oglethorpe to Trustees, April 24, 1736, *CRG*, XXI, 217; Curnock, *Wesley's Journal*, I, 168, n. 2.

55. Fitzwalter to Oglethorpe, July 5, 1735, MS. CRG, XX, 457-59.

56. Gapen to Trustees, June 13, 1735, *ibid.*, 395-402.

57. Causton to Trustees, July 25, 1735, *ibid.*, 225-26; Stephens to Trustees, Jan. 19, 1737/8, *CRG*, XXII, Pt. I, 77-78.

58. *Egmont Diary*, II, 314.

59. John Brownfield to Verelst, April 13, 1736, *CRG*, XXI, 137, 145; Brownfield to Trustees, May 17, 1737, *ibid.*, 465-66; Curnock, *Wesley's Journal*, I, 323; *LES*, 1, No. 22; 61, No. 16; 90, No. 906.

60. *Egmont Diary*, II, 370; Moore, *A Voyage to Georgia*, 31.

61. Causton to Trustees, April 25, 1737, *CRG*, XXI, 401; Verelst to Causton,

Aug. 11, 1737, MS. CRG, XXIX, 432.

62. Stephens to Trustees, Dec. 20, 1737, *CRG*, XXII, Pt. I, 44.

63. *Egmont Diary*, II, 466; *LES*, 41, No. 164.

64. Stephens to Trustees, Jan. 19, 1737/8, *CRG*, XXII, Pt. I, 77-78; II, 251, 293; *LES*, 22, No. 635-38; 24, No. 695.

65. Robert Potter to Egmont, April 15, 1735, MS. CRG. XX, 345; *Egmont Diary*, II, 276; *LES*, 62, No. 21-25.

66. *CRG*, II, 156, 164, 221; *Egmont Diary*, II, 276, 278, 294, 447, 451; Martyn to Oglethorpe, Aug. 4, 1736, MS. CRG, XXIX, 295-96; Verelst to Hugh Anderson, Dec. 14, 1737, *ibid.*, 495-96; *ibid.*, XXXII, 483-84.

67. Anderson to Egmont, Aug. 10, 1737, *CRG*, XXI, 500-01; II, 182-83; Anderson's memorial to Trustees, Aug. 10, 1737, Egmont Papers, 14203, pp. 80-83.

68. Martyn to Anderson, May 19, 1738, MS. CRG, XXI, 508-09; *Egmont Diary*, II, 487.

69. Stephens to Trustees, Aug. 26, 1738, *CRG*, XXII, Pt. I, 229.

70. Anderson to Egmont, March 3, 1739, *ibid.*, Pt. II, 93-105; II, 302; V, 227-28; *Egmont Diary*, III, 82-83.

71. Stephens to Trustees, Jan. 19, 1737/8, *CRG*, XXII, Pt. I, 78.

72. *CRG*, IV, 80-81.

73. *Ibid.*, 98; Thomas Jenys to Trustees, April 24, 1738, XXII, Pt. I, 137.

74. *Egmont Diary*, II, 476.

75. *Ibid.*, 495-96.

76. *CRG*, IV, 107, 157, 189.

77. *LES*, 16, No. 435.

78. Passenger List, Egmont Papers, 14207, p. 61; Martyn to Bailiffs and Recorder of Savannah, July 27, 1734, MS. CRG, XXIX, 59; Martyn to John Vanderplank, July 27, 1734, *ibid.*, 58; John Brownfield to Trustees, May 17, 1737, *CRG*, XXI, 467.

79. *LES*, 58, No. 1643-46.

80. Stephens to Trustees, Aug. 26, 1738, *CRG*, XXII, Pt. I, 229.

81. Martyn to Causton, Oct. 28, 1734, MS. CRG, XXIX, 67.

CHAPTER IX

1. *CRG*, II, 8-11; Martyn to Causton, Oct. 28, 1734, MS. CRG, XXIX, 64-65; *ibid.*, 41, 60, 62, 75-76; XXXI, 37; XXXII, 5-7, 22-27, 30-33, 414-16.
2. Recorder of Savannah to Oglethorpe, *S. C. Gazette*, April 20, 1734; Christie to Oglethorpe, Dec. 14, 1734, MS. CRG, XX, 85; Verelst to Bailiffs and Recorder of Savannah, May 15, 1735, XXIX, 105; Martyn to John Pye, April 24, 1741, XXX, 328-29; Fallowfield to Trustees, Jan. 1, 1740/1, *CRG*, XXII, Pt. II, 481.
3. Passenger list, Egmont Papers, 14207, p. 61; *LES*, 67, No. 209.
4. Christie to Oglethorpe, Dec. 14, 1734, MS. CRG, XX, 82-90.
5. Gordon to Trustees, May 7, 1735, *ibid.*, 492.
6. Verelst to Bailiffs and Recorder of Savannah, May 15, 1735, MS. CRG, XXIX, 105-07; Verelst to Causton, May 15, 1735, *ibid.*, 103-04.
7. Christie to Trustees, May 28, 1735, MS. CRG, XX, 328-31; Christie to Oglethorpe, July 31, 1735, *ibid.*, 228-30. (The letter of May 28 is mixed with another. It is answering a letter written in London on May 15 and was probably written in July. See *ibid.*, 468.)
8. Martyn to Causton, Oct. 28, 1734, MS. CRG, XXIX, 69-70; *LES*, 45, No. 1290; Jones to John Lyde, Sept. 18, 1740, Egmont Papers, 14205, p. 129.
9. Coulter, *Journal of William Stephens, 1743-1745*, 200; *CRG*, I, 573; II, 520; VII 9-10; Martyn to President and Assistants, March 8, April 7, 1752, MS. CRG, XXXI, 572, 589; Martyn to Russell, April 7, 1752, *ibid.*, 593; XXXIII, 531-33.
10. *CRG*, IV, 19-21.
11. *CRG*, II, 208; Verelst to Causton, Aug. 11, 1737, MS. CRG, XXIX, 420.
12. *CRG*, IV, 21-22, 32-33, 65.
13. *Ibid.*, 44-45, 54, 80; Stephens to Trustees, Feb. 27, 1737/8, XXII, Pt. I, 96; John Brownfield to Trustees,

May 17, 1737, XXI, 468; Egmont Papers, 14203, pp. 33, 214.
14. *Egmont Diary*, II, 476.
15. *Ibid.*, 488; *CRG*, II, 240-41; IV, 234; Verelst to Oglethorpe, Aug. 11, 1738, MS. CRG, XXX, 4.
16. *LES*, 70, No. 299; Tailfer and others, *True and Historical Narrative*, 34.
17. *CRG*, II, 233; *LES*, 75, No. 440-42; *Egmont Diary*, II, 483, 485-86; Verelst to Causton, March 23, 1736/7, May 19, 1738, MS. CRG, XXIX, 355, 530; Verelst to Stephens, May 20, 1738, *ibid.*, 520; XXXII, 579-81.
18. *LES*, 88, No. 806-10.
19. Delamotte to Wesley, Feb. 23, 1737/8, Egmont Papers, 14203, 106-09; Norris to Trustees, Dec. 12, 1738, *CRG*, XXII, Pt. I, 352.
20. *CRG*, IV, 213; Stephens to Trustees, Sept. 27, 1738, XXII, Pt. I, 263.
21. *CRG*, IV, 212; *Egmont Diary*, III, 54.
22. *CRG*, IV, 214.
23. Tailfer and others, *True and Historical Narrative*, 34.
24. *CRG*, II, 282, 284; IV, 418; *Egmont Diary*, III, 63, 66, 71, 80; Martyn to Gilbert, July 11, 1739, MS. CRG, XXX, 100; Verelst to Oglethorpe, July 14, 1739, *ibid.*, 102.
25. *CRG*, IV, 645.
26. *CRG*, III, 425; Martyn to Magistrates of Savannah, June 20, 1739, *ibid.*, 431-32; *Egmont Diary*, III, 51-53, 74.
27. *CRG*, IV, 160, 190, 200, 256; Stephens to Verelst, Jan. 3, 1738/9, XXII, Pt. II, 5.
28. *CRG*, IV, 256, 299; Stephens to Verelst, Jan. 3, 1738/9, XXII, Pt. II, 7.
29. *CRG*, IV, 233.
30. *Ibid.*, 319-22, 331-33; Stephens to Trustees, May 19, 1739, XXII, Pt. II, 140-41.
31. Stephens to Trustees, May 19, 1739, *CRG*, XXII, Pt. II, 141.
32. *Ibid.*, 141-42; Jones to Verelst, Feb. 17, 1738, *ibid.*, 84-85.

33. *CRG*, I, 352; II, 282-84, 298; MS. CRG, XXXIII, 32-38, 53-55; *Egmont Diary*, III, 65, 70-71, 76.

34. Verelst to Jones, Sept. 14, 1739, MS. CRG, XXX, 165; *Egmont Diary*, III, 81.

35. Verelst to Christie, July 14, 1739, MS. CRG, XXX, 141-42.

36. Verelst to Stephens, July 14, 1739, *ibid.*, 114; Verelst to Oglethorpe, July 14, 1739, *ibid.*, 102; Verelst to Williamson, July 14, 1739, *ibid.*, 140-41.

37. *CRG*, IV, 421, 428; Oglethorpe to Verelst, June 15, 1739, MS. CRG, XXX, 154-55; Martyn to Newcastle, Aug. 28, 1739, *ibid*, 152-54; Oglethorpe to Trustees, July 16, 1739, *CRG*, XXII, Pt. II, 179; Oglethorpe to Verelst, Sept. 5, 1739, *ibid.*, 208; Newton D. Mereness, ed., *Travels in the American Colonies* (New York, 1916), 218-25; *S. C. Gazette*, Aug. 11, 1739.

38. *CRG*, IV, 406-07, 412-13, 419; Stephens to Verelst, Sept. 10, 1739, XXII, Pt. II, 209-11; Oglethorpe to Verelst, Oct. 9, 1739, *ibid.*, 231-36; *The St. Augustine Expedition of 1740* (Columbia, S.C., 1954), 8-10 Edward McCrady, *History of South Carolina under the Royal Government, 1719-1776* (New York, 1899), 185-87.

39. *CRG*, IV, 426-28; Tailfer and others, *True and Historical Narrative*, 89.

40. *CRG*, IV, 415, 417-18, 430-31.

41. *Ibid.*, 431-32.

42. *Ibid.*, 443-49; Oglethorpe to Trustees, Nov. 16, 1739, XXII, Pt. II, 269; *Egmont Diary*, III, 120.

43. *CRG*, IV, 495; John Fallowfield to Trustees, Dec. 1739, XXII, Pt. II, 294-96.

44. Christie to Trustees, Dec. 2, 1739, Jan. 1739/40, *CRG*, XXII, Pt. II, 278-79, 310-11; Stephens to Trustees, Jan. 28, 1739/40, *ibid.*, 304; II, 322-23; IV, 476-77, 482-83; *Egmont Diary*, III, 130-31.

45. Stephens to Trustees, Jan. 28, 1739/40, *CRG*, XXII, Pt. II, 306-09;

46. *CRG*, II, 315; *Egmont Diary*, III, 119-20, 122-25; Martyn to Causton, March 25, 1740, MS. CRG, XXX, 206-07; Verelst to Jones, March 29, 1740, *ibid.*, 228-29; XXXIII, 98-101.

47. *CRG*, IV, 589-90; John Pye to Trustees, Nov. 13, 1740, XXII, Pt. II, 433.

48. *CRG*, IV, 641-43.

49. *Ibid.*, 430-31; *Egmont Diary*, III, 123.

50. *CRG*, IV, 58-59, 66, 430-31; Stephens to Trustees, Sept. 29, 1738, XXII, Pt. I, 268; *LES*, 53, No. 1528-30; Egmont Papers, 14203, p. 215.

51. *CRG*, IV, 449.

52. *Ibid.*, 452, 499, 505, 517; V, 324.

53. *CRG*, IV, 530.

54. Jones to John Lyde, Sept. 18, 1740, Egmont Papers, 14205, pp. 140-41.

55. *Ibid.*, 141; *Egmont Diary*, III, 135.

56. *CRG*, II, 338; V, 373-74; *Egmont Diary*, III, 150, 152.

57. *CRG*, II, 344-46, 349-50, 352-54; IV, 482; MS. CRG, XXXIII, 124-31; *Egmont Diary*, III, 159, 167.

58. *Egmont Diary*, III, 172, 196-97, 207, 211; *CRG*, V, 491-92; Verelst to Stephens, April 27, 1741, MS. CRG, XXX, 324-25; a copy of this pamphlet is in Peter Force, *Tracts and Other Papers . . .* (Washington, 1838), II, last item in vol.

59. *CRG*, II, 371; V, 545.

60. *CRG*, V, 585, 667; Christie to Vernon, July 20, 1742, XXIII, 380.

61. Coulter, *Journal of William Stephens, 1741-1743*, 145, 154-55, 177; *CRG*, V, 657-86.

62. *CRG*, V, 658; Stephens to Verelst, Jan. 22, 1742/3, XXIII, 467-68.

63. *S. C. Gazette*, Oct. 31, 1743; Coulter, *Journal of William Stephens, 1741-1743*, 170; *CRG*, V, 658; *The Weekly History* (London), Aug. 7, 14, 1742 (No. 70, 71).

64. *CRG*, VI, 333-34; VII, 837.

65. *CRG*, VIII, 54, 142, 145; *Georgia Gazette*, Nov. 24, 1763, Jan. 12, Sept. 13, 1764.

CHAPTER X

1. *CRG,* IV, 655.
2. *Ibid.,* 131-32, 318-22, 599; *Supplement,* 130; Coulter, *Journal of William Stephens, 1741-43,* 68-69; *ibid., 1743-45,* 96, 218.
3. *CRG,* IV, 153-54; *Supplement,* 164; Coulter, *Journal of William Stephens, 1741-43,* 92, 215; *ibid., 1743-45,* 112; Causton Journal, Egmont Papers, 14203, pp. 25, 27.
4. *CRG,* IV, *Supplement,* 11, 19, 261; Coulter, *Journal of William Stephens, 1741-43,* 1, 132; *ibid., 1743-45,* 26, 30, 246.
5. *CRG,* IV, 55.
6. *Ibid.,* 250, 475; Causton to Trustees, March 8, 1736/7, XXI, 379; Samuel Montaigut to Oglethorpe, Dec. 17, 1734, MS. CRG, XX, 78; Coulter, *Journal of William Stephens, 1741-43,* 152; *ibid., 1743-45,* 53, 181, 264.
7. Elisha Dobree to Trustees, Feb. 10, 1734/5, MS. CRG, XX, 259.
8. Elisha Dobree to Trustees, Feb. 13, 1734/5, *ibid.,* 262.
9. Anon., Jan. 26, 1733/4, Egmont Papers, 14200, p. 153.
10. Causton to Trustees, Sept. 8, 1735, MS. CRG, XX, 301.
11. Coulter, *Journal of William Stephens, 1741-43,* 26-27.
12. *CRG,* IV, 433-34, 447.
13. Eveleigh to Oglethorpe, Oct. 19, 1734, MS. CRG, XX, 641.
14. *CRG,* IV, 40, 235-36, 462; Coulter, *Journal of William Stephens, 1741-43,* 145; Curnock, *Wesley's Journal,* I, 299.
15. *CRG,* IV, 45, 417, 482-83, 531, 655; V, 395; Stephens to Trustees, Jan. 28, 1739/40, XXII, Pt. II, 307, 308; Stephens to Trustees, Dec. 31, 1741, XXIII, 162-95; Thomas Jones to John Lyde, Sept. 18, 1740, Egmont Papers, 14205, p. 140; *S. C. Gazette,* Jan. 15, 1740/1.
16. Jones to Lyde, Sept. 18, 1740, Egmont Papers, 14205, p. 134.
17. Elisha Dobree to Trustees, Jan. 15, 1734/5, MS. CRG, XX, 104; Francis Percy [Piercy] to Oglethorpe, Feb. 16, 1734, *ibid.,* 238.
18. Amatis to Trustees, June 6, July 24, 1735, *ibid.,* 373, 383; Anon. to "My Lord," June 5, 1735, *ibid.,* 369.
19. Parker to Trustees, n. d., *ibid.,* 481.
20. Causton's Journal, Egmont Papers, 14203, p. 41.
21. *CRG,* IV, 361.
22. *CRG,* V, 179.
23. *CRG,* IV, 57; Parker to Robert Hucks, Dec. 24, 1734, MS. CRG, XX, 486; Curnock, *Wesley's Journal,* I, 307.
24. *CRG,* IV, 251-52, 257.
25. *Ibid.,* 117, *Supplement,* 117, 118, 147; Coulter, *Journal of William Stephens, 1741-43,* 67; *ibid., 1743-45,* 86-87, 103, 216.
26. *CRG,* IV, 604-06, 609.
27. *Ibid.,* 495-96; Jones to John Lyde, Sept. 18, 1740, Egmont Papers, 14205, p. 134.
28. Pye to Trustees, Sept. 23, 1743, *CRG,* XXIV, 111; Dobell to Trustees, Nov. 4, 1743, *ibid.,* 171.
29. *A New Voyage to Georgia,* By a Young Gentleman (2nd ed., London, 1737), 3, 34, 35; Coulter, *Journal of William Stephens, 1743-45,* 158.
30. Coulter, *Journal of William Stephens, 1743-45,* 176.
31. *Ibid.,* 208; *ibid., 1741-43,* 98; *Memoirs and Anecdotes of Philip Thicknesse* (Dublin, 1790), 15; Causton to his wife, March 12, 1732/3, Egmont Papers, 14200, p. 56; Curnock, *Wesley's Journal,* I, 237, 242.
32. *CRG,* IV, 212; Jones to Verelst, Feb. 8, 1738/9, XXII, Pt. II, 51.
33. Jones to Lyde, Sept. 18, 1740, Egmont Papers, 14205, pp. 129-30.
34. *Memoirs and Anecdotes of Philip Thicknesse,* 29.
35. *CRG,* I, 211; II, 36; III, 129; Brownfield to Verelst, Feb. 11, 1735/6, XXI, 112-13; Samuel Montaigut to Oglethorpe, Dec. 17, 1734, MS. CRG, XX, 77-78; Christie to Oglethorpe, Dec. 17, 1734, *ibid.,* 88; XXIX, 600, 612, 617, 620.
36. Gordon to Trustees, May 7, 1735, MS. CRG, XX, 489-90; XXIX, 610,

614. Prices for 1737-38, *ibid.*, 609-20; for 1740, Jones to John Lyde, Sept. 18, 1740, Egmont Papers, 14205, p. 130; for 1743, Dobell to Egmont, Jan. 5, 1742/3, *CRG*, XXIII, 462.

37. MS. CRG, XXIX, 612-15; inventory in Egmont Papers, 14203, pp. 259-78.

38. MS. CRG, XXIX, 610.

39. *CRG*, IV, 343, 450.

40. Eveleigh to Oglethorpe, May 30, 1735, MS. CRG, XX, 356-57.

41. *Ibid.*, XXIX, 615.

42. *Ibid.*, 609; Egmont Papers, 14203, p. 266.

43. Egmont Papers, 14203, pp. 254-56, 266; *CRG*, I, 253; III, 130.

44. MS. CRG, XXIX, 609, 610, 612, 614; Egmont Papers, 14203, pp. 254, 257.

45. Verelst to Causton, May 15, 1735, MS. CRG, XXIX, 101-02.

46. *CRG*, II, 192, 240; IV, 21, 32-33; John Pye to Verelst, June 29, 1737, *ibid.*, XXI, 490; *Egmont Diary*, II, 488; Causton to his wife, March 12, 1732/3, Egmont Papers, 14200, p. 56.

47. Oglethorpe to Verelst, Nov. 2, Dec. 3, 1735, *CRG*, XXI, 36, 50; Verelst

to Oglethorpe, n. d. (probably Nov., 1735), MS. CRG, XXIX, 189.

48. Verelst to Stephens, Sept. 17, 1741, MS. CRG, XXXI, 381; Jones to Trustees, April, 1739, *CRG*, XXII, Pt. II, 132.

49. *S. C. Gazette*, April 16, 1737; May 19, June 16, 1739.

50. *Ibid.*, Nov. 2, 1734; Jan. 25, 1734/5; Oct. 4, 1735; Sept. 10, 1743.

51. *Ibid.*, May 18, 1734; March 22, 1734/5; March 5, 1740/1; March 12, 1743/4; Feb. 18, 1744/5; June 17, Dec. 2, 1745.

52. *Ibid.*, May 18, Nov. 2, 1734; Jan. 4, 18, 1734/5; Oct. 4, 1735; Feb. 26, 1740/1.

53. *Ibid.*, Sept. 26, 1743; Jan. 2, 1743/4; Aug. 20, 1744.

54. *Ibid.*, June 13, 1743; Feb. 13, 1743/4.

55. *Ibid.*, Aug. 30, 1735; July 22, 1745.

56. *CRG*, IV, 630; Thomas Hawkins to Trustees, May 23, 1736, *ibid.*, XXI, 157; passenger list, Egmont Papers, 14207, p. 62, reproduced in *GHQ*, XXXI, 282-88.

CHAPTER XI

1. *LES*, 5, No. 117-19; *CRG*, II, 32; Martyn to Oglethorpe, May 11, 1733, MS. CRG, XXIX, 26.

2. *LES*, 98, No. 1134; Causton to Oglethorpe, Jan. 16, 1734 (incorrectly dated; probably written in July, 1735), MS. CRG, XX, 639; Susan Bowling to Peter Gordon, March 20, 1734, *ibid.*, 335-37.

3. Verelst to Causton, May 19, 1738, MS. CRG, XXIX, 534; *CRG*, IV, *Supplement*, 119-20.

4. *CRG*, VI, 13, 31, 70, 140-41, 151, 159.

5. *Ibid.*, 194.

6. *Ibid.*, VIII, 210, 595.

7. *CRG*, III, 426; *LES*, 20, No. 542-44; Egmont Papers, 14203, p. 348.

8. *CRG*, III, 426.

9. *LES*, 8, No. 192-93; Causton to Trustees, April 2, 1735, MS. CRG, XX, 575-76.

10 *LES*, 20, No. 453.

11. Elbert to Trustees, April 20, 1742, *CRG*, XXIII, 282-84.

12. *Ibid.*

13. *CRG*, I, 404; VI, 24; Verelst to Stephens, MS. CRG, XXX, 478; Stephens Journal, Egmont Papers, 14219, p. 6.

14. *LES*, 10, No. 262; 96, No. 1091; *CRG*, III, 426; II, 339-40; V, 344, 377, 389, 391; *Egmont Diary*, III, 135, 159; Egmont Papers, 14203, p. 354; Verelst to Stephens, Oct. 25, 1740, MS. CRG, XXX, 297; Stephens to Verelst, April 4, 1741, *CRG*, XXIII, 5.

15. *LES*, 11, No. 276-78; 95, No. 1054; Dobree to Trustees, March 28, 1735, MS. CRG, XX, 327.

16. *LES*, 67, No. 188; 80, No. 567; 91, No. 907.

17. *CRG*, III, 425; IV, 410-11; VI, 15, 46, 51; Pye to Trustees, Nov. 24, 1743, XXIV, 179; Stephens to Verelst, Oct. 28, 1743, *ibid.*, 150; Egmont Papers, 14203, p. 354; 14204, p. 45.

18. Coulter, *Journal of William Stephens, 1741-43*, 93, 124, 182-83, 214-15, 222.
19. *Ibid., 1743-45*, 159.
20. *Ibid.*, 163-65, 175.
21. *Ibid.*, 192.
22. *CRG*, I, 405; II, 406; VI, 17-18, 22-23, 160; Verelst to Stephens, Aug. 10, 1742, MS. CRG, XXX, 478-79; Martyn to Stephens, May 10, 1743, *ibid.*, 503; Verelst to President and Assistants, March 24, 1746, XXXI, 152.
23. Dobree to Trustees, March 28, July 8, 1735, MS. CRG, XX, 327, 655.
24. *LES*, 11, No. 282; 69, No. 258; Verelst to Causton, March 23, 1736, MS. CRG, XXIX, 356.
25. *LES*, 10, No. 248; 51, No. 1477.
26. *LES*, 69, No. 270; *CRG*, III, 426; Egmont Papers, 14203, p. 342; Delamotte to Wesley, Feb. 23, 1737/8, *ibid.*, 106, 108.
27. *LES*, 69, No. 268; 94, No. 1031, *CRG*, VII, 203; VIII, 237-38, 378; White, *Historical Collections of Georgia*, 334.
28. *LES*, 8, No. 210-11; 67, No. 187.
29. Oglethorpe to Trustees, Sept. 17, 1733, Egmont Papers, 14200, p. 113; *LES*, 41, No. 1179-82.
30. *LES*, 95, No. 1045; Christie to Trustees, March 19, May 28, 1734/5, MS. CRG, XX, 263, 329-30.
31. *LES*, 8, No. 210; Dobree to Trustees, July 8, 1735, MS. CRG, XX, 655; Causton to Trustees, June 20, 1735, *ibid.*, 524.
32. *CRG*, IV, 506, 509, 573-74; White, *Historical Collections of Georgia*, 332.
33. *CRG*, IV, 205, 416-17; *S. C. Gazette*, April 12, 1739.
34. *LES*, 10, No. 265; *CRG*, IV, 23, 39, 41, 46; Stephens to Trustees, Dec. 30, 1737, XXII, Pt. I, 43; Causton's Journal, Egmont Papers, 14203, pp. 20, 46, 60.
35. *S. C. Gazette*, April 12, 1739.
36. Fox to Trustees, July 6, 1735, MS. CRG, XX, 649-50.
37. *CRG*, III, 425; John Brownfield to Trustees, May 17, 1737, XXI, 465-66; Causton's Journal, Egmont Papers, 14203, pp. 11, 27, 48, 71; *ibid.*, 214.
38. Fox to Trustees, Aug. 1, 1741, *CRG*, XXIII, 81-83.
39. Coulter, *Journal of William Stephens, 1741-43*, 26.
40. *LES*, 23-24, No. 670-71; *CRG*, II, 11; Martyn to Bailiffs and Recorder of Savannah, July 27, 1734, MS. CRG, XXIX, 59; Martyn to Causton, Oct. 28, 1734, *ibid.*, 67.
41. Martyn to Oglethorpe, Nov. 22, 1733, MS. CRG, XXIX, 40; Causton to Oglethorpe, Jan. 16, 1734 (incorrect date), XX, 638.
42. Martyn to Vanderplank, July 27, 1734, *ibid.*, XXIX, 58.
43. *CRG*, II, 452, 455-56; MS. CRG, XX, 569; Paul Hamilton to Causton, May 27, 1734, *ibid.*, 529.
44. *LES*, 65, No. 142; 74, No. 418; *S. C. Gazette*, Jan. 26, 1737/8.
45. Peter Gordon to Trustees, May 7, 1735, MS. CRG, XX, 491.
46. *LES*, 24, No. 672; 82, No. 649.
47. *LES*, 82, No. 650; 24, No. 672; *CRG*, IV, 111, 624; V, 471; *Egmont Diary*, III, 200; Verelst to Causton, Aug. 4, 1738, MS. CRG, XXIX, 586; Verelst to Stephens, Sept. 28, 1739, *ibid*, XXX, 172.
48. Townsend to Trustees, April 21, 1743, *CRG*, XXIII, 287.
49. *LES*, 99, No. 1186.
50. *CRG*, IV, 188-89; George Whitefield, *A Journal of a Voyage from Gibraltar to Georgia* (London, 1738), 10.
51. *CRG*, IV, 61-62, 426; *LES*, 99, No. 1186.
52. Mary Townsend to Trustees, May 29, 1739, *CRG*, XXII, Pt. II, 145-50.
53. *CRG*, I, 371, 404; II, 404; V, 353-54; VI, 24; Townsend to Trustees, April 21, 1742, XXIII, 286-88; Verelst to Stephens, Aug. 10, 1742, MS. CRG, XXX, 478; *Egmont Diary*, III, 143-44.
54. *CRG*, IV, 623-25.
55. *LES*, 24, No. 671, 674.
56. *CRG*, IV, 630-31.
57. *CRG*, IV, Supplement, 61, 75-77; *S. C. Gazette*, May 7, 1741.
58. *CRG*, IV, Supplement, 78-79.
59. *Ibid.*, 177-78.

60. Thomas Jones to Trustees, Feb. 23, 1742/3, *CRG*, XXIII, 496; MS. CRG, XXX, 544; Coulter, *Journal of William Stephens, 1741-43*, 115; A. S. Salley, Jr., ed., *Register of St. Phil-* ip's *Parish, Charles Town, S. C., 1720-1758*, 209; *CRG*, VIII, 150-51; Bonds, Bills of Sale, Etc., 1755-1762 (Ga. Dept. of Archives and History), p. 426.

CHAPTER XII

1. *CRG*, II, 94, 96, 98; *Egmont Diary*, II, 170, 172; Verelst to Bailiffs and Recorder of Savannah, May 15, 1735, MS. CRG, XXIX, 113; XXXII, 272-76; *LES*, 41, No. 1178; 65, No. 123.
2. *CRG*, I, 207; II, 11; Robert Parker Jr., to Peter Gordon, March 2, 1734 (O.S.), MS. CRG, XX, 232; Samuel Quincy to Verelst, Aug. 28, 1735, *ibid.*, 292-93; Causton to Oglethorpe, Jan. 16, 1734 (O. S.), incorrectly dated, *ibid.*, 632, 639; Christie to Trustees, March 19, May 28 (incorrectly dated), 1734/5, *ibid.*, 624, 330; Causton to Trustees, March 10, 1734 (O. S.), *ibid*, 565; Elisha Dobree to Verelst, July 8, 1735, *ibid.*, 655; President and Assistants to Verelst, July 19, 1750, *CRG*, XXVI, 16; *LES*, 37, No. 1056.
3. *CRG*, II, 100; Verelst to Bailiffs and Recorder of Savannah, May 15, 1735, MS. CRG, XXIX, 113; *LES*, 4, No. 104.
4. *CRG*, IV, 570; James Carwell to Trustees, Oct. 15, 1741, *ibid.*, XXIII, 113; Christie to Trustees, March 19, 1734/5, MS. CRG, XX, 621-22.
5. *LES*, 9, No. 220; 67, No. 195-96.
6. Isaac Chardon to Oglethorpe, Oct. 26, 1734, MS. CRG, XX, 32; Edward Jenkins and John Dearne to Oglethorpe, n. d. (written in 1735), *ibid.*, 629; *LES*, 9, No. 219; *CRG*, IV, *Supplement*, 139; V, 346; *Egmont Diary*, III, 137.
7. James Carwell to Trustees, Oct. 15, 1741, *CRG*, XXIII, 113-16.
8. *LES*, 37, No. 1057-58; 58, No. 1642; 90, No. 894; Egmont Papers, 14203, p. 350.
9. Causton to Trustees, March 24, 1734 (O. S.), MS. CRG, XX, 550-51; Eveleigh to Oglethorpe, Oct. 19, 1734, *ibid.*, 641.

10. Peter Gordon to Trustees, May 7, 1735, *ibid.*, 491-92.
11. *LES*, 72, No. 333; *CRG*, III, 426; Verelst to Causton, Nov. 28, 1735, MS. CRG, XXIX, 192; *S. C. Gazette*, Jan. 26, March 30, 1737/8; Egmont Papers, 14203, p. 352.
12. *CRG*, IV, 416-17; VIII, 211; *LES*, 37, No. 1057.
13. Elisha Dobree to Verelst, July 28, 1735, MS. CRG, XX, 655.
14. *CRG*, I, 417; II, 409, V, 691; John Brownfield to Trustees, May 17, 1737, XXI, 465, 468-69; Martyn to Stephens, May 10, 1743, MS. CRG, XXX, 503-04; *ibid.*, 540; *LES*, 20, No. 541.
15. *LES*, 36, No. 1031, 1034; 58, No. 1638; 102, No. 1275; William Gough to Oglethorpe, Nov. 11, 1736, *CRG*, XXI, 252; John Brownfield to Trustees, May 17, 1737, *ibid.*, 468-69; Causton to Oglethorpe, Jan. 16, 1734 (O. S.), incorrectly dated, MS. CRG, XX, 637; XXX, 540.
16. Stephens to Trustees, Jan. 19, 1737/8, *CRG*, XXII, Pt. I, 75; Martyn to Stephens, May 19, 1738, MS. CRG, XXIX, 506-07.
17. Verelst to William Bradley, Dec. 14, 1737, MS. CRG, XXIX, 493.
18. *CRG*, IV, *Supplement*, 51-52; Egmont Papers, 14207, p. 61.
19. *CRG*, VIII, 595; Egmont Papers, 14219, p. 6.
20. *LES*, 52, No. 1504-07; 73 No. 388; 96, No. 1066.
21. *CRG*, IV, 543.
22. *CRG*, III, 425; Egmont Papers, 14203, pp. 214, 354; 14219, p. 7.
23. *CRG*, IV, 543-44.
24. Stephens to Martyn, Aug. 31, 1745, *ibid.*, XXIV, 418-19; *LES*, 45, No. 1291-94.
25. John Dobell to Trustees, Oct. 31, 1743, *CRG*, XXIV, 159-60; Coulter,

Journal of William Stephens, 1743-45, 33.

26. *CRG*, VII, 208, 323.
27. *CRG*, VI, 374; VIII, 211.
28. *LES*, 45, No. 1299; 95, No. 1055; John Brownfield to Trustees, May 17, 1737, *CRG*, XXI, 467-68.
29. *LES*, 66, No. 179; 69, No. 253; 71, No. 329; 102, No. 1283.
30. Oglethorpe to Trustees, Aug. 12, 1733, Egmont Papers, 14200, p. 108; *LES*, 33, No. 940; *Egmont Diary*, II, 370.
31. Elizabeth Stanley to Oglethorpe, Jan. 16, 1734/5, MS. CRG, XX, 129-30.
32. *Egmont* Diary, II, 370, 375, 404; Verelst to Causton, March 23, 1736 (O. S.), May 20, 1737, MS. CRG, XXIX, 357, 382; *CRG*, II, 198.
33. Egmont Papers, 14203, p. 354.
34. *CRG*. IV, 630; *LES*, 50, No. 1429.
35. *CRG*, I, 456-57; Coulter, *Journal of William Stephens, 1743-45*, 59, 182-83.
36. *CRG*, VI, 404; VII, 311.
37. *CRG*. II, 11.
38. George Symes to Oglethorpe, Jan. 2, 1734 (O. S.), MS. CRG, XX, 97.
39. George Symes to Oglethorpe, n. d., *ibid.*, 451.
40. *LES*, 51-52, No. 1478-81; 77, No. 487-88; Causton Journal, Egmont Papers, 14203, p. 47.
41. *LES*, 26, No. 730; 52, No. 1480; 70, No. 290; 80, No. 582.
42. *LES*, 40, No. 1138.
43. *CRG*, II, 345; *LES*, 40, No. 1138-39; Causton to Oglethorpe, Jan. 16, 1734 (O. S.), incorrectly dated, MS. CRG, XX, 638.
44. *CRG*, II, 11; Verelst to Causton, Aug. 11, 1737, MS. CRG, XXIX, 426; XXXII, 28-33.
45. Joseph Hetherington to Oglethorpe, March 22, 1734/5, MS. CRG, XX, 530; *CRG*, II, 127; *LES*, 75, No. 447.
46. Peter Gordon to Trustees, May 7, 1735, MS. CRG, XX, 491-92; Samuel Marcer to Trustees, April 25, 1735, *ibid.*, 349-50; Verelst to Causton, May 15, 1735, *ibid.*, XXIX, 103.
47. *CRG*, II, 363; 410; IV, 140, 143, 207, 211-12, 222, 327, 361-62, 365;

IV, *Supplement*, 153, 158, 159, 163, 174; Eveleigh to Verelst, May 1, 1736, XXI, 149; MS. CRG, XXX, 541-44; XXXIII, 89; XXXV, 256; Egmont Papers, 14203, p. 352.
48. *Egmont Diary*, III, 58.
49. Stephens to Verelst, Nov. 20, 1740, *CRG*, XXII, Pt. II, 444-47.
50. *CRG*, I, 404; III, 426 V. 664; VI, 17; John Brownfield to Trustees, May 17, 1737, XXI, 468; Verelst to Stephens, Aug. 10, 1742, MS. CRG, XXX, 478; Egmont Papers, 14203, p. 352; 14207, p. 61.
51. *CRG*, IV, 655.
52. *CRG*, IV, *Supplement*, 34, 130, 195, 258.
53. *CRG*, IV, 655-56; V, 395; *LES*, 40, No. 1139.
54. *CRG*, IV, *Supplement*, 102-03.
55. *CRG*, VI, 30-31.
56. *Ibid.*, 92-93; Coulter, *Journal of William Stephens, 1743-45*, 69.
57. Coulter, *Journal of William Stephens, 1743-45*, 7.
58. *Ibid.*, 70, 100-01.
59. *Ibid.*, 142, 144, 148-49, 189, 231.
60. *CRG*, VI, 176, 440; VII, 228, 718, 863.
61. *CRG*, I, 549; II, 509; VI, 315; Martyn to Henry Parker, July 14, 1750, MS. CRG, XXXI, 420; Verelst to Henry Parker and Assistants, Aug. 16, 1750, *ibid.*, 451.
62. James Habersham to Martyn, Jan. 24, 1750 (O. S.), *CRG*, XXVI, 137-39.
63. *CRG*, VI, 430; VII, 718; *Georgia Gazette*, Jan. 12, Sept. 13, 1764.
64. *LES*, 58, No. 1643; Martyn to John Vanderplank, July 27, 1734, MS. CRG, XXIX, 58; Martyn to Bailiffs and Recorder of Savannah, July 27, 1734; *ibid.*, 59; Stephens to Trustees, Aug. 26, 1738, *CRG*, XXII, Pt. I, 229.
65. Egmont Papers, 14207, p. 61; *CRG*, VI, 17, 74, 106-07; J. Norton Wright to Trustees, June 12, 1743, XXIV, 37; Coulter, *Journal of William Stephens, 1743-45*, 118-19, 123-24.
66. *CRG*, VI, 30-31; Thomas Jones to Trustees, April, 1739, XXII, Pt. II, 132.
67. *CRG*, IV, 676.

68. Causton to Trustees, Dec. 1, 1741, *CRG*, XXIII, 157.
69. *CRG*, IV, *Supplement*, 207.
70. *Ibid*, 207-10.
71. *CRG*, V, 574; VI, 20-21, 30-31.
72. Coulter, *Journal of William Stephens, 1741-43*, 32.
73. *Ibid.*, 151; *CRG*, VI, 51.
74. Coulter, *Journal of William Stephens, 1741-43*, 95-96.
75. *CRG*, VII, 101.
76. *CRG*, V, 656; VI, 49; Coulter, *Journal of William Stephens, 1741-43*, 131.
77. *CRG*, VI, 51, 74.
78. Coulter, *Journal of William Stephens, 1741-43*, 201.
79. *Ibid.*, *1743-45*, 78.
80. *CRG*, VI, 231; President and Assistants to Martyn, Nov. 5, 1748, XXV, 337-38.
81. Egmont Papers, 14207, p. 61.
82. *CRG*, VII, 706, 790.
83. Store accounts, in "Bonds, Bills of Sale," Book HH (Ga. Dept. of Archives and History), p. 4.
84. *LES*, 5, No. 120-23; 103, No. 1303; Egmont Papers, 14207, p. 61.
85. *LES*, 14, No. 395; 58, No. 1661; *CRG*, I, 187; II, 72-73; Causton to Oglethorpe, Jan. 16, 1734 (O. S.) incorrectly dated, MS. CRG, XX, 633; Martyn to Causton, Oct. 28, 1734, XXIX, 70.

86. Thomas Young to Oglethorpe, Jan. 13, 1734/5, MS. CRG, XX, 124-25.
87. Young to Trustees, June 22, 1735, *ibid.*, 394-95.
88. Causton to Trustees, June 20, 1735, *ibid.*, 520-23.
89. Verelst to Causton, Aug. 7, 1735, *ibid.*, XXIX, 149; William Gough to Oglethorpe, Nov. 13, 1736, *CRG*, XXI, 251, 253; *LES*, 76, No. 454.
90. Verelst to Stephens, Aug. 4, 1738, MS. CRG, XXIX, 566-67.
91. *CRG*, IV, 231; Stephens to Trustees, Nov. 21, 1738, XXII, Pt. I, 323.
92. *CRG*, IV, 246, 248.
93. Stephens to Verelst, Dec. 31, 1740, *CRG*, XXII, Pt. II, 472; *LES*, 38, No. 1093.
94. *LES*, 48, No. 1387, 1389.
95. *CRG*, II, 391; V, 597-98; Martyn to Stephens, March 3, 1741, (O.S.), MS. CRG, XXX, 432-33.
96. Stephens to Martyn, Oct. 16, 1742, *CRG*, XXIII, 401-02; V, 656.
97. John Dobell to Trustees, Sept. 1; 1743, *CRG*, XXIV, 89.
98. *CRG*, III, 426; IV, 676.
99. *CRG*, VI, 108.
100. *Ibid.*, 164.
101. *Ibid.*, 166.
102. *Ibid.*, 343; VII, 809.
103. *CRG*, VII, 524, 551, 685; VIII, 291, 408, 595; IX, 593-94; X, 4-5, 416, 459, 646, 911.

CHAPTER XIII

1. *LES*, 55, No. 1585; Egmont Papers, 14207, p. 61; *GHQ*, XLIV, 223-24.
2. *LES*, 55, No. 1585; 56, No. 1587-89; Oglethorpe to Trustees, Sept. 17, 1733, Egmont Papers, 14200, p. 115.
3. *LES*, 8, No 202; *Egmont Diary*, II, 69; Oglethorpe to Trustees, July 16, 1739, *CRG*, XXII, Pt. II, 178; V, 209.
4. Martyn to Oglethorpe, March 27, 1734, MS. CRG, XXIX, 49.
5. *Egmont Diary*, II, 69-70.
6. *LES*, 55-56, No. 1586; 79, No. 546; 102, No. 1280; *CRG*, 11, 88; Verelst to Oglethorpe, Jan. 9, 1735 (O. S.), MS. CRG, XXIX, 220.
7. Verelst to Causton, May 20, 1737, MS. CRG, XXIX, 381-82.

8. Verelst to Causton, Aug. 11, 1737, *ibid.*, 424.
9. *Ibid.*, 423-34; *CRG*, XXI, 442-43.
10. Stephens to Verelst, Aug. 13, 1737, *CRG*, XXI, 441; Journal of the ship Mary Ann, Captain Thomas Shubrick, 1737, *ibid.*, 443-45; Stephens to Trustees, Oct. 26, 1737, *ibid.*, 512.
11. Stephens to Trustees, Oct. 26, 1737, *ibid.*, 512.
12. *CRG*, IV, 7-11; Stephens to Trustees, Oct. 26, 1737, XXI, 513; *S. C. Gazette*, Nov. 5, 1737.
13. White, *Historical Collections*, 332-33.
14. *LES*, 19, No. 519; 75-76, No. 448-50; 94, No. 1006.
15. *CRG*, I, 304-05, 318; *Egmont Diary*, II, 365, 484; Martyn to Whitefield,

May 19, 1738, MS. CRG, XXIX, 509-10; XXXII, 553-54.

16. Whitefield to Verelst, May 17, June 3, 1737, CRG, XXI, 394-96; Verelst to Whitefield, June 30, 1737, MS. CRG, XXIX, 394-95; Verelst to Causton, Jan. 6, 1737 (O. S.), ibid., 496; Egmont Diary, II, 417; S. C. Gazette, May 4, 1738; George Whitefield, A Journal of a Voyage from Gibraltar to Georgia (London, 1738), 33; CRG, IV, 142; Causton to Trustees, May 26, 1738, XXII, Pt. I, 160-61.

17. George Whitefield, A Continuation of the Reverend Mr. Whitefield's Journal, from his arrival at Savannah, to his Return to London (London, 1737), 2-5.

18. Anon. (undoubtedly Whitefield) to James Habersham, June 10, 1738, Georgia Records, Miscellaneous 1732-96, Force Transcripts, Library of Congress; Whitefield, Continuation of Whitefield's Journal, 6.

19. Whitefield, Continuation of . . . Whitefield's Journal, 11-12; Whitefield, A Continuation of the Reverend Mr. Whitefield's Journal, from his arrival at London, to his departure from thence on his way to Georgia (London, 1739) passim; Whitefield, A Continuation of the Reverend Mr. Whitefield's Journal, from his embarking after the Embargo to his arrival at Savannah in Georgia (London, 1740), 7, 11; CRG, I, 333-34, 348; II, 259-60, 273-74; IV, 487-88; V, 74, 79-81, 83, 85-86; Stephens to Trustees, Aug. 26, 1738, XXII, Pt. 230; Martyn to Stephens, June 1, 1739, MS. CRG, XXX, 83-84; Verelst to Oglethorpe, June 11, 1739, ibid, 90; S. S. Gazette, July 14, Aug. 11, 1739; Egmont Diary, II, 512-13, 516; Egmont Papers, 14209, pp. 383-85.

20. CRG, I, 327, 329-30; IV, 212, 487, 490; Martyn to Norris, July 11, 1739, MS. CRG, XXX, 98-99; XXXII, 607-08; XXXIII, 20-23.

21. Whitefield to Verelst, Jan. 16, 1739/40, Egmont Papers, 14204, pp. 301-02.

22. Whitefield, A Continuation of the Reverend Mr. Whitefield's Journal, after his arrival at Georgia, to a few days after his second return thither from Philadelphia (London, 1741), 4; CRG, IV, 491.

23. White, Historical Collections, 332-33.

24. Ibid., 332-35.

25. Ibid., 331; Whitefield to a friend at Bethesda, March 21, 1745/6, ibid.

26. [Jonathan Barber and James Habersham], Orphan-Letters to the Reverend Mr. Whitefield (Glasgow, 1741), 23-24.

27. CRG, IV, 532; Whitefield, Continuation of . . . Whitefield's Journal . . . arrival at Georgia . . . return thither from Philadelphia, 10.

28. Whitefield, ibid., 5, 14; S. C. Gazette, March 8, 1739/40.

29. CRG, IV, 627; Supplement, 15, 21, 53; Thomas Jones to John Lyde, Sept. 18, 1740, Egmont Papers, 14205, p. 138.

30. CRG, IV, 636, 644-45; S. C. Gazette, Aug. 30, 1740; Barber and Habersham, Orphan-Letters, 3.

31. LES, 38, No. 1100; CRG, I, 387-88; Stephens to Verelst, Feb. 4, 1741/2, XXIII, 211; Orton to Trustees, March 4, 1741/2, ibid., 228-29; Verelst to Stephens, Sept. 17, 1741, MS. CRG, XXX, 369; XXXIII, 180-81.

32. Coulter, Journal of William Stephens, 1741-43, 29-34, 36-37; Whitefield to Trustees, Aug. 17, 1742, CRG, XXIII, 391-92; Thomas Jones to Verelst, April 26, 1742, ibid., 301.

33. Martyn to Habersham, May 10, 1743; MS. CRG, XXX, 490-91.

34. Coulter, Journal of William Stephens, 1741-43, 119; John Dobell to Trustees, Nov. 30, 1742, CRG, XXIII, 436.

35. Coulter, Journal of William Stephens, 1741-43, 41-42, 76-77; Martyn to Stephens, May 10, 1743, MS. CRG, XXX, 516.

36. CRG, I, 371; IV, 506, 509; Supplement, 166-68; V, 359-60; Whitefield to Trustees, March 10, 1739/40, XXII, Pt. II, 359; White, Historical Collections, 332; MS. CRG, XXIII,

109-11; Verelst to Whitefield, June 11, 1740, XXX, 269.

37. George Whitefield, *A Short Account of God's Dealings with the Reverend Mr. George Whitefield . . . From His Infancy to the Time of His entering into Holy Orders . . .* (London, 1740), 9-10.

38. Whitefield, *Journal of a Voyage from Gibraltar to Georgia*, 26-27.

39. Whitefield, *Journal from Embarking after the Embargo to Arrival in Georgia*, 24.

40. June, 1740, marginal note in Egmont Papers, 14204, pp. 417-20; Barber and Habersham, *Orphan-Letters*, 21.

41. CRG, V, 358-59.

42. *Ibid.*, 360, 450; Whitefield to Trustees, March 10, 1739/40, XXII, Pt. II, 359; Verelst to Whitefield, June 11, 1740, MS. CRG, XXX, 271; Martyn to Bailiffs and Recorder of Savannah, June 6, 1740, *ibid.*, 110; *Egmont Diary*, III, 204; Whitefield to Egmont, Jan. 28, 1739 (O. S.), Egmont Papers, 14204, 317-18; *S. C. Gazette*, March 8, 1739/40.

43. Habersham to Whitefield, n. d., Barber and Habersham, *Orphan-Letters*, 7.

44. Barber to Whitefield, March 21, 1740/1, *ibid.*, 3-5.

45. *Ibid.*, 9.

46. *Ibid.*, 10-11.

47. *Ibid.*, 12; White, *Historical Collections*, 334.

48. Barber and Habersham, *Orphan-Letters*, 14-15; White, *Historical Collections*, 332.

49. Barber and Habersham, *Orphan-Letters*, 19-20; White, *Historical Collections*, 334.

50. Barber and Habersham, *Orphan-Letters*, 15-16.

51. Barber to Whitefield, *ibid.*, 3.

52. *LES*, 10, No. 241-43; 2 letters from Edward Jenkins and John Dearne to Thomas Siddons, the first dated March 18, 1734/5, the second undated but from internal evidence, written in 1735, MS. CRG, XX, 335, 629.

53. Stephens to Verelst, Dec. 31, 1740, CRG, XXII, Pt. II, 473.

54. Barber and Habersham, *Orphan-*

Letters, 13-14; White, *Historical Collections*, 332-35.

55. CRG, IV, *Supplement*, 59.

56. Barber and Habersham, *Orphan-Letters*, 17; White, *Historical Collections*, 335.

57. CRG, VI, 40-41; Coulter, *Journal of William Stephens, 1741-43*, 110.

58. Coulter, *Journal of William Stephens, 1741-43*, 116; CRG, V, 655.

59. Coulter, *Journal of William Stephens 1741-43*, 112, 117-18; CRG, V, 631-32.

60. White, *Historical Collections*, 332.

61. *Ibid.*, 333.

62. CRG, VIII, 276-77, 686.

63. *Georgia Gazette*, Nov. 24, Dec. 15, 1763.

64. *LES*, 30, No. 871-74; 57, No. 1610; Egmont Papers, 14200, p. 61; Oglethorpe to Trustees, Aug. 12, 1733, *ibid.*, 108.

65. Oglethorpe to Trustees, about Dec., 1733, Egmont Papers, 14200, p. 129.

66. *Ibid.*; Martyn to Causton, Oct. 28, 1734, MS. CRG, XXIX, 68-69.

67. Jenkins to Oglethorpe, Jan. 20, 1734/5, MS. CRG, XX, 155.

68. CRG, II, 93-94; *Egmont Diary*, II, 170.

69. CRG, II, 94; instructions about William Little, May 1, 1735, MS. CRG, XXXII, 271-72; Verelst to Bailiffs and Recorder of Savannah, May 15, 1735, XXIX, 114-15.

70. Thomas Christie to Trustees, May 28, 1735 (incorrectly dated), MS. CRG, XX, 331, 460; Jenkins and Dearne to Oglethorpe, n. d., *ibid.*, 630.

71. CRG, IV, 508-09.

72. Dobell to Trustees, Sept. 1, 1743, CRG, XXIV, 89.

73. CRG, VII, 276; VIII, 118, 200.

74. CRG, II, 11; MS. CRG, XXXII, 28-33; Oglethorpe to Trustees, May 14, 1733, Egmont Papers, 14200, p. 65.

75. *LES*, 39, No. 1120; *S. C. Gazette*, Aug. 25, 1733.

76. *LES*, 35, No. 991-92; 39, No. 1121.

77. *LES*, 35, No. 993; CRG, I, 126-27; II, 35; Martyn to Oglethorpe, June 13, 1733, MS. CRG, XXIX, 27-28.

78. Moore, *Voyage to Georgia*, 26-27.
79. Mercer to Trustees, April 25, 1735, MS. CRG, XX, 346-51.
80. *LES*, 35, No. 992; William Gough to Oglethorpe, Nov. 13, 1736, *CRG*, XXI, 248.
81. Coulter, *Journal of William Stephens 1743-45*, 22.
82. *CRG*, IV, 54, 63-64, 84; Stephens to Trustees, Jan. 19, 1737/8, XXII, Pt. I, 70-71.
83. *CRG*, VI, 379.
84. Whitefield to Verelst, Jan. 28, 1739/40, *CRG*, XXII, Pt. I, 350; IV, 317; *Egmont Diary*, III, 119.
85. Egmont Papers, 14203, p. 214.
86. *CRG*, IV, 217.
87. *CRG*, III, 425-26; character of the persons who signed the representation for Negroes, Dec. 9, 1738, Egmont Papers, 14203, p. 350.
88. *CRG*, IV, 336.
89. *LES*, 41, No. 1174; *Egmont Diary*, III, 176; Potter to Oglethorpe, Dec. 16, 1734, MS. CRG, XX, 70; *CRG*, IV, 434, 473.
90. Potter to Egmont, Dec. 17, 1734. MS. CRG, XX, 73; Samuel Quincy to Egmont, Dec. 17, 1734, *ibid.*, 74; *CRG*, IV, 471-73, 483, 492, 511.
91. *CRG*, IV, 533.
92. *Ibid.*, 492, 598, 642, 676; V, 356; Oglethorpe to Trustees, Jan. 24, 1739/40, XXII, Pt. II, 301-02; Stephens to Verelst, Nov. 20, 1740, *ibid.*, 443; *Egmont Diary*, III, 135.
93. *CRG*, I, 385; II, 367-68; IV, *Supplement*, 253-57; Verelst to Stephens, MS. CRG, XXX, 344; Verelst to Mercer, Sept. 17, 1741, *ibid.*, 387; XXXII, 154-59, 169-75; *Egmont Diary*, III, 215, 222, 224; *S. C. Gazette*, Nov. 7, 1741.
94. Coulter, *Journal of William Stephens, 1741-43*, 12; *CRG*, VI, 4; John Dobell to Trustees, Nov. 4, 1743, XXIV, 169.
95. Coulter, *Journal of William Ste-

phens, 1741-43*, 117; *CRG*, V, 655; *LES*, 39, No. 1121-23.
96. *CRG*, VII, 386-87; IX, 186; John Dobell to Trustees, Nov. 4, 1743, XXIV, 169-70.
97. *CRG*, I, 490, 503, 527; .VI, *passim;* Stephens to Verelst, Dec. 15, 1746, XXV, 145-46; Verelst to Stephens, March 1, 1745 (O. S.), July 25, 1746, March 24, 1746 (O. S.), MS. CRG, XXXI, 60, 84, 153; Martyn to President and Assistants, March 11, 1748/9, *ibid.*, 278; XXXIII, 350-52.
98. *CRG*, I, 557-58, 573-74; II, 510-11, 520; VI, 315-16, 337, 353, 549, 638; XXVI, 32-35, 40-41, 266; MS. CRG, XXXI, 419-20, 571-72, 575, 580-81, 589.
99. *CRG*, VI, 379; VII, 205, 410, 434, 481; XIII, 165.
100. *LES*, 39, No. 1124; *CRG*, VI, 347, 397-98; VII, 161, 204, 810.
101. *LES*, 18-19, No. 514-17.
102. *S. C. Gazette*, Aug. 25, 1733; Oglethorpe to Trustees, Aug. 12, 1733, Egmont Papers, 14200, p. 508.
103. Oglethorpe to Trustees, Aug. 12, 1733, Egmont Papers, 14200, p. 508.
104. Jenkins to Oglethorpe, Jan. 20, 1734/5, MS. CRG, XX, 155-56.
105. *LES*, 9, No. 220; 67, No. 195; Jenkins and Dearne to Oglethorpe, n. d. [1735], MS. CRG, XX, 629.
106. *Ibid.*, Fitzwalter to Oglethorpe, Jan. 16, 1734/5, MS. CRG, XX, 113.
107. *CRG*, II, 344-45; Christie to Trustees, May 24, 1737, XXI, 429-30; Jenkins to Oglethorpe, Jan. 20, 1734/5, MS. CRG, XX, 155; *LES*, 18-19, No. 516-17.
108. *S. C. Gazette*, Sept. 6, 1742.
109. *CRG*, V, 659; Stephens to Verelst, March 8, 1742/3, XXIII, 535-38; Stephens to Verelst, Oct. 18, 1743, XXIV, 139-40; British Public Record Office, Treasury I, Bundle 393, fos. 19-20, Library of Congress transcripts.

CHAPTER XIV

1. *LES*, 36, No. 1022.
2. *Ibid.*, No. 1018-24; Martyn to Causton, Oct. 28, 1734, MS. CRG, XXIX,

69; PRO, Treasury I, Bundle, 393, fos. 22-23, Library of Congress transcripts.

3. E. Merton Coulter, ed., "A List of the First Shipload of Georgia Settlers," *GHQ*, XXXI, 282-88.
4. *Ibid.*, *S. C. Gazette*, Aug. 25, 1733.
5. *S. C. Gazette*, Aug. 25, 1733.
6. *LES*, 36, No. 1018; 88, No. 828; Oglethorpe to Trustees, Aug. 12, 1733, Egmont Papers, 14200, pp. 106, 108.
7. *LES*, 99, No. 1173; Oglethorpe to Trustees, about Dec., 1733, Egmont Papers, 14200, pp. 127-29.
8. *LES*, 36, No. 1019.
9. *S. C. Gazette*, May 11, 1734.
10. *LES*, 36, No. 1022; *CRG*, II, 71; *Egmont Diary*, II, 128; Martyn to Causton, Oct. 28, 1734, MS. CRG, XXIX, 69.
11. *LES*, 36, No. 1021.
12. *CRG*, II, 72-73; Martyn to Causton, Oct. 28, 1734, MS. CRG, XXIX, 70.
13. Martyn to Causton, Oct. 28, 1734, MS. CRG, XXIX, 68-69.
14. *LES*, 47, No. 1366; 63-64, No. 76-81; *CRG*, I, 190-91; II, 70, 79.
15. *Egmont Diary*, II, 157; *CRG*, I, 209.
16. Oglethorpe to Trustees, about Dec., 1733, Egmont Papers, 14200, p. 129; Oglethorpe, "State of the Colony of Georgia," March, 1734/5, *ibid.*, 519.
17. Jenkins and Dearne to Oglethorpe, n. d. (1735, from internal evidence), MS. CRG, XX, 629.
18. John Brownfield to Trustees, May 17, 1737, *CRG*, XXI, 466; Edward Jenkins to Oglethorpe, Jan. 20, 1734/5, MS. CRG, XX, 155.
19. *LES*, 47, No. 1366; Verelst to Bailiffs and Recorder of Savannah, May 15, 1735, MS. CRG, XXIX, 106-07; Verelst to Causton, March 23, 1736 (O. S.), *ibid.*, 349.
20. *CRG*, IV, 512-13; *LES*, 51, No. 1453.
21. *CRG*, IV, 487, 491; Whitefield to Verelst, Jan. 28, 1739/40, XXII, Pt. II, 351.
22. White, *Historical Collections*, 332, 334. This age for Richard does not agree with *LES*, 36, No. 1023.
23. *CRG*, IV, 505-09; Whitefield to Trustees, March 10, 1739/40, XXII, Pt. II, 359; MS. CRG, XXXIII, 23, 29.
24. Oglethorpe to Trustees, April 2, 1740, *CRG*, XXII, Pt. II, 339-41.
25. *CRG*, IV, 523, 539-41.
26. *Ibid.*, 544, 546; Whitefield, *Continuation of . . . Whitefield's Journal . . . Arrival at Georgia, to . . . second return from Philadelphia*, 16.
27. White, *Historical Collections*, 332-33.
28. Whitefield to Trustees, May 19, 1740, *CRG*, XXII, Pt. II, 372-74.
29. *CRG*, V, 352.
30. *CRG*, IV, 588.
31. *Ibid.*, 596-97.
32. *CRG*, V, 333-34; *Egmont Diary*, II, 133.
33. *CRG*, I, 370; II, 323-24; IV, *Supplement*, 57-58; V, 332-35, 351; Verelst to Stephens, June 11, 1740, MS. CRG, XXX, 252; Verelst to Oglethorpe, June 11, 1740, *ibid.*, 266; instructions about orphans to Bailiffs and Recorder of Savannah, XXXIII, 109-11; *Egmont Diary*, III, 144, 204.
34. *CRG*, IV, 676; V, 554; VI, 5.
35. Jones to Verelst, July 1, 1741, *CRG*, XXIII, 53-54; Stephens to Verelst, June 9, 1742, *ibid.*, 341-42.
36. *CRG*, IV, 427.
37. *Ibid.*, 574.
38. *Ibid.*, *Supplement*, 11-12.
39. Coulter, *Journal of William Stephens, 1741-43*, 70.
40. Philip Thicknesse to his mother, Nov. 3, 1736, *CRG*, XXI, 255-56.
41. Coulter, *Journal of William Stephens, 1741-43*, 70, 110; Oglethorpe, Proceedings, MS. CRG, XXXV, 528.
42. Coulter, *Journal of William Stephens, 1741-43*, 110.
43. *Ibid.*, 110-112.
44. *CRG*, V, 657; List of Military Strength of Georgia, MS. CRG, XXXV, 556, 558.
45. Oglethorpe to Newcastle, Nov. 24, 1742, MS. CRG, XXXV, 544; Declaration of Nottaway, Nov. 22, 1742, XXXVI, 54-55; John Dobell to Trustees, Nov. 30, 1742, *CRG*, XXIII, 437-38; Coulter, *Journal of William Stephens, 1741-43*, 142-43.
46. Coulter, *Journal of William Stephens, 1741-43*, 166-67, 177, 179; Oglethorpe to Newcastle, March 12, 21, 1742/3, MS. CRG, XXXVI, 97-98; 104-05; one of Oglethorpe's officers

to a friend, March 25, 1743, *ibid.*, 154-56.

47. *S. C. Gazette*, April 18, 1743.

48. Coulter, *Journal of William Stephens, 1741-43*, 200, 210.

49. *Ibid.*, 202; *1743-45*, 55, 102.

50. Coulter, *Journal of William Stephens, 1743-45*, 105, 112, 160-61, 164, 166, 189.

51. *Ibid.*, 44; *1741-43*, 131, 156; *LES*, 43, No. 1238.

52. *LES.*, 43, No. 1238; Thomas Stephens to Verelst, Dec. 15, 1737, *CRG*, XXII, Pt. I, 31; "The Humble Petition of the German & French Inhabitants of Savannah to Gen. Oglethorpe," June, 1743, XXIV, 32-34.

53. *CRG*, VI, 34; Stephens to Verelst, Feb. 4, 1741/2, XXIII, 212; Coulter, *Journal of William Stephens, 1741-43*, 130-31, 133.

54. *CRG*, I, 444, 534; II, 437, 494; VI, 63, 69, 111; Martyn to Stephens, Feb. 2, 1743 (O. S.), MS. CRG, XXX, 583; Verelst to Stephens, Feb. 11, 1743 (O. S.), *ibid.*, 588; Martyn to Stephens, July 7, 1749, XXXI, 300; Verelst to Nicholas Rigby, July 6, 1749, *ibid.*, 319; Martyn to President and Assistants, July 10, 1749, *ibid.*, 327.

55. Coulter, *Journal of William Stephens, 1743-45*, 83-85.

56. *CRG*, II, 498; Stephens and Assistants to Martyn, July 19, 1750, XXVI, 19-20; William Spencer to Martyn, July 18, 1750, *ibid.*, 8-9.

57. Rigby to Verelst, July 26, 1750, *CRG*, XXVI, 39-41.

58. *CRG*, VIII, 247; Noble Jones to Noble Wimberly Jones, July 14, 1760, Georgia Records, Miscellaneous, 1732-96, Force Transcripts, Library of Congress; *Georgia Gazette*, Sept. 3, 1766.

59. *CRG*, VI, 17.

60. *Ibid.*, 122, 125; V, 574; Coulter, *Journal of William Stephens, 1743-45*, 189-90.

61. *CRG*, I, 437, 439-40, 491-92; II, 433, 435-36; Stephens to Verelst, March 31, Sept. 15, 1746, XXV, 35-36, 112-14; James Habersham to Verelst, Sept. 30, 1746, *ibid.*, 127-29; Martyn to Stephens, July 18, 1746, MS. CRG, XXXI, 72.

62. *CRG*, I, 494; II, 479; VI, 190; Martyn to President and Assistants, March 16, 1746, MS. CRG, XXXI, 111.

63. *CRG*, I, 398-401, 506-09; Martyn to Stephens, July 18, 1746, MS. CRG, XXXI, 79; instructions from Trustees against Negroes, March 17, 1747 (O. S.), *ibid.*, 361-62.

64. *CRG*, I, 497, 522-23, 533-34; Petition of Trustees to House of Commons, Feb. 2, 1748 (O. S.), MS. CRG, XXXIII, 374-76, 393.

65. President and Assistants to Martyn, May 4, 1748, *CRG*, XXV, 290-94.

66. *CRG*, I, 530-33, 543-44, 550; II, 504; President and Assistants to Martyn, Jan. 10, 1748/9, XXV, 347-52; Martyn to President and Assistants, May 19, 1749, May 3, 1750, MS. CRG, XXXI, 386-88, 397-98; Martyn to Henry Parker, July 14, Aug. 15, 1750, *ibid.*, 416-17, 442-43; XXXIII, 467-68.

67. President and Assistants to Martyn, Oct. 2, 1749, *CRG*, XXV, 430-37.

68. *CRG*, VI, 261-65.

69. *Ibid.*, 268-279.

70. *Ibid.*, 285, 328.

71. Representation of President and Assistants, Magistrates and Other Principal Inhabitants to Trustees, July 7, 1750, MS. CRG, XXXVI, 495-97.

72. Martyn to Henry Parker and Assistants, March 11, 1750/1, *ibid.*, XXXI, 481-82.

73. *CRG*, VI, 344; VII, 655.

74. Representation to the Trustees, July 7, 1750, *CRG*, XXVI, 512-15.

75. *CRG*, I, 547; II, 498-500; James Habersham to Martyn, Dec. 31, 1750, XXVI, 113-14; Martyn to President and Assistants, July 14, Aug. 15, 1750, MS. CRG, XXXI, 423, 441-42; XXXIII, 427-31.

76. *CRG*, VI, 410; VII, 166, 655, 783, 834; VIII, 43, 108-09, 247, 354, 390, 546-47, 601, 618, 642, 696, 712, 764; IX, 147-48, 164, 225, 338; X, 120-21, 226, 395; XII, 19-20.

CHAPTER XV

1. *LES,* 26, No. 735-38; 14, No. 401; 11, No. 284; 67, No. 203; *CRG,* II, 11; *Egmont Diary,* I, 295; Egmont Papers, 14207, p. 61.
2. *LES,* 26, No. 735; *S. C. Gazette,* Aug. 25, 1733; Egmont Papers, 14207, p. 61; Oglethorpe to Trustees, Aug. 12, 1733, *ibid.,* 14200, p. 106.
3. In the possession of Jones' descendant, W. W. DeRenne, Athens, Georgia.
4. Martyn to Causton, Oct. 28, 1734, MS. CRG, XXIX, 65-66, 70; Martyn to Jones, May 15, 1735, *ibid.,* 131; *Egmont Diary,* II, 189; *Extract of the Journals of Mr. Commissary Von Reck . . . ,* 19-20.
5. Martyn to Causton, Oct. 28, 1734, MS. CRG, XXIX, 65.
6. Verelst to Bailiffs and Recorder of Savannah, May 15, 1735, *ibid.,* 113.
7. Martyn to Causton, Oct. 28, 1734, Jan. 25, 1734/5, *ibid.,* 70, 78-80; *CRG,* II, 82-83.
8. Causton to Trustees, April 2, 1735, MS. CRG, XX, 572; Bathurst to Trustees, March, 1735, *ibid.,* 525-27.
9. Christie to Oglethorpe, Dec. 14, 1734, *ibid.,* 82; Gordon to Trustees, May 7, 1735, *ibid.,* 489-90.
10. Parker to Peter Gordon, March 2, 1734 (O. S.), MS. CRG, XX, 332, 334; Parker to his wife's brother, Jan. 30, 1734/5, *ibid.,* 555; *CRG,* II, 102.
11. Verelst to Causton, May 15, 1735, MS. CRG, XX, 103-04; Verelst to Bailiffs and Recorder of Savannah, May 15, 1735, *ibid.,* 111; Martyn to Jones, May 29, 1735; XXIX, 131-32.
12. Jones to Trustees, July 1, 1735, MS. CRG, XX, 421-28.
13. *CRG,* II, 65.
14. Causton to Trustees, Jan. 16, 1734 (O. S.), incorrectly dated, MS. CRG, XX, 634.
15. George Dunbar to Oglethorpe, Jan. 23, 1734 (O. S.), *ibid.,* 158-61.
16. Jones to Oglethorpe, July 6, 1735, *ibid.,* 201-06.
17. Tomochichi to Trustees, Feb. 24, 1734 (O. S.), *ibid.,* 246-47.

18. Thomas Gapen to Trustees, June 13, 1735, *ibid.,* 398; John Brownfield to Trustees, March 6, 1735/6, *CRG,* XXI, 140; II, 114-15; *Egmont Diary,* II, 189, 287.
19. *CRG,* II, 112, 114; XXI, 473; Verelst to Causton, July 18, 1735, MS. CRG, XXIX, 143; Verelst to Bailiffs and Recorder of Savannah, May 15, 1735, *ibid.,* 109-10.
20. Causton to Trustees, April 2, 1735, MS. CRG, XX, 572; Martyn to Causton, Oct. 28, 1734, XXIX, 70; *CRG,* II, 76; Von Reck to Oglethorpe, Feb. 18, March 7, 1736, XXI, 90, 129-30; John Vat to Oglethorpe, March 10, 1735 (O. S.), *ibid.,* 135-36; Oglethorpe to "Revd Sir," March 16, 1735 (O. S.), *ibid.,* 133; Oglethorpe to Causton, March 17, 1735/6, *ibid.,* 126; Martyn to Bolzius, June 10, 1736, MS. CRG, XXIX, 294.
21. John Brownfield to Trustees, Feb. 10, 1736/7, *CRG,* XXI, 321-22.
22. Instructions of Oglethorpe to Jones and others, June 11, 1736, Egmont Papers, 14202, pp. 1-3.
23. Oglethorpe to Jones, June 14, 1733, *ibid.,* 4.
24. Oglethorpe to Lacy, June 11, 1736, *ibid.,* 2; *S. C. Gazette,* June 26, July 3, 10, 17, 1736.
25. *S. C. Gazette,* July 24, 31, Aug. 14, Nov. 13, 1736; Samuel Eveleigh to Verelst, Aug. 9, 1736, *CRG,* XXI, 206-07; *Egmont Diary,* II, 307.
26. Causton to Trustees, Dec. 14, 1736, April 25, 1737, *CRG,* XXI, 289, 401; John Wesley's account of forts and settlements in Georgia, Sept., 1737, Egmont Papers, 14203, p. 88.
27. Causton Journal, Egmont Papers, 14203, pp. 9, 12, 26, 33; John Brownfield to Trustees, June 19, 1737, *CRG,* XXI, 481.
28. *CRG,* IV, 46-47; Causton Journal, Egmont Papers, 14203, p. 35.
29. Causton Journal, Egmont Papers, 14203, pp. 49-50.
30. *Ibid.,* 51, 68, 72; Bolzius to Trustees, July 28, 1737, *CRG,* XXI, 493; Verelst to Causton, Aug. 11, 1737, MS. CRG, XXIX, 427.

31. MS. CRG, XXIX, 433; Verelst to Causton, Oct. 10, 1737, *ibid.*, 456; *LES*, 61, No. 17.

32. Martyn to Causton, Aug. 3, 1737, MS. CRG, XXIX, 407.

33. *CRG*, IV, 11; MS. CRG, XXXII, 540-43.

34. Stephens to Trustees, Jan. 19, 1737/8, *CRG*, XXII, Pt. I, 79-80.

35. *CRG*, IV, 31, 35-37, 46, 48, 51.

36. *Ibid.*, 54-56, 67, 70-71, 86-87; II, 119; Causton to Trustees, March 1, 1738/9, XXII, Pt. I, 103-06; Verelst to Causton, Sept. 17, Oct. 10, 1737, MS. CRG, XXIX, 446, 456; *LES*, 61, No. 17.

37. *CRG*, IV, 120-22.

38. *Ibid.*, 69-70; II, 226-27; *Egmont Diary*, II, 313, 477, 513.

39. *CRG*, IV, 213-14.

40. *Ibid.*, 31, 618-19; VI, 340; *LES*, 26, No. 735; Causton to Trustees, Feb. 19, 1741, Egmont Papers, 14205, p. 200.

41. *CRG*, IV, 266; *Supplement*, 174.

42. *CRG*, IV, 676.

43. *Ibid.*, 272, 278-79; *S. C. Gazette*, Feb. 22, 1739.

44. *Egmont Diary*, III, 1-2.

45. *CRG*, IV, 475-76, 478.

46. *CRG*, II, 317; Verelst to Thomas Jones, March 29, 1740, MS. CRG, XXX, 229; Tailfer and others, *True and Historical Narrative*, 111.

47. *CRG*, IV, 535-36, 638; Oglethorpe to Newcastle, April 1, 1740, MS. CRG, XXXV, 248-50; *S. C. Gazette*, April 4, 11, 1740.

48. *CRG*, IV, 556-59, 562, 638.

49. *Ibid.*, 637-38; *Supplement*, 33, 43, 56; Stephens to Trustees, Dec. 31, 1741, XXIII, 184; Oglethorpe to Newcastle, MS. CRG, XXXV, 374-77.

50. *CRG*, IV, 651-52, 655.

51. *Ibid.*, *Supplement*, 14.

52. *Ibid.*, 15-17, 19-20; *S. C. Gazette*, Oct. 16, 1740.

53. *S. C. Gazette*, Jan. 22, 1741; *CRG*, IV, *Supplement*, 91-93, 117.

54. *CRG*, IV, *Supplement*, 118-19.

55. *Ibid.*, 124-25, 133-34; *LES*, 98, No. 1139.

56. *S. C. Gazette*, Aug. 29, 1741; Coulter, *Journal of William Stephens*, 1741-43, 4.

57. *CRG*, IV, *Supplement*, 140, 148-49, 166, 228, 235-36, 240-41, 255, 262-63; Coulter, *Journal of William Stephens*, 1741-43, 1-2, 18-20.

58. *CRG*, II, 367; IV, *Supplement*, 233, 249, 252-53; Stephens to Verelst, Oct. 29, 1741, March 20, 1741/2, XXIII, 142, 269-70; Verelst to Stephens, April 27, 1741, MS. CRG, XXX, 321; Verelst to Oglethorpe, April 27, 1741, *ibid.*, 330-33.

59. Coulter, *Journal of William Stephens*, 1741-43, 2-4.

60. *Ibid.*, 45-46.

61. *Ibid.*, 78, 122-23.

62. *Ibid.*, 96; *S. C. Gazette*, May 15, 1742.

63. *S. C. Gazette*, June 14, 1742; Oglethorpe to Newcastle, June 7, 1742, MS. CRG, XXXV, 454; Francis Moore's Journal of Spanish Proceedings, *ibid.*, 493.

64. Coulter, *Journal of William Stephens*, 1741-43, 96, 99-101; Francis Moore's Journal of Spanish Proceedings, MS. CRG, XXXV, 495-96.

65. Coulter, *Journal of William Stephens*, 1741-43, 111-12, 122-23; Thomas Jones to Verelst, Feb. 23, 1742 (O. S.), *CRG*, XXIII 508; Egmont Papers, 14206, p. 198.

66. *S. C. Gazette*, March 21, April 4, 1743; Oglethorpe to Newcastle, March 12, 1742/3, MS. CRG, XXXVI, 97-98.

67. Coulter, *Journal of William Stephens*, 1741-43, 186, 218-19; *CRG*, V. 659, 687.

68. Coulter, *Journal of William Stephens* 1741-43, 225-27; 1743-45, 20-21, 40-41, 45-50, 54-55.

69. *Ibid.*, 1741-43, 36-37; 1743-45, 21-22, 27, 29-32, 38, 41-42.

70. *Ibid.*, 1741-43, 46, 53-54, 96, 132, 135-40.

71. *Ibid.*, 148, 159-61.

72. *Ibid.*, 184-85, 187-88, 198; 1743-45, 6.

73. *Ibid.*, 1743-45, 6-9; Dobell to Trustees, Sept. 1, Oct. 21, 1743, *CRG*, XXIV, 85, 145.

74. Coulter, *Journal of William Stephens*, 1743-45, 127-29.

75. *Ibid.*, 145-46; 1741-43, 146-49, 178-79; Verelst to Stephens, Feb. 11, 1743

(O. S.), MS. CRG, XXX, 586; *CRG*, II, 450.

76. *CRG*, I, 548-49, 556; II, 509-10; Martyn to Henry Parker, July 14, 1750, July 10, 1751, MS. CRG, XXXI, 420, 498; Martyn to Noble Jones, July 16, 1750, *ibid.*, 410, XXXIII, 433-35, 499-501.

77. Martyn to Henry Parker, Aug. 15, 1750, MS. CRG, XXXI, 445-46; Martyn to James Habersham, Aug. 15, 1750, *ibid.*, 445; Stephens and Assistants to Martyn, July 19, 1750, *CRG*, XXVI, 27; Habersham to Martyn, Dec. 15, 1750, *ibid.*, 90.

78. *CRG*, VI, 353-54, MS. Council Journal, 1749-51, Georgia Records, Force Transcripts, Library of Congress, f. 42, p. 86.

79. *CRG*, I, 547; II, 498-500; Martyn to Henry Parker, Aug. 15, 1750, MS. CRG, XXXI, 441; XXXIII, 427-31; MS. Council Journal, fo. 42, pp. 86-87.

80. MS. Council Journal, fo. 43, pp. 87-88.

81. *Ibid.*, 88, fo. 44, p. 91; Henry Parker to Martyn, Jan. 3, 1750 (O. S.), *CRG*, XXVI, 127.

82. MS. Council Journal, fo. 45, pp. 91-92.

83. *Ibid.*, fo. 52 pp. 106-07.

84. *Ibid.*, fo. 48-49, p. 99, *CRG*, XXVI, 155-63, 166-72, 178-79; Martyn to Henry Parker, July 10, 1751, MS. CRG, XXXI, 489, 491-92; Martyn to Habersham, Feb. 18, 1750/1, *ibid.*, 471.

85. Noble Jones and Robinson to Martyn, Feb. 27, 1750/1, Dec. 19, 1751, *CRG*, XXVI, 165-66, 321-22; Robinson to Martyn, March 27, Dec. 19, 1751, *ibid.*, 186-87, 322-23; Haber-sham to Martyn, June 13, 1751, Jan. 31, 1752, *ibid.*, 234-35, 329.

86. Habersham to Martyn, May 3, 1751, *ibid.*, 202.

87. MS. Council Journal, fos. 55-59, *passim*; fos. 59-60, pp. 119-20.

88. *Ibid.*, fos. 62-64, pp. 126-29.

89. *CRG*, I, 555-56; II, 510; Habersham to Martyn, Aug. 19, 1751, XXVI, 274-75; Martyn to Parker, July 10, 1751, MS. CRG, XXXI, 497-98; Memorial of Trustees to Board of Trade, Feb. 10, 1752, XXXIII, 539; *Ibid.*, 493-99.

90. *CRG*, I, 578; representation to King from Board of Trade, Jan. 17, 1753, MS. CRG, XXXIII, 591; memorial to King from Trustees, May 6, 1751, *ibid.*, 502-13; other memorials of Trustees, *ibid.*, 538-81.

91. Board of Trade to President and Assistants, July 16, 1752, MS. CRG, XXXIII, 582-83; President and Assistants to Board of Trade, Jan. 27, 1753, *CRG*, XXVI, 411-13; VI, *passim*.

92. Representation of Board of Trade to King, July 27, 1754, MS. CRG, XXXIII, 614-15; Order in Council, Aug. 6, 1754, *CRG*, XXVI, 453-54; Reynolds to Board of Trade, Dec. 5, 1754, MS. CRG, XXVII, 69.

93. *CRG*, VI, 460-61.

94. *CRG*, VII, 9-17; royal instructions to Reynolds, MS. CRG, XXXIV, 27; *Acts of Privy Council, Colonial Series*, IV, 785.

95. On the subsequent career of Noble Jones, see E. Merton Coulter, *Wormsloe: Two Centuries of a Georgia Family* (Athens, Ga., 1955), 82-107.

Bibliography

I. MANUSCRIPTS

A. University of Georgia Library
    Egmont Papers from Phillipps Collection. (Letters pertaining to Georgia.)

B. Georgia Department of Archives and History
    Bonds, Bills of Sale, Deeds, Powers of Attorney, Etc.
    Estate Inventories
    Letters of Guardianship
    Miscellaneous loose papers
    Register of Grants
    Store Accounts
    Wills

C. Library of Congress
    Georgia, Miscellaneous, 1732-1865
    Georgia Proclamations, 1754-1778
    Transcripts from Bodleian Library, British Museum, and British Public Record Office

II. CONTEMPORARY TRACTS AND MEMOIRS

Anonymous
    An Account Shewing the Progress of the Colony of Georgia in America. London, 1741. (Reprinted in Allen D. Candler, ed., *The Colonial Records of the State of Georgia*, III [Atlanta, 1905], 367-432.)
    An Account Shewing what Money has been received by the Trustees for the use of the Colony of Georgia, and how they Discharged Themselves thereof, with Observations thereon. London, 1742[?].
    Both Sides of the Question: or, a Candid and Impartial Enquiry into a Certain Doubtful Character. London, 1749.

A New Voyage to Georgia, by a Young Gentleman. London, 1737.
*Some Account of the Designs of the Trustees for Establishing the
  Colony of Georgia in America.* London, 1732[?]. (Reprinted
  in Peter Force, *Tracts,* 1835, I, No. 2 [Washington, 1835],
  under the title, *A Brief Account,* etc.)
Barber, Jonathan and James Habersham. *Orphan-Letters to the Rev-
  erend Mr. Whitefield.* Glasgow, 1741.
Cadogan, George. *The Spanish Hireling Detected.* London, 1743.
[Martyn, Benjamin]. *An Impartial Enquiry into the State and Utility
  of the Province of Georgia.* London, 1741.
[Martyn, Benjamin]. *Reasons for Establishing the Colony of Georgia,
  with Regard to the Trade of Great Britain.* London, 1733.
Montgomery, Sir Robert. *A Discourse Concerning the Design'd Estab-
  lishment of a New Colony to the South of Carolina.* London, 1717.
  (Reprinted in Peter Force, *Tracts,* I, No. 1. Washington, 1835.)
Moore, Francis. *A Voyage to Georgia begun in the Year 1735.* London,
  1744.
[Oglethorpe, James Edward]. *A Full Reply to Lieut. Cadogan's Spanish Hireling, &c. and Lieut. Mackay's Letter Concerning the Action at Moosa.* London, 1743.
[Oglethorpe, James Edward, attributed to]. *A New and Accurate Ac-
  count of the Province of South-Carolina and Georgia.* London,
  1732.
Reck, Georg Philipp Friedrich, Baron von, and Johann Martin Bolzius. *An Extract of the Journals of Mr. Commissary von Reck . . .
  and of the Reverend Mr. Bolzius.* London, 1734.
South Carolina General Assembly. *The Report of the Committee
  Appointed to Examine into the Proceedings of the People of
  Georgia.* Charleston, 1736.
South Carolina General Assembly. *The Report of the Committee of
  Both Houses of the Assembly of . . . South Carolina Appointed
  to enquire into the Causes of the Disappointment of Success in
  the late Expedition against St. Augustine under the command
  of General Oglethorpe.* Charleston, 1742. Several other editions.
  (Reprinted, Columbia, S. C.: Archives Department, 1954.)
[Stephens, Thomas]. *A Brief Account of the Causes that have Re-
  tarded the Progress of the Colony of Georgia in America.* London,
  1743.
[Stephens, Thomas]. *The Castle-Builders; or, the History of William
  Stephens, of the Isle of Wight, Esq., lately deceased.* London, 1759.
[Stephens, Thomas]. *The Hard Case of the Distressed People of
  Georgia.* London, 1742.
[Stephens, William] *A State of the Province of Georgia.* London,
  1742.

Tailfer, Patrick, Hugh Anderson, David Douglass, and others. *A True and Historical Narrative of the Colony of Georgia in America.* Charles Town, 1741. Several other editions. (Reprinted with comments by the Earl of Egmont. Athens: Univ. of Ga. Press, 1960.)

Thicknesse, Philip. *Memoirs and Anecdotes of Philip Thicknesse.* Dublin, 1790.

Whitefield, George.

A Journal of a Voyage from Gibraltar to Georgia. London, 1738.

A Continuation of the Reverend Mr. Whitefield's Journal, from His Arrival at Savannah, to His Return to London. London, 1739.

A Continuation of the Reverend Mr. Whitefield's Journal, during the Time he was Detained in England by the Embargo. London, 1739.

A Continuation of the Reverend Mr. Whitefield's Journal, from his Arrival at London, to his Departure from thence on his way to Georgia. London, 1739.

A Continuation of the Reverend Mr. Whitefield's Journal, from his Embarking after the Embargo, to his Arrival at Savannah in Georgia. London, 1740.

A Short Account of God's Dealings with the Reverend Mr. George Whitefield . . . from his Infancy to the Time of his Entering into Holy Orders. London, 1740.

A Continuation of the Reverend Mr. Whitefield's Journal, after his Arrival at Georgia, to a Few Days after his Second Return thither from Philadelphia. London, 1741.

An Account of Money Received and Disbursed for the Orphan-House in Georgia. London, 1741.

A Continuation of the Reverend Mr. Whitefield's Journal, from a Few Days after his Return to Georgia, to his Arrival at Falmouth on the 11th of March 1741. London, 1741.

A Continuation of the Account of the Orphan-House in Georgia. Edinburgh, 1742.

A Continuation of the Account of the Orphan-House in Georgia, from January 1740/1 to January 1742/3. London, 1743.

III. NEWSPAPERS AND PERIODICALS

The Daily Advertiser (London).
Gentleman's Magazine (London).
The South-Carolina Gazette.

IV. OTHER PRINTED SOURCES

Candler, Allen D. and Lucian Lamar Knight, eds. *The Colonial Records of the State of Georgia.* 26 vols. Atlanta: State printers, 1904-1916. (Vols. 20, 27-39, in manuscript, available at Georgia Department of Archives and History, Atlanta.)

Carroll, Bartholomew R. *Historical Collections of South Carolina.* 2 vols. New York: Harper, 1836.

Coulter, E. Merton and Albert B. Saye, eds. *A List of the Early Settlers of Georgia.* Athens: Univ. of Ga. Press, 1949.

Coulter, E. Merton, "A List of the First Shipload of Georgia Settlers," in *Georgia Historical Quarterly,* XXXI (Dec., 1947), 282-88.

Coulter, E. Merton, ed. *The Journal of William Stephens, 1741-1743.* Athens: Univ. of Ga. Press, 1958.

Coulter, E. Merton, ed. *The Journal of William Stephens, 1743-1745.* Athens: Univ. of Ga. Press, 1959.

Curnock, Nehemiah. *The Journal of the Rev. John Wesley, A. M., Sometime Fellow of Lincoln College, Oxford.* 8 vols. London: Robert Culley and Charles H. Kelley, 1910-1916.

Force, Peter, ed. *Tracts and Other Papers Relating Principally to the Origin, Settlement, and Progress of the Colonies in North America, from the Discovery of the Country to the Year 1776.* 4 vols. Washington: Peter Force, 1836-1846. (Reprinted, 1947.)

Grant, W. L. and James Munro, eds. *Acts of the Privy Council, Colonial Series, 1613-1783.* 6 vols. London: H. M. Stationery Office, 1908-1912.

Habersham, James. *The Letters of the Hon. James Habersham, 1756-1775.* Vol. VI, of *Collections of the Georgia Historical Society.* Savannah: Georgia Historical Society, 1904.

Historical Manuscripts Commission. *Diary of Viscount Percival, afterwards First Earl of Egmont.* 3 vols. London: H. M. Stationery Office, 1920-1923.

Kingsbury, Susan Myra, ed. *The Records of the Virginia Company.* Washington, 1906.

McPherson, Robert G., ed. "The Voyage of the *Anne*—A Daily Record," in *Georgia Historical Quarterly,* XLIV (June, 1960), 220-30.

Salley, A. S., Jr., ed. *Death Notices in the South-Carolina Gazette, 1732-1755.* Columbia: S. C. Historical Commission, 1917.

Salley, A. S., Jr., ed. *Narratives of Early Carolina.* New York, Scribner's, 1911.

Salley, A. S., Jr., ed. *Register of St. Philip's Parish, Charles Town, 1720-1758.* Charleston: Walker, Evans & Cogswell, 1904.

Salley, Harriet Milledge, ed. *Correspondence of John Milledge, Governor of Georgia, 1802-1806.* Columbia, S. C.: Privately printed, 1949.

White, George. *Historical Collections of Georgia.* New York: Pudney & Russell, 1854.

V. Secondary Accounts

Bruce, Philip Alexander. *Economic History of Virginia in the Seventeenth Century.* New York: Macmillan, 1895. (Reprinted, New York: Peter Smith, 1935.)

Corry, John Pitts. *Indian Affairs in Georgia, 1732-1756.* Philadelphia: Privately printed, 1936.

Crane, Verner W. "The Promotion Literature of Georgia," in *Bibliographical Essays, a Tribute to Wilberforce Eames.* Cambridge, Mass.: Harvard Univ. Press, 1924.

Crane, Verner W. *The Southern Frontier, 1670-1732.* Durham: Duke Univ. Press, 1928. (Reprinted, Ann Arbor: Univ. of Mich. Press, 1956.)

DeBrahm, John Gerar William. *History of the Province of Georgia.* Wormsloe: Privately printed, 1849.

Estill, John Holbrook. *The Old Lodge. Freemasonry in Georgia in the Days of the Colony.* Savannah, 1885.

Ettinger, Amos A. *James Edward Oglethorpe: Imperial Idealist.* Oxford: University Press, 1936.

Fries, Adelaide L. *The Moravians in Georgia, 1735-1740.* Winston-Salem, N. C., 1905.

Gosse, Philip. *Dr. Viper, the Querulous Life of Philip Thicknesse.* London: Cassell, 1952.

Hewatt, Alexander. *An Historical Account of the Rise and Progress of the Colonies of South Carolina and Georgia.* 2 vols. London, 1779. (Reprinted in B. R. Carroll, *Historical Collections of South Carolina,* Vol. 1. New York: Harper, 1836.)

Hodge, Frederick W. *Handbook of American Indians North of Mexico.* 2 vols. Washington: Govt. Print. Office, 1907-10. (Smithsonian Institution, U. S. Bureau of Ethnology, Bulletin 30.)

Johnston, Edith Duncan. *The Houstouns of Georgia.* Athens: Univ. of Ga. Press, 1950.

Johnston, Elizabeth Lichtenstein. *Recollections of a Georgia Loyalist.* New York and London: Bankside Press, 1901.

Lanning, John Tate. *The Diplomatic History of Georgia.* Chapel Hill: Univ. of N. C. Press, 1936.

McCall, Hugh. *The History of Georgia.* 2 vols. Savannah: Seymour & Williams, 1811-1816. (Reprinted, 1 vol. Atlanta: A. B. Caldwell, 1909.)

McCrady, Edward. *The History of South Carolina under the Proprietary Government, 1670-1719.* New York and London: Macmillan, 1897.

McCrady, Edward. *The History of South Carolina under the Royal Government, 1719-1776.* New York and London: Macmillan, 1899.

Mereness, Newton Dennison, ed. *Travels in the American Colonies.* New York: Macmillan, 1916.

Northen, William J., ed. *Men of Mark in Georgia.* 3 vols. Atlanta: A. B. Caldwell, 1907-1911.

Rand, Benjamin. *Berkeley and Percival.* Cambridge: University Press, 1916.

Redding, Mrs. J. H. *Life and Times of Jonathan Bryan, 1708-1788.* Published by *Savannah Morning News,* 1901.

Smith, Abbot Emerson, *Colonist in Bondage: White Servitude and Convict Labor in America, 1607-1776.* Chapel Hill: Univ. of N. C. Press, 1947.

Stephens, William Bacon, *History of Georgia.* 2 vols. New York and Philadelphia, 1847-1859.

Strobel, P. A. *The Salzburgers and their Descendants.* Baltimore: T. Newton Kurtz, 1855. (Reprinted. Athens: Univ. of Ga. Press, 1953.)

Stokes, Anthony. *A View of the Constitution of the British Colonies, in North-America and the West Indies* . . . London, 1783.

Swanton, John R. *Early History of the Creek Indians and Their Neighbors.* Washington: Govt. Print. Office, 1922. (Smithsonian Institution, Bureau of American Ethnology, Bulletin 73.)

Tyerman, Luke. *The Life and Times of Rev. John Wesley, M. A., Founder of the Methodists.* 3 vols. London: Hodder and Stoughton, 1870-1871.

Tyerman, Luke. *The Oxford Methodists.* New York: Harper, 1873.

Index

Note: Women are indexed under their last name when they first came to Georgia and not under subsequent married names.

Abercorn, 44, 60

Abercromby, James, South Carolina attorney general, 117-18

Aglionby, William, 116, 189

Agriculture, importance in Georgia, xiv-xv, 37, 74, 121, 147; described, 14-16, 110, 123, 146; of Salzburgers, 59-61; delayed by Spanish alarm, 99; Hugh Anderson fails at, 141; failure (1738), 151

Alarm bell, and Red String Plot, 80-81

Alligators, 16, 168-69

Amatis, Catherine, 138

Amatis, Nicholas, 33, 127

Amatis, Paul, Trustees' gardener at Charles Town, 122-23; differences with Fitzwalter over garden, 126-34; silk culture, 127, 128, 132; ill temper, 129-31; Red String Plot, 130-31; given control of garden by Trustees, 132; removal and death, 138, 165-66, 295

Amory, John, 276-77

Amusements, at early Savannah, 14

Anderson, Adam, 140

Anderson, Hugh, inspector of public garden, 139-41, 164

Anderson, James, marriage, 163-64; 195

Ann, brings original settlers to Georgia, 2-7; passenger list, 295-99

Anniversaries, celebration of, 161-62

Assembly, called by Trustees, xii; regulates militia, 288

Assistants, salaries, 290

Augusta, founded, xvii; surveyed and described, 274-75

Avery, Joseph, surveyor, 42, 282

Bailiffs, 20, 145, 149-53, 153-57

Baillie, John, Scotch settlers, 43, 164, 202

Baillie, Thomas, Scot, 164, 226

Baillou, Peter, 36, 196, 205

Balls, in Savannah, 162

Barber, Rev. Jonathan, 223, 229, 232

Barnard, Sir John, 38

Barner, John, constable, 34

Bathurst, Sir Francis, poor living conditions, 172-73, 270

Beaufain, Hector de, on agriculture, xiv-xv

Beaufort, South Carolina, 7-8

Beer and wine, 3, 164

Bethesda, 50, 220-34, 238

Bills of exchange, 96-98

Birth, first in colony, 22

Bishop, Philip, 30-31

Bliss, Mrs. Ann, public nurse, 194

Blitheman, William, carpenter on Tybee lighthouse, 48

Bloody Marsh, Battle of, xvii, 283

Board of Trade, 290

Boat building, 205

Bolton, Mary, 233

Bolzius, Rev. John Martin, minister to Salzburgers, 57-61, 163, 263

Bolzius Orphan House, 220

Bosomworth, Rev. Thomas, 210, 263

CPSIA information can be obtained at www.ICGtesting.com
Printed in the USA
LVOW06s1237140814

399007LV00002B/181/P